# The Magazine

"Your book is one of a kind. It does exactly what it sets out to do—clearly, competently, valuably."

—Norman Cousins

"The book . . . works both as a complete primer for the novice and as a cobweb sweeper for the expert in search of new ideas. . . . It's everything you need to effectively manage your own magazine into the 1990s."

—*Magazine Week*

"It's the best . . . book I have read on the subject."

—Lee F. Young, William Allen White School of Journalism, University of Kansas

"A masterful job. I don't know how you did it, but you did it beautifully.... I'm keeping this book prominently displayed on my desk."

—Peter G. Diamandis

"Well worth reading and studying for students of publishing, potential entrepreneurs, and present editors and publishers. . . . It conveys not only the realities but the excitement of the magazine business."

—Christine D. Urban, Graduate School of Business Administration, Harvard University

"After reading . . . your delightful and comprehensively informative book, I wonder how we ever managed to publish successful magazines!"

—William M. Gaines, *MAD* magazine

# The Magazine

Third Edition

*Everything You Need to Know to Make It in the Magazine Business*

*by*

Leonard Mogel

A *Folio:* Book

Old Saybrook, Connecticut

Library of Congress Cataloging-in-Publication Data

Mogel, Leonard.
    The magazine : everything you need to know to make it in the magazine business / by Leonard Mogel.—3rd ed.
        p.    cm.
    Includes bibliographical references and index.
    ISBN 1-56440-086-7
    1. Periodicals, Publishing of.    I. Title.
Z286.P4M63 1992
070.5'72—dc20                            92-19213
                                              CIP

Manufactured in the United States of America
Third Edition/First Printing

To my wife Ann, whose love I have cherished for forty-three years, for her patience and understanding and for her unremitting dedication to this project.

# CONTENTS

# ACKNOWLEDGMENTS

I wish to thank the following people at *Folio:* for their excellent support: Hershel Sarbin, Joe Hanson, Barbara Love, Michelle Weber, Suzanne Zelkowitz, Robert M. Steed, Diane Cyr, Liz Horton, and the entire staff.

My sincere appreciation to Linda Kennedy, Bruce Markot, Kevin Lynch, Nancy Freeborn, Mary Ballachino, and all the other people at The Globe Pequot Press.

To Daniel A. Ross for his outstanding contribution to the chapter "Magazine Publishing and the Law."

To all my interviewees for their splendid cooperation: Valerie Salembier, Howard Rauch, Bruce Brandfon, Irving Herschbein, John Klingel, Howard Greene, Stacy Gordon, and Jim Kobak.

To Dr. Kathleen Endres of the University of Akron for permission to use her excellent study in the chapter "The Fascinating Business of Business Magazines."

To John Peter, Judy Jorgenson of the American Society of Magazine Editors, Terilyn McGovern, Bride Whalen, Phyllis Reed, Peter Jacobi, Larry Bodine, Rip Georges, Helen Berman, Janet Libert, John Plunkett, Kate Salovaara Brower, Lindsay Davidson, Mediamark Research Inc., Alex White, Robert Moore, Gordon Haight, and Charlotte Kelly Veal for the use of their research materials and for their general support.

To Barbara Grahn of the Standard Rate and Data Service for permission to reprint a portion of their Consumer and Business Publication Listings.

# INTRODUCTION

Time Warner, with annual revenues exceeding $12 billion, is a titan in the communications industry. The company's vast network extends to film entertainment, music, book publishing, and cable television businesses, as well as magazine publishing—a field in which it owns twenty-five publications that together produce annual revenues of $3 billion.

In magazine publishing, advertising sales account for the largest portion of a company's revenues. In this area Time Warner's magazines are superstars. In 1991, its *People* magazine was number two among all magazines with $345 million in ad sales, followed by the company's *Time* magazine with $326 million and *Sports Illustrated* with $323 million. Time Warner seldom makes mistakes. Yet even a giant stumbles.

In the early 1980s Time Inc. (now a part of Time Warner) attempted to launch *TV Cable Week* as a competitor to *TV Guide*. It applied the most advanced research and test marketing to this effort, but all was for naught. The magazine failed after only twenty-five weeks of publication. The result was a reported loss of $47 million, a tidy sum for misjudging the market.

Undaunted, and flush with the success of its *People* magazine, Time Inc. started *Picture Week*, another newsweekly, in 1985. By the time the company was ready to publish, however, it decided to kill the project, this time for a reported loss of $30 million.

The global media baron Rupert Murdoch stormed these shores in the early 1980s, determined to launch a broadcast, film, and magazine publishing empire. In one megadeal he bought *TV Guide*, *Seventeen*, and the *Daily Racing Form* from the Annenberg family for the huge sum of $3 billion.

In the period 1976–86 Murdoch accumulated almost a dozen other magazines and in the process amassed a mountain of debt. By 1991 Murdoch, facing a recessionary climate, had to sell nine of these publications to K-III Holdings for more than $600 million. Included in the transaction were the profitable *Seventeen* and *New York* magazines. Clearly, the astute Mr. Murdoch had goofed.

These losses indicate the volatility of the magazine business. If talented giants like Time Inc. and Murdoch make mistakes, what about the 500-odd new magazines (with such names as *Bathroom Journal, Inside the Mafia,* and *Ninja Combat Training Manual*) launched each year? Most are underfinanced. Many have vague concepts and inexperienced management. How will most fare? Dismally. Only 10 percent will make it into the second year, and, of these survivors, many will take longer than four years to reach a break-even point.

On the positive side, magazines are being acquired for record prices. Time Inc. paid $480 million for the company that owns the highly profitable *Southern Living* magazine.

In June 1989 the supermarket tabloid *National Enquirer* was sold for $412 million. The giant Cahners Publishing Company added to its substantial network of sixty-seven business magazines by purchasing the consumer magazines *American Baby* and *Modern Bride*. Diamandis Communications bought CBS's large magazine division for $650 million and then sold it to the French Hachette Publications six months later for a far greater sum. Condé Nast, owner of many fine consumer magazines, filled its stable with the prestigious *New Yorker*. It also revitalized *Vanity Fair* and, with Tina Brown at the helm, made it a great success.

Yet even for established magazines these are bad times and good. The cautious economic climate has forced many national advertisers to cut back sharply on their ad spending. A number of well-established magazines have folded. Others have cut staffs and consolidated their operations. Desktop publishing has revolutionized magazine production. International publishing has become a reality.

This book is intended for two audiences—those planning to start new magazines and those who wish to enter this exciting field. In either case you must learn the trade.

If you intend to beat the odds and launch a new magazine, an essential first step is conducting extensive research to determine whether there is a true editorial need for your magazine. Assuming there is, you must then address these vital questions: Do you have sufficient experience and talent to steer this ship? Do you have adequate capital for this launch? New publishers must be fully conversant with the financial aspects of magazine publishing, know the best structure for a venture to take, and know how to go about raising the vast amounts of money required. Lack of capital and lack of ability are the primary reasons for failure in the magazine business.

This book attempts to answer the prospective publisher's questions; it is a primer for actually starting your own magazine. And perhaps more realistically, it also provides you with the facts, figures, and concepts you need to know to enter and become successfully employed in the magazine business.

Can the reader build a house by reading a book? Of course not. But the fundamentals are here. The reader will learn how to prepare a dummy issue and how to write a business plan, the sine qua non for financing a new magazine. The book also contains candid interviews with industry leaders, case histories of failures and successes, and descriptions of the job opportunities in the various phases of magazine publication. Most important, in these pages I share with the reader the expertise gained from my personal experience of more than thirty-five years in this wonderful world of magazines.

# What Is a Magazine?

In 1991 we celebrated the 250th anniversary of American magazine publishing. The first magazine, *American Magazine,* was published by Andrew Bradford in 1741, beating Benjamin Franklin and his *General Magazine* by three days. Both folded within a few months of their first issues. By 1800 there were already one hundred magazines; by 1850, six hundred.

Many magazines that originated in the 1800s are still with us. Some examples: *American Banker,* the *Atlantic, Cosmopolitan, Harper's Magazine, Ladies' Home Journal,* and *McCall's.* Today there are more than 13,000 consumer magazines alone in this country.

In the trade a magazine is sometimes called a "magazine" and sometimes a "publication," a "periodical," a "title," a "journal," or even a "book." The last designation has gained many adherents in recent years and is used as frequently as "magazine." "How are things at your *book*?" "I hear that *book* is in trouble." "It's a beautiful *book* but it won't cut the mustard." If there's confusion over when a book is a book and when it is a magazine, no one in the magazine business really minds. It's an understood term.

The *Random House Dictionary of the English Language* defines a magazine as "a publication that is issued periodically, usually bound in a paper cover, and typically containing stories, essays, poems, etc., by many writers, and often photographs and drawings, frequently specializing in a particular subject or area, as hobbies, news or sports." The same source classifies a periodical as "a magazine or other journal that is issued at regularly recurring intervals."

Within the broad spectrum of magazines are two major subdivisions—*consumer* magazines, which are publications of general or specialized interest either sold or given free to the public, and *business* magazines, sometimes called *trade* magazines, which deal with the commercial and financial aspects of particular industries or businesses. (See chapter 12 for extensive coverage of this division of magazines.) A third subdivision is the smaller literary journal, sometimes published under university auspices; the fourth, newsletters.

A breakdown in the consumer magazine category according to these magazines' specialization is provided in Standard Rate and Data Service (SRDS), a monthly directory of the advertising rates, production specifications, circulation data, and so on of hundreds of publications. This directory is invaluable to media people in advertising agencies as a guide in advertising placement and in the analysis of magazines for their clients' advertising campaigns. SRDS publishes similar directories for newspapers, radio and TV stations, and business publications. (See chapter 12 for classification groupings in SRDS business magazines.)

## CLASSIFICATION GROUPINGS

The individual magazines in SRDS's consumer magazine listing are grouped within fifty-one separate classifications, beginning alphabetically with *Airline Inflight* and ending with *Youth.* The term *audited* indicates that these magazines are members of Audit Bureau of Circulations (ABC) and are paid-circulation magazines that have their circulation figures audited once a year.

Any discussion of consumer magazines should consider the trend away from the general-editorial classification and toward the specialized. The generals can't match the immediacy of TV. When Jack Ruby killed Lee Oswald at the time of the Kennedy assassination, it was live TV that captured the incident for its multimillion viewers. When the Persian Gulf War started, we saw it live on TV. No newspaper, let alone magazine, was able to convey these events as they actually happened. TV is tough competition for the mass-circulation, general consumer magazine; it provides easy relaxation, plus a blend of entertainment, information, and news—and it's free.

From an advertising viewpoint TV and also radio offer larger total audiences at a cost per thousand usually lower than that of the general magazines (see chapter 5). Advertising effectiveness, loyalty of readers, and selectivity should be formidable arguments in favor of these magazines, but it makes for a difficult sell when TV is the adversary.

The specialized magazine offers a direct appeal to its readers that other mass media cannot match. A TV special about jogging cannot compare to a subscription to *Runner's World,* even though TV reaches a much larger audience. A reader supports his or her interest in a sport or activity by buying a specialized magazine. This reader wants the depth and perspective that only that particular magazine can bring to the subject.

For a wider understanding of the range of consumer magazines, we list all the magazines in the SRDS classifications.

## Business Publications

The business or trade magazine of forty years ago was a small, poorly designed journal that served primarily as an advertising medium and had a limited editorial content. Today, however, we have some giant business publications of superior quality, many selling thousands of advertising pages a year. (For a greater understanding of this important area of magazine publishing, see chapter 12.)

## Literary Reviews and Academic Journals

The category of literary reviews and academic journals encompasses hundreds of publications of small circulation, generally nonprofit and funded by universities, grants, and foundations. Often these magazines do not accept advertising. They may publish bimonthly or less frequently. Some have been published for generations and enjoy an eminent position in our intellectual structure, despite their limited circulation. The *Kenyon Review,* for example (published in Gambier, Ohio), is an outstanding academic journal founded in 1939. Its broad literary spectrum covers the fields of physics, anthropology, history, and even the culinary and horticultural arts.

The chapters in this book on production, subscriptions, editorial, and art will be of interest to those pursuing careers in academic publishing.

# Classification Groupings - U.S. Consumer Magazines

**1. AIRLINE INFLIGHT/TRAIN ENROUTE**
(See also: Hotel Inroom.)

**AUDITED**
Aboard Inflight Magazines
America West Airlines Magazine
American Way
Continental Profiles
Delta Sky
East/West Network, Inc.
Pan Am Clipper
Southwest Spirit
TWA Ambassador
United Vis a Vis
USAir Magazine

**NON-AUDITED**
Air Destinations
Air Travel Journal
Alaska Airlines Magazine
American Eagle Latitudes South
Amtrak Express
Crain's Detroit Business International Edition
Hawaiian Airlines Magazine
Horizon Air Magazine
Japan Airlines Winds
LACSA'S World
Midflight
Northwest Compass Readings
Shuttle Quarterly
SkyWritings
Spirit of Aloha
St. Petersburg News—Aeroflot Inflight

**1A. ALMANACS & DIRECTORIES**

**NON-AUDITED**
Almanac for Farmers & City Folk, The
Blum's Farmers & Planters Almanac and Turner's Carolina Almanac
Grier's Almanac
J. Gruber's Hagers-Town Town and Country Almanack
Ladies Birthday Almanac, The
Old Farmer's Almanac, The
Trail Blazers' Almanac and Pioneer Guide Book

**2. ART & ANTIQUES**
(See also: Crafts, Games, Hobbies & Models; Entertainment Guides & Programs; Literary, Book Reviews & Writing Techniques; Music.)

**AUDITED**
American Artist
Antiques, The Magazine
Art & Antiques
Art in America
Artist's Magazine, The
Artnews
Collectors' Showcase
Museum & Arts Washington
Southwest Art

**NON-AUDITED**
American Collector's Journal
Antique Monthly
Antique Trader Weekly, The
Antiques & Fine Art
Antiques Directory, The
AntiqueWeek
Art & Auction
Art Now Gallery Guide
Art of California
Art Today
Art/World
Artforum
Collector Editions
Collectors Mart
Collectors News
Contemporanea International Art Magazine
Fiberarts
FMR
Horizon
Official Museum Directory, The*
Plate World
Shuttle Spindle & Dyepot
Treasure Chest
Vue
Wildlife Art News

**3. AUTOMOTIVE**
(See also: Crafts, Games, Hobbies & Models; Mechanics & Science; Motorcycle; Sports; Travel.)

**AUDITED**
American Rodder
Auto Club News
Automobile Magazine
AutoWeek
Car and Driver
Car Craft
Cars & Parts Magazine
Circle Track
Dune Buggies & Hot VWs
European Car
4-Wheel
Four Wheeler

Hemmings Motor News
Hot Rod
Motor Trend
Mustang & Fords
Off-Road
Open Wheel
Popular Hot Rodding
Road & Track
Sport Truck
Sports Car International
Stock Car Racing Magazine
Street Rodder
Super Chevy
Super Stock & Drag Illustrated
Truckin'

**NON-AUDITED**
Alfa Owner
Auto Racing Digest
Automundo Magazine
Bracket Racing USA
British Car
California Sports Car
Car Collector/Car Classics
Cars & Parts Annual
Chevrolet High Performance
Chrysler Power
Classic Auto Restorer
Collector Car Trader
Corvette Fever Magazine
Corvette Quarterly
du Pont Registry
Fabulous Mustangs and Exotic Fords
4WD Sport Utility
Grassroots Motorsports
Guide To Muscle Cars
High Performance Mopar
IMSA Arrow
IMSA Yearbook
Kit Car
Kit Car Illustrated
Mini Truckin'
Mopar Muscle
Motor Trend's New Car Buyer's Guide
Motor Trend's Road Tests
Motor Trend's Sports Cars of the World
Motor Trend's Truck & Van Buyer's Guide
Muscle Car Review
Muscle Cars
Muscle Cars of the '60s/'70s
Muscle Mustangs & Fast Fords
Musclecar Classics
Mustang Monthly
National Dragster
National Speed Sport News
1992 Car and Driver Buyers Guide
1992 Car and Driver Road Test Annual
Official NASCAR Yearbook and Press Guide
Old Cars News & Marketplace
Old Cars Price Guide
On Track
Pontiac
Popular Argus Group
RaceTime
Road & Track Specials
Rod & Custom Magazine
Special Interest Autos
SportsCar
Super Ford
Super Street Truck
Turbo
Vette
VW Trends
Wheel, The

**4. AVIATION**
(See also: Crafts, Games, Hobbies & Models; Travel.)

**AUDITED**
AOPA Pilot
Flying
Kitplanes
Plane&Pilot
Private Pilot

**NON-AUDITED**
Air Line Pilot
Air Progress
General Aviation News & Flyer
Rotorcraft
Soaring
Sport Aviation
Ultralight Flying!
Wings West
World Airshow News

**5. BABIES**
(See also: Children's; Women's.)

**AUDITED**
American Baby
Baby On The Way
Baby Talk
Bounty InfantCare Guide, The
Child Magazine's Guide to Having a Baby
Childbirth
Expecting
First Year of Life
Guide for Expectant Parents
Healthy Kids: Birth-3

5

Lamaze Parents' Magazine
Organized Pregnancy, The
Parenting*
Parents Baby Care - Birth Edition
Twins

**NON-AUDITED**
Baby Times
Beginnings
Bounty Pregnancy Guide, The
Embarazo
First Visit
Get Ready for Baby!
Mi Bebe
Organized Parent, The
Parents Baby Care
Pediatrician
Prenatal Educator
That's My Baby
Una Nueva Vida
Woman's Day MotherChild: The Early Years

**5A. BLACK/AFRICAN-AMERICAN**

**AUDITED**
Black Collegian, The
Essence*

**NON-AUDITED**
Aim
American Visions
Black Elegance
Black Pages
Career Focus
College Preview
Dawn
Excel
First Opportunity
Journal of the National Technical
 Association
New Orleans Tribune, The
Right Choices
SuccessGuide 1992

**6. BOATING & YACHTING**
**(See also: Fishing & Hunting; Sports.)**

**AUDITED**
Boating
Cruising World
Ensign, The
Florida Sportsman*
Lakeland Boating
Motor Boating & Sailing
Power And Motoryacht
Sail
Sailing World
Salt Water Sportsman
Sea Magazine
Trailer Boats
WoodenBoat
Yachting
Yachtsman's Guide to the Virgin Islands

**NON-AUDITED**
American Sailor
Boatbuilder
Boating World
Chesapeake Bay Magazine
Eastern/Southeast Boating Newspaper
Embassy's Complete Boating Guide to
 Florida's East Coast
Embassy's Complete Boating Guide to
 Long Island Sound
Embassy's Complete Boating Guide to
 Rhode Island & Massachusetts
Great Lakes Boating
Great Lakes Sailor
Heartland Boating
Hot Boat
Jet Skier Magazine
Log, The
Long Island Power & Sail
MotorBoat Magazine
Ocean Navigator
Offshore
Pacific Boating Almanac
Personal Watercraft Illustrated
Pleasure Boating
Powerboat
Sailboat & Equipment Directory
Sailing
Santana
Soundings
Southern Boating
Southern Saltwater*
Splash
Water Scooter
Waterway Guide
Yachtsman's Guide To The Bahamas

**7. BRIDES, BRIDAL**
**(See also: Home Service & Home;
Women's; Women's/Men's Fashions,
Beauty & Grooming.)**

**AUDITED**
Bridal Guide
Bride's and Your New Home
Elegant Bride
Modern Bride

**NON-AUDITED**
Bridal Crafts
Bridal Fair
National Bridal Publications, Inc.
New England Bride
New Jersey Bride
Weddings West

**8. BUSINESS & FINANCE**
**(See also: Fraternal, Professional
Groups, Service Clubs, Veteran's Or-
ganizations & Associations.)**

**AUDITED**
Barron's-National Business and Financial
 Weekly*
Better Investing

Black Enterprise*
Business Week*
Cahners Magazine Network*
D & B Reports*
Economist, The North America Edition
Entrepreneur
Financial World*
Forbes
Fortune
Frequent Flyer
Governing*
Harvard Business Review
Hispanic Business
Home Office Computing*
Inc.
Institutional Investor*
Kiplinger's Personal Finance Magazine*
Medical Economics
Money*
Nation's Business
New Woman*
Professional Managerial Network, The*
Real Estate Today*
Scientific American*
Success
Wall Street Journal, The*
Working Woman*
World Monitor*
Worth

**NON-AUDITED**
Across the Board
Dollars & Sense*
Entrepreneurial Woman
Europe
Extra Income
Franchise Opportunities Guide
Income Opportunities
Income Plus
Individual Investor
Jay Schabacker's Mutual Fund Guides and
 Directory
Make Money
Opportunity Magazine
Small Business Opportunities
SRDS Media and Market Planner: Financial
 Markets*
Your Money

**8A. CAMPERS, RECREATIONAL
VEHICLES, MOTOR HOMES &
TRAILERS
(See also: Camping & Outdoor Recrea-
tion; Fishing & Hunting; Sports; Travel.)**

**AUDITED**
Motorhome
Trailer Life

**NON-AUDITED**
Coast to Coast Magazine
Family Motor Coaching
Highways
Northeast Outdoors
RV West
Trailblazer
Woodall's 1992 RV Buyer's Guide

**8B. CAMPING & OUTDOOR
RECREATION
(See also: Campers, Recreational
Vehicles, Motor Homes & Trailers;
Fishing & Hunting; Sports; Travel.)**

**AUDITED**
AAA CampBook
Backpacker
Sierra*

**NON-AUDITED**
American Park Network
Camping and RV Magazine
KOA Directory Road Atlas and Camping
 Guide
Lost Treasure
National Park Guide
Summit
Texas Parks & Wildlife Magazine
Trailer Life Campground & RV Services
 Directory
Treasure
Wheelers RV Resort & Campground Guide
Woodall's 1992 Campground Directory
Woodall's 1992 Tent Camping Guide

**9. CHILDREN'S
(See also: Babies; Education &
Teacher; Women's; Youth.)**

**AUDITED**
Fantastic Flyer Magazine

**NON-AUDITED**
Essential News
Pack-O-Fun

**9A. CIVIC**

**AUDITED**
Kiwanis Magazine
Rotarian, The

**NON-AUDITED**
Lion, The

**9B. COLLEGE & ALUMNI**

**AUDITED**
Advance
Business Today
Campus Connection
College Outlook
Directions
U. The National College Newspaper

**NON-AUDITED**
Alcalde
AllCampus Media

Breaker's Guide
BYU Today
California Monthly
Career Futures
Careers & Majors
Carolina Alumni Review
Collegiate Insider Magazine
Collegiate Sports/Alumni Network
Columns
Directory of Classes
Drew Magazine
Florida Leader Magazine
For Graduates Only
Harvard Magazine
Ivy League Magazine Network, The
Key—College Transfer
Missouri Alumnus
Montanan
Ole Miss Alumni Review
Penn Stater, The
Rutgers Magazine
Shout Magazine
Stanford Magazine, The
Term Planner
U.S. Foreign Student Magazine
UCLA Magazine
University Alumni Report, The

**10. COMICS & COMIC TECHNIQUE**

**AUDITED**
Archie Comic Group
Marvel Comics Group
Superman Group

**NON-AUDITED**
Cartoons
DC Group

**10A. COMPUTERS
(See also: Science/Technology.)**

**AUDITED**
AmigaWorld
CompuServe Magazine*
Compute
Computer Buyer's Guide and Handbook
Computer Shopper*
Data Based Advisor*
Digital Review*
InCider/A+
PC Computing
PC Magazine*
PC Novice
PC Today

**NON-AUDITED**
ComputerCraft
Game Player's PC Entertainment
Link-Up
MPC World
Online Access
PCM, The Premier Personal Computer
 Magazine for Tandy Computer Users
Rainbow, The
Run
Video Games & Computer Entertainment
Windows Magazine*

**11. CRAFTS, GAMES, HOBBIES &
MODELS
(See also: Art & Antiques; Automotive;
Aviation; Mechanics & Science.)**

**AUDITED**
Crafts 'N Things
Crafts Magazine
Dell Puzzle Magazine Group
Flying Models
Game Player's Nintendo Guide
Model Railroader
Radio Control Car Action
Railroad Model Craftsman
Trains
Workbasket

**NON-AUDITED**
American Woodworker
Basically Buckles
Better Homes and Gardens Special Interest
 Publications Bunnies, Bears & Cats
Better Homes and Gardens Special Interest
 Publications Christmas Cross Stitch
Better Homes and Gardens Special Interest
 Publications Christmas Ideas
Better Homes and Gardens Special Interest
 Publications Christmas Ornaments
Better Homes and Gardens Special Interest
 Publications Country Crafts
Better Homes and Gardens Special Interest
 Publications Dollmaker
Better Homes and Gardens Special Interest
 Publications Holiday Crafts
Blade Magazine, The
Ceramic Arts & Crafts
Ceramics
Ceramics Monthly
Classic Toy Trains
Coin Prices
Coin World
Coinage
Coins
Comics Buyer's Guide
Comics Buyer's Guide Price Guide
Contemporary Doll Magazine
Contract Bridge Bulletin, The
Creative Quilting
Crochet World
Cross Stitch Sampler
Cross Stitcher
Cross-Stitch Plus
Decorative Artist's Workbook
Decorative Arts Digest
Doll Crafter
Doll Designs
Doll Reader
Dolls
Dragon
FineScale Modeler

**Classification 11—Continued**
Fine Woodworking
Game Player's Sega Genesis Strategy
 Guide
Game Player's The Leading Magazine of
 Video and Computer Entertainment
Home Shop Machinist, The
Horoscope
International Doll World
Knitting World
Lapidary Journal
Linn's Stamp News
Live Steam
Llewellyn New Times, The
Magical Blend
Mainline Modeler
Miniature Collector
Miniatures Showcase
Model Airplane News
Needlepoint Plus
Numismatic News
Numismatist, The
Nutshell News
Old-Time Crochet
Passenger Train Journal
Popular Ceramics
Popular Magazine Group
Popular Woodworking
Quick & Easy Crafts
Quick & Easy Crochet
Quick & Easy Quilting
Quilt World
Radio Control Boat Modeler
Railfan & Railroad
Scott Stamp Monthly
Southwest Crafts
Stitch 'N Sew Quilts
Teddy Bear and Friends
Teddy Bear Review
Tole World
Toy Farmer
Toy Shop
Toy Trucker & Contractor
Tropical Fish Hobbyist
Woman's Day Best Ideas for Christmas
Women's Circle Crochet
Wood
Woodshop News
Woodsmith Sourcebook
Woodworker's Journal, The
World Coin News

**12. DANCING**

**NON-AUDITED**
American Square Dance Magazine

**13. DOGS & PETS
(See also: Fishing & Hunting.)**

**AUDITED**
Cat Fancy
Cats Magazine
Coonhound Bloodlines
Dog Fancy
Dog World
Gun Dog*
I Love Cats
Pure-Bred Dogs American Kennel Gazette

**NON-AUDITED**
American Cage-Bird Magazine
American Field
Animals
Aquarium Fish
Better Beagling
Bird Talk
Birds U.S.A.
Cat Companion From Friskies
Dogs USA
Hounds and Hunting
Kennel Review
Off-Lead

**14. DRESSMAKING & NEEDLEWORK
(See also: Women's; Women's/Men's
Fashions, Beauty & Grooming.)**

**AUDITED**
McCall's Needlework & Crafts
Sew News
Vogue Patterns

**NON-AUDITED**
Sew Beautiful
Threads
Woman's Day Holiday Crafts & Granny
 Squares

**15. EDITORIALIZED & CLASSIFIED
ADVERTISING**

**NON-AUDITED**
Classified, Inc.

**16. EDUCATION & TEACHER
(See also: Art & Antiques; Children's;
Mechanics & Science; Music; Women's;
Youth.)**

**AUDITED**
Instructor
Learning92*
NEA Today

**NON-AUDITED**
Florida Leader Magazine for High School
 Students
Mangajin
PMLA
Teacher Magazine*

## 17. ENTERTAINMENT GUIDES & PROGRAMS
(See also: Art & Antiques; Entertainment & Performing Arts; Hotel Inroom; Metropolitan/Entertainment, Radio & TV; Music; TV & Radio/Communications & Electronics.)

### NON-AUDITED
American Repertory Theatre Guide
Around San Diego
Arts & Leisure Publications
Arts Alive!
Bank of Boston Celebrity Series Guide
Bienvenidos a Miami
Boston Ballet Guide
Boston Ballet's "The Nutcracker" 1992
Boston Classical Network, The
Capital Magazine
Coastal Guide
Colorado Arts Programs
Encore
Encore! Magazine
Entertainment
Fine Arts Folio
Focus: New York
Guide, The
Inside Hollywood
Key Magazines
Official Visitors Guide to Central Florida
Performing Arts Network
Playbill Magazine
Program Magazine of the Boston
  Symphony Orchestra, The
Promenade
Ravinia Festival Program
Regional Center for the Arts Magazine
Showtime
Soundcheck
Southern California Guide
Stagebill
Universal Amphitheatre Concert Program
  Guide
Welcome to Miami and the Beach

## 17A. ENTERTAINMENT & PERFORMING ARTS
(See also: Entertainment Guides & Programs; Media/Personalities; Metropolitan/Entertainment, Radio & TV; Music.)

### AUDITED
American Film
Cineaste
Coming Attractions
Entertainment Weekly*
Movies USA
Opera News
Premiere
SCENE
Take One
Us
Video Event

### NON-AUDITED
Blockbuster
Center Stage
Center, The
Dance Magazine
DancScene
Drama Review, The
Dramatics
Film Comment
Houston Symphony Magazine
Model & Performer
Movieline
Overture
Rave
Washington Opera Magazine, The

## 18. EPICUREAN

### AUDITED
Best Recipes
Bon Appetit
Food & Wine
Gourmet*
Wine Spectator, The

### NON-AUDITED
All About Beer
American Brewer
Chile Pepper, The
Chocolatier
Cookbook Digest
Eating Well
Heads Up
Kosher Gourmet Magazine, The
Quarterly Review of Wines, The
Quick 'N Easy Country Cookin'
Simply Seafood
Spotlight's Wine Country Guide
Uncle Dutchie's Gourmet Co-op
Vegetarian Times*
Wine & Spirits
Wine Enthusiast

## 19. FISHING & HUNTING
(See also: Boating & Yachting; Dogs & Pets; Horses, Riding & Breeding; Sports.)

### AUDITED
American Handgunner
American Hunter, The
American Rifleman
Aqua-Field Publications
Bassin'
Bassmaster
Bowhunter
Chevy Outdoors
Deer & Deer Hunting

Ducks Unlimited
Field & Stream
Fishing & Hunting News
Fishing Facts
Fishing World
Florida Sportsman
Fly Fisherman
Full Cry
Fur-Fish-Game
Game & Fish Magazine
Gun Dog
Guns & Ammo
Guns Magazine
Handguns
Hunting
In-Fisherman, The
Michigan Out-Of-Doors
Midwest Outdoors
New York Sportsman
North American Fisherman
North American Hunter
North American Whitetail
Outdoor Life
Pennsylvania Sportsman, The
Salt Water Sportsman*
Shooting Times
Southern Outdoors
Sport Fishing
Sports Afield
Texas Fish & Game
Western Outdoors
Wildfowl
Wing & Shot

### NON-AUDITED
American Handgunner's Annual Book Of
  Handguns
Angling America Magazine
Arizona Hunter & Angler
Bama Hunting Classic/Volunteer State
  Hunting Classic Bulletin
Bassmasters Classic Report
Bow & Arrow Hunting
Bowhunting World
California Angler
Crappie
Dakota Country
Dakota Outdoors
Deer Trail, The
Discovering and Exploring New Jersey's
  Fishing Streams
Dixie Gun Works Blackpowder Annual
Eastern Bowhunting
Fish and Game Finder Magazines
Fish Sniffer, The
Fisherman, The
Fishing in Maryland
Fly Rod & Reel
Flyfishing
Gray's Sporting Journal
Gulf Coast Fisherman
Gun List
Gun Show Calendar
Gun Week
Gun World
Guns & Ammo Annual 1992
Guns Magazine's 1992 Annual
Handloader Magazine
Hunt
Hunter Education Instructor
Hunting Annual 1992
In-Fisherman Walleye Guide, The
International Bowhunter
Marlin
Michigan Deer Spectacular Bulletin
Muzzle Blasts
New Alaska Outdoors, The
Northwoods Group
Outdoor America
Outdoor Press, The
Pheasants Forever
Rifle
Safari
Salmon Trout Steelheader
Shotgun Sports
Skeet Shooting Review
South Carolina Rules & Regulations for
  Hunting & Fishing Licensees
South Florida's Angler's Guide
Southern Saltwater
Sporting Classics
Tide
Trap & Field
Trapper and Predator Caller, The
Trout
Turkey Call
Turkey Hunter, The
Walleye
Western Outdoor News
Wisconsin Outdoor Journal
Wisconsin Whitetail Deer Expo Bulletin
Woods & Waters Protector

## 19A. FITNESS
(See also: Health; Men's; Sports; Women's.)

### AUDITED
Muscle & Fitness
Personal Fitness & Weight Loss

### NON-AUDITED
American Fitness Magazine
Fitness Plus
Flex
New Body
New Living
Woman's Day Guide to Your Body, Your
  Health
Woman's Day 101 Ways To Lose Weight
  and Stay Healthy

## 20. FRATERNAL, PROFESSIONAL GROUPS, SERVICE CLUBS, VETERAN'S ORGANIZATIONS & ASSOCIATIONS
(See also: Business & Finance; Civic; Military & Naval (Air Force, Army, Navy & Marines); Religious & Denominational; Women's.)

### AUDITED
American Legion Auxiliary's National News,
  The
Elks Magazine, The
Federal Times
Hadassah Magazine
Junior League Review
Reform Judaism
Scouting
VFW Magazine

### NON-AUDITED
B'nai B'rith International Jewish Monthly,
  The
California Veteran
D.A.C. News
Discovery YMCA
Eagle Magazine
GFWC Clubwoman
Jonathan
M.A.C. Gopher, The
National Fraternal Club News
Paraplegia News
SAR Magazine, The
Saving Social Security
Telephone Pioneer, The
Toastmaster, The

## 20A. GAMING

### NON-AUDITED
Bingo Bugle
Casino Player
Loose Change
Lottery Player's Magazine
New Jersey Casino Journal
Win Magazine
Winning!

## 21. GARDENING (HOME)
(See also: Home Service & Home.)

### AUDITED
Flower & Garden
Horticulture, The Magazine of American
  Gardening
National Gardening
Organic Gardening

### NON-AUDITED
American Horticulturist
American Rose, The
Better Homes and Gardens Special Interest
  Publications Garden Ideas and Outdoor
  Living
Carolina Gardener
Fine Gardening
Garden Design
Gardens & More
Herb Quarterly, The
Texas Gardener

## 21A. GAY PUBLICATIONS

### NON-AUDITED
Advocate, The
Genre
Guide Magazine

## 22. GENERAL EDITORIAL

### AUDITED
Air & Space/Smithsonian
American Heritage
American Legion Magazine, The
Americana
Archaeology
Architectural Digest*
Atlantic, The
Avenue
Bon Appetit*
Conde Nast Ltd., The
Connoisseur, The
Consumers Digest
Country America
Ebony
European Travel & Life*
Globe
Grit
Harper's Magazine
Harrowsmith Country Life
Hispanic
Hispanic Business*
Historic Preservation
Kiplinger's Personal Finance Magazine
Life
Mas
Metropolitan Home*
Modern Maturity*
Money
Mother Jones
National Enquirer
National Examiner
National Geographic Magazine
Natural History
New Age Journal
New Choices*
New Woman*
New Yorker, The
Parade
Private Clubs
Reader's Digest
Robb Report, The
Rolling Stone*
Saturday Evening Post, The
Sierra*
Smithsonian
Spy
Star
Town & Country
Utne Reader
Vanity Fair
Washington Post Magazine, The*
Wildlife Conservation
World Monitor
World Press Review

### NON-AUDITED
Adelante Magazine

American Scholar, The
Body, Mind & Spirit
Buzzworm
Celebrate Life!
Class
Commentary
Die Hausfrau-Das Fenster nach druben
Emerge
FAD
Feelin' Good
Futurist, The
Human Potential
Leadership Network, The
Lifestyles 5752
Monk
Natural Health
New Dimensions
New Republic - National Review Joint Buy
Joe Franklin's Nostalgia
Philip Morris Magazine
Reader's Digest Hispanic Edition
Trilogy
21st Century, The
24Hours
USA Today
USA Weekend
Wilson Quarterly, The
World & I, The

## 22A. GROUP BUYING OPPORTUNITIES

### AUDITED
American Express Publishing Corporation
  Group Advertising Incentive Plan
Conde Nast Ltd., The*
Conde Nast Package of Women, The*
Hachette Magazine Network
Hearst Power Packages
K-III Magazines Group Performance Plan
Knapp Signature Collection, The
Lang Communications Women's Lifestyle
  Network*
Macfadden Women's Group
Meredith Custom Marketing
Newsweek/Meredith Family Connection
Newsweek/Times Mirror Ad-Vantage
Professional Women's Network
Ser Padres Network
SpanAmerica

### NON-AUDITED
Creativity Network, The
Empire Press History Group, The
Leadership Network, The*
New York Times Company Magazine
  Group, The
Senior Publishers Media Group*
Times Mirror Magazine Network*

## 23. HEALTH
(See also: Fitness.)

### AUDITED
American Health
Better Nutrition for Today's Living
Changes
Diabetes Self-Management
Health Journal
Healthy Kids: 4-10*
In Health
Longevity
Prevention
Walking Magazine, The

### NON-AUDITED
Accent on Living
Arthritis Today
Bounty DiabetesCare Guide, The
Coping
Delicious!
Diabetes Countdown
Diabetes Forecast
Diabetes in the News
Eating Well*
Exceptional Parent
Generations
Health World
HeartBeat
Illustrated Directory of Handicapped
  Products, The
Independent Living
Just For You
Let's Live
Living Right
Mainstream
Ostomy Quarterly
Positive Approach, A
Saint Raphael's Better Health
Sober Times
Total Health
Vegetarian Times
Vim & Vigor
Vitality
Voice, The
Whole Life
Yoga Journal

## 23A. HISTORY

### NON-AUDITED
America's Civil War
American History Illustrated
Aviation Heritage
Civil War Times Illustrated
Highlander, The
Military History
Old West
True West
Vietnam
Wild West
World War II

## 24. HOME SERVICE & HOME
(See also: Gardening (Home); Women's.)

### AUDITED
Architectural Digest
Better Homes and Gardens

Better Homes and Gardens Special Interest
    Publications
Capper's
Colonial Homes
Country Home
Country Journal
Country Living
Country Sampler
Decorating Remodeling
Early American Life
Elle Decor
Family Handyman, The
Fine Homebuilding
Home
Home Mechanix
House Beautiful
House & Garden
Housing Guides of America
Metropolitan Home
Midwest Living
Northern California Home & Garden
Old-House Journal
Practical Homeowner
San Diego Home/Garden
Southern Accents
Southern Homes
Southern Living
Sunset
Traditional Home
TwentyOne Magazine
Unique Homes
Victorian Sampler
Workbench

**NON-AUDITED**

American Dream, The
Bay Area Homestyle Resource Magazine
Better Homes And Gardens Bedroom And
    Bath Ideas
Better Homes and Gardens Special Interest
    Publications Building Ideas
Better Homes and Gardens Special Interest
    Publications Country Kitchen Ideas
Better Homes and Gardens Decorating
    Ideas
Better Homes and Gardens Special Interest
    Publications Do-It-Yourself
Better Homes And Gardens Special Interest
    Publications Holiday Appetizers
Better Homes and Gardens Holiday
    Cooking
Better Homes and Gardens Special Interest
    Publications Home Plan Ideas
Better Homes and Gardens Special Interest
    Publications Home Products
    Guide
Better Homes and Gardens Low Calorie
    Recipes
Better Homes and Gardens Remodeling
    Ideas
Better Homes and Gardens Special Interest
    Publications Kitchen & Bath Ideas
Better Homes and Gardens Special Interest
    Publications Window and Wall Ideas
Builder's Best Home Designs
California Homes & Lifestyles
Country Accents
Country Almanac
Country Decorating Ideas
Country Living Kitchens
Country Style Homes, Plans & Designs
Decorating Remodeling Best Home Plan
    Designs
Decorating Remodeling Kitchen & Bath
    Custom Planner
Designers' Collection Home Plans
Distinguished Home Plans
Extra Equity for Homebuyers
FMO News
Hearst Special Publications
Home & Condo
Home Planner
HomeBuyer's Guide—Dallas/Fort Worth
Homestyles Group
Homestyles Home Plans
House Beautiful's Home Building
House Beautiful's Home Remodeling &
    Decorating
House Beautiful's Houses & Plans
House Beautiful's Kitchen/Baths
House Plans
Kansas City Homes & Gardens
Log Home Living
Magazine Publishing Company Network
Metropolis
New Homeowner
Northwest Kitchen & Bath Quarterly
Owner Builder, The
Poolife
Prime Real Estate
Renovator's Supply, The
Residential and Commercial SunSpaces
Seattle Home and Garden
Shop-At-Home Directory, The
Southwest Sampler
Temas—U. S. Edition
Timber Frame Homes
Victorian Homes
Washington Home & Garden
Welcome Homeowner Magazine
Woman's Day Gardening & Outdoor Living
    Ideas
Woman's Day Home Decorating Ideas
Woman's Day Home Improvement New
    Product Ideas 1991
Woman's Day Home Improvements
Woman's Day Kitchen & Bath New Product
    Ideas 1992
Woman's Day Kitchens & Baths

## 25. HORSES, RIDING & BREEDING
(See also: Fishing & Hunting.)

**AUDITED**

Blood-Horse, The
Chronicle of the Horse, The
Equus
Horse & Rider
Horse Illustrated
Horseplay
Practical Horseman

Quarter Horse Journal, The
Quarter Racing Journal, The
Spur
Western Horseman

**NON-AUDITED**

Appaloosa Journal
Arabian Horse World
Backstretch, The
California Horse Review
Equine Images
Garri's Horse World USA
Hoof Beats
Horse and Horseman
Horse Show
Horse World
Horsemen's Journal
Horsetrader, The
Hunter & Sport Horse
Maryland Horse
Modern Horse Breeding
Paint Horse Journal
Polo
Quarter Horse News
Quarter Racing Record, The
Rural Heritage
Saddle & Bridle
Saddle Horse Report
Thoroughbred Times
Voice of the Tennessee Walking Horse
Walking Horse Report
Western Horse, The

## 25A. HOTEL INROOM
(See also: Airline Inflight/Train
Enroute; Entertainment Guides &
Programs; Travel.)

**AUDITED**

Inn Room Magazine
Travelhost
Washington, D.C. Visitor's Guide
Where Magazine

**NON-AUDITED**

Arrived
Guest Guide
Guest Informant
Guestlife
Pinnacle
SRDS Media and Market Planner: Travel &
    Tourism Industries*
SV Entertainment
This Is Indianapolis
Traveler, The

## 27. LABOR, TRADE UNION

**NON-AUDITED**

Labor Press
Milwaukee Labor Press AFL-CIO

## 28. LITERARY, BOOK REVIEWS &
WRITING TECHNIQUES

**AUDITED**

Writer's Digest

**NON-AUDITED**

Antaeus
Granta
New York Review of Books, The
Parabola
Story
West Coast Review of Books
Writers' Journal
Yellow Silk

## 28A. MATURE MARKET

**AUDITED**

AARP Bulletin
Golden Years
Mature Outlook
McCall's Silver Edition
Modern Maturity
New Choices
Senior Spectrum Newspapers
Southern California Senior Life
VFW Auxiliary

**NON-AUDITED**

Arizona Senior World
Arthritis Today*
California Senior Citizen
Fifty Something Magazine
Good Old Days
Retired Officer, The*
Retirement Life
Senior Ads U.S.A.
Senior Magazine
Senior Publishers Media Group
Senior Spotlite
Senior Times
Sun Life
Vantage
Where to Retire

## 29A. MEDIA/PERSONALITIES
(See also: Entertainment Guides &
Programs; Entertainment & Performing
Arts; Music; Romance.)

**NON-AUDITED**

Sterling Women's Group

## 30. MEN'S
(See also: Automotive; Civic; Fishing &
Hunting; Fitness; Fraternal,
Professional Groups, Service Clubs,
Veteran's Organizations &
Associations; Mystery, Adventure &
Science Fiction; Sports.)

**AUDITED**

Details
EM: Ebony Man
Esquire
Field & Stream*

Gentlemen's Quarterly
M
Men's Fitness
Men's Health
National Lampoon
Outdoor Life*
Outside*
Penthouse
Petersen Magazine Network
Playboy
Popular Mechanics
Rolling Stone*

**NON-AUDITED**

American Survival Guide
Gallery
Genesis
Geomundo
Hombre De Mundo
Mecanica Popular
MGF
Oui
Players
Soldier of Fortune
Times Mirror Magazine Network

## 30A. METROPOLITAN / REGIONAL /
STATE
(See also: Entertainment Guides &
Programs; Metropolitan/Entertainment,
Radio & TV.)

**AUDITED**

Alabama Living
Alaska
Arkansas Times
Atlanta Magazine
Baltimore Magazine
Beverly Hills (213)
Boston Magazine
Bostonia Magazine
California City Group
Cape Cod Life
Carolina Country
Chicago
Chicago Life
Cleveland Magazine
Colorado Homes & Lifestyles
Columbus Monthly
Connecticut Magazine
Country Living Magazine
D Magazine
Delaware Today Magazine
Detroit Monthly
Diablo
Facets
Family Living
Grand Rapids Magazine
Hawaii Magazine
Honolulu Magazine
Houston Metropolitan Magazine
Hudson Valley
Imagen
Indianapolis Monthly
Kansas City Live!
Kentucky Living
L.A. West
Los Angeles Magazine
Louisville
Media Networks, Inc.
Memphis
Metro Magazines
Miami Mensual
Michigan Country Lines
Mid-Atlantic Country
Milwaukee Magazine
Minnesota Monthly
Monterey Bay
Mpls.-St. Paul
New Jersey Goodlife
New Jersey Monthly
New Mexico Magazine
New Orleans Magazine
New York Woman
Newport Beach (714)
North Dakota REC Magazine
North Shore
Northern Ohio Live
Ohio Magazine
Orange Coast
Orlando Magazine
Pacific Northwest
Palm Beach Life
Palm Springs Life
Palm Springs Life's Desert Guide
Peninsula
Penn Lines
Philadelphia Magazine
Phoenix Home & Garden
Pittsburgh Magazine
Ranch & Coast
Rhode Island Monthly
Rural Living
Sacramento Magazine
St. Louis Magazine
San Diego Magazine
San Francisco Focus
Seattle Weekly
South Florida
Southern Homes*
Spotlight Magazine
Sunrise Publications
Tampa Bay Life
Tennessee Magazine, The
Texas Monthly
Tucson Lifestyle Monthly Magazine
Ultra
Valley Magazine
Washington Flyer Magazine
Washington Post Magazine, The*
Washingtonian Magazine, The
Yankee

**NON-AUDITED**

Adirondack Life
Annapolitan
Aspen Magazine
Atlanta Lake Life Magazine
Atlantic City Magazine
Back Home in Kentucky

Blue Ridge Country
Boca Raton
Buffalo Spree
Cape Cod Home & Garden
Center
Charleston Magazine
Charlotte
CITI, Charlotte's Magazine of Fine Living
Coast & Country
Colorado Magazine
Colorado Official State Vacation Guide
Coral Springs Monthly
Delaware Valley
Denver Magazine
Down East
Eastsideweek
Escape Magazine
Exclusively Yours, Greater Milwaukee
516 Magazine
Florida Keys Magazine
Florida Living
Fort Lauderdale Magazine
Fox Valley Living
Georgia Journal
Georgia Magazine
Georgia Magazine
Great Lakes Travel & Living
Greenwich Magazine
Gulfshore Life
Hartford Monthly
Hi Class Living
House
Houston People
Illinois Farm Bureau Almanac
Inland Empire
Inside
Inside Chicago
Jacksonville Magazine
Jacksonville Today
Japanese-American Yellow Pages
KNOW Atlanta Magazine
L.A. Style
Long Beach Monthly
Louisiana Life
Manhattan
Metro
Midwest City Network
Mississippi Magazine
Missouri Magazine
Montana Magazine
Monthly, The
Nantucket Journal
Nashville Visitor's Guide
Network Publications
New Dominion
New Hampshire Profiles
New York Alive
Nightlife Magazine
Northeast Ohio Avenues
NorthwestLiving!
Oh! Idaho
On The Avenue
On The Town
Orange County Magazine
Oregon Coast
Oregon Trail Magazine
Palm Beach Illustrated
Peachtree Magazine
Phoenix
Plantation Monthly
Richmond Flyer Magazine
Richmond Surroundings
Roanoker
Rockford Magazine
Rural Living
Salt Lake City
San Antonio Monthly Magazine
San Francisco's The City Magazine
Santa Barbara Magazine
Sarasota Magazine
Social Pictorial Review
Southern California Magazine
Southwest Profile
STL: The Art of Living in St. Louis
Tampa Bay Magazine
Utah Holiday Magazine
Vail Magazine
Valley Magazine, The
Vermont Magazine
West Virginia - It's You!
Willamette Week
Winston-Salem Magazine
Wisconsin Trails

## 30B. METROPOLITAN/ENTERTAINMENT,
RADIO & TV
(See also: Entertainment Guides &
Programs; Entertainment & Performing
Arts; Metropolitan / Regional / State.)

**AUDITED**

Cable Guide, The
Eleven

**NON-AUDITED**

Cable TV Magazine Network
Fine Tuning
KPBS On Air
Nine Magazine
Public Broadcasting Magazine Network
Public Broadcasting National Print Network,
    The
San Antonio Focus
WETA

## 31. MILITARY & NAVAL (AIR FORCE,
ARMY, NAVY & MARINES)

**AUDITED**

Air Force Times
Army Times
Army Times Military Group
Family
Military Lifestyle
Navy News
Navy Times
Off Duty
Salute

## Classification Groupings - U.S. Consumer Magazines continued

**NON-AUDITED**
Armed Forces Communications, Inc.
Base Paper Company, The
CASS Military Base Newspaper Network
Leatherneck
Marine Corps League
Military
Military Base Paper Division, EBM Military Consumer Group
Military Media Inc.
Military Newspapers of Virginia
Naval History
Retired Officer, The

**31A. MOTORCYCLE**
(See also: Automotive.)

**AUDITED**
American Motorcyclist
Cycle News
Cycle World
Dirt Bike
Dirt Rider Magazine
Dirt Wheels
Easyriders
Motocross Action
Motorcyclist
Rider

**NON-AUDITED**
Biker
Cycle World 1991 Annual & Buyer's Guide
Harley Women
Hot Bike
Motorcycle Road Racer Illustrated
Motorcyclist's Post, The
SuperCycle
3&4 Wheel Action

**33. MUSIC**
(See also: Education & Teacher; Entertainment Guides & Programs; Entertainment & Performing Arts; Literary, Book Reviews & Writing Techniques; TV & Radio/Communications & Electronics.)

**AUDITED**
Audio
Bam
Car Audio and Electronics
CD Review
Circus Magazine
Country Music
Electronic Musician
Guitar For The Practicing Musician
Guitar Player
Keyboard
Metal Edge
Music Express
Musician Magazine
New Route
Pulse!
Request
Rip
Rolling Stone
Spin
Stereo Review
Stereophile

**NON-AUDITED**
Absolute Sound, The
Acoustic Guitar
Audio/Video Interiors*
Bam Network, The
Bass Player
Bluegrass Unlimited
Car Stereo Review
Compact Disc Buyers' Guide
Contemporary Christian Music
Country Song Roundup
Down Beat
Drum Corps World
Faces Rocks/Metal Muscle Combination
Guitar School
Guitar World
Hit Parader
Home & Studio Recording
Illinois Entertainer
Jazziz
Jazztimes
Keyboard Classics
Modern Drummer
Music & Sound Buyer's Guide
Music City News
OnlyMusic
Ovation
Rock
Rocket, The
Sheet Music Magazine
Stereo Buyers' Guide
Today's Music Educator
Video Buyers' Guide
Word Up!

**34. MYSTERY, ADVENTURE & SCIENCE FICTION**

**NON-AUDITED**
Davis Reader Group, The
Fate
Heavy Metal
Magazine of Fantasy and Science Fiction, The

**35. NATURE & ECOLOGY**

**AUDITED**
Audubon
National Parks
Sierra
Wildbird Magazine

**NON-AUDITED**
American Birds
American Forests
Bird Watcher's Digest
Birder's World
Birding

**Classification 35—Continued**
E Magazine
Earthwatch
Garbage
Pacific Discovery
Sea Frontiers
Zoo Life

**36A. NEWS - WEEKLIES**
(See also: News - Biweeklies, Dailies, Semimonthlies.)

**AUDITED**
American Medical News
Entertainment Weekly
Insight On The News
Jet
Maclean's-Canada's Weekly Newsmagazine
New York Magazine
New Yorker, The*
Newsweek
People Weekly
Sports Illustrated
Time
TV Guide
U.S. News & World Report
Washington Post National Weekly Edition, The

**NON-AUDITED**
T.L.C.

**36B. NEWS - BIWEEKLIES, DAILIES, SEMIMONTHLIES**
(See also: News - Weeklies.)

**AUDITED**
USA Today*
Village Voice*

**NON-AUDITED**
European*
San Antonio Current

**36C. NEWSWEEKLIES (ALTERNATIVES)**

**AUDITED**
Chico News & Review
City Pages
Creative Loafing
Dallas Observer
East Bay Express
Isthmus
L.A. Weekly
Memphis Flyer, The
Nashville Scene
New Times
San Jose Metro
Tucson Weekly, The
Westword

**NON-AUDITED**
Baltimore City Paper
Casco Bay Weekly
Coast Weekly
Houston Press
In Pittsburgh
Independent, The
Maine Times
Metroland
Paper, The
Philadelphia City Paper
Random Lengths
Santa Fe Reporter, The
Syracuse News Times
Welcomat

**37. NEWSLETTERS**

**NON-AUDITED**
ARN News
In the Groove
Krefeld Immigrants and Their Descendants
NASCAR News
National Coalition News
Newsletter of the Institute for Studies in American Music
Odyssey
Outdoor Woman
Suds 'n Stuff
Visibility

**38. NEWSPAPER DISTRIBUTED MAGAZINES**

**AUDITED**
Chicago Tribune Magazine
Chicago Tribune TV Week Magazine
Los Angeles Times Magazine
The New York Times Magazine
Parade*
San Francisco Examiner Image
Sunday Magazine Network
Vista
Washington Post Magazine, The

**NON-AUDITED**
USA Weekend*

**38A. PARENTHOOD**

**AUDITED**
Disney Channel Magazine, The
Healthy Kids: 4-10*
Mickey Mouse Magazine
Parenting*
Parents*
Sesame Street Magazine*

**NON-AUDITED**
All About Kids
Bay Area Parent

Boston Parents' Paper, The
CASS Metropolitan Parenting Publications Network
Chicago Parent Newsmagazine
Childsplay
Grand Rapids Parent Magazine
Long Island Parenting News
MetroKids
Minnesota Parent
Mothering
Northwest Parent
Our Kids Houston
Our Kids San Antonio
Parents' Press
Rhode Island Parents' Paper, The
San Diego Family Press
San Francisco Peninsula Parent
South Florida Parenting
Today's Family
Working Moms & Dads

**39. PHOTOGRAPHY**

**AUDITED**
American Photo
Camera & Darkroom Photography
Darkroom & Creative Camera Techniques
Outdoor Photographer
Petersen's Photographic Magazine
Photographer's Forum
Popular Photography
Shutterbug

**NON-AUDITED**
Outdoor & Travel Photography
Picture Perfect
PSA Journal

**41. POLITICAL & SOCIAL TOPICS**
(See also: News - Weeklies; News - Biweeklies, Dailies, Semimonthlies.)

**AUDITED**
American Spectator, The
Foreign Affairs
Nation, The
National Review
New Republic, The
Reason
Washington Journalism Review

**NON-AUDITED**
Commonweal
Crisis, The
Diplomatic World Bulletin
Foreign Service Journal
Human Events
Issues in Science and Technology
National Interest, The
Political Science Quarterly
Responsive Community, The
Spotlight, The
Washington Monthly, The

**42. RELIGIOUS & DENOMINATIONAL**
(See also: Fraternal, Professional Groups, Service Clubs, Veteran's Organizations & Associations.)

**AUDITED**
Catholic Digest

**NON-AUDITED**
America
Bible Review
Biblical Archaeology Review
Catholic Answer, The
Catholic Twin Circle
Chai Today
Charisma
Christian Century, The
Christian Herald
Christian Ministry, The
Christian Reader, The
Christianity Today
Church Herald, The
Discipleship Journal
Episcopal Life
Group
Group's Jr. High Ministry
Jacobs Religious List
Kashrus
Leadership
Living Church, The
Lutheran, The
Marriage Partnership, The
Moment
Moody
National Catholic Register
Nor'easter
Official Catholic Directory, The*
Our Sunday Visitor
PCA Messenger, The
Presbyterian Survey
Quest, The
Saint Anthony Messenger
This People
Word of Life Quarterly

**43. SCIENCE/TECHNOLOGY**
(See also: Computers; Mechanics & Science.)

**AUDITED**
Astronomy
Discover
Omni
Popular Science
Science News
Sciences, The
Scientific American
Spectrum Magazine, IEEE

**NON-AUDITED**
Earth
Final Frontier
Science Probe!
Scientist, The*
Sky & Telescope
Technology Review

**43B. SEX**

**NON-AUDITED**
Chic
Hustler
Swank

**44. SOCIETY**

**AUDITED**
City & Country Club Life
Interview

**NON-AUDITED**
Bay Window
Palm Beach Society Magazine

**45. SPORTS**
(See also: Automotive; Aviation; Boating & Yachting; Fishing & Hunting; Fitness; Horses, Riding & Breeding; Motorcycle; Snowmobiling.)

**AUDITED**
Baseball Digest
Bicycle Guide
Bicycling
Bill Mazeroski's Baseball
BMX Plus
Bowling Digest
California Bicyclist
California City Sports
Dick Vitale's Basketball
Don Heinrich's College Football
Don Heinrich's Pro Preview
Executive Golfer
Football Digest
Golf Digest
Golf Magazine
Golf World
Great Golf Resorts of the World
Inside Sports
Lindy's Football Annuals
Mountain Bike Action
Outside
Petersen's Pro Football
Rodale Active Network
Runner's World
Scholastic Coach
Ski
Skiing
Skin Diver Magazine
Snow Country
Snow Week
SnoWest
Snowmobile
Southern Links/Western Links
Sport
Sporting News
Street & Smith's Baseball
Street & Smith's College Basketball
Street & Smith's College Football
Street & Smith's Pro Basketball
Street & Smith's Pro-Football
Surfing
Tennis
Transworld Skateboarding
Triathlete
Underwater USA
VeloNews
Volleyball
Water Ski
Winning: Bicycling Illustrated
Women's Sports and Fitness
WWF Magazine

**NON-AUDITED**
ACC Basketball Handbook
Action Pursuit Games
Amateur Athlete
American Hockey Magazine
American Rowing
American Snowmobiler
American Woman Magazine
Athlon Sports Communications Inc.
Balloon Life
Balls & Strikes
Baseball America
Baseball Card News
Baseball Card Price Guide Monthly
Baseball Cards
Basketball Digest
Basketball Weekly
Bear Report
Beckett Baseball Card Monthly
Bicycle Guide's Buyers' Annual
Bicycle Paper, The
Bicycle USA
Billiards Digest
Black College Sports Review
Bowling
Bullpen
Canoe
Canoe & Kayak Racing News
Card Collector's Price Guide
Chicago District Golfer
Chicago Sports Profiles
Chicagoland Golf
Clell Wade Coaches Directory, Inc.
Climbing
College Basketball Yearbooks
Country Club, The
Cross Country Skier
Cycling USA
Dave Campbell's Texas Football
Dive Training
Ehlert Outdoor Enthusiast Group
Fairway Guide
Fairways & Greens
Fantasy Baseball
Fisheye View Scuba Magazine

Florida Golfer
Florida Sports Magazine
Football News
Football, Basketball and Hockey Collector
Fore
Giants Newsweekly, The
Go
Golf For Women
Golf Georgia
Golf Tips
Golf Traveler
Golfweek
Greater Hartford Open Spectator Guide
Gulf Coast Golfer
Hockey Digest
Host Creative Communications Sports
    Publications
Hummer Trail & Touring Guide
Inside Karate
Inside Kung-Fu
Inside Kung-Fu Presents Inside Tae Kwon
    Do
International Gymnast
L. A. Sports Profiles
Lacrosse
Let's Play Hockey
Let's Play Softball
Majors Series, The
Met Golfer, The
MetroSports Magazine
Michigan Golfers Map & Guide
Minnesota Hockey
Minnesota Soccer Times
NASTAR Guide
National Croquet Calendar, The
National Directory of College Athletics
    (Men)
National Directory of College Athletics
    (Women)
National Masters News
National Sports Review, The
NCGA News
Network
New England Golf
New England Runner
New York Running News
1992 Western Open
North Texas Golfer
Northern California Schedule, The
Pacific Diver
Packer Report
Paddler
Paintball Magazine
Palaestra
Parachutist
Petersen's College Basketball
Petersen's College Football
Petersen's Pro Baseball
Petersen's Pro Basketball
Philadelphia Golf Magazine
Powder
Professional Sports Publications
Professional Team Publications
Pro Football Weekly
Prorodeo Sports News
Racquet
Racquetball Around Ohio
Racquetball Magazine
Referee
Rocky Mountain Sports Magazine
Rugby
Running Times
Scuba Times
Show, The
Silent Sports
Skating
Ski America
Skier's Pocket Guide
Skybox
Skydiving
Slo-Pitch News
Snow Goer
Snowboarder
Snowmobiler's Race & Rally
Soccer California
Soccer Digest
Southwest Cycling
The Sporting News Baseball Yearbook
The Sporting News College Basketball
    Yearbook
The Sporting News College Football
    Yearbook
The Sporting News Fantasy Baseball
    Owner's Manual
The Sporting News Hockey Yearbook
The Sporting News Pro Basketball
    Yearbook
The Sporting News Pro Football Yearbook
Sports 'N Spokes
Sports Card Trader
Sports Collectors Digest
Sports Media, Inc.
Sports View College Basketball Preview
Sports View College Football Preview
Spring Training
Surfer Magazine
Swimming World-Junior Swimmer
Taekwondo World
Tavern Sports International
Tennis West
Texas Bicyclist
Texas Coach
Track & Field News
Trading Cards
Tuff Stuff
U. S. Croquet Gazette Annual
U.S. Roller Skating
U.S. Senior Open Magazine
U.S. Sports Magazine
UMI's Southeastern Basketball Handbook
USA Gymnastics
Vermont Sports Today
Volleyball Monthly
Water Skier, The
Wind Surfing
Windy City Sports
Wisconsin Golf
Wisconsin Golf Directory
Wisconsin Snowmobile News
Woman Bowler

Yellow Jersey Group Publications
Youth Soccer News

## 46. TRAVEL
(See also: Airline Inflight/Train
Enroute; Automotive; Aviation;
Entertainment Guides & Programs;
Hotel Inroom.)

### AUDITED
AAA TourBooks
AAA World
Adventure Road
Aloha
Avis Traveler
Business Traveler International
Cape Cod Guide
Caribbean Travel & Life Magazine
City Guide
Conde Nast Traveler
Cruise Travel Magazine
Departures
Discovery
Diversion
Endless Vacation
European Travel & Life
Friendly Exchange
Friends
Gourmet
Home and Away
Islands
Michigan Living
Motorland
National Geographic Traveler
Physicians' Travel & Meeting Guide
See Magazines
Sierra*
Tours & Resorts
Travel & Leisure
Travel Holiday
Vacations
Vista USA
Westways

### NON-AUDITED
AAA Going Places Magazine
AAA Today
AsiaPacific Travel
Berlitz Cruise Guides
Best Read Guide
British Heritage
Connecticut Traveler
Country Inns Bed & Breakfast
Cruise Passenger Network
Cruises & Tours
Destination Washington
Finger Lakes Travel Guide
Florida World Magazine
Ford Times
Ford's Freighter Travel Guide and
    Waterways of the World
Georgia On My Mind
Golden State
Hawaii Drive Guides
Humm's Guide To The Florida Keys
International Living
International Travel News
Interval International Traveler
Japanese City Guide
Keys Guide, The
Midwest Magazine Network
Midwest Motorist, The
Milepost, The
Nashville City Guide
National Motorist
Nevada Magazine
New England Living Travel Guide
New York Motorist
New York Social Calendar
Northwest Travel
Ohio Motorist, The
Pacific Companion
Preferred Traveller
Rand McNally Road Atlas
Rand McNally's Deluxe Road Atlas and
    Travel Guide
Rocky Mountain Motorist
SRDS Media and Market Planner: Travel &
    Tourism Industries*
State, The
Student Travel Catalog
Tennessee Visitor Guide
Touring America
Tours!
Travel South
Travel 50 & Beyond
Vacation Reviews
Washington Motorist, The
Worldwide Travel Planner, The
Yankee Magazine's Travel Guide To New
    England

## 47. TV & RADIO/COMMUNICATIONS &
ELECTRONICS
(See also: Mechanics & Science;
Music.)

### AUDITED
ON SAT
Popular Electronics
Radio-Electronics
Satellite Orbit
Satellite TV Week
Video
Video Review
Videomaker

### NON-AUDITED
Audio/Video Interiors
Camcorder
CQ
Monitoring Times
Movie Marketplace
Palmer Video News
Popular Communications
Popular Electronics Hobbyists Handbook
QST
Radio-Electronics Electronics Experimenters
    Handbook
73 Amateur Radio Today

Worldradio

## 49. WOMEN'S
(See also: Babies; Brides; Bridal; Chil-
dren's; Dressmaking & Needlework;
Education & Teacher; Fitness;
Fraternal, Professional Groups, Service
Clubs, Veteran's Organizations & As-
sociations; Health; Home Service &
Home; Romance; Sports; Women's/
Men's Fashions, Beauty & Grooming;
Youth.)

### AUDITED
American Baby*
Baby Talk*
Child
Conde Nast Package of Women, The
Cooking Light
Cosmopolitan
Cosmopolitan En Espanol
Elle*
Episodes
Essence
Executive Female
Family Circle
First for Women
Glamour
Good Housekeeping
Harper's Bazaar*
Harper's Bazaar En Espanol
Healthy Kids: 4-10
Ideas Para Su Hogar
Ladies' Home Journal
Lady's Circle
Lang Communications Women's Lifestyle
    Network
Lear's
Longevity*
Mademoiselle*
McCall's
Mirabella
New Woman
Parenting*
Parents
Redbook Magazine
Sassy
Self
Ser Padres
Sesame Street Magazine
Seventeen
Shape
Soap Opera Digest
Soap Opera Weekly
'Teen
True Story
TV y Novelas U.S.A.
Us*
Vanidades Continental
Victoria
Vogue*
W
Weight Watchers Magazine
Woman's Day
Woman's Day Family Celebrations
Woman's Day Light Meals in Minutes
Woman's World
Working Mother
Working Woman
YM

### NON-AUDITED
Allure
American Woman
Buenhogar
Business Women Leadership Media
Christian Parenting Today
Fairfield County Woman
Family Circle Great Ideas
Family Circle Great Ideas Christmas Helps
    And Holiday Baking
Family Circle Great Ideas Light & Easy
    Meals
Family Circle Great Ideas Now! Fitness
Fast & Healthy Magazine
Home Cooking
Playgirl
Quarante
Soap Opera Update
Today's Chicago Woman
Today's Lifestyles
Today's Christian Woman
Tu International
Virtue
Woman's Day Special Interest Publications
Woman's Day Great Holiday Baking
Women's Circle
Women's Household
Women's Record, The

## 50. WOMEN'S/MEN'S FASHIONS,
BEAUTY & GROOMING
(See also: Brides, Bridal; Dressmaking
& Needlework; Women's.)

### AUDITED
Elle
Harper's Bazaar
Mademoiselle
New Woman*
Vogue

### NON-AUDITED
Model News
Models & Talent International Network
Swimwear Illustrated

## 51. YOUTH
(See also: Children's; Education &
Teacher; Religious & Denominational;
Women's.)

### AUDITED
Boys' Life
Careers
Fast Times
Junior Scholastic
Kid City Magazine
On Target
Right On! Group

**December, 1991**

Scholastic Teen Network
16 Magazine
Sports Illustrated for Kids
Sterling Teen Network
Teen Beat
3-2-1 Contact
Trends

### NON-AUDITED
Barbie
Campus Life
Career Success
Cheer News Today
Children's Magazines
Disney Adventures
Disney Comics
Eye, The
For Seniors Only
Game Player's Sports for Kids
GamePro
Journey
Key--High School Junior
Key--High School Senior
KidSports
New Expression
NYC
Purple Cow
School Guide
Splice
Surprises
Talbot's Student Planning Book
Teen Times
Teens Today
Thrasher
Topps Magazine
Tuff Stuff Jr.
VICA JOURNAL
Visions
Your Prom

(Courtesy *Consumer Magazine and Agri-Media Rates and Data*, December 1991 edition; reproduced with permission from Standard Rate and Data Service, Inc.)

### Newsletters

A newsletter is generally defined as a publication that is sold by subscription or distributed free. It is usually four to eight pages long, printed in one color, and often set in a typewriter face so as to help convey the immediacy of the newsletter's message.

There are approximately 4,500 subscription newsletters, covering a great variety of subjects. Some examples are *Hideaway Report, Retirement Letter, Sludge, Platt's Oilgram Report, Tightwad Gazette, Laughing Bear Newsletter, Cat Mews, Wrestling Observer Newsletter,* and *Jukebox Collector Newsletter.*

For the editors of newsletters, there is even the *Newsletter on Newsletters,* costing $120 for a year's subscription and published twice monthly by the Newsletter Clearinghouse, 44 West Market Street, Rhinebeck, NY 12572. *Time* magazine called it the bible of the industry.

Newsletters, usually high priced, can be very profitable for their publishers. A genuine service to their subscribers, newsletters often fill a need not met by business publications in the same fields. Getting started as a publisher of a newsletter is difficult, however, since it often takes years for the report to establish its credentials and its usefulness to readers. The newsletter field would not be our recommendation as an avenue for a new publishing venture.

In addition to paid-subscription newsletters, there are many free newsletters. These are sent to members of associations, organizations, or special groups.

In this chapter we have defined and categorized the various classes of magazines. Now we can approach the broader subject—how do magazines really work?

# THE SCOPE OF MAGAZINE PUBLISHING TODAY

According to a statistic developed by the Magazine Publishers of America (MPA), an average of 1.3 new magazines are launched every day of the year. Of these, about half are consumer magazines. Is it overkill? Yes. Will it continue? Yes again, though probably on a reduced basis. The reason for this proliferation is what one commentator calls "niche-itis"—the need to inform and entertain readers who share a special interest, be it a consumer life-style or a business specialization.

But as we know, many new magazines will not find their niche. In 1990 about a dozen magazines published by experienced publishers bit the dust. The list includes *Taxi, Model, Memories, 7 Days, Business Month,* and Forbes's *Egg.* Also in 1990 the following magazines were either sold or merged with other magazines:

| | |
|---|---|
| *American Health* | *McCall's Needlework* |
| *Cable Vision* | *& Craft* |
| *Compute!* | *National Examiner* |
| *Consumer Electronics* | *Sail* |
| *Globe* | *Sunset* |
| *M. inc.* | *Workbasket* |

Again in 1990 Time Warner, in the interest of satisfying the public's unquenchable thirst for coverage of the entertainment industry, kicked off a new magazine, *Entertainment Weekly.* It is estimated that this publication will take five years and $150 million to break even.

In 1991 the following magazines were sold or merged:

| | |
|---|---|
| *Broadcasting* | *Mother Earth News* |
| *Daily Racing Form* | *Psychology Today* |
| *Discover* | *Smart* |
| *Golf Illustrated* | *Spy* |

Yet this bold adventurism is what makes magazine publishing such a fascinating endeavor, one that attracts investors and entrepreneurs on an almost-endless search for publishing's gold medal.

### Who Dominates Publishing?

As in most fields, a handful of large publishers dominate the magazine industry. Here is a list of some of the top parent companies in magazine publishing and their prominent offspring:

*Time Inc. Magazines*
Approximate Annual Revenues—$2 billion
| | |
|---|---|
| *People* | *Sports Illustrated* |
| *Time* | *Fortune* |

*Condé Nast*
Approximate Annual Revenues—$1.2 billion
| | |
|---|---|
| *Parade* | *Glamour* |
| *Vogue* | *Vanity Fair* |

*Hearst Corp.*
Approximate Annual Revenues—$1.1 billion
| | |
|---|---|
| *Good Housekeeping* | *Redbook* |
| *Cosmopolitan* | *Esquire* |

*Hachette Publications*
Approximate Annual Revenues—$585 million
| | |
|---|---|
| *Women's Day* | *Car & Driver* |
| *Elle* | *Popular Photography* |

*Reed International*
Approximate Annual Revenues—$422 million
(Cahners Magazines)
| | |
|---|---|
| *Publishers Weekly* | *Professional Builder* |
| *Emergency Medicine* | *Restaurants & Institutions* |

*Reader's Digest Association*
Approximate Annual Revenues—$515 million
| | |
|---|---|
| *Reader's Digest* | *Family Handyman* |
| *American Health* | *Travel-Holiday* |

We have highlighted a half-dozen major magazine companies. There are a total of fifteen publishing organizations whose annual revenues exceed $300 million. Clearly, large publishers dominate this industry. In terms of individual magazines, about forty have annual revenues of more than $100 million.

## Some Statistics on Magazine Readership

The leading research organization, Mediamark Research Inc. (MRI), has conducted surveys on magazine readership. Its significant conclusions show that nearly everyone reads magazines:

—88 percent of the U.S. population eighteen years of age or older read one or more magazines during an average month.

—The average magazine copy has just under five readers per copy.

—The median age of magazine readers is thirty-nine years; 40 percent are at least high school graduates, and 62 percent are married.

## How Much Do Advertisers Spend in Magazines?

In 1991, advertisers spent more than $7 billion in consumer magazines. Of this total, automotive advertisers spent the most, $940 million, with toiletries and cosmetics next at $629 million.

Philip Morris and its various companies was the top spender with $167 million, followed by General Motors with $162 million and Procter & Gamble with $111 million.

Now that we have touched on the scope of magazine publishing, we will discuss its individual functions.

# 2

# Functions and Responsibilities of the Publisher and Business Staff

It was said that at the *New Yorker* editorial types coexisted peacefully with members of the business side while maintaining a safe distance of three floors between them. At some magazines the editor outranks the publisher; at others the reverse is the case.

The division of the roles of editor and publisher has been characterized as a church-and-state relationship: Thou shalt not tread on the other's ground. This caveat seems to be breaking down, however, at least at Time Inc. magazines. There the managing editor of *Sports Illustrated* was also named publisher, and so his duties include counseling his top editors as well as running the business side of the magazine.

At *Life* magazine the same system prevails. *Rolling Stone's* Jann Wenner is both editor in chief of the magazine and chairman of the company. Ed Kosner is the editor and president of *New York* magazine. With the increasing complexity of magazine operations today, we may see the old system of role separation eliminated.

The publisher generally is responsible for the key areas of advertising sales, newsstand circulation, subscriptions, production, promotion, and finance. On most magazines the publisher is also charged with budgeting, making financial projec-

tions, and preparing profit-and-loss statements for the magazine's board of directors or top management. In short, the publisher controls all business aspects of the magazine, with the tactful cooperation of the editorial side.

The following chart shows the structure of the business arm of a magazine and includes all the departments reporting to the publisher. Bear in mind that the sizes of staffs vary and that at a large consumer magazine a hundred people or more may answer to the advertising director, while at a small business magazine the entire noneditorial department may number six or eight.

## Advertising Director

The position of advertising director is usually number two on the business side of a magazine, with the individual reporting directly to the publisher. He or she is responsible for management of the advertising sales department, sets department policy and procedures, and is accountable for attaining advertising goals or quotas. The ad director is also responsible for recruiting and training sales personnel and for supervising branch managers. Sales promotion and research also fall into the advertising director's domain.

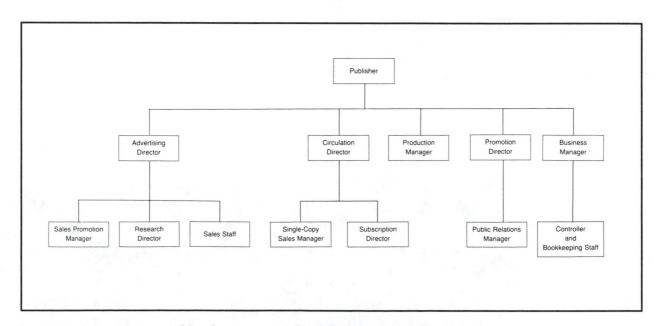

**Table of organization for the business arm of a magazine**

A magazine I published had annual advertising sales of $8 million. Supervising this advertising staff was the publisher and, under him, the advertising director, who had five full-time salespeople based in New York (two men and three women). We had a branch office in Chicago with one salesperson, and we used independent sales representatives in Los Angeles and Atlanta to cover the West and Southeast. In addition to these sales personnel, we employed a sales promotion manager who doubled in public relations. Larger magazines may have as many as thirty to forty salespeople covering just the New York area.

On a day-to-day basis the advertising director will perform a variety of functions, among them making key sales calls with the salespeople, developing sales strategy for new business, and analyzing call reports (reports on the results of a sales visit) submitted weekly by the house staff and the branch offices.

The advertising director also evaluates research and meets with his or her own staff to discuss problem areas—such as how to break into a new product classification or cover an industry convention—or to plan coordination of the efforts of the home-office salespeople and the out-of-town representatives. The advertising director additionally consults with editors concerning future editorial tie-ins. He or she will also direct the creation of sales promotion material relating to the sales of advertising; in this respect the advertising director will meet with the sales promotion manager, exchange ideas, and then approve copy and layouts before the material is printed.

This position on the business side of a magazine is demanding, highly coveted, and well paid. On even a small magazine, an advertising director will be paid about $40,000 to $45,000 a year. This figure can exceed $100,000 on a major publication.

## Sales Promotion Manager

A magazine's sales-promotion department is responsible for the creation of printed material and programs used to develop advertising sales. The work is varied and may include the writing of the publisher's letter that is bound into the free copies of each issue mailed to advertisers and prospects. This letter covers such subjects as the results of new surveys, new advertisers in the magazine, increased circulation figures, and awards won by the magazine. The sales department's work also includes the preparation of mailing pieces alerting possible advertisers to special issues of the publication, the coordination of contests or tournaments tied in to the advertising sales effort, and, from time to time, the creation of a sustained campaign to bring one large advertiser into the book. On a large consumer or business magazine, the department will have many employees headed by a creative director. (See chapter 10 on promotion for a further definition of this function.) At a smaller magazine one or two people are the entire staff. To understand the role of the sales promotion manager, or SPM, consider the following example, based on an actual sales promotion effort.

The advertising-space salesperson of a youth-oriented publication is having difficulty attracting a jeans manufacturer into the magazine. The SPM learns that the manufacturer is having its national sales meeting in Miami. The SPM arranges for the advertising director of the publication—an expert on the youth market—to address the group. The ad director, the SPM, and the space salesperson fly to Miami, where the ad director delivers a hip, no-nonsense, twenty-minute talk punctuated at the end with a soft sell for the magazine. Each of the jeans manufacturer's salespeople is given a copy of the speech, which contains a subtle reference to the fact that this magazine "delivers the jeans market efficiently and economically." A contest is also launched for the manufacturer's sales staff by the magazine.

The job is well done. The jeans salespeople applaud the ad director's speech. The manufacturer's sales manager is impressed and recommends to his own advertising manager that the company schedule ads in the magazine. The publication's space salesperson gets an extra commission, the ad director gets a sense of self-satisfaction from a job well done, and the SPM gets a pat on the back.

### Research Director

The job of selling advertising becomes more complex and sophisticated every day. Advertisers, in evaluating media, have an increasing need for knowledge about audience characteristics, since the problem is not only in choosing among TV and radio stations, newspapers, billboards, and business and consumer magazines but in selecting from the thousands of choices within each media group.

Many consumer magazines subscribe to syndicated field studies, such as those prepared by Mediamark Research Inc. (MRI) and Simmons, which evaluate these magazines' audiences according to demographic (social and economic) criteria. (See chapter 5.) This body of information can then be processed by advertising agency computers and ultimately utilized for the making of media decisions.

The important function of coordinating the mountain of readership information at a magazine is the responsibility of the research director. Research involves numbers, projections, and audience-sampling procedures. The research director and staff plan, develop, and execute all research projects (primary and secondary) to analyze existing and potential markets. Research is also concerned with improving a magazine's image and content, as well as generating advertising sales.

One needs to have a strong background in mathematics and statistics to fill this demanding role. A creative research director has the ability to locate the pertinent data and to compare the magazine's strengths with those of the competition. Effective presentation of this information by a magazine's sales force can often be the decisive factor in the determination of ad schedules.

### Sales Staff

Of all the personnel reporting to the advertising director, the people who sell the space are the most important. Armed with reams of promotion, research, and other sales tools, they forge their way each morning to the Madison Avenues of our land. For many magazines, whether consumer or business, advertising sales are the most significant

source of revenue, and the sales staff must deliver the goods.

Since we devote a whole chapter in this book to advertising sales, it is not necessary to define the precise workings of a sales staff at this point. It is helpful, however, to understand that the sales staff, composed of in-house salespeople and independent representatives, report directly to the advertising director.

### Circulation Director

When the advertising director says to the publisher at an executive-board meeting, "I must have a circulation of one million for the next ABC period or our competitors will knock our brains out," the message is clear: Find the circulation director, and let her or him figure out how to get 50,000 new subscriptions and 30,000 more single-copy sales in six months.

The circulation director, we soon learn, is a heavyweight in the magazine's pecking order. He or she is responsible for getting the magazine in the hands of the reader. For publications that sell both by the single copy and by subscription, the function assumes even greater importance. (See chapter 8 on subscriptions and chapter 9 on single-copy sales.)

### Single-Copy Sales Manager

We now call this category "single-copy sales," when just a few years ago we referred to it as "newsstand sales." Old-timers like me still use the latter phrase, even though "there ain't hardly no newsstands anymore." Newsstands have been replaced by racks in supermarkets, convenience stores, liquor stores, and air and rail terminals. There are 150,000 such outlets across the United States and Canada, and the imposing job of developing sales in these outlets falls on the usually broad back of the single-copy sales manager.

On a magazine this person will work to promote sales with the national distributor, the wholesalers, and the dealers. (See chapter 9.) The single-copy network has become extremely complex, crammed with problems of overcrowding, monopoly, censorship, and the like. For some inexplicable reason the job of single-copy sales manager is not highly paid and often does not command the esteem it deserves.

## Subscription Director

Many magazines do not lend themselves to newsstand (oops) or single-copy sales. Business publications, literary journals, and newsletters depend primarily on subscriptions for their circulation. Later on, in the chapter on subscriptions, we will find that there are a score of different approaches to subscription sales. In the field of direct mail alone exist hundreds of businesses that create, write, buy lists, print, and so on. The subscription director, usually a senior officer of the magazine, runs this total effort.

For those readers who want to make magazine publishing a career, we offer the tip that the field of subscriptions presents many opportunities for ambitious people. A flair for writing helps but is not essential, since there are many specialists performing this service. Many MBAs entering publishing choose the field of circulation, since it often leads to the top.

## Production Manager

In the past decade the cost of paper has almost doubled, typesetting and printing costs have gone up 6 to 8 percent a year, and all other material used in a magazine has been subject to the inflationary spiral. Small wonder, then, that production managers constantly wear a harried look. When you add the responsibility for quality control and the increasing sophistication of desktop publishing and other technologies to the production manager's work load, the job can become overpowering.

The production manager buys paper, negotiates printing contracts, and works with the art department on selecting color separators and typesetters. In addition, this person must make frequent visits to printing plants to oversee the actual running of the magazine at press time. To some the job is not much fun, and often it doesn't

pay well. The production manager is like an offensive lineman in football: He or she doesn't carry the ball (the editors think *they* do), but without this expert you couldn't run a magazine.

## Promotion Director

Earlier in this chapter we talked about the job of the sales promotion manager, who works primarily with the advertising sales department. Now we introduce the promotion director. What does she do? (More women than men work in this capacity.)

Let us suppose we are publishing a women's fashion magazine. Since department stores are of key importance to apparel and cosmetic manufacturers, we are producing a touring fashion show with the "look" that epitomizes our magazine's fashion philosophy. The show will be presented in various cities in cooperation with local department stores. Who is in charge of transporting the clothes, arranging for the music, placing ad tie-ins, coordinating window displays, serving as liaison with the national advertisers, and 101 other details incumbent in a promotion of this kind? The promotion director, of course.

Now suppose we are promoting newsstand sales. A magazine wholesalers' convention in California presents a prime opportunity to impress 500 decision makers with our totally new editorial concept. The promotion director arranges an exciting fashion show and a presentation by our editor as part of the convention program. It is a wonderful occasion for our magazine to make lots of points.

## Public Relations Manager

Many magazines use outside PR counsel. Some have in-house public relations staffs who coordinate their operations with outside counsel, but more often the PR manager operates without outside counsel. The public relations manager is responsible for the magazine's image with both the trade and the consumer.

If the magazine is involved in a lawsuit, the public relations manager handles press relations. If the magazine runs a particularly noteworthy story, this individual will try to break it in the national media. Is the magazine suffering from a flat editorial image? Then send the editor on an extensive tour of the country, visiting ten or twelve key cities. The PR manager will arrange for local TV, radio, newspaper, and magazine interviews. Publicity can be many times more effective than any advertising campaign—and it's a lot cheaper.

Writing courses and work on college newspapers are good preparation for entering the field of public relations. Professional PR writing is concise and contains no flowery phrases or opinions. The prospective PR person must also be persuasive and assertive without being too pushy, since "selling" a release to media members is a highly competitive task.

## Business Manager and Accounting Staff

And now a few words for the unheralded people who perform the voluminous financial tasks that keep the magazine operating as a business. Attending to cash flow, developing budget projections, producing monthly operating statements, investing the company's surplus cash, preparing the quarterly and annual reports, and, yes, even demanding a receipt for the $10 the art director is claiming for the cab he took home the night he worked until 11:00 P.M.—these are just some of the duties of the accounting department. The business manager of the publication or magazine company is in charge of this staff.

## The Young and the Powerful

In the advertising business today, young people are making the important ad-buying decisions at agencies and client advertisers. Or, as *MEDIA-WEEK* puts it, "How do you handle a 25-year-old buyer if you're a 45-year-old seller?" The answer? Appoint a young publisher. The following publishers of major magazines were all thirty-six or under as of April 1992:

Tom Florio, *Condé Nast Traveler,* thirty-five
Jay MacDonald, *Inc.,* thirty-five
John Skipper, Disney Publishing, thirty-six
Tony Glaves, *Southern Accents,* thirty-two

Lori Zelikow Florio, *New Woman,* thirty-three
Randy Jones, *Esquire,* thirty-six
Bob Guccione, Jr., *Spin,* thirty-six
Barbara Newton, *Organic Farming,* thirty-three

More and more, magazine publishing is becoming a young person's game.

In the next chapter we focus on the key role of the editor in the publishing process.

## Interview

Valerie Salembier is the first woman publisher in the sixty-year history of *Family Circle,* one of the world's largest-selling magazines for women. Breaking new ground is, in fact, the hallmark of her career.

After starting her publishing career in promotion at Time Inc., Salembier moved to *Newsweek,* where in 1972 she became the first woman hired on the advertising sales staff. Salembier then joined *Ms.* magazine and rose from advertising sales director to associate publisher. Later, at *USA TODAY,* Salembier played a key role in one of the country's most heralded media launches. During her five-year tenure as senior vice-president/advertising, advertising revenues at the national newspaper increased from $38 million to $140 million.

Her next step was a quantum leap to publisher of Rupert Murdoch's newly acquired *TV Guide.* From there she moved to the newspaper business, with the daunting challenge of guiding the *New York Post* at a time when its very existence was threatened. In March 1991 Salembier was named publisher of *Family Circle,* a publication of The New York Times Company Magazine Group.

She is a participant in many civic and professional organizations, such as the New York Sports Commission, the New York City Police Foundation, the United Jewish Appeal, and the Advertising Club of New York.

*Do you see magazine publishing as a growth area for the 1990s?*

Difficult as it may be to believe, with more than 11,000 magazines currently in print, there is still room for growth in magazine publishing in the

1990s. While the number of new launches may diminish slightly due to the overall economic slowdown, there are still many niches yet to be filled by specialized magazines. In contrast to the past, however, these magazines will be *reader-driven*—that is, designed to meet reader needs, rather than advertiser needs, since readers will be increasingly responsible for a magazine's profitable bottom line.

*Are there any departments of a magazine, such as ad sales, circulation, promotion, or editorial where, in your opinion, the demand for talent exceeds the supply?*

The critical word here is *talent*. For magazines to thrive we must constantly seek out and cultivate innovative people who will bring new ideas and solutions into every department. People of this caliber are always in demand, and increasing the pool of talent is vital to the continued health of our industry.

*Consumer magazines are generally considered more glamorous than business or trade magazines. Do you agree with this premise?*

Define "glamorous"! If by glamorous you mean a high profile with the average reader, then consumer magazines probably have a significant edge. Some would argue, though, that an editorial mention in *Variety, Women's Wear Daily,* or the *Wall Street Journal* is far more glamorous than in most consumer magazines. Glamour, I suppose, is really in the eye of the beholder.

*Do you think there are sufficient opportunities in magazine publishing outside New York City?*

There is no question that New York is the publishing capital, especially in terms of consumer magazines. There are certainly excellent opportunities in other markets as well. For example, the Meredith Corporation is headquartered in Des Moines, Iowa; the Southern Progress group is located in Birmingham, Alabama; Weider Publishing and the new Disney Publishing group are in Los Angeles. From an editorial standpoint many major magazines have bureaus in major metropolitan areas,

and some—like *U.S. News & World Report*—are headquartered outside New York. In addition, most major publishers have advertising sales offices in many of the top markets like Los Angeles, Chicago, and Detroit. And, of course, magazine printing is handled predominantly outside the New York area.

*The odds against succeeding with a new magazine are great. What areas do you think still offer opportunities?*

Wherever there are emerging demographic or psychographic trends, there are strong opportunities for magazine development. In terms of demographic trends, the growing minority population in the United States and the "graying" of the population overall should open new niches to serve the special interests of these readers. Similarly, rising interest in health and fitness should spark more mainstream entries in these fields. For example, *Fitness*—a new magazine from the New York Times Magazine Group's Women's Publishing Division—is designed for women who view fitness not as a passing fad but as a way of life.

*Career books generally conclude that an applicant must go through the personnel or human resources department in applying for a job, even though other approaches can be tried. Do you have any ideas about how someone applying for a magazine publishing position can circumvent this traditional approach?*

Naturally, personal contacts with people already in publishing can help open doors, but not everyone has such ready-made networking capabilities. These can be created, however, with some hard work and innovative thinking. Attend industry seminars, and follow up with a personal letter to one of the speakers who most impressed you. Read trade publications, and follow up with a personal letter to someone whose interview you found particularly insightful. Opportunities can be created, but you need to make the most of them by ensuring you don't waste the time someone may afford you. Do your homework: Be prepared with appropriate questions, be focused on your interests and direction, and don't expect a job offer on the spot!

*You made it in magazine publishing as a woman. In your opinion, have women achieved parity in this field?*

While I'm reluctant to declare parity at this point, there is little doubt that women have made enormous strides in virtually every aspect of magazine publishing. Perhaps more than any other industry, magazines have begun to dismantle the "glass ceiling" and have enabled women to rise to positions of fiscal responsibility and real decision-making power. And while few magazine companies have women at the helm (Christie Hefner at *Playboy* is a noteworthy exception), it may only be a matter of experience—and time.

# 3

# The Role of the Editor

The late Harold Ross of the *New Yorker* was a great editor. He never attended college and was not an outstanding writer, yet the standards he set during his long reign never compromised excellence. This tradition has been maintained for more than sixty years at the *New Yorker*. Recently, Tina Brown became only the fourth editor in the magazine's history. She proved to be a brilliant innovator in her eight years at *Vanity Fair*.

A portion of this magazine's editorial profile as it appears in SRDS provides the key to an understanding of the greatness Ross infused into the publication: "*The New Yorker*'s fiction pieces are selected for imagination and style: its articles exhibit candor, impartiality, intelligence, and where appropriate, a sense of humor."

There have been and are at present many fine editors at business and consumer magazines. John Mack Carter is an editorial giant who has brought fame to *McCall's*, the *Ladies' Home Journal*, and *Good Housekeeping*. Helen Gurley Brown made

*Cosmopolitan* the success it is today. Norman Cousins was a legend in his many years at the *Saturday Review*. William F. Buckley, Jr., brings erudition and wit to his controversial *National Review*.

The trendy Anna Wintour has revitalized *Vogue*. Tina Brown's gossipy, chic editorial style made another Condé Nast magazine, *Vanity Fair*, a big winner.

From the past, not to be overlooked are Hedley Donovan of *Time*, Edward Thompson of *Smithsonian*, Gilbert Grosvenor of *National Geographic*, and the Wallaces of *Reader's Digest*.

What can the neophyte editor learn from these greats? The answers are numerous, yet two overriding principles have been adhered to by all these editors. First, all have established distinct identities for their publications. Rather than "me too" publishing, they have developed unique personalities for their respective magazines. And second, they never forgot that a great editor knows and understands the magazine's audience. This factor, above all, is the essence of success in the

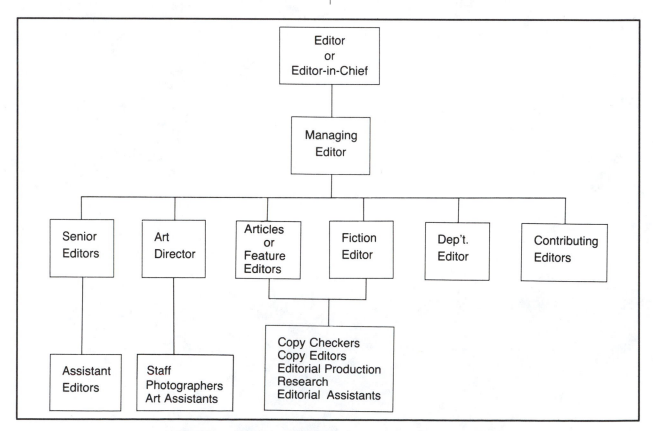

**Table of organization for the editorial arm of a magazine**

publishing of a magazine.

To better understand the craft of editing a magazine, we first need to understand the role of an editor. Simply speaking, the editor is the person having managerial and sometimes policymaking responsibility for the editorial portion of the magazine. Let us now track a month in the life of an editor of a monthly magazine.

## First Week

A general meeting is held with the associate and assistant editors, the staff writers, and the art directors. A future October issue with an on-sale date of September 20 is discussed. At this time the staff decides on the theme for this issue.

Very often the editor, or editor in chief, as he or she is sometimes called, will assign a senior or associate editor to be in charge of this issue. Usually two or three issues are in the works at one time under the overall supervision of the editor in chief.

At the same meeting subjects for articles or fiction are discussed. Obviously, business magazines would not have fiction editors; they employ staff writers, who are seldom used on consumer magazines. The size of a magazine's staff varies as to the number of people in each function. Everyone present is urged to participate in this session by contributing ideas for this October issue. Although the consensus of the group is sought, it is the editor's viewpoint that prevails and ultimately decides what goes into the magazine. Also considered at this meeting are cover treatments.

## Second Week

About a week later a follow-up meeting is held, this time with fewer participants. Usually the editor, the issue editor, the art director, some senior and associate editors, and the managing editor will attend. The managing editor has a critical function on the magazine. He or she directs the day-to-day flow of copy—from the writers, through copyreading, typesetting, layout, and, finally, to press.

At this second meeting the ideas and suggestions are crystallized, and a go-ahead is given by the editor for the total editorial content of this im-

pending October issue. At this point articles and fiction are assigned to in-house and free-lance writers, and assignments are also made for art, illustrations, and photography for the inside pages and the cover. Both the editorial and the art people are working on a fixed budget of dollars and pages. Since it is difficult to predict the size (number of pages) of an issue so far in advance, an estimate is made based on the previous year's issue for that month and on the current trend.

If any material is assigned and not used in the issue planned, it is held for inventory and possibly run at a later date. Most magazines operate on a fixed ratio of advertising to editorial content. Many use the formula of 60 percent editorial to 40 percent advertising. The news magazines like *Time* and *Newsweek* often carry 65 percent advertising to 35 percent editorial. Business publications operate on a similar basis.

Simultaneously, the editor is receiving copy for the August and September issues, which are well into production.

When free-lance writers are used, they coordinate their work with a specific assistant or associate editor who guides the pieces through to their final stage. Even so, the editor invariably reads every word of copy before it is typeset and will either make necessary changes or redirect the work to one of the associates for other changes.

During this hypothetical typical month, we must realize that the editor is also concerned with the current July issue, which goes to press in two weeks. Since this issue is in its final form, it is the editor's job to approve all the layouts in order to have a final fix on everything before it goes to press. Now we begin to picture the editor as some master chef, poking a finger into many pots, directing the whole editorial kitchen.

## Third Week

In the third week the July issue is in its mechanical stage. That is, type is set and color separations are made for the inside of the book and the cover. In these days of desktop publishing, much of this work is done on the computer. The editor approves the page proofs or suggests certain changes.

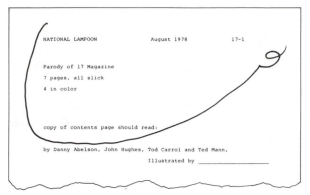

Figure 3-1. This is a title page for an actual article that ran in the *National Lampoon*. This article is a major piece, written by four people. The initials, PJ, are the chief editor's initials, and they indicate that he is in charge of getting the article through to completion. The date submitted, May 24, is rather late for an August issue that goes to press on June 20.

Figure 3-2. Here, the art people who are planning the layouts learn that the seven-page article will be printed on slick (coated) paper. (This magazine uses newsprint as well as slick paper.) Four of the pages are to be printed in full color. The bylines ("by Danny Abelson," etc.) are copy that is actually to be typeset; the five lines on top are merely instructive.

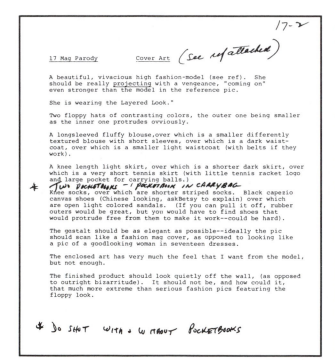

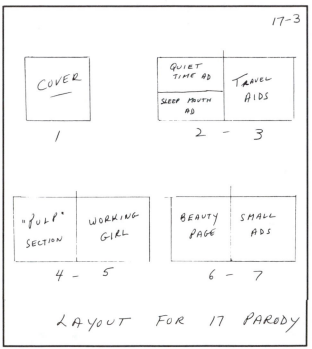

Figure 3-3. On the left we see the detailed "art notes." These are instructions to the art director on how writers and the editor visualize the cover of this parody of *Seventeen*. Notice the attention to small matters, seemingly unimportant, such as description of the black canvas shoes the model will wear. The emphasis on detail not only will make the art people's work simpler but will help them come up with just what the editorial people had in mind. The little boxes on the right identify the contents of each of the seven pages in the article. Pacing is important. This page gives the writers and the designers a fix on what goes where.

*17-4*

Art Ref for 17 Par Cover

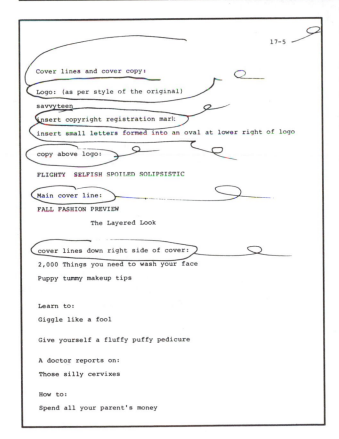

YOUNGER FACE

BUT EVEN MORE

VIVACIOUS

"HEY FELLA

17-5

Cover lines and cover copy:

Logo: (as per style of the original)
savvyteen
insert copyright registration mark:
insert small letters formed into an oval at lower right of logo

copy above logo:

FLIGHTY  SELFISH SPOILED SOLIPSISTIC

Main cover line:
FALL FASHION PREVIEW
            The Layered Look

cover lines down right side of cover:
2,000 Things you need to wash your face
Puppy tummy makeup tips


Learn to:
Giggle like a fool

Give yourself a fluffy puffy pedicure

A doctor reports on:
Those silly cervixes

How to:
Spend all your parent's money

Figure 3-4. The photo clipped from another magazine is a visual expression of what the cover shot should look like. The "hey fella" instruction evidently describes the message the model should convey through her facial expression and body language. Cover lines are integral as sell copy for the actual *Seventeen* magazine. Therefore, the parody *Seventeen* attempts to emulate this approach. Items deleted will not be typeset.

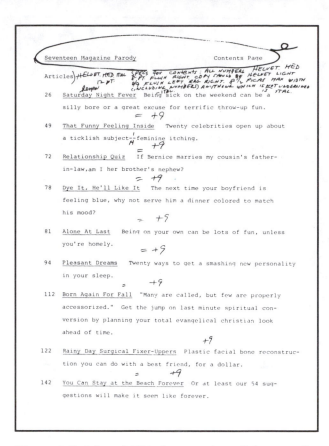

Figure 3-5. (above) This is a portion of the actual contents to be typeset. The copyreader's corrections appear on this preliminary typing of the copy, and the copy has also been typemarked. The specifications are explicit, including instructions that the page numbers are to be set flush right, and the titles of the articles flush left.

Figure 3-6. We see here a typesetter's proof ready for reproduction. The writer's work is now in print. Usually, a rough proof is run off by the typesetter before going into final proofs, but in this case there was not enough time. If there were any changes on these proofs, the typesetter would pull an additional set of proofs.

Figure 3-7. We now see the printed contents page with all the elements in place, including the two parody ads. These ads had to be set so they would resemble actual ads appearing in *Seventeen*. It is interesting to note the development from idea to layout to repro to the printed page—the efforts of a number of individuals, culminating in an effective graphic presentation.

FLIGHTY SELFISH SPOILED SOLIPSISTIC          AUGUST 1978          $1

*savvyteen*

**FALL FASHION PREVIEW**

**THE LAYERED LOOK**

Learn to: Giggle like a fool

2,000 things you need to wash your face

Puppy tummy makeup tips

How to: Spend all your parents' money

Oodles of ads

Gobs of product plugs

Shamelessly self-serving merchandise promotions

Savvyteen's **NATIONAL HAIR-DRYING COMPETITION**

Figure 3-8. Here is the printed cover of *Savvyteen*, a parody of *Seventeen*. The details of the cover, from logo to cover lines to photograph, are authentic reproductions of the parodied magazine's style. This page was in color and incurred very high production costs.

Meanwhile, the editor is appraising and approving work in progress for the August, September, and October issues. The process may take the form of short meetings with the individual-issue editors.

## Fourth Week

We are now in the fourth week of this editor's typical month, with the July issue about to go to press. The printer (or in-house desktop production manager) will submit blueprints, or brownlines, as they are sometimes called. These are merely final proofs of each page with all the elements in place. Changes can still be made. The managing editor and a proofreader may also read these page proofs for any errors that have been overlooked. Now the issue is put to bed, and everyone can breathe a brief sigh of relief.

The editor, however, must immediately focus attention on the August issue, which may be in type-proof form, and the September and October issues, which are in various stages of development. Not much fun, is it?

The cycle we have described involves a rather automatic procedure that the editor must follow. It does not take into account other aspects of the editor's role that are no less important than his or her routine functions.

The editor, for example, can even help in the sale of advertising. At a number of magazines I published, I encouraged the editor to attend meetings with the ad sales staff at agencies. Such meetings have been fruitful, for who can best present the publication's editorial viewpoint? The editor, of course.

Although the editor is not directly responsible for the magazine's physical production, he or she is nonetheless vigilant on the quality of reproduction. A little goading of the production people goes a long way toward maintaining high standards.

The editor should visit the marketplace. Taking trips across the country to meet people can be productive. Such trips can often be tied in to lectures to students and other groups and, of course, have public relations value. Editors of business publications constantly attend conventions or sales conferences in order to gain valuable insight into the activities of their industry.

Figures 3-1 through 3-8 show the stages of development of a typical article. Throughout, the editor's guidance and close attention are essential to achieving professional results, readability, and interest.

## What Will You Make in an Editorial Job?

If you want to get rich, get a job as an investment banker. Editorial people on magazines are not highly paid. It is a simple case of supply and demand: There are many more people yearning for these jobs than there are jobs.

*Folio:*, the preeminent magazine for magazine publishers, ran a recent Robert M. Steed survey on editorial compensation. Here are the highlights:

### Average Salaries for:

#### Editorial Manager

| | |
|---|---|
| All respondents | $59,914 |
| Business magazines | 66,227 |
| Consumer magazines | 52,409 |

#### by Region

| | Average | Business | Consumer |
|---|---|---|---|
| Northeast | $67,475 | $73,619 | $57,233 |
| South | 57,008 | 57,554 | 56,364 |
| North Central | 59,421 | 61,589 | 55,873 |
| West | 50,417 | 67,857 | 42,788 |

#### by Editorial Pages Produced Annually

| | | | |
|---|---|---|---|
| To 499 | $54,706 | $57,796 | $52,057 |
| 500 to 999 | 56,976 | 64,860 | 49,880 |
| 1,000 to 1,499 | 67,744 | 67,744 | — |
| 1,500 to 2,999 | 90,333 | 90,444 | 90,000 |

#### by Number of Editorial Employees Supervised

| | | | |
|---|---|---|---|
| 2 to 5 employees | $51,258 | $56,592 | $45,719 |
| 6 to 10 employees | 69,024 | 68,856 | 69,231 |
| More than 10 | 88,913 | 92,717 | 77,500 |

#### by Sex

| | | | |
|---|---|---|---|
| Male | $63,146 | $68,552 | $55,474 |
| Female | 54,000 | 60,842 | 48,091 |

Note: A top editor working for a magazine with a circulation of 500,000 or more will be paid twice as much as an editor working for a publication selling 50,000 or less.

## Average Salaries for:

### Editor

| | Average | Business | Consumer |
|---|---|---|---|
| All respondents | $46,898 | | |
| Business magazines | 49,226 | | |
| Consumer magazines | 44,260 | | |

**by Region**

| | Average | Business | Consumer |
|---|---|---|---|
| Northeast | $55,309 | $56,257 | $55,800 |
| South | 41,604 | 40,283 | 43,980 |
| North Central | 44,168 | 49,300 | 36,640 |
| West | 37,778 | 38,600 | 37,462 |

**by Editorial Pages Produced Annually**

| | Average | Business | Consumer |
|---|---|---|---|
| To 499 | $40,669 | $43,182 | $37,530 |
| 500 to 999 | 46,475 | 48,061 | 44,543 |
| 1,000 to 1,499 | 54,955 | 57,438 | 48,333 |
| 1,500 and over | 68,075 | 80,750 | 61,738 |

**by Number of Editorial Employees Supervised**

| | Average | Business | Consumer |
|---|---|---|---|
| 1 | $37,762 | $40,767 | $32,700 |
| 2 to 5 | 43,265 | 45,179 | 41,118 |
| More than 10 | 87,536 | 82,222 | 97,100 |

**by Sex**

| | Average | Business | Consumer |
|---|---|---|---|
| Male | $52,934 | $57,147 | $49,280 |
| Female | 39,122 | 39,494 | 38,681 |

## Average Salaries for:

### Managing Editor

| | Average | Business | Consumer |
|---|---|---|---|
| All respondents | $37,803 | | |
| Business magazines | 39,665 | | |
| Consumer magazines | 35,704 | | |

**by Region**

| | Average | Business | Consumer |
|---|---|---|---|
| Northeast | $42,664 | $44,570 | $40,228 |
| South | 33,583 | 36,187 | 29,577 |
| North Central | 35,322 | 38,275 | 28,571 |
| West | 37,722 | 37,917 | 37,629 |

**by Number of Editorial Employees Supervised**

| | Average | Business | Consumer |
|---|---|---|---|
| 1 | $31,461 | $32,888 | $29,083 |
| More than 10 | 57,425 | 42,967 | 66,100 |

**by Sex**

| | Average | Business | Consumer |
|---|---|---|---|
| Male | $41,226 | $44,349 | $37,623 |
| Female | 35,345 | 36,239 | 34,355 |

## Average Salaries for:

### Senior Editor/Associate Editor

| | Average | Business | Consumer |
|---|---|---|---|
| All respondents | $36,437 | | |
| Business magazines | 34,686 | | |
| Consumer magazines | 39,007 | | |

**by Sex**

| | Average | Business | Consumer |
|---|---|---|---|
| Male | $38,491 | $37,547 | $39,509 |
| Female | 33,859 | 31,363 | 38,293 |

## Average Salaries for:

### Copy Editor

$29,000*

*Estimated. Not tabulated in survey.

# EDITORIAL JOB DESCRIPTIONS

**Editorial Management.** A manager (editor and publisher, editor in chief, editorial director) sets editorial policy. He or she may hold other titles and may be in charge of other products and departments in addition to editorial ones. The editor reports to this individual.

**The Editor.** The editor is responsible for editorial direction and editorial content, including both art and text, as well as cover of the magazine.

**The Managing Editor.** This editor coordinates the editorial and the art and production departments to ensure that the magazine is put out on time and in an acceptable form. He or she oversees the copyediting and proofreading staff to make sure the magazine is factually and grammatically correct.

**Senior Editor.** This editor heads the editorial feature department. This person plans and writes features in specialty areas. He or she is responsible for all editorial work in that subject area and may oversee associate editors, free-lance writers, and designers.

**Copy Editor.** This editor copy-edits, proofreads, and prepares copy for the printer. He or she is responsible for the accuracy of all editorial copy, as well as for the flow of editorial copy from the editorial department to the printer. This individual is under the supervision of the managing editor.

Following are random comments from editorial respondents in the *Folio:* survey:

"I love my job. I would pay them to let me work here, but do not tell them that." (Editor in the Midwest working on a business magazine and earning $38,000.)

"Staying on time is hard because I always want to make the issue better." (Editorial manager in the West earning $100,000 in salary and roughly $70,000 in bonuses.)

"How do you find topnotch writers? Even when I offer huge sums of money, I find the state of writers nationwide to be deplorable!" (Editor in the West with seven years' experience and earning a salary and bonus in the high thirties.)

"Sustaining a creative spark for myself and staff amid so many routine duties required to produce each issue is a great challenge." (Editor in the Midwest earning $50,000.)

"The trick is to find outstanding writers and get them to work cheap." (Senior editor in the Northeast earning a salary and bonus in the midtwenties.)

"The lack of foresight among editorial management staffs creates complex problems for the copy-editing department. Maintaining accuracy during deadline pressure is also a concern." (Copy editor in the Northeast with one year's experience.)

Here are comments from Robert M. Steed on these findings:

Editorial managers who supervise a staff of more than ten earn almost 2.4 times as much in salary, and four times as much in total compensation, as those who are not supervisors.

The disparity between compensation of men and women is largest in the editor category. Women's salaries average 74 percent of

men's and their total compensation is only 62 percent of their male counterparts'.

## Other Magazine Jobs

**Bureau Chief.** A newsmagazine with offices in various locations will designate a bureau chief to supervise the staff of reporters and correspondents, identify the topics of interest, and assign coverage.

**Staff Writer/Reporter.** These are the people who write and edit material in assigned subject areas. They may attend functions and shows and keep current on the other media in the area assigned. They may also check layouts and pasteups.

## The Art of Editing

Peter Jacobi is a professor of journalism at Indiana University who writes often about magazines. He has been an editor, writer, and critic. In an excellent article in *Folio:*, he delineates the role of a successful editor. Here are some highlights from Jacobi's article:

The editor must give it [a magazine] spirit and flesh, must make of concept a three-dimensional object with designs and colors and words and a profusion of new concepts that then manifest themselves in the minds of perhaps many thousands of people.

The editor builds an environment and choreographs the movements of necessary editorial elements that will cause a reader to consider the publication his own. The editor designs the blend of the predictable and the surprising, of the constant and the dynamic, of the continuing and the innovative so that the reader will be both comfortable and stimulated in the reading.

Success comes when an editor is so close in taste and temperament, in predilection and passion to his reader that emotionally and intellectually they become as one.

In the same article Jacobi quotes Phil Kunhardt, former editor of *Life:*

Figure 3-9. When I was writing the first edition of this book, I came across an interesting column in an issue of *Texas Monthly*. It describes in detail the functions of research and fact-checking. Since such work is essential to a magazine's accuracy, I reprint the column here. This is one magazine, by the way, that subscribes to a policy of job stability. Ann Dingus and David Moorman are still there, Ann as contributing editor, David as assistant editor. (Reprinted with permission of *Texas Monthly* magazine. Copyright © 1978 by Mediatex Communication Corporation.)

# THE INSIDE STORY

**D**avid Moorman is one of those orderly and precise people whose sense of procedure, while very clear to him, is confusing to everyone else. David is our research editor and, along with his assistant, Anne Dingus, has the job of making sure that every fact in every story in every issue is correct in every respect. Since our issues on the average contain 60,000 words, and since the information in any issue can range from nineteenth-century methods of sausage making to technical details of the latest NASA mission, and since the time to check all this is something less than a month, David has need of being orderly and precise.

He begins with a clean set of galleys (editor's proof sheets) for every story. As he works he marks the galleys in a complicated color code, underlining long passages with red, blue, green, yellow, or black felt-tipped pens, drawing long arrows from one word to another, slashing jagged check marks across names, until the galleys begin to look like the work of some obsessive but dramatic modern painter. No one but David understands his color code. At times I have been tempted to ask him to explain it, but I always relent. Arcane mysteries are better simply appreciated than resolved.

Most magazines have some sort of research and fact-checking department for two reasons. The first is that libel is a constant concern, and good fact checking reduces that worry. But more than that, any publication wants to be right not just in its judgments and analyses of people and events but also in all the small particulars that lead to those judgments. It is one of the cruel truths of journalism that you cannot be right if your facts are wrong.

David began with us as a proofreader in September of 1975. A native of Fort Worth, he had come to Austin seven years earlier to attend the University of Texas, where he discovered what remain the consuming interests in his life—art, jazz, and literature, especially poetry. *Texas Monthly* at that time had published 32 issues, and for each one we had felt the lack of a research department. David's meticulous proofreading made him seem the most likely candidate for the job.

In his new role, he developed such demanding standards and procedures that as time went on he found that it was impossible to check an entire issue by himself. To assist him he hired Anne Dingus, a graduate of Rice University who had been working for a petroleum trade publication. Although David did not explain his color code to Anne, he did outline for her his fact-checking

*Dingus (l), Moorman: just the facts, ma'am*

procedure: "(1) Read the story at hand. (2) Mark all statements of fact that should be checked. (3) Find out if David Anderson [our libel lawyer] has made any comment about libel. (4) Contact the editor of the story for a brief discussion of it. (5) Contact the author of the story. Discuss sources. Be sure to ask if anything or anyone mentioned in the story is confidential or sensitive. Ask the author if there is anything in particular that he or she would like for you to check. (6) Contact sources and check the facts until you are satisfied that our story is correct in all of its particulars. (7) Transfer all ordinary changes through the copy desk. Confer, however, with the editor and the author about any passage that must be rewritten as a consequence of your research. (8) *Keep detailed records of all the checking that is done on a story.*"

In accomplishing all this, David's most important tool is the telephone. "Everyone in the world has a telephone," he told me once. "And no matter who they are, you can just call them. I've talked to everyone from felons to nudists to evangelists to blues singers." Regarding the personal qualities that a fact checker needs, David considers an obsession for correctness and order very important, but he rates that below other qualities: "Your intuition and imagination are the important things. You have to be able to feel when something's wrong. Sometimes two or three people will tell me something's right and for no particular reason I'll keep checking it and find out it *was* wrong."

*Gregory Curtis*

"The magazine editing process is pure theater, with different acts and scenes, different players and costumes and scenery, which taken all together make a brand new production each time out."

## Ten Ways to Increase Editorial Productivity

Larry Bodine, in a *Folio: Sourcebook 1992* article, gives ten short maxims for effective editorial management:

1. Hire people who are smarter than you are.
2. Hire people who are both journalists and experts.
3. Spell out the editorial focus [of the magazine] in 35 words or less.
4. Draft writers' guidelines.
5. Know your reader.
6. Don't micro-manage [delegate].
7. Spell out the editor's noneditorial duties [for example, speaking and attending conventions and conferences, going on sales calls, conducting public relations].
8. Capture their [the editorial staff's] imagination with an idea.
9. Be your staff's advocate.
10. Create an atmosphere safe for ideas.

## Care and Nurturing of the Free-Lance Writer

Many magazines rely heavily on the free-lance writer. He or she is someone who chooses to work at home on an assignment basis. The compensation usually is not great, but these writers prefer the freedom of free-lance work to the restriction of being cooped up in an office from nine to five. A free-lancer who does a lot of work for a particular magazine may visit the office about once a month, making appointments in advance to see a number of editors about assignments. This day is a major event for the writers, and the wise editor will treat it as such, sometimes taking the writer to lunch, or at least chatting for a half-hour or more.

At such a meeting the editor may suggest an assignment to the writer, trying to be as direct as possible in describing what he or she has in mind,

the length of the piece, and how much can be paid for it. Payment is usually done on a per word basis—from as little as 25 cents a word for a small trade magazine to an average of $1.25 a word on consumer magazines. It is reported that at *Vanity Fair*, editor Tina Brown paid $15,000 for certain features.

If travel or special research is necessary to write the article, the editor will discuss guidelines for this additional expense. Often the piece will require art or photography, in which case the art director may be brought into the discussion. A good editor is an efficient matchmaker in giving assignments to free-lance writers. By matching the *right* writer to an assignment, an editor is using "people skills" to the fullest—to the benefit of the magazine. Good initial communication means less rewriting and fewer missed deadlines.

Some magazines follow a policy that in my opinion is extremely unfair to the free-lance writer: They will pay for an article or a piece of fiction only on publication, sometimes months after the completed work has been submitted. A more equitable policy is payment on acceptance. Out-of-pocket expenses should be paid to the writer in advance. If the piece is lengthy and the fee large, many magazines will give the writer an advance when the assignment is made and final payment on acceptance.

A recent survey conducted for *Publishing News* turned up these significant findings:

- On the issue of rights, 40 percent of business magazine editors say they buy "all rights," and 31 percent of consumer magazine editors seek the same option. In an "all rights" situation, the free-lancer does not receive additional fees if the piece runs in a foreign publication or in an anthology.
- Some 43.3 percent of business magazines and 44.8 percent of consumer magazines pay for free-lance work on receipt. Most of the others pay on publication or later.
- Relatively few editors send authors edited manuscripts or galley proofs to indicate how their copy has been amended or cut. Obviously, editors wish to avoid the delay of discussions with their free-lancers.

Sometimes an editor chooses not to run an article, even though it has been completed and approved. An almost-standard practice is for the writer to be paid a "kill fee," which can be the full rate or a percentage of it. The same payment practices are followed when editors deal with outside photographers or artists.

How does one go about becoming a free-lance writer? For those wishing to do so, possibly as a stepping-stone to editing or a full-time editorial position, a number of recommendations can be made. First, we suggest subscribing to two excellent journals published by F & W Publications, 1507 Dana Avenue, Cincinnati, OH 45207–1005. These journals' editorial profiles express their value to writers.

*Writer's Digest* is edited for writers and editorial workers, including those individuals who aspire to become professionals, as well as those who have earned this status. The prime concern is to help readers become better writers and to tell them where they can sell what they write. Articles cover commercial forms of writing, from verse to novel writing. Monthly departments cover photojournalism, TV, cartooning, poetry, New York market news, and questions about and answers to writer's problems. *Writer's Yearbook* is edited for beginning and professional writers—anyone with an interest in writing for publication. The main editorial features are the markets to which writers can sell manuscripts, articles on various phases of instruction, in-depth interviews with well-known writers, and a travel piece on a "Writer's Paradise."

Each year *Writer's Digest* conducts a survey of 400 editors on their treatment of free-lancers. It then publishes a list, based on various criteria, of the best magazines for free-lancers. Consistently at the top of the list are *Redbook, Reader's Digest, American Legion, Playboy,* and *Cosmopolitan.*

Another source of information for the free-lance writer is the American Society of Journalists and Authors (ASJA), 1501 Broadway, New York, NY 10036. This group is the nationwide organization of professional nonfiction writers. Its membership includes more than 800 leading free-lance writers of magazine articles, trade books, and other forms of nonfiction, each of whom has met exacting standards of professional achievement.

ASJA sponsors an annual nonfiction writers' conference that brings together some of America's leading authors, publishers, editors, and agents. These persons then explore with professional and aspiring writers current publishing markets and trends in books and magazines, newspapers, television, and other media.

Free-lance people are integral to the creative flow and growth of most magazines. They allow for a much broader body of talent than is available in-house. They should be respected, wooed, and, yes, nurtured—things a perceptive editor will take care to do.

The better-established free-lance writers and artists have agents who do their bidding for them. Submissions from agents are well received. But what of the hundreds of manuscripts that pass over the transom? Do the authors of unsolicited manuscripts get a fair hearing? Usually not. In these cases, however, an editor's personal encouragement on a rejection note may be all that's necessary to buoy the spirit of a neophyte writer. Certainly, a basic rule for a good editor to follow is that unsolicited manuscripts should be read by a responsible member of the editorial staff.

## Editors on Editing

A magazine editor is given the awesome responsibility of dealing in thoughts, ideas, and information. How the editor responds to this task affects the readers of the magazine as well as the financial success of the publication. Here are thoughts on the subject from some major editors:

"Editors occupy a position comparable to that of the literary critic—forever evaluating the passing human parade from a perspective and with a moral agenda often invisible to their readers." —Lewis Lapham, editor of *Harper's.*

"My job entails overall direction and perspective. I must make as sure as possible that the magazine holds value for the reader. I must give it an integrated viewpoint and personality. To get it done, I have to inspire my staff and thereby make the most of its talent and enthusiasm." —Alan Ternes, editor of *Natural History.*

"Like Gaul, the editor's job is divided into

three parts—creative, administrative, and ceremonial. And the editor himself *is* the magazine, its living embodiment." —Robert Hood, retired editor of *Boy's Life*.

"The editor gives a magazine expression through her staff, putting it all together. And that "all" is all for the reader and for readership growth. We do what we do for naught if we do not attract readers." —Myrna Blyth, editor in chief of *Ladies' Home Journal*.

"The key job is to establish the personality of the magazine and to make sure that everything—from story selection to editing and graphic presentation—is true to that personality. I see myself as a colonel. I direct/command the staff, but still I must have combat responsibilities—those of writing, editing, traveling." —Frank Anton, formerly editor and now publisher of *Builder*.

"There ain't no magazine without the editor. Anything else is not a magazine, but merely a corporation." —T. George Harris, former editor of *American Health*.

## The Editor Should Take Chances

Nothing is more boring than the magazine that is totally predictable, with everything fitting nicely into neat packages. Of course, if you are publishing magazines on the order of the mass-circulation *National Enquirer* or *Star*, your readers enjoy and expect the same thing—articles on diet, cancer cures, and TV stars—week after week. A good editor, however, should be an innovator, constantly testing new formulas, using fiction where none was previously carried, taking a stab at humor by placing cartoons in large bodies of text, making good use of photography to dramatize the visual effect. This creative approach to editing holds true for business as well as consumer magazines.

Too often we see a publication moving along from year to year, improving its circulation, ultimately reaching a high point, but then starting a gradual decline. In such a case numerous editorial meetings are held to diagnose the creeping malady, and readership studies are conducted to seek out the root cause of the circulation drop. Emergency measures—such as low-rate subscription

efforts and newsstand promotion campaigns—are attempted, when what is really called for is a dramatic editorial face-lift.

I personally experienced that kind of situation when I published a magazine that climbed to a circulation of almost a million in just five years. With no apparent reason, the circulation began to drop about 10 percent a year. After some deep soul-searching we realized that our audience was changing, as were the times. Fortunately, we reacted quickly to cope with this problem—changing the cover style and hiring a new editorial team. Our existing staff was just too complacent. New free-lance writers were sought. The prescription worked—we were able to avert the disease of aging.

A magazine has a lifetime—ten, twenty, or fifty years. (Witness the death of the original *Life*, *Look*, and *Saturday Evening Post*.) The editor must constantly infuse the magazine with the dynamism that will keep readers stimulated. There must always be an atmosphere of excitement in the magazine—in its graphics and in its writing. Many readers subscribe to magazines out of force of habit, year after year. Compare them with the readers who eagerly await each issue. The successful editor is the one who innovates, who takes chances all the time.

## The National Magazine Awards

Each year the American Society of Magazine Editors sponsors the National Magazine Awards for editorial excellence. The awards are administered by the Graduate School of Journalism, Columbia University, and are supported by the Magazine Publishers of America. Following are the prizes for 1992, given according to circulation size:
General excellence and photography, more than 1 million circulation: *National Geographic*
General excellence, 400,000 to 1 million circulation: *Mirabella*
General excellence, 100,000 to 400,000 circulation: *Texas Monthly*
General excellence, less than 100,000 circulation: *The New Republic*
Various lesser awards are given. In the same year *Creative Classroom* won the award for per-

sonal service, *Sports Afield* for special interests, *Sports Illustrated* for feature writing, *Story* for fiction, *The Nation* for essays and criticism, and *Business Week* for single-topic issue.

### Awards for Excellence in Business Magazine Journalism

American Business Press (ABP) sponsors the annual Neal Editorial Achievement Awards for outstanding writing in business magazines. The prizes in 1992 for magazines with ad revenues in excess of $5 million went to: *Jewelers' Circular-Keystone, Builder, National Jeweler, Restaurant Business,* and *Restaurants & Institutions.*

For business magazines with ad revenues between $2 and $5 million, the awards were given to: *Transmission & Distribution, Architecture, RN,* and *Pork '91.* For publications with ad revenues up to $2 million, the awards went to: *Business Atlanta, Truckers News, Apparel Industry Magazine, Seafood Business,* and *Convenience Store Decisions.*

Certificates of Merit were given to another group of magazines including: *Geriatrics, Contemporary Pediatrics, Direct, Medical Economics,* and *Professional Builder & Remodeler.*

Reading these articles, one is struck with the high quality of their treatment of real contemporary issues. Writers and editors of business magazines are not asked to entertain their readers. Instead, they must suggest solutions to help their readers do the best possible job.

# LEARNING TO BE AN EDITOR OR WRITER

I sincerely doubt that a poll taken of our fifty top magazine editors would reveal that many of them, when they were in college, had a master plan for becoming magazine editors. It is possible that no more than a few were even dedicated to becoming writers. How, then, does it happen? Where can one train for this exalted profession?

A liberal arts background at college is valuable in the sense that it may stimulate intellectual growth. Writing courses, if led by competent professionals, can certainly be rewarding. Voracious reading of books and quality magazines will develop a feeling for the nuances of style. Completing all these prerequisites, however, does not guarantee a successful editorial or writing career.

### The Association for Education in Journalism

The Magazine Division is a subunit of the Association for Education in Journalism (AEJ), which is a national journalism educators' organization. Its membership of about 150 comprises college faculty members who teach one or more magazine journalism courses or who have some other interest in the magazine field (consulting, research, free-lance writing). Many of these faculty members also teach courses in the newspaper field or in special, related areas, such as law, history, or graphic arts.

Each division of the AEJ offers individual programs in teaching and research in conjunction with AEJ's national program and annual conventions. A recent national convention devoted six separate sessions to magazine journalism.

Professional groups like the Magazine Publishers of America (MPA), the American Business Press (ABP) (trade and business publications), and the Society of National Association of Business Communicators are affiliate members of AEJ and its Magazine Division. Representatives of these groups sometimes appear on this division's programs.

There are no exact data on the number of schools or departments of journalism that offer magazine courses or on the number or quality of courses provided by them.

A recent AEJ directory shows that five schools have accredited "sequences" (noncomprehensive programs) in magazine journalism: the University of Missouri, Northwestern University's Medill School of Journalism, Ohio University, Syracuse University, and the University of Texas at Austin.

Several other schools offer more comprehensive programs in magazine instruction, programs known as "emphases" rather than "sequences."

They include the following:

- Ball State University
- Bowling Green State University
- California State University at Fullerton
- Drake University
- University of Georgia
- University of Kansas
- Kansas State University
- University of Minnesota
- University of North Carolina
- University of Oregon
- San Jose State University
- Temple University

A recent survey conducted by AEJ's Magazine Division determined that writing is the most important ingredient in the education of a magazine professional. The panel was composed of magazine editors, educators from the AEJ, and recent graduates.

Experience in all kinds of writing, the survey concluded, would be best achieved in college. Excellent writing ability was considered essential for any entry-level magazine job and just as critical for any movement up the editorial ladder. Editing ability was the second most frequent response to the question, What does it take to move up into magazine management?

Respondents endorsed a broad liberal arts background and any course that would improve general language skills. They also approved the usual academic structure of a core, special sequence requirements, electives, and background courses.

The three groups in the survey strongly recommended meaningful internships—those giving students an opportunity to write on demand and on deadline. Such internships also help students understand the profit-making aspects of commercial magazines.

Several of the schools produce laboratory magazines to give students practical experience in magazine production. Students at the excellent journalism school of the University of Kansas produce a magazine for the alumni. This school requires all students to take the following courses:

Beginning Newswriting (Reporting I)
Advanced Newswriting (Reporting II)
Editing
History of American Journalism
Law of Communications

The magazine-emphasis majors then take specific magazine courses, as well as journalism electives in such areas as photography, editorial and interpretive writing, and marketing. There is a wide range of elective courses, and the magazine major's journalism education is not limited to magazine courses.

At an accredited school or department of journalism, a student is restricted as to the number of journalism courses he or she can take. Approximately 70 percent of the total course work leading to a bachelor's degree must be nonjournalism course work, mostly in the liberal arts. This restriction exists to prevent a journalism education from following a "trade school" approach.

Further information on AEJ's Magazine Division can be obtained by writing to any of its member schools.

The graduate magazine publishing program of Northwestern's Medill School is excellent, comprising about twenty master's candidates. It actually produces a magazine in a twelve-week period. The students write and edit the magazine, target the circulation and advertising sales campaign, and handle design and production chores—all on a fixed budget. Students must also confirm the magazine's commercial viability by preparing a six-year business plan. The Medill School additionally conducts "Magazine Fairs," at which job and internship recruiters from many leading magazine publishers are in attendance.

## Summer Magazine Seminars and Workshops

Several colleges offer comprehensive summer seminars and workshops in publishing. The oldest is the Radcliffe six-week book and magazine program conducted every July since 1949. The Radcliffe program attracts recent graduates as well as working professionals. For information write to Radcliffe Publishing Course, Radcliffe College, 77 Brattle Street, Cambridge, MA 02138.

Stanford University sponsors a thirteen-day

book and magazine seminar. Applicants must have a minimum of three years in book or magazine publishing to qualify for the program. Many publishing companies have sent employees to the course. For information, write to Stanford Professional Publishing Course, Stanford Alumni Association, Bowman House, Stanford, CA 94305–4005.

New York University's School of Continuing Education runs an annual Summer Magazine Publishing Institute that I originated about fifteen years ago. It combines book and magazine publishing and runs for seven weeks, beginning in early June. The program is geared to those entering the profession, not professionals. A major plus for this program is its access to about a hundred leading industry professionals who conduct the lectures. For information, write to Management Institute, Center for Publishing, New York University, School of Continuing Education, 48 Cooper Square, New York, NY 10003.

## Writers' Conferences

There are many writers' conferences that may be of help to potential editors as well. Readers are advised to check dates and addresses of these programs. A partial list follows:

Santa Barbara Writers Conference, c/o Barnaby Conrad, Box 304, Carpinteria, CA 93014

Wesleyan-Writers Conference, Wesleyan University, Middletown, CT 06459

Newsletter Association of America, c/o Donna Civin, 2626 Pennsylvania Avenue, NW, Washington, DC 20037

Christian Writers Institute Conference and Workshop, c/o Helen Kidd, CW1, Gundersen Drive and Schmale Road, Wheaton, IL 60187

Cornell University Summer Session, B12 Ives Hall, Ithaca, NY 14853–3910

International Congress of Crime Writers, Mystery Writers of America, 105 East Nineteenth Street, #3D, New York, NY 10003

Philadelphia Writers Conference, c/o Emma S. Wood, Box 834, Philadelphia, PA 19105

Reader's Digest/Utah State University Magazine Article Writers Workshop, c/o Dick Harris, Utah State University, UMC 01, Logan, UT 84322

Bread Loaf Writers Conference, Middlebury College, Middlebury, VT 05753

Rhinelander School of Arts, c/o Robert E. Gard, University of Wisconsin Extension, 720 Lowell Hall, Madison, WI 53706

An organization of interest to writers and editors is the Council of Literary Magazines and Presses, 154 Christopher Street, Suite C, New York, NY 10014–2839. Of special interest to editors and publishers of small magazines is COSMEP (Committee of Small Magazine Editors and Publishers), P.O. Box 703, San Francisco, CA 94101. Although COSMEP doesn't have printed membership lists, it sponsors the *International Directory of Little Magazines and Small Presses* ($19.95), published by Dustbooks, P.O. Box 100, Paradise, CA 95969. Another useful function of COSMEP is its rental service of mailing lists of 2,900 libraries and 3,900 bookstores.

The R. R. Bowker Company, 121 Chanlon Road, New Providence, NJ 07974, issues a free catalog of books on book and magazine design.

The Literature Program of the National Endowment for the Arts, Washington, DC 20506, gives grants to writers and to literary magazines.

## Metropolitan Magazines: A New Opportunity for Writers and Editors

A category of magazines showing recent growth is "metropolitan." Some of the magazines in this category have achieved exceptional editorial and financial success. *Washington, Philadelphia,* and *Texas Monthly* are examples of metropolitan magazines with provocative editorial content—a far cry from the chamber-of-commerce-subsidized magazines that dominated this classification a few years ago. Competing head-on with the daily newspapers, they must project a unique image beyond their slickness. Some of the finest investigative reporting and most spirited muckraking has been undertaken by these publications.

There were 191 metropolitan (once commonly known as city) magazines listed in the October 27, 1991, issue of Standard Rate and Data's Consumer edition. This is definitely a growth area in the magazine business.

The would-be editor or magazine writer should become familiar with the local city magazine. What may begin as a small free-lance assignment can often lead to a full-time editorial job. These magazines' staffs function very much like those of any other magazine but frequently rely on local stringers (part-time reporters) for leads and ideas for new articles. As a training ground for editors and writers, the metropolitan magazine is excellent—and it doesn't require writers to leave home and relocate to New York to find employment at a quality magazine.

# FINAL THOUGHTS ON MAKING IT AS AN EDITOR

One route to success in the magazine editorial field is to take any job you can get on a magazine as long as it isn't too far from the editorial department. Then learn all you can about the editorial function. If your interest lies in editing a consumer magazine, don't feel that work on a business publication is not good training. It is, since it inculcates in the beginning employee the need for clarity and precision without sacrificing creativity.

As in other fields, the ambitious, talented individual will ultimately be discovered by management and rewarded with promotions leading to the top editorial positions. This advice may sound like pure old rugged individualism, yet it still holds true.

Often asked in my classes was the question, Is it necessary for the editor to be a fine writer? My answer invariably was that, while being a fine writer may be helpful, far more important is that the editor be an organized, critical thinker, one who can evaluate good writing and generate ideas and excitement into the editorial package.

In closing this chapter on the vital subject of the editor's role, I offer a few additional thoughts on editorial success.

One of an editor's prime concerns is maintaining readers' interest and loyalty. Studies have indicated that the average issue of a consumer magazine is read for little more than an hour. This finding implies that readers are scanning and not digesting the total editorial and advertising package of their magazines. Why? Because most magazines are just not interesting enough to capture their audience. In considering readership problems a magazine publisher should ask a number of questions:

1. Who is the audience? Does the editor know the audience, and are the readers' interests served?
2. Has the editor made an effort to understand our rapidly changing society and how it affects readers?
3. Has the editor ever stopped to think seriously about why 30, 40, or even 50 percent of the magazine's subscribers don't renew their subscriptions? Could the reason be the magazine's repetitive editorial aspects or its lack of vitality?
4. Does the magazine lack a sense of humor? Too many publications are deadly dull and needn't be so. Why not try cartoons? They're inexpensive, and even serious financial journals have used them effectively.
5. Has the magazine a staff of professionals? Are writers functioning as editors? Should they be home doing free-lance writing instead of editing and evaluating other people's copy?

For the would-be entrepreneur wishing to start a new magazine, I give further advice: If you are not a brilliant, experienced editor yourself, go out and join forces with the best one you can find. Nothing is more important for a new magazine than the editorial concept and its execution.

## Interview

Howard S. Rauch is a former vice-president and editorial director of Gralla Publications, a leading business magazine publisher. In his twenty-odd years with Gralla, he served as editor or publisher on five of its magazines and developed its training program. Today he is a leading editorial consultant.

Rauch is a sought-after speaker on trade magazine editorial topics and has addressed many workshops sponsored by *Folio:,* the American Society of Business Press Editors, and the New York Society of Business Press Editors.

Rauch holds an MBA in marketing from New York University's Graduate School of Business Administration.

*What college or postcollege training do you recommend for those seeking business magazine editorial jobs?*

Majoring in journalism or some other variation of communications arts seems to be the logical route. I have had modest success with business majors who had writing ability. I have also seen successful candidates at Gralla following careers at newspapers, investment brokerage firms, advertising agencies, and, of course, other business magazine publishing companies.

The common thread for all candidates includes a possible interest in writing about business, an interest in the specific industries covered by the publisher in question, and, following that, such obvious items as writing *and* editing capability. Many business magazines expect all its writers to have copy-editing skills, knowledge of layout, pasteup, and production as well as some photography skill.

*What is the career path generally followed by those who ultimately become editors in chief at a business magazine?*

Some publishers look to hire an individual with professional experience in the field the magazine covers, as opposed to professional experience as a journalist. This professional experience can also be exploited by an alert sales and promotion staff.

Many publishers do not follow the above path. They find that a capable journalist can learn a new field very quickly and that a journalist editor is much more equipped to manage other editors. It is still possible for someone to come through a training program and work his or her way up to editor in chief of a business magazine within a four- to five-year period.

With respect to specific rungs on the editorial career ladder, at Gralla the individual moved from trainee to assistant editor to associate editor to se-

nior associate editor to senior editor. This last title upgrade can be achieved three years from the time the individual joins the training program, if the individual has the required talent. From senior associate or senior editor, one could advance to assistant managing editor (on a larger magazine), managing editor, executive editor, and then editor in chief.

*Are salary ranges for editorial people on business magazines equal to those at consumer magazines?*

It is impossible to generalize on an answer. Based on surveys I have seen published in *Folio:*, my guess is that the top editors' salaries are comparable to what a top editor at a consumer magazine can earn. Of course, there are many small consumer publications too, where the editors do not fare that well. To them a trade magazine could represent a financial oasis.

With respect to junior staff editors, consumer magazines may have a slight edge on compensation, but I believe the opportunity to advance is far greater if you are speaking in terms of a progressive business magazine publisher.

It certainly is possible for editors in chief and executive editors to earn between $50,000 and $100,000 a year. Generally speaking, editorial salaries at all levels are being upgraded.

*In what area of magazines will one find the greatest opportunity for writing as opposed to straight editing?*

At many trade publishing companies, you never stop writing; however, as you enter the realm of management—for example, when you are promoted to managing editor—you do less straight writing and a great deal more editing.

Some editorial types cannot adjust to the management regimen and ask to be returned to the straight-writing ranks. In so doing they knowingly forfeit financial gain and the ultimate opportunity to become an editor in chief.

There are many companies, of course, where the straight editing function falls to one or more staff copy editors. This allows other staff members to concentrate on writing but perhaps not at all on editing.

We view this setup as a disadvantage. A copy editor can become a crutch. Without such an individual many writers cannot function in an atmosphere—such as at Gralla—where they are expected to do some basic editing of their own manuscripts.

This problem is best illustrated if I tell you that we had a one-hour written test that was part of our screening process. The failure rate for junior editors freshly graduated from college was 77 percent. The failure rate was much higher for editors with two to five years of experience, who had worked at organizations where they were never required to edit their own manuscripts at any stage.

Trade magazine publishers offer journalists a career in publishing, not just in writing and reporting. Writing is the background you need in order to move toward becoming an industry authority. When you are authoritative enough, you also should be in a position to enter the publisher ranks.

*Can free-lancers make a living just writing for magazines? How much per word were they paid on your magazines?*

"Making a living" is beauty in the eye of the beholder. It is possible to make $25,000 to $35,000 a year, I suppose, writing for trade magazines. But some free-lancers who get involved in special projects, or who are retained to be in charge of, say, a quarterly magazine, and who carry various other assignments as well earn upwards of $40,000 or $50,000.

While some editors may still pay by the word, many pay based on the difficulty of the assignment. A free-lancer can earn anywhere from $150 to $750 for a single article. With respect to special projects, the fee a free-lancer receives can range from $1,000 to in excess of $3,000.

*What percentage of business magazine editing jobs do you think exist outside New York City?*

The percentage is very small by comparison; I cannot begin to guess. After New York City I would guess that Chicago, Cleveland, Minneapolis, Boston, and Philadelphia house some large trade magazine publishing companies. Of course, there are scattered opportunities elsewhere.

For many journalism graduates who would like a crack at a trade magazine job in a big city, the paramount problem they confront is the cost of relocation. Unfortunately, many graduates end up settling for a less preferable job because they cannot afford to move. Others who do not believe they can afford to move do it anyway; they recognize that taking the chance is probably the only way to become affiliated with a major publishing company.

*What are the entry-level jobs for magazine editing?*

Many publishers really do not offer entry-level positions. More experience is sought at the outset, because no training vehicle exists. Gralla is one of the few major trade publishing companies that has maintained a formal training program for candidates fresh out of school.

Our program combined job rotation, a series of workshops, and "second opinions" on all feature articles written while a trainee. Each trainee received a ten-week agenda that involved assignments on four or five of our magazines. Additional ten-week schedules were prepared by our training program coordinator until such time as the trainee moved onto one magazine as an assistant editor.

At the outset of being a trainee, an individual did some feature writing but was more often involved in writing news, writing material for departments (such as that on new products or other new literature), pasting up pages (on those magazines without staff artists), or assisting other editors who were preparing full-length features.

Workshops were scheduled monthly during regular office hours and ran as long as two hours. Instructors included the editorial director, associate editorial director, editors in chief with special expertise, and department heads (such as our research director or circulation director).

In the workshops we addressed how to cover a trade show, how to understand statistics, editorial "goofs" to avoid (my favorite—I gave this one), how to write for a retail magazine, interviewing techniques, sources of story leads, headline and lead writing, graphics for tabloids, graphics for standard-size magazines, editorial performance measurement, understanding production, plus much more.

We also sent our editors to *Folio*: "Face-to-Face" seminars. These sessions, of course, are excellent and complement the "curriculum" we offered at Gralla.

*How important is market research in magazine editing?*

Any trade publication company that is a class act invests heavily in market research. As a result, readers receive hundreds of thousands of dollars of statistical material *free* in various issues of the magazine in question. Gralla, through its own research department as well as in conjunction with major market research companies, conducts in excess of one hundred studies a year. These range from highly comprehensive consumer studies covering such areas as kitchen remodeling and jewelry purchases to diversified investigations of the business practices of our readers. In many cases highly valued estimates of market size and market direction are available only from business magazine publishers. The data often are so critical that editors are invited to review them during presentations at major industry conventions or to give private presentations to leading corporations across the country. Any college graduate attempting to evaluate the worth of a trade publisher as an employer should definitely ask questions about market research activity and ask to see examples.

*How much travel was necessary on the part of your editorial people?*

Candidates for positions in our business must be prepared to travel. Our top editors were in demand with respect to personal appearances all over the world. The average junior editor at Gralla traveled 1.9 to 2.3 days a month; senior editors traveled out of town as often as 6 to 8 days a month.

*Can college writing courses and those offered in summer programs really teach one to write?*

Perhaps, but not necessarily to write for business magazines. I went on record many years ago that a special course must be developed to focus on trade journalism as a career. That curriculum should include courses on "How to Write about Retailing," "How to Write about Financial Matters," "How to Write about the Computer Field," "How to Write about the Travel Market," and on and on.

I also find that the instructor of a writing course may choose to focus on newspapers or newsstand magazines. Trade magazine writing remains a mystery to many colleges that offer journalism programs.

You have not asked me a question about whether or not trade magazine careers really are so great.

For those people with excellent writing skills, high energy levels, the ability to make friends easily and build confidence among executives at large or small companies, some sense of graphics, and a keen interest in the business world there is the prospect of becoming a nationally recognized authority in some major industry. Aside from directing the development of editorial content, trade magazine editors are sought-after speakers; often develop audiovisual shows for special presentations before large audiences; are consulted by key executives on major business decisions; and are important sources of information for major consumer media.

Many publishers have stepped up their recruitment efforts at the college level. The industry needs more graduates who exhibit management potential because, down the line, there is definitely a place to put them.

In 1987 Gralla developed its first recruitment kit to present at college career days. In 1988 we organized our first recruitment committee, which allowed us to visit over forty key schools in six months. We found several college guidance people who had no knowledge of trade publishing careers and had to be sold before they would allow us to address classes of graduating journalism majors.

The careers in trade publishing are terrific. I have been at it for over thirty years, and I can assure anyone that there is never a dull moment in our business!

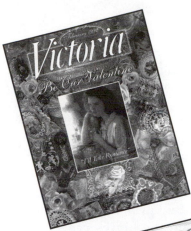

# 4

# Art, Layout, and Design

This chapter is about magazine art and the people who make it—the art directors. In fact, magazine art direction may be as important as its editorial thrust.

Art people work at a frenetic pace, often with impossible deadlines. Consider their responsibility on a magazine that makes heavy use of illustration, photography, color, and complex layouts.

Let's start with the cover. This element is especially important if the publication sells on the newsstand (or in the supermarket or at the airport). There all magazines are on consignment, which means that the publisher gets paid only for those copies actually sold. If you publish *Cosmopolitan* and your newsstand distribution is more than two million, the difference between an average cover and a brilliantly executed one can be as much as $500,000 in unrealized profits.

Not all magazines play for such staggering stakes, yet all are concerned with their graphics. Talented art directors can make the pedestrian article come alive by the clever use of type, photographs, or illustrations. Yet good art need not be expensive. Some magazines do not even employ a full-time artist or designer. Instead, they engage the services of a free-lance art director or designer who establishes graphic guidelines that can then be implemented by less experienced in-house people.

One need only examine the work of such premier designers as Milton Glaser, Walter Bernard, Steve Phillips, John Peter, and Rip Georges to appreciate the significant role of art direction in magazines.

## The Cover

The next time you're in a supermarket that has a large magazine rack, study the covers for a few minutes. What is really more important—the photo (or illustration) or the blurbs that dominate the covers of most newsstand publications? Art directors generally detest these cover blurbs, claiming that they detract from the intended visual effect. Circulation managers and some editors, with an eye on profits, insist that these cover lines, not the art, are what really attract the busy shopper to the magazine. A case can be made for both viewpoints.

Newsstand purchasers of magazines are casual buyers. They do not buy every issue of a magazine, or else they would subscribe. Cover blurbs can inform the buyer of the actual contents of that issue. If these lines are exciting and provocative, they may encourage impulse buying; if there is too much clutter, however, the blurbs cancel themselves out.

*Cosmopolitan,* a very successful newsstand publication, never varies from its standard cover design—a beautiful, sexy woman displaying an alluring amount of cleavage. Exposing a little more cleavage might change the magazine's image, something the publishers are reluctant to do.

Yet covers are no less important for a business magazine. Most busy executives receive dozens of these magazines. The cover treatment of the magazine's subject matter makes the difference between its being read and its being tossed into the wastebasket.

Although a roomful of twenty top art directors would achieve little unanimity on the subject of covers, some of these professionals' theories on cover design make good sense. Here are the principles they adhere to when creating a magazine cover:

1. Do not tell a complicated story that is difficult for the reader to understand. Reading time for a cover may be three seconds.
2. Make certain the cover logo (the name of the magazine in type or art) is easily identifiable. If a light color is used for the logo, a dark color should be used for the background.
3. Think of the cover as a poster. Would the reader want to hang it on his or her wall?
4. Even magazines that are sold by subscription rather than on newsstands require exciting graphics. Worse than insulting readers is to bore them.
5. Experiment with *fewer* cover lines. Sometimes one brilliant, catchy, topical phrase can have a better pulling effect than a half-dozen blurbs.
6. Experiment with backgrounds. For some audiences white works best; for others, red or another high-key color is more effective.

Later in this chapter we will offer a brief analysis of some award-winning covers.

## Luring the Reader into an Article

The other day I picked up a consumer magazine I subscribe to. I glanced at the cover and was unimpressed by the picture of a sports star in a gaucho hat and two cover blurbs about pieces inside. On browsing through the issue, I stopped at an article entitled "Why I Was Fired from the CIA." The headline was set in a simple typeface, as was the byline, and underneath was a three-line subhead. No graphic ostentation here, just a well-written first-person article. I read the piece because the subject interested me. I needed no meretricious ploy to lead me into the article.

The same issue carried an article about a successful European watercolorist. This article was introduced by a striking poster by the artist on the left-hand page and a full page of his work on the right. I read this piece, too, but I might not have had the layout been treated only with type. This situation again proves that there are no fixed rules in magazine design. While most articles need layouts that will draw readers into the story, others can be best handled with attractive typography.

We must remember that most readers do not read all the pages of a magazine; it is therefore necessary for the art staff to utilize many means to attract readership. All the elements of a layout are important—the headline, the choice of typeface, the use of white space, the blending of the headline with the body typeface, the quality of the photography, the glamour of color illustrations, and, finally, the judicious positioning of all these elements in the space allotted.

## Rip Georges on Art Direction

Rip Georges is an art director whose list of credits reads like the Magazine Hall of Fame for Design. His work at *Esquire* in 1989 and 1990 earned him the National Magazine Award for Best Design and the Society of Publication Designers' Gold Award for cover design as well as six Silver Awards in other categories. A few years prior to the *Esquire* as-

signment, Georges won the Gold Award in the Society of Publication Designers' competition for the design of an entire issue for his work on *L.A. Style*.

He has been involved in start-ups at *New West* and *Revue,* a relaunch at *Arts+Architecture,* and, in 1991, the launch of Condé Nast's new "journalistic beauty book," *Allure.*

Georges was interviewed by Suzanne Zelkowitz in the August 1990 issue of *Folio:* and later by Diane Cyr in the December 15, 1991, issue of *Folio:'s Publishing News.* We offer his random comments on how he artfully translates the editorial message:

> The nice thing about magazines is that you get to take chances. . . . I would much rather see a magazine in which that happens than one that plays it safe with a stock approach to imagery.
>
> A good relationship between an art director and an editor is absolutely critical—there needs to be some sort of rapport and combustibility—I know there are adversarial relationships, but I've never worked on a project that has produced good work that way.
>
> I tend to work like an architect—doing blueprints. . . . The transition to designing on the computer should be easy. I like anything that makes my job easier, and desktop publishing will do that.
>
> I am not of the school that holds that the golden age of magazine design has passed. . . . There's still great design. I'm bullish about the times we're in.
>
> A wonderful asymmetrical or hand-rendered type design is often not remembered except by other designers, and that's not my constituency. Readers will remember a good portrait.
>
> There's nothing better than a great picture, except a great, big picture.
>
> The content of the magazine is going to be driven by the editor. The designer's function is to give it visual shape. Certainly we (designers) have input in story ideas—especially story ideas that are driven visually.
>
> It's more difficult now to produce good magazines because of the economy and the intrusion of advertising. But I think that the

photographers now are just as good as ever; so are the illustrators. And the advantage of electronic page design enables you to control your product better.

If you've failed to communicate the editorial idea, you've failed, period. As a designer, I should be able to create a form that enables the reader to get to the content of an article with the least possible resistance and with a design that's still interesting and original.

All art directors have got to be prepared to take chances and be prepared to fall flat on their faces every once in a while. You've got to be prepared to take risks. Even when you fail, you learn a lot from your mistakes. There's too much safe work going on right now and not enough risk-taking.

On the facing page is an example of Rip George's award-winning design in the 1987 Society of Publication Designers' competition. The comments are those of the competition's judges.

## How to Find an Art Director

Unfortunately, there is no test one can give for determining the talent and skill of a prospective art director. Hiring one presents problems, especially if the job is for a new magazine. The simplest avenue is to raid the staff of some other publication whose design you admire. That approach usually doesn't work, however, for top art directors at successful magazines are paid very well and are reluctant to take chances with a new venture.

A sounder approach is to seek out the number two person at a well-designed magazine—a staff member who does not expect to move into the top spot in the immediate future. The excitement of a new venture may be all that is necessary to entice this designer to your magazine.

There are some key questions to be asked when interviewing to fill an art director's slot. In an article that ran in *Folio:*, the noted designer and art consultant John Peter suggested the following:

1. Ask about publication experience. It is most important that the AD (art director) have production know-how and a solid magazine

background. I would not choose someone for a new magazine who has worked primarily at ad agencies.

2. Ask for references. These are sometimes difficult to check, especially if the person is working at another job at the time of the interview.

3. Ask for and look at the magazines the designer has worked on. If the concept and execution are completely different from your own, it may be best to keep looking.

4. Ask about the thinking behind these designs.

5. Ask about format and layout.

6. Ask about typography, photography, illustration, and graphics. An incomplete facility with any of these elements should eliminate an applicant.

7. Ask about paper, printing, and production. Here you are playing for big chips. An art director skilled in production techniques can save the cost of a full-time production person for the new venture.

8. Ask about scheduling and budgets.

9. Ask about the designer's proposed procedure in designing your magazine.

10. Ask about the designer's interest in your project. I would expect enthusiasm and confidence. You'll need it.

11. Ask about the designer's facility and understanding of computer-generated design techniques.

## How to Become an Art Director

The field of commercial art and design is broad, offering numerous outlets for talented people. Design is used in packaging, fabrics, apparel, interiors, architecture, and urban planning. Thousands of artists are employed as illustrators, photographers, and art directors on magazines and in advertising agencies.

What is the best preparation for an art career in magazine publishing? Many high schools and most colleges offer art courses. The official accrediting organization for art schools is NASA (National Association of Schools of Art), 11250 Roger Bacon Drive, Reston, VA 22090. Send $10.00 plus $1.00 for postage for its directory.

(Reprinted courtesy *L.A. Style*)

## *L.A. Style*
Untitled
Award: Design/entire issue
Art Director: Rip Georges

Consistent high quality and a clear design vision make *L.A. Style* one of the best publications in the country. It visually fulfills one of the many possible images for a Los Angeles identity; it's young and sophisticated at the same time. Rip Georges turns this publication to pure gold. His feeling for type and space is unparalleled. It is a design primer. "At last," observed one judge, "an alternative (for the time being) magazine with a little respect (dammit) for the classic elements of great design. Big, bold photographs with clear, classy (and oh so easy-to-read) type. And what style." Seconded another, "It's so handsome and it looks so easy. But you know, if they charged for leading by the linear foot, the magazine would be bankrupt."

Some of the outstanding colleges offering graphic design programs are the Art Center College of Design, Pasadena, California; Philadelphia College of Art, Philadelphia, Pennsylvania; Moore College of Art, also in Philadelphia; Rhode Island School of Design, Providence; and in New York City, Cooper Union, Parson School of Design, Pratt Institute (Brooklyn), and the School of Visual Arts.

Pratt is a superior institution, famed as the spawning ground for countless ad agency and magazine designers. It offers a four-year program leading to the degree of BFA (Bachelor of Fine Arts). Students can major in graphic design, illustration, or art direction.

The art-direction major at Pratt covers a broad range of courses, including visual communications, design procedures, typographic design, illustration, typography, graphic and advertising design, package design, and design for publications.

The School of Visual Arts in New York City has trained many of our top art directors and photographers. The school sponsored the publication of a unique, large-format magazine, *ON SEEING,* featuring the fine-art photography of a number of its students.

## A Sad Word about Submissions

A pitiful sight in a magazine's reception room is that of a young artist carrying his or her twenty-pound portfolio of illustrations and photography, waiting a half-hour for an appointment with an assistant art director. Too often all that is forthcoming is a two-minute scan and the comment "Leave your card, and we'll be in touch." Frequently the quality of this commercial art is equal to that of the magazine's regular contributors.

"Cronyism" prevents the walk-in artist from getting a break, resulting in a sameness that is pervasive in many of our current publications.

## American Institute of Graphic Arts

The American Institute of Graphic Arts, or AIGA, located at 1059 Third Avenue, New York, NY 10021, does a great deal to foster interest in the graphic arts. It sponsors four exhibitions a year at its headquarters gallery in New York and awards outstanding magazine covers and layouts. Each year the Type Directors Club stages a show at AIGA to showcase exceptional efforts by its members.

The AIGA also offers opportunities to participate in its traveling, slide-presentation programs. These presentations reflect standards established in competitive shows by jurors of unique experience and capabilities who select the best graphics from entries numbering in the thousands.

## The Society of Publication Designers Awards

The Society of Publication Designers Awards honors innovative magazine, tabloid, and newspaper design. Each year the judges sift through more than 5,000 entries to come up with their selection of award winners. Awards are bestowed for such design elements as cover, story presentation, photography, and illustration.

The following pages highlight some recent winners in the competition. Although consumer magazines dominate, there are many business publications with outstanding art direction. Some notable examples: *School Arts, Institutions* (covering the food service industry), *Geriatrics Learning, Emergency Medicine,* and *Professional Builder.*

## *Graphis*

**Award:** Merit
**Design Director:** B. Martin
Pederson
**Art Director:** Randell Pearson
**Designer:** B. Martin
Pederson

Art directors from here to Switzerland, where it is edited, hail *Graphis* as the design bible. We won't even attempt to estimate how many layouts have been "borrowed" from its pages during the last 40 years.

Here, the designers have injected a bit of whimsy into a piece about the creators of the Swatch watch. The photograph is charming, though the type is a bit hard to read in its sans serif form. The net effect, however—it works wonderfully.

THE ATLANTIC MONTHLY

*The Great Alaskan Oil Spill was a drama in which the main characters played out their roles according to the script for an elaborate charade—the pretense that a major oil spill can be controlled. The principal props in the charade are the "contingency" plans written to assure the public that organizations know what to do when a spill occurs or one is imminent. In real life, however, contingency plans are barely worth the paper they're written on*

# OIL-SPILL FANTASIES

BY LEE CLARKE

WITHIN HOURS OF THE EXXON VALDEZ GROUNDING, IN PRINCE WILLIAM Sound in March of last year, officers from the Alaska Department of Environmental Conservation were aboard the stricken vessel. To the extent possible, ADEC officials surveyed the damage and began nudging numerous bureaucracies into action. The night was dark, so officials could not tell how badly damaged the ship was, but they knew the spill would be large. "The oil was several feet deep *on top of the water*," an eyewitness told me (probably with some exaggeration) not long ago. "You could have put a hose in the stuff and sucked it up." One of the first ADEC officials to board the vessel used the ship's radiophone to awaken the terminal superintendent of Alyeska Pipeline Service, the corporation owned by the seven oil companies that oversee the Alaska pipeline. He reported that the spill was "a bad one" and advised that airplanes with oil dispersants be readied immediately. A sense of urgency, even panic, was appropriate, because some of the airplanes and dispersants were in Arizona.

ADEC notified Alyeska first because the consortium bore the greatest organizational and legal responsibility for immediate response to an oil spill in Prince William Sound. The elements of that response are detailed in oil-spill contingency plans, particularly one written by Alyeska and approved by ADEC. Alyeska's contingency plan called, chiefly, for two measures: the use of a containment boom (like a long curtain, partly submerged in

NOVEMBER 1990      ILLUSTRATIONS BY J. OTTO SIEBOLD      65

## *The Atlantic Monthly*

**Award:** Merit
**Design Director:** Judy Garlan
**Art Directors:** Judy Garlan/
Robin Gilmore Barnes
**Designers:** Judy Garlan/Robin Gilmore Barnes
**Illustrator:** J. Otto Siebold

Oil spills are major disasters, yet to attract the reader into the story, the designers chose to illustrate the title page of this article with a humorous line drawing of the captain of the *Exxon Valdez* asleep at the switch.

The headline is small but effective; and, although the page is somewhat busy, the contrast of the three different typefaces creates interest. Note how the first six lines of the text lead into the smaller body type.

## *Life*

**Award:** Merit
**Art Director:** Tom Bentkowski
**Designer:** Tom Bentkowski
**Photographer:** Alfred Eisenstaedt
**Photo Editor:** Peter Howe

(top) This is an issue of *Life* in 1990 heralding the triumphs of its great photographer, Alfred Eisenstaedt, who was still making camera art at the age of ninety-one. His career spanned seven decades, the greater part of them at *Life*.

What better way to illustrate the contents page than a half-dozen of Eisenstaedt's memorable photos. My favorite is the one in the center, New York's Penn Station during rush hour (1943). Bentkowski pulls it off brilliantly—six photos, no clutter, great design.

(bottom) The title page is a gem, distinguished by the artistry of the photo of a German town in the 1930s. Eisenstaedt shot this using a vintage camera and glass-plate negative. The photo at the right is of a horse-drawn cab in Milan in 1934.

The headline, with its classical serifs, lends grace to the article. This issue of *Life* featured eight pages of Eisenstaedt's photography, accompanied by an article on the great photographer himself.

## What Will You Make as an Art Director?

The art director oversees all editorial art and design work for the magazine, as well as the art production. He or she also heads photography and illustration. For all this, art directors are paid about as much as managing editors. From my experience, I think they are underpaid.

Following are random comments from art department respondents in the *Folio:* survey:

"Dealing with copy-heavy, nonvisual editors is the hardest part of my job." (Art director in the Northeast earning $30,000.)

"The division between editorial and design—the 'who's responsible for what'—is unclear. Can an art director change 'heads' to look better?" (Art director in the West with twenty years' experience, earning about $40,000.)

"My motto is to keep fresh, avoid complacency, think like a reader of the magazine, and always make a better magazine each month." (Art director in the Northeast with ten years' experience, earning about $55,000.)

We have examined in this chapter the complex and demanding function of the art director. Good design need not be expensive. A talented art director with a small budget can, by the use of type alone, infuse excellence into a business or consumer magazine, an academic journal, or a house organ.

Fortunately, there are many schools to prepare young people for entry into this exciting field. And after the training period is over, in this as in other crafts the best experience is to work under the tutelage of talented professionals.

A word about the role of women in art direction: Women's entry into this field is recent. Even ten years ago there were only a handful of women art directors. Today there are almost as many female art directors as male ones.

Although the average salary for women in the *Folio:* study is about 83 percent that of men, the figures are a statistical average of magazines of all sizes. When we examine the larger circulation magazines in the study, salaries for men and women are almost equal.

From my experience, there is today no bias in the hiring of women as art directors on consumer or business magazines.

### Average Salaries for:

#### Art Director

| | | |
|---|---|---|
| All respondents | $39,975 | |
| Business magazines | 36,466 | |
| Consumer magazines | 42,505 | |

**by Region**

| | Average | Business | Consumer |
|---|---|---|---|
| Northeast | $47,979 | $44,500 | $49,577 |
| South | 34,021 | 29,167 | 38,875 |
| North Central | 36,243 | 39,957 | 32,529 |
| West | 39,825 | 34,556 | 44,136 |

**by Editorial Pages Produced Annually**

| | Average | Business | Consumer |
|---|---|---|---|
| To 499 | $35,767 | $26,800 | $38,971 |
| 500 to 999 | 43,037 | 36,536 | 50,038 |
| 1,000 to 1,499 | 42,318 | 35,500 | 50,500 |

**by Sex**

| | Average | Business | Consumer |
|---|---|---|---|
| Male | $43,885 | $42,667 | $44,646 |
| Female | 36,509 | 32,422 | 39,935 |

**by Years in Business**

| | Average | Business | Consumer |
|---|---|---|---|
| Up to three | $28,512 | $23,857 | $32,133 |
| 4 to 10 | 40,100 | 37,235 | 42,313 |
| 11 to 20 | 44,714 | 49,000 | 42,077 |

# Developing Advertising Sales

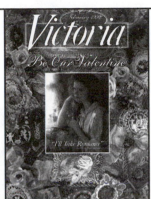

The following scenario depicts the way in which a person on the editorial side of a magazine perceives a day in the life of an advertising salesperson. The perception is based on the apparently opulent life-style led by these fortunate individuals.

The salesperson arrives at the office at about 9:30 A.M. and scans the sports pages of his newspaper while having his Danish and coffee. He confirms his lunch date for that day. Lunch is preeminent in the mind of an ad salesperson. He makes calls to ad agency people, setting lunch dates for later in the week.

Then it is off by foot (but $4.00 taxi fare recorded on the expense account) for an 11:00 A.M. meeting eight blocks away. The ad agency media director he is to meet with is tied up, and so he passes some time in the reception area with an old buddy from another magazine.

Then it's time for lunch at New York's posh Four Seasons restaurant with an advertising agency account supervisor, whom he first meets at the bar for two fast drinks before being seated. He is careful to greet the maitre d', a captain, two waiters, and at least three diners, thus establishing his familiarity in these plush digs and, he hopes, impressing his client.

Two hours, two more drinks, and $116 later, he is back at the office, where he announces to his boss, the advertising director, "We look good for eight four-color pages from [the name of his lunch date] next year."

He then makes a half-dozen phone calls to set up future lunch appointments. By then it is 4:50 P.M. and time to walk the few blocks to Grand Central Station to catch the 5:04 P.M. train to Westport, Connecticut, where he will have a couple of drinks at the station cafe before his wife picks him up. All this for $110,000 a year, plus whatever he can steal on his expense account. . . .

There may be a few advertising space salespeople who function this way, but, as we'll see in this chapter, the life and times of most people in ad sales are at best difficult. The work entails a great deal of rejection—people who don't return calls, or those who just cannot be seen. Many ad salespeople are on sales quotas. If they miss their quota too often, they are replaced.

In a larger sense a magazine sells in competition not only with other magazines in its classification but also with TV, radio, and newspapers. Moreover, large multimagazine or multimedia companies such as Time Warner are able to approach major advertisers with attractive packages that involve favorable rates as well as merchandising possibilities.

## The Scope of Magazine Advertising Sales

Advertising sales for all consumer magazines are now more than $7 billion a year; for business magazines, more than $4 billion. The top ten consumer magazines sell a total of $2.6 billion a year. The tenth-ranking book, *Better Homes and Gardens,* sells about $160 million.

## The Top Ten Consumer Magazines in Advertising Revenue

For 1991, a poor year for ad sales, these ten lead all the rest:

| Rank | Magazine | 1991 Revenues (millions) |
|---|---|---|
| 1. | Parade | $388.7 |
| 2. | People | 344.9 |
| 3. | Time | 326.6 |
| 4. | Sports Illustrated | 323.1 |
| 5. | TV Guide | 279.2 |
| 6. | Newsweek | 228.5 |
| 7. | Business Week | 220.1 |
| 8. | U.S. News & World Report | 172.5 |
| 9. | Good Housekeeping | 165.5 |
| 10. | Better Homes & Gardens | 160.0 |

*Source: PIB*

Six out of this top ten, *People, Time, Sports Illustrated, TV Guide, Newsweek,* and *Business Week,* were down in revenues for the year. *Parade,* the leader, is a weekly newspaper supplement that is classified as a consumer magazine.

## Top Advertisers in Magazines

In 1991 the top five advertisers spent $616 million out of the total revenue of about $7 billion for all consumer magazines for that year. Here is the ad dollar breakdown:

| Rank | Advertiser | 1991 Spending (millions) |
|---|---|---|
| 1. | Philip Morris | $167.1 |
| 2. | General Motors | 162.1 |
| 3. | Procter & Gamble | 111.5 |
| 4. | Ford Motor Company | 94.1 |
| 5. | Toyota | 81.8 |

Procter & Gamble, the nation's largest advertiser, with total expenditures in excess of $2 billion, spent only 111.5 million on magazines. The major portion of its budget goes for TV advertising.

In terms of categories, here are the ten leading groups in magazine advertising revenues:

1. Automotive
2. Toiletries and Cosmetics
3. Direct Response
4. Business and Consumer Services
5. Food and Food Products
6. Apparel, Footwear, and Accessories
7. Cigarettes, Tobacco, and Accessories
8. Travel, Hotels, and Resorts
9. Computers and Office Equipment
10. Beer, Wine, and Liquor

## The Importance of Advertising Sales

Before we discuss the role of the advertising director, we must emphasize the significance of advertising sales. Many business magazines operate on a controlled-circulation basis; that is, their readers get the magazine free. This policy is the publisher's decision, predicated on the belief that in his or her particular industry it is more important to reach everyone than to charge a subscription rate and thereby reach only a portion of the market. Accordingly, it is incumbent on management to recover the cost of production and make a profit from the sale of advertising.

On consumer magazines, although revenue is received from subscriptions and sometimes newsstand sales, in order to yield a profit it is almost always necessary to sell advertising because production, editorial, and overhead costs are so high.

Most magazines base their rates on circulation. For example, a given magazine has an ABC circulation of 100,000. (ABC stands for the Audit Bureau of Circulations and attests to the fact that this magazine's circulation is audited once a year by ABC.) The publication decides to charge $3,000 for a black-and-white page and $3,600 for a four-color page. We then divide 100,000 into $3,000 and say that the book has a CPM (cost per thousand) of $30. This figure usually refers to its CPM for a black-and-white ad; if we want to determine its CPM for a four-color ad, we divide the 100,000 into $3,600 and come up with a figure of $36. There are many other conditions and standards to be considered in media selection, among them demographics and pass-along readership.

To prepare advertising, conduct research, and evaluate the media, the advertiser (often called "the account") employs an advertising agency. The agency's compensation is usually in the form of a 15 percent commission from the media, so that when an agency is billed by a magazine for that $3,000 black-and-white ad, the publication automatically credits the agency with the 15 percent and agrees to accept $2,550 for the ad. The agency thus keeps $450 of the $3,000 paid by the advertiser for the full-page ad. This practice is standard in other media as well. In addition, the agency is usually reimbursed for creative and out-of-pocket costs in the preparation of the ad.

A magazine's advertising director employs sales-oriented people to accomplish the difficult task of bringing accounts and agencies into the magazine. A good deal of sophistication and marketing know-how is required for this effort. In fact, on major magazines specialists are employed, so that a *Time* or a *Newsweek* will have salespeople with expertise in the fields of automotive, liquor, apparel, tobacco, electronics, and a dozen other product categories. These specialists have an intimate knowledge of their industries, giving them a decided edge in making sales. Competition demands that the advertising-space salesperson utilize many tools of the trade and offer much more than competitive rates.

### The Rate Card and Media Kit

A *rate card* is a simple or detailed listing of a publication's advertising rates and other data. It is issued by the publication for the benefit of its advertisers and their agencies. It is also published in a monthly directory called SRDS (Standard Rate and Data Service), along with the rate cards of hundreds of other magazines in its subdivisions. There are SRDS directories for consumer magazines and business magazines and separate directories for radio and TV stations.

# FOCUS ON *FORTUNE*

*Fortune* is one of our leading consumer magazines, selling more than $150 million in advertising in 1991. It is a member of the Time Inc. Magazine Company family. *Fortune* has a North American circulation of 665,000 and is published biweekly.

Let's consider its 1991 *Media and Rate Information* booklet, a handsome presentation of seventy pages. Rate cards and media kits take many forms, but basically they serve as ammunition for space salespeople making sales calls on either an advertiser or an ad agency.

Although advertising rates are a significant portion of *Fortune*'s kit, many other areas are covered as well. Figure 5–1 shows the contents pages of the kit.

**General Information.** This section covers *Fortune*'s birth in 1930, a gutsy time to launch a business magazine. These pages detail high points in the magazine's editorial history.

**Syndicated and Audience Studies.** Here *Fortune* quotes from two readership studies conducted among executives and corporate managers, comparing *Fortune* with its prime competition, *Business Week* and *Forbes*.

## CONTENTS

| | Page |
|---|---|
| **GENERAL INFORMATION** | |
| Editorial Statement | 3 |
| FORTUNE History | 4 |
| **SYNDICATED AND AUDIENCE STUDIES** | |
| ORC Executive Caravan | 9 |
| Top Managers' Readership | 11 |
| **EDITORIAL AND ADVERTISING CALENDAR** | |
| Editorial and Special Advertising Sections | 13 |
| 1991 Closing Dates | 22 |
| **ADVERTISING RATES** | |
| FORTUNE Advertising Editions | 23 |
| Worldwide and North America | 24-25 |
| U.S. Regional Editions Map | 26-27 |
| Demographic Editions | 28 |
| Regional Editions | 29 |
| Metro and International | 30 |
| Europe and Asia | 31 |
| Combined Editions | 32 |
| Special Advertising Availabilities | 33 |
| Special Advertising Opportunities | 34 |
| Frequency Discounts | 35 |
| Worldwide Rates | 35 |
| Renewal Programs | 35 |
| Leadership and Preferred Advertiser Plans | 36 |
| "500" Package | 36 |
| EPIC | 37 |
| General Provisions | 38 |
| Commission and Cash Discounts | 38 |
| **SPECIAL CATEGORY OPPORTUNITIES** | |
| Financial Package | 40-41 |
| Travel Package | 42-43 |
| Consumer Package | 44-45 |

1

Figure 5–1

The publisher may change the rates published herein at any time, provided that no increase in rates will apply to advertising the closing date of which precedes the announcement of increased rates.

**FORTUNE/Published by The Time Inc. Magazine Company**
**Time & Life Building**
**Rockefeller Center**
**New York, New York 10020**
**(212) 522-1212**

© 1991 The Time Inc. Magazine Company. Printed in U.S.A. #90185

2

*Reproduced with permission from Fortune*

**Editorial and Advertising Calendar.** Special editorial issues and special advertising sections are the lifeblood of many magazines. Such issues and sections are the means by which a magazine encourages advertisers to increase their commitment. An example of a special editorial issue is "Special Report—The New Europe"; of a special advertising section, "Managing Business Travel Costs." In 1991 *Fortune* produced fifty-one of these special issues and sections.

**Advertising Rates.** *Fortune* has five basic advertising editions: Worldwide, circulation 780,000; International, circulation 115,000; North America, circulation 665,000; Europe, circulation 60,000; and Asia, circulation 45,000. An advertiser may buy space in any one of these editions. In addition, *Fortune* has six U.S. regional editions and two demographic editions—Industrial Management and Global Financial.

Advertisers use regional editions if their product or service is sold only in a specific territory or if they wish to test-market a new product.

Figure 5–2 shows the rate schedule for *Fortune's* Worldwide and North America editions.

Worldwide is the largest edition *Fortune* offers, with a total circulation of 780,000. At $38,550 for a one-time black-and-white page, the CPM is $49.42, a competitive rate for a magazine in this classification. When an advertiser buys space in the North America edition, he or she pays $35,060 for a black-and-white page, or a CPM of $52.72.

Note also that *Fortune* provides substantial discounts for frequency buyers. Back covers are always a premium position on a magazine. *Fortune's* rate for an ad on the back cover of its North American edition is $16,090 higher than its rate for a four-color page in that edition.

**Special Category Opportunities.** This section relates to packages *Fortune* offers that combine various editions with similar editorial focus. If the advertiser buys the Consumer Package, the ad will be in five issues and the advertiser will receive a substantial discount.

## WORLDWIDE

### CIRCULATION: 780,000

Includes all circulation in North America, Europe, Asia, Africa, the Middle East, Latin America, and the South Pacific.

| FULL PAGE | 1X | 6X | 12X | 18X | 25X | 39X | 50X | 64X |
|---|---|---|---|---|---|---|---|---|
| Black & White | 38,550 | 36,240 | 34,700 | 33,920 | 33,540 | 33,150 | 32,770 | 32,380 |
| 2 Color | 48,570 | 45,660 | 43,710 | 42,740 | 42,260 | 41,770 | 41,280 | 40,800 |
| 4 Color Process | 58,980 | 55,440 | 53,080 | 51,900 | 51,310 | 50,720 | 50,130 | 49,540 |
| **COVERS** | | | | | | | | |
| 2nd Cover | 64,880 | 60,990 | 58,390 | 57,090 | 56,450 | 55,800 | 55,150 | 54,500 |
| 3rd Cover | 58,980 | 55,440 | 53,080 | 51,900 | 51,310 | 50,720 | 50,130 | 49,540 |
| 4th Cover | 76,670 | 72,070 | 69,000 | 67,470 | 66,700 | 65,940 | 65,170 | 64,400 |
| **TWO-THIRDS PAGE** | | | | | | | | |
| Black & White | 28,270 | 26,570 | 25,440 | 24,880 | 24,590 | 24,310 | 24,030 | 23,750 |
| 2 Color | 35,620 | 33,480 | 32,060 | 31,350 | 30,990 | 30,630 | 30,280 | 29,920 |
| 4 Color Process | 43,250 | 40,660 | 38,930 | 38,060 | 37,630 | 37,200 | 36,760 | 36,330 |
| **JUNIOR PAGE** | | | | | | | | |
| Black & White | 24,830 | 23,340 | 22,350 | 21,850 | 21,600 | 21,350 | 21,110 | 20,860 |
| 2 Color | 31,280 | 29,400 | 28,150 | 27,530 | 27,210 | 26,900 | 26,590 | 26,280 |
| 4 Color Process | 37,980 | 35,700 | 34,180 | 33,420 | 33,040 | 32,660 | 32,280 | 31,900 |
| **HALF-PAGE (HORIZONTAL ONLY)** | | | | | | | | |
| Black & White | 22,740 | 21,380 | 20,470 | 20,010 | 19,780 | 19,560 | 19,330 | 19,100 |
| 2 Color | 28,650 | 26,930 | 25,790 | 25,210 | 24,930 | 24,640 | 24,350 | 24,070 |
| 4 Color Process | 34,800 | 32,710 | 31,320 | 30,620 | 30,280 | 29,930 | 29,580 | 29,230 |
| **ONE-THIRD PAGE** | | | | | | | | |
| Black & White | 14,640 | 13,760 | 13,180 | 12,880 | 12,740 | 12,590 | 12,440 | 12,300 |
| 2 Color | 18,460 | 17,350 | 16,610 | 16,240 | 16,060 | 15,880 | 15,690 | 15,510 |
| 4 Color Process | 22,410 | 21,070 | 20,170 | 19,720 | 19,500 | 19,270 | 19,050 | 18,820 |

## NORTH AMERICA

### CIRCULATION: 665,000

Includes the U.S. and Canada.

| FULL PAGE | 1X | 6X | 12X | 18X | 25X | 39X | 50X | 64X |
|---|---|---|---|---|---|---|---|---|
| Black & White | 35,060 | 32,960 | 31,550 | 30,850 | 30,500 | 30,150 | 29,800 | 29,450 |
| 2 Color | 44,170 | 41,520 | 39,750 | 38,870 | 38,430 | 37,990 | 37,540 | 37,100 |
| 4 Color Process | 53,630 | 50,410 | 48,270 | 47,190 | 46,660 | 46,120 | 45,590 | 45,050 |
| **COVERS** | | | | | | | | |
| 2nd Cover | 59,000 | 55,460 | 53,100 | 51,920 | 51,330 | 50,740 | 50,150 | 49,560 |
| 3rd Cover | 53,630 | 50,410 | 48,270 | 47,190 | 46,660 | 46,120 | 45,590 | 45,050 |
| 4th Cover | 69,720 | 65,540 | 62,750 | 61,350 | 60,660 | 59,960 | 59,260 | 58,560 |

ON AN AVAILABILITY BASIS ONLY:

| TWO-THIRDS PAGE | 1X | 6X | 12X | 18X | 25X | 39X | 50X | 64X |
|---|---|---|---|---|---|---|---|---|
| Black & White | 25,700 | 24,160 | 23,130 | 22,620 | 22,360 | 22,100 | 21,850 | 21,590 |
| 2 Color | 32,390 | 30,450 | 29,150 | 28,500 | 28,180 | 27,860 | 27,530 | 27,210 |
| 4 Color Process | 39,330 | 36,970 | 35,400 | 34,610 | 34,220 | 33,820 | 33,430 | 33,040 |
| **JUNIOR PAGE** | | | | | | | | |
| Black & White | 22,570 | 21,220 | 20,310 | 19,860 | 19,640 | 19,410 | 19,180 | 18,960 |
| 2 Color | 28,450 | 26,740 | 25,610 | 25,040 | 24,750 | 24,470 | 24,180 | 23,900 |
| 4 Color Process | 34,540 | 32,470 | 31,090 | 30,400 | 30,050 | 29,700 | 29,360 | 29,010 |
| **HALF-PAGE (HORIZONTAL ONLY)** | | | | | | | | |
| Black & White | 20,680 | 19,440 | 18,610 | 18,200 | 17,990 | 17,780 | 17,580 | 17,370 |
| 2 Color | 26,060 | 24,500 | 23,450 | 22,930 | 22,670 | 22,410 | 22,150 | 21,890 |
| 4 Color Process | 31,640 | 29,740 | 28,480 | 27,840 | 27,530 | 27,210 | 26,890 | 26,580 |
| **ONE-THIRD PAGE** | | | | | | | | |
| Black & White | 13,320 | 12,520 | 11,990 | 11,720 | 11,590 | 11,460 | 11,320 | 11,190 |
| 2 Color | 16,780 | 15,770 | 15,100 | 14,770 | 14,600 | 14,430 | 14,260 | 14,100 |
| 4 Color Process | 20,380 | 19,160 | 18,340 | 17,930 | 17,730 | 17,530 | 17,320 | 17,120 |

**Figure 5–2**

Reproduced with permission from *Fortune*

**Advertising Support.** This section of *Fortune's* rate card details the many marketing services available to advertisers. The phrase "value-added services" has received great emphasis in recent years. Simply stated, it refers to what a magazine can do for an advertiser in addition to running his or her advertising. *Fortune* offers an impressive list of value-added services, including the following:

| | |
|---|---|
| custom mailings | seminars |
| ad reprints | speakers |
| sales contests | showroom displays |
| outings | customer loyalty programs |
| custom publishing | research and trade- |
| broadcast support | show peripherals |

**Subscriber Profile.** Here, *Fortune* gives demographic and other information about its typical reader. This person's average net worth is a whopping $1,218,600, and the average value of his or her investment portfolio is $770,990. The median age of readers is forty-five, and 76 percent of them graduated from college.

**Production.** This section is the nuts-and-bolts of the rate card. When an agency is preparing an ad for *Fortune,* these pages cover all the specifications.

**Personnel.** This section lists all of *Fortune's* domestic and foreign offices, in addition to the key editorial and business personnel at the home office in New York.

## Research: a Vital Component

Advertising agencies depend heavily on syndicated research for much valuable statistical information. The two major research organizations, Simmons and MRI (Mediamark Research Inc.), measure this information. Once a magazine agrees to participate in these studies, it is committed to the results, which are then submitted to the advertising agencies that subscribe.

Simmons and MRI collect information from a cross-section of the population on a statistical and geographic basis. These organizations measure people's heavy to light usage of products in more than 900 categories and their heavy to light usage of all print and broadcast media. The organizations also collect personal data, such as education, income, age, and property ownership. Finally, they measure magazine-reading time and how long a magazine is kept in the home. This information is compiled for approximately 160 different consumer magazines.

Another important factor measured is pass-along readership. That is, although a magazine has a given number of primary buyers, it has an added number of readers who do not buy the magazine but instead read the buyer's copy. To qualify as pass-along readers, these secondary (pass-along) readers are checked for their recall of a recent issue of a magazine.

The Simmons or MRI interviewer visits a home and spends about twenty minutes asking questions, generally demographic ones. Primary readers and accepted pass-along readers are then given questionnaires measuring the data outlined above.

Consequently, a publication can have 500,000 primary readers and as many as five or six pass-along readers per copy, giving it a total audience of 3,000,000 to 3,500,000. This total is used by the magazine's research team as sales ammunition to show its efficiency as compared with that of competitive magazines. For example, Magazine A has a primary circulation of 100,000 and four pass-along readers per copy, for a total audience of 500,000. Its black-and-white page rate is $1,000. Thus, instead of a CPM of $10.00 ($1,000 divided by 100,000), the magazine has a *total audience* CPM of $2.00 ($1,000 divided by 500,000). Magazine B has a primary circulation of 150,000 and two pass-along readers per copy, for a total audience of 450,000. Its black-and-white page rate is $1,400. Instead of a CPM of $9.33 ($1,400 divided by 150,000), the magazine has a *total audience* CPM of $3.22 ($1,400 divided by 450,000).

The conclusion? Magazine A is more efficient than Magazine B even though magazine B's primary circulation is 50 percent higher than magazine A's.

Once a magazine subscribes to participation in an MRI or Simmons study, it may call on the service for specialized information derived from the study. Let's say that *Fortune* is competing with *Forbes* and *Business Week* for scotch whiskey advertising. If these two competitors are part of the same Simmons or MRI field study, *Fortune* can ask the research organization to compute its efficiency in reaching scotch drinkers vis-à-vis the other two magazines. Since this information is part of the service's syndicated research, it is simple for the research organization to fulfill the magazine's request.

In addition to the semiannual syndicated field studies conducted by MRI and Simmons, these services are often called on to undertake custom studies on behalf of individual magazines.

Advertising agencies also subscribe to these field studies so that the research data will be readily available to them.

Advertisers are becoming even more sophisticated in their evaluation of media and now measure the psychographics as well as the demographics of a magazine's readers. Broadly stated, the term *psychographics* refers to the attitudinal relationships of a publication's readers to the publication. This factor measures how respondents rate themselves on each of twenty adjective clusters, such as whether they consider themselves affectionate (which includes "passionate," "loving," and "romantic"), broad-minded (which includes "liberal" and "tolerant"), creative (encompassing "inventive," "imaginative," and "artistic"), and stubborn (including "hardheaded," "headstrong," and "obstinate"). It also measures "buying style"—respondents' attitudes toward shopping, brand choice, and a product's advertising effectiveness.

Although there are obvious discrepancies in this syndicated research, it is nonetheless a valuable adjunct to a space salesperson's selling story.

The total audience factor is examined in the chart. *Sports Illustrated,* for example, has a circulation of 3,439,000. With its pass-along of 6.72 adult readers per copy, it has a total audience in column one of 23,096,000 adults. One of its competitors, *Sports Afield,* has a circulation of only 530,000, but with its pass-along of 9.63 readers per copy it has a total audience of 5,102,000. Under certain circumstances *Sports Afield* may then be a more efficient buy for particular advertisers.

Note the median age and income shown. Income is for the whole household the survey respondent lives in. MRI measures many other demographic factors in its complete study; only a capsulized version is presented here.

It is also significant to note the unqualified success of Time Inc. Magazine's *People*. At the time of this MRI study, *People* had a circulation of 3,202,000 and a total audience of 35,141,000—about two of every fifteen Americans.

## Target Marketing: A Dynamic Trend in Magazine Advertising

When I started in magazine publishing some forty years ago, the only selectivity magazines could offer advertisers was in the form of regional editions. Later a bit more sophistication was developed—doctors' or students' editions were offered, as was reaching subscribers in large or small counties.

Today's printing technology has enabled magazines to offer advertisers options never even thought about fifteen or twenty years ago. The technique is called "target marketing"; the capability involves selective binding and ink-jet print-

ing. Its use may revolutionize magazine advertising in the coming decade.

A recent ad for Volkswagen in *Newsweek* is shown in an article by Cary Peyton Rich in *Folio:*. Under the headline "FAHVERGNUGEN FOR FIVE" and a photo of the car and a smiling young family of five appears the following *personalized* message:

LEWIS MOTORS, INC.

1325 SHELBURNE RD, SOUTH BURLINGTON, VT

ATTENTION: EDWARD COYLE

YOU ARE INVITED TO TEST DRIVE THE ALL NEW 1990 VOLKSWAGEN PASSAT AT LEWIS MOTORS INC. AND RECEIVE A COMPLIMENTARY 3-VOLUME RAND MCNALLY TRAVEL SET. TO ARRANGE FOR AN APPOINTMENT PLEASE CALL MARK BENDIT OF LEWIS MOTORS INC. AT (802) 658–1130. OFFER ENDS MAY 31, 1990.

(Edward Coyle is a fictitious name used for this example. Other copies of the magazine would carry similar personalized offers.)

Further target marketing of this nature enables advertisers to reach specific segments of a magazine's circulation—young suburban families,

| | AUDIENCE (000) | | | MEDIAN AGE | | | MEDIAN H/D INCOME | | | CIRCU-LATION | READERS PER COPY | | |
|---|---|---|---|---|---|---|---|---|---|---|---|---|---|
| | TOTAL ADULTS | TOTAL MEN | TOTAL WOMEN | ADULTS | MEN | WOMEN | ADULTS | MEN | WOMEN | (000) | ADULTS | MEN | WOMEN |
| Total Adult Population | 184,274 | 87,875 | 96,399 | 40.9 | 40.3 | 41.6 | 33,975 | 36,393 | 31,777 | - | - | - | - |
| Popular Science | 7,283 | 5,850 | 1,433 | 39.4 | 38.4 | 43.1 | 40,819 | 39,962 | 44,442 | 1,750* | 4.16 | 3.34 | .82 |
| Practical Homeowner | 1,431 | 769 | 662 | 41.0 | 42.2 | 39.2 | 44,692 | 47,558 | 43,350 | 675 | 2.12 | 1.14 | .98 |
| Premiere | 1,479 | 753 | 726 | 30.7 | 31.5 | 28.6 | 47,004 | 51,250 | 45,313 | 474 | 3.12 | 1.59 | 1.53 |
| Prevention | 9,792 | 2,351 | 7,441 | 46.2 | 46.1 | 46.3 | 36,743 | 38,857 | 35,895 | 3,121 | 3.14 | .75 | 2.38 |
| Reader's Digest | 52,074 | 21,663 | 30,411 | 46.4 | 46.2 | 46.6 | 34,613 | 37,063 | 32,912 | 16,680 | 3.12 | 1.30 | 1.82 |
| Redbook | 14,135 | 1,500 | 12,635 | 40.7 | 41.9 | 40.5 | 35,035 | 37,862 | 34,536 | 3,825* | 3.70 | .39 | 3.30 |
| Road & Track | 5,585 | 5,246 | 339 | 31.7 | 31.2 | 37.2 | 44,319 | 43,852 | 61,979 | 687 | 8.13 | 7.64 | .49 |
| Rodale Active Network (Gr) | 5,941 | 4,245 | 1,696 | 35.7 | 34.7 | 37.9 | 49,526 | 50,822 | 46,307 | 1,524 | 3.90 | 2.79 | 1.11 |
| Rolling Stone | 7,852 | 4,609 | 3,243 | 25.5 | 26.2 | 24.7 | 40,996 | 40,716 | 41,234 | 1,190 | 6.60 | 3.87 | 2.73 |
| Runner's World | 1,891 | 1,057 | 834 | 38.5 | 39.1 | 37.9 | 59,519 | 65,000 | 48,889 | 415 | 4.56 | 2.55 | 2.01 |
| Saturday Evening Post | 3,604 | 1,388 | 2,216 | 48.9 | 48.6 | 49.0 | 33,848 | 35,461 | 32,222 | 468 | 7.70 | 2.97 | 4.74 |
| Scientific American | 2,774 | 2,041 | 733 | 40.4 | 40.4 | 40.4 | 55,078 | 54,170 | 57,813 | 500 | 5.55 | 4.08 | 1.47 |
| Self | 3,396 | 329 | 3,067 | 31.1 | 34.5 | 30.3 | 45,207 | 55,000 | 44,164 | 1,155* | 2.94 | .28 | 2.66 |
| Sesame Street Magazine | 6,249 | 1,582 | 4,667 | 32.5 | 33.1 | 32.2 | 45,623 | 45,709 | 32,797 | 1,316 | 4.75 | 1.20 | 3.55 |
| Seventeen | 6,178 | 916 | 5,262 | 28.5 | 33.1 | 27.2 | 37,081 | 41,528 | 35,926 | 1,866 | 3.31 | .49 | 2.82 |
| Shape | 2,890 | 668 | 2,222 | 29.1 | 29.4 | 29.0 | 46,145 | 47,589 | 44,455 | 670* | 4.31 | 1.00 | 3.32 |
| Ski | 2,152 | 1,480 | 672 | 29.3 | 26.6 | 34.7 | 55,837 | 53,767 | 58,889 | 434 | 4.96 | 3.41 | 1.55 |
| Skiing | 1,907 | 1,343 | 564 | 29.1 | 26.4 | 34.7 | 57,306 | 56,573 | 58,538 | 435 | 4.38 | 3.09 | 1.30 |
| Smithsonian | 8,481 | 4,306 | 4,175 | 43.5 | 42.5 | 44.6 | 45,679 | 47,298 | 43,644 | 2,342* | 3.62 | 1.84 | 1.78 |
| Soap Opera Digest | 7,604 | 892 | 6,712 | 31.7 | 27.6 | 32.1 | 31,323 | 33,817 | 30,931 | 1,377 | 5.52 | .65 | 4.87 |
| Southern Living | 12,098 | 3,275 | 8,823 | 45.8 | 48.0 | 44.6 | 38,530 | 46,913 | 36,541 | 2,416 | 5.01 | 1.36 | 3.65 |
| Sport | 4,116 | 3,608 | 508 | 33.6 | 33.0 | 39.7 | 38,398 | 38,757 | 36,479 | 858* | 4.80 | 4.21 | .59 |
| The Sporting News | 3,909 | 3,389 | 520 | 33.9 | 33.6 | 34.6 | 40,423 | 39,516 | 50,574 | 629 | 6.21 | 5.39 | .83 |
| Sports Afield | 5,102 | 4,374 | 728 | 40.8 | 40.0 | 44.3 | 34,339 | 35,132 | 32,420 | 530* | 9.63 | 8.25 | 1.37 |
| Sports Illustrated | 23,096 | 17,999 | 5,097 | 34.2 | 33.5 | 37.1 | 40,663 | 40,525 | 41,104 | 3,439 | 6.72 | 5.23 | 1.48 |
| Star | 10,860 | 3,264 | 7,596 | 34.9 | 31.7 | 36.8 | 29,908 | 31,987 | 29,257 | 2,813* | 3.86 | 1.16 | 2.70 |

**Figure 5–3. Magazine Audience Estimates Spring 1992**

affluent seniors, college students, recent movers, and so on.

Of course, this technology is expensive, both for the advertiser and for the magazine. Results have to be evaluated to warrant the expense. In the final analysis, if more targeted *Newsweek* readers come into their Volkswagen dealers for a test drive than other magazines' readers do, the program works.

As Rich points out in the article, "Eventually advertisers might merge their lists with publishers' lists and come up with a targeted segment. There is incredible potential." Target marketing in magazines is an exciting new development in magazine sales.

## Cross-Media Deals: The Octopus Approach

When the high-voltage team from Time Warner visits a major automaker, it may be pitching $100 million worth of advertising for a half-dozen of its publications. But Time Warner is in many other businesses—movies, TV, records, amusement parks. The team members' objective is to get the magazine advertising, but they are also aiming at cross-media deals involving the other tentacles of their octopus. Some have called these "large-scale kitchen sink deals." The results are revolutionizing the way advertising is sold.

Multimagazine companies without other media subsidiaries are nonetheless visiting large advertisers and offering special discounts, merchandising, and value-added packages. What about single-magazine operations? Are they shut out from these opportunities? No. These magazines are joining with other magazine companies in presenting joint-buy deals.

For the big guys with their multimillion-dollar sales potentials, these are heady times. But for the little guys without the muscle, the going can be tough.

## The Tribulations of an Ad Salesperson

I've sold ad space myself. Success can provide glorious highs, but, alas, there are frequent low points. Advertisers and their agencies can find dozens of reasons for not buying advertising in your magazine. The publishing sales consultant Helen Berman has offered a list of more than two dozen common objections. Here is a sampling from her list:

1. I don't believe in advertising.
2. The agency says, "I don't decide where to place the space—talk to the client."
3. The client says, "I don't handle advertising decisions—talk to my agency."
4. Your rates/CPM are too high.
5. We can only afford one publication—your competitor's.
6. Let me think it over—call me next week/month/year/century.
7. I don't believe in your magazine.
8. I haven't time to see you.

If you can overcome these objections, you belong in ad sales.

## Page Brokers: Sales Reps Outside a Magazine's Own Staff

When a publisher wants to broaden its market in an area where it has a small potential, it will generally hire a sales representative for that territory. Yet opening an office with one's own salesperson involves rent, secretarial help, phones, and other expenses. The alternative is to engage a rep for the territory, which entails no such cost outlay. Reps are independent sales organizations representing a number of magazines in a given territory.

Similarly, these independent sales reps are used for categories not considered primary by a magazine. A fashion magazine, for example, would consider automotive and financial advertising to be secondary categories. Here the magazine might employ reps on a commission basis rather than have its own staff pursue these accounts.

Reps traditionally work on commissions only—10, 15, or 20 percent, depending on their status. Sometimes the rep demands a fixed monthly guarantee against commission, especially if the initial sales effort is costly. The rep may work for a dozen or more publishers and employ a number of salespeople to cover the area. If the magazine represented is important enough, one person may cover that publication exclusively. In other, more usual situations, one rep covers a number of magazines; however, this arrangement may present a problem to the publisher, as we will explain.

The advantages of using a rep are many, including the following:

1. Little or no investment of hard dollars has to be made by the publication.
2. A rep usually has more influence among accounts and agencies in the territory or category than a publication's own salesperson does.
3. A rep can be an excellent sounding board for testing new ideas and investigating new markets for the magazine.

The disadvantages are these:

1. There is a lack of direct contact with the magazine because of the division of a rep's responsibility.
2. Costs can run higher than if a magazine opens its own office.
3. There is the danger of the "peddler effect," whereby a rep makes many offerings to a buyer and sells whatever comes easiest. To avoid this situation, I always incorporated into my contracts veto power over the rep's handling competitive magazines.

My feeling about reps in general is that they can be a successful adjunct to a magazine's own efforts but to be effective must receive the same attention and attitude as the magazine's own staff.

## Selling Advertising for a New Magazine

For readers of this book who intend to start their own magazines, this subject is of singular importance. When even existing magazines encounter so much sales resistance, imagine how much this resistance is compounded for the new publication. Hardhearted agency and account people often will not even see salespeople for new magazines, telling them to return after they have been in business for a year. Without any advertising sales, how can they last that long? Some important tips from someone who has been there:

1. Be prepared to make your entire sales presentation in fifteen minutes.
2. If you do not yet have your first issue, you must have a professionally produced dummy, which connotes clearly the look of the proposed magazine. (See chapter 14.)
3. Discuss in detail the background of the new publication's founders. If impressive, it can override other negative factors.
4. Emphasize the substantial financial structure of the venture. No advertiser likes to be burned by advertising in a magazine that dies after three issues for lack of capital.
5. Seek out those advertisers who are known in the industry as pioneers. These are people who will gamble and advertise in a new book if promised special positions and other considerations.
6. Do not make deals. A special charter rate is perfectly acceptable, but offering one advertiser lower rates than another is lethal. Word gets around quickly, and the rate-cutting reputation of the magazine persists for a long time. This does not preclude a firm offer to all advertisers of, say, three free ads for a thirteen-time contract, or one ad free after an advertiser signs up for a four-time contract. The important principle to follow is consistency in maintaining the established rate.
7. Take an honest position about circulation. Discuss only the figure you can actually guarantee, not the number you expect to reach if the newsstands sell out. Tell advertisers when you will be audited and how you propose to document your circulation.
8. Hire the most experienced ad people you can afford, and be candid with them about the publication's financial structure. Consider offering a piece of the action to a star salesperson who only by this means may be weaned away from another situation.

9. Don't use boring slide presentations. Instead, use a fast-paced professional video.
10. Work hard at selling the most important account in a particular product classification. Others will surely follow because they will assume the leader knows something they don't know.
11. Do not have your salespeople call on too many accounts. Specialize in the categories you feel are most logical for immediate business. Once those ads are sold, you can go on to other primary classifications.
12. Set up meetings at the large advertising agencies. Invite the key people on accounts you feel are appropriate for your new magazine. Bring along the editor of your publication. He or she can best articulate the editorial concept. This meeting is very significant and should be carefully rehearsed before it takes place.

Since magazines often lose money on their subscription efforts and many do not have a newsstand potential, advertising sales bear the burden of providing the primary source of profit. (See chapter 8 on subscriptions.) For new magazines this income is of supreme importance.

## Selling the Account versus Selling the Agency

Here is a hypothetical situation that demonstrates a typical problem in selling space: The salesperson for a women's magazine is interested in breaking into the camera classification, since research tells her that her readership makes heavy use of this product. She visits the account executive, or AE, at an agency that handles a major camera account to tell her impressive story. The AE listens intently but then suggests that she see the media buyer at the agency.

This she does, only to be informed that the agency's media director is really the decision maker, and so it's off to see him to make the pitch for the third time. The media director seems to accept the salesperson's convincing presentation but now tells her that judgment on the acceptance of new media rests at the account level.

### Getting into Advertising Sales: Seven Short Tips

1. If you're still in school, get a job selling advertising space for your college newspaper. Getting turned down by the local record-store owner will be good training for getting turned down by more important people later on.
2. Consider where you would like to work. The "big three" advertising sales markets are New York, Chicago, and Los Angeles, in that order, but there are advertising agencies all over the country and therefore opportunities for a salesperson who is willing to relocate.
3. If you're a woman, note that space-selling opportunities have increased enormously in recent years. Nowadays women can (and indeed do) become advertising directors at major magazines. Consider sales training courses designed specifically for women (such as those at David King's Careers for Women, 80 Fifth Avenue, New York, NY 10011).
4. On the West Coast Kathy Aaronson runs a sales training service for men and women similar to that of David King's. She calls it "The Sales Athlete." Aaronson has lectured at the *Folio:* seminars and has trained more than 300,000 experienced and inexperienced sales and marketing executives coast to coast. Her address: The Sales Athlete, 9808 Wilshire Boulevard, Beverly Hills, CA 90212.
5. Get a job selling classified advertising for your local yellow pages directory. This source offers an excellent entry-level base, and these jobs are easier to get than selling jobs on a magazine are.
6. Take any space-sales job at a consumer *or* business magazine, even if it's at the low end of the totem pole. A successful record on one magazine will lead to either a promotion there or opportunities with increased salary and responsibilities at another magazine.
7. Get a job as an associate media planner at an advertising agency, an entry-level job where you'll be involved in developing the media plan. This work entails evaluating the various media. If you're good, you'll no doubt be promoted in short order to media planner. Then you'll be taken out to lunch every day by advertising-space salespeople. You can learn about their jobs and even get leads about job opportunities.

Leonard Mogel, *Making It in the Media Professions.* Copyright © 1988.

The indefatigable space salesperson next drives out to New Jersey to see the advertising manager of the camera company. This gentleman is polite and attentive as he informs her that although he would recommend scheduling her book, final evaluation of media belongs to the agency. "After all," he submits, "why do we have an agency if not for this function?" Now back to the agency for more of the same runaround. This story is repeated hundreds of times every day in the lives of space salespeople.

What is the best approach to selling space? There are no general rules. In my opinion the salesperson should make every effort to first see the highest level at the account and then be prepared to drop down a few echelons when requested to do so. It is still the client's money. No matter how strong the agency recommendation, it is the client who makes the final decision. Of course, if the client is insistent, all bases at the agency should be touched. That may mean a presentation to eight or ten different individuals, but this is how sales are made.

## What Will You Make as a Space Salesperson?

*Folio:*'s 1991 advertising sales compensation survey is summarized by Suzanne Zelkowitz in the September 1991 issue. Some general conclusions:

- Rate cutting on the part of many magazines suffering from the down economic climate makes ad selling a very difficult occupation.
- Bonus/commission increases to heavy hitters were better in 1991 than in the previous years.
- Women regional/branch category managers earn more than men in both salary and total compensation, whereas in every other ad sales category they earn significantly less.
- You'll make more money in the Northeast than in other parts of the country.

### Average Salaries for:

#### Ad Sales Director

| All respondents | $89,583 |
|---|---|
| Business magazines | 92,630 |
| Consumer magazines | 86,327 |
| Top third | 140,468 |
| Middle third | 80,827 |
| Bottom third | 48,769 |

**by Region**

| | Average | Business | Consumer |
|---|---|---|---|
| Northeast | $112,020 | $113,200 | $111,036 |
| South | 71,710 | 72,458 | 71,018 |
| North Central | 83,465 | 93,632 | 57,030 |
| West | 72,882 | 72,750 | 69,417 |

**by Number of Respondent's Employees**

| | Average | Business | Consumer |
|---|---|---|---|
| None/1 | $57,340 | $72,344 | $32,333 |
| 2 to 5 | 69,993 | 73,846 | 67,211 |
| More than 5 | 105,314 | 105,923 | 104,402 |

**by Sex**

| | Average | Business | Consumer |
|---|---|---|---|
| Male | $101,175 | $106,019 | $96,144 |
| Female | 74,598 | 71,366 | 75,250 |

### Average Salaries for:

#### Ad Sales Manager

| All respondents | $76,945 |
|---|---|
| Business magazines | 69,617 |
| Consumer magazines | 87,803 |
| Top third | 121,554 |
| Middle third | 68,702 |
| Bottom third | 40,579 |

**by Ad Revenue**

| | Average | Business | Consumer |
|---|---|---|---|
| Up to $999,999 | $46,221 | $43,254 | $52,650 |
| $1 million to $3 million | 72,322 | 75,507 | 62,767 |
| $20 million and over | 114,769 | 99,500 | 117,545 |

**by Sex**

| | Average | Business | Consumer |
|---|---|---|---|
| Male | $84,616 | $76,775 | $96,770 |
| Female | 65,089 | 57,939 | 74,008 |

| Average Salaries for: | |
|---|---|
| Branch/Regional Category Manager | |
| All respondents | $70,910 |
| Business magazines | 66,855 |
| Consumer magazines | 77,609 |
| Top third | 100,060 |
| Middle third | 67,965 |
| Bottom third | 45,952 |

| Average Salaries for: | | | |
|---|---|---|---|
| Ad Salesperson | | | |
| All respondents | $49,380 | | |
| Business magazines | 53,334 | | |
| Consumer magazines | 44,910 | | |
| Top third | 78,588 | | |
| Middle third | 43,002 | | |
| Bottom third | 27,436 | | |
| **by Sex** | | | |
| | Average | Business | Consumer |
| Male | $60,147 | $62,856 | $55,311 |
| Female | 42,263 | 44,518 | 40,360 |

# SALES JOB DESCRIPTIONS

**Ad Sales Director.** The director (in some cases this person may have the title of publisher) is the top ad sales executive. He or she manages the ad sales department, sets policies and procedures, is responsible for reaching goals and quotas, and hires and trains personnel.

**Ad Sales Manager.** This manager is generally the second level of management in the ad sales department; he or she reports to the ad sales director (or publisher) and has management but not policy responsibility for personnel within the department.

**Branch/Regional/Category Manager.** This individual is responsible for selling ad pages to accounts from specific categories (liquor, tobacco, cosmetics, and so on) or to accounts in specific regions. He or she may supervise some staff.

**Ad Salesperson.** The salesperson (who may be called the account executive) calls on clients and agencies, makes presentations, maintains current accounts, and develops new accounts.

Following are random comments from advertising sales respondents in recent *Folio:* surveys:

"The autonomous working environment is appealing. I'm free to create and produce results." (Ad sales director in the West, earning approximately $120,000 in salary and bonuses/commissions.)

"I'm always learning new things and passing that knowledge on and watching the sales staff develop into real pros." (Ad sales director in the West, working on a business weekly and earning a salary and bonuses/commissions of more than $150,000.)

"The editorial product is wonderful to sell. You always believe in what you're doing." (Ad sales manager in the South, working on a consumer monthly and earning approximately $75,000 in salary and bonuses/commissions.)

"The thrill of having a prospective client see my way and run a full program in my book, not in the competitor's, is tremendous." (Branch manager in the Northeast, with almost ten years' experience and earning a salary and bonuses/commissions in the high nineties.)

"We're a hot book with tremendous momentum as reflected by an avalanche of new contracts for next year." (Ad sales director with thirty-two years' experience, working on a business weekly and earning roughly $150,000 in salary and bonuses/commissions.)

"The never-ending challenge of managing ten very different individuals, all focusing on a common goal, makes the days just fly by." (Branch manager in the West, working on a consumer weekly and earning a salary and bonuses/commissions in the mid eighties.)

## Interview

We interviewed Bruce Brandfon, ad manager of *Fortune* in the District of Columbia and the neighboring territory, about his thoughts on the ad sales function.

Bruce graduated from the University of Virginia with honors in English. Later he attended the Fordham University Graduate School of Business. He is married, has two sons, and lives in Bethesda, Maryland.

*What was your career path to attaining your present position at* Fortune?

My first job selling ad space was as mail order advertising manager for the *New Ingenue,* which ended mercifully with my termination just prior to the demise of the publication. I took a self-imposed hiatus from ad sales for several years to work as a musician, a more gratifying experience at least from an artistic, if not financial, standpoint.

In 1976, I was hired to sell space for *Combustion* magazine, a trade publication for power plant engineers. My next position was at *Dun's Review,* a monthly business magazine. My customers included banks, financial clients, and corporate advertisers. In August 1978 I was hired by *Fortune* as a salesman in the New York office handling a variety of accounts, including the North and South Carolina territory. Next step was as *Fortune's* alcoholic beverage advertising manager. I was then promoted to *Fortune* associate New York manager in 1984, division manager in '85, and New York advertising director in 1987. In 1992, I became Washington, D.C., advertising manager.

*Do many people move into magazine ad sales from ad agencies? Is this a good route to take?*

People do move from the agency business into ad sales, usually from the media planning side. As a rule, direct selling experience at a publication is a prerequisite at most major magazines. Agency experience is an alternative route. As the agency business has been forced to downsize, more and more sales applicants come from agencies.

*Have opportunities for women in magazine ad sales achieved parity with those for men?*

Yes. Clearly, there are a great many women in the business selling successfully, and an increasing number of women have risen into the ranks of management. The publisher of *Sports Illustrated for Kids* as well as the ad director of *Money* (to name two within my own company alone) are women.

*If you had to do it all over again, what would you have majored in at college to prepare you for your career?*

My feeling is that a broad liberal arts curriculum is an excellent background for ad sales. My own major was English Literature, and I believe that it has served me well. Courses in Marketing, even an MBA in Marketing, definitely are a plus, particularly if you are looking for the fast track route to management.

*What are the benefits of working for a giant multi-publication company such as Time Inc. Magazines? Are talented people often moved from one magazine to another?*

There are numerous benefits associated with working for a huge company like Time Warner. There is a great depth to the resources at your disposal, such as research, sales support, and marketing. Increasingly, many of our big customers are looking for multimedia campaigns that take advantage of our stable of magazines as well as our cable TV, video, books, movies, and direct marketing capabilities. Benefits also include excellent health, profit sharing, stock savings, and education plans.

Movement from one magazine to another is somewhat limited, with the exception of senior level managers such as ad directors and publishers. Ad sales management at individual titles prefer keeping the best people where they are, producing results for the good of the publication.

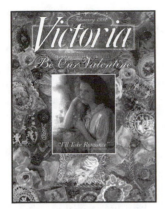

# How a Magazine is Produced

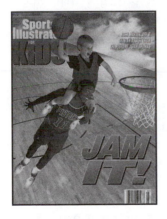
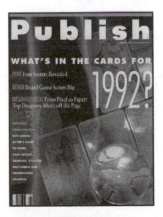
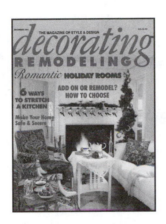

The purpose of this chapter is not to train readers as production people but rather to orient them in the various phases of the production process of a magazine. Practical, hands-on experience is really the only way to fully comprehend the steps necessary to produce a magazine. Within the limitations of one chapter, however, we will present some basics. Let us begin with the three printing systems in use today—letterpress, gravure, and offset. An understanding of each is necessary for anyone in the magazine industry. Let us start with the oldest.

## Letterpress

Although printing from movable type dates back to eleventh-century China, we owe to Johannes Gutenberg the development of printing as a process of graphic reproduction. His invention in 1440 of movable type using separate pieces of metal made it possible to print different pages of a book by using the same pieces of type over and over again. Today's letterpress printing uses type directly on paper or from cast metal plates on to the paper. (Consult *Pocket Pal,* a guide to the printing process, published by the International Paper Company.)

In letterpress, printing is by the raised, or *relief,* method. For short runs sheet-fed presses that print on sheets of paper are used; for longer runs web-fed rotary presses print from rolls. The continuous roll, or web, is printed on both sides at the same time at high speeds. The printed web is either sheeted or folded at the delivery end of the press into signatures (or sections) of eight or sixteen or thirty-two pages. These signatures may be printed in one, two, or four colors, depending on the capacity of the press. By the use of special inks and dryers, high speeds are attainable. A simple way of determining if a book or magazine has been printed by the letterpress method is to look for a slight denting on the reverse side of the paper. Few major magazines are printed in letterpress because of the economies in preparation for the other processes.

## Gravure

Gravure uses a sunken, or *depressed,* surface for the image. The paper moves between an impression cylinder, which rotates in a counterclockwise direction, and the plate cylinder, which rotates in a clockwise direction. The image areas consist of small pits or wells etched into a copper cylinder or wraparound plate, which rotate in a bath of ink. The excess is wiped from the surface by a flexible steel blade. The ink remaining in the thousands of recessed cells form the image, which is transferred to the paper under pressure. Gravure printing offers a greater variety of shadings from light to dark than is possible with either letterpress or offset. When gravure printing is done on a rotary press, the process is called *rotogravure.* Most Sunday newspaper magazine sections are printed in rotogravure on groundwood paper, which is slightly finer than newsprint.

## Offset Lithography

We know now that letterpress prints from a raised surface and gravure from a depressed surface. Offset is a method of printing from a *flat* surface. The process is based on the principle that water and grease do not mix. The part of the printing surface that carries the design (words and pictures) is treated chemically to attract greasy ink. The surrounding surface is dampened with water so that it will reject the ink.

A rotary press with three large cylinders, one above the other, is used for offset printing. The printing plate is fastened to the top cylinder, which rolls against a water roller and an ink roller. It then transfers, or *offsets,* the inked image to the middle cylinder, which is covered with rubber. The design is printed as the paper passes between the rubber-covered cylinder and the third cylinder.

There are offset presses for short, medium, and long runs. Both sheets and rolls are used, depending on the capability of the presses. On high-speed web offset presses, where rolls of paper are used, speeds of up to 1,800 feet per minute are possible. The major advantage of the offset process is the simplicity of preparation. The camera shoots the copy, either line (as in type matter) or halftone (as in black-and-white photographs), and transfers it by an inexpensive photochemical process to a plate that is used for the printing. No expensive molded or cast plates are required.

There are other printing processes, such as silk screen, photogelatin, and xerography, but these are not used in the printing of magazines.

## Typesetting

For more than 400 years after Gutenberg's invention of movable type, all type was set by hand—a tedious, slow process. Each letter or character was a separate piece, made at first of wood and later of metal. In 1886 typesetting was revolutionized by Ottmar Mergenthaler's invention of the Linotype™. Now, for the first time, a full "line of type," in one piece of metal, or *slug,* could be set by machine, at reasonably high speeds.

In the traditional Linotype system the operator types out the copy on a keyboard that looks much like that of a large typewriter. The machine arranges *matrices* (individual type molds) into a line of words. When a complete line of matrices has been set, the machine pours molten-type metal into the molds. The metal hardens quickly, and the finished slug drops out of the machine. The brass matrices return on a distribution bar to a *magazine* (a metal case). Only one type style, or face, is housed in this magazine, requiring the operator to remove the case and insert another to typeset a different typeface.

There are hundreds of different typefaces, divided into two basic styles, *roman* (straight up and down) and *italic* (slanted).

Most faces come in both roman and italic. Type is further classified by its breakdown into *serif* (letters that have fine lines finishing off the main strokes) and *sans serif* (letters with no such fine lines). Type is further delineated between *bold, medium,* or *light* face.

Typefaces are usually available in sizes from 6 to 72 *points* (72 points to the inch, top to bottom). We also measure type in *picas.* The pica (6 picas to the inch) expresses the width of a line of type. Space between lines can be varied. For example,

the art director may specify 6 point on 7, 12 picas wide. This merely means that there is 1 point of space between the lines of 6-point type and that the line of type is to be 2 inches wide (6 picas to the inch).

Typefaces are designed to serve the imagination and creativity of the art director or designer. Many faces that were designed more than 200 years ago are still in use.

*Display type* is used for headlines, ads, titles, and the like. The designer can choose from a wide variety of typefaces. Modern faces each express a unique purpose.

## The Art of Type Selection

Following are some thoughts on type selection by an authority in this field, Alex White. White maintains a full-time free-lance design practice and is a professor of graphic design at the University of Hartford; he is the author of two books on the subject of type selection: *How to Spec Type* and *Type in Use.*

Here are some of White's selections for headlines and his comments on their use. Note how effective these choices are in conveying the mood of the pieces and drawing the reader into the body of the article:

The best way to improve the look of your publication is to redefine the structure of its columns. That gets at the root of the "sameness" problem. But if you aren't ready to make a structural overhaul, the next best way to upgrade the appearance of your magazine is to develop more compelling, more involving primary display typography.

Headlines create the *apparent* personality of printed material (the underlying structure, or grid, actually does most of the work). As primary typography, headlines are intended to stop the reader and persuade him or her to get into the secondary (subheads, liftouts, and captions) and tertiary (text) levels of typography.

Headline treatments fall into three broad categories: alignment, contrasting type styles, and the integration of type and

# members
## of the
### Wedding

*Courtesy of Folio:*

*Above*: The "W" was chosen to echo the scalloped ruffles of the wedding gown shown on the facing page of this opening spread. The initial is well placed and integrated with the entire headline, not only with the last line. Strong designs such as this can and should be used on subsequent pages of an article. Initials can be found in clip books or bought as transfer type.
*Pacific Northwest*; Shauna Narciso, Art Director

*Below*: This headline/subhead combination uses vastly different members of the same type family. All-caps contrast with U/lc. The 1/2-point rules and fl/rr setting give these typographic elements a simple, clean environment.
*Medical Economics*; John Newcomb, Design Director

## Type in Use
*Headlines*

*Below*: Contrasting typefaces are used here to great effect—in *addition* to width alignment. Notice that the overscore's width matches the photo's below.
*BP America*; NorthShore Group, Design Director

# CHEMICALS
## LINKS IN AN INDISPENSABLE CHAIN

■ One of the country's most important industries is thriving making products you use every day but don't see...

Says BPCA President Doug Campbell, "The marriage satisfied each ... organization's ...

# Pickin' and Singin'

*The misty blue ridges of the Appalachian mountains fostered the traditional music that evolved into bluegrass.*

changed slowly and entertainment consisted mostly of families and neighbors getting together to play music. That music has evolved into an American tradition—bluegrass.

Today, the sometimes happy, sometimes sad and lonely, always lively sounds of bluegrass can be heard throughout the land. In Colorado, it's groups like the Bluegrass Patriots that help keep bluegrass alive.

"There are about six bluegrass groups in Colorado," says Glenn Zankey, lead vocalist and guitarist for the Fort Collins-based Bluegrass Patriots. With names like "Turtle Creek", "Grain of Salt", "Front Range" and "Hot Rize", they play at festivals, weddings, fund raisers and other social events. With the

*Bluegrass Has Become an American Music Tradition*

*by Bill Ciesla*

The Appalachian mountains. For years they were a barrier to westward expansion. The rugged folk who settled in those hills lived in isolation. Traditions

## CAN THE AMA SELL ITS OWN BRAND OF MALPRACTICE REFORM?

Organized medicine contends its radical plan is fair, workable, and constitutional. But even some defense attorneys have reservations.

By Carol Stevens WASHINGTON EDITOR

If the American Medical Association hoped to cause a stir with its self-proclaimed "radical" solution to the malpractice crisis, it certainly succeeded. When the proposal—endorsed by 32 medical specialty societies—was unveiled ... this ... orts in the

pected legal challenges. And if it gets past those hurdles, the plan will still have to prove capable of delivering stable malpractice awards and administrative savings sufficient to persuade insurance carriers to moderate their premiums.

'MA prop al suc-

to help other states that want to try all or part of the plan. "We're not going to go out and beat on statehouse doors," Todd says. "Some states have solved their malpractice problems through tort reform and have no need for a program like this. But we'll be happy to help any

*Above*: A clear order of importance is visible here: headline, subhead, caption, then text. This blend of typefaces and type sizes is appealing and leads the reader into the story. The very tight letterspacing on the headline is intentional.
*Colorado Country Life*; W.B. Cole, Art Director

# Type in Use

*Headlines*

# ENOUGH HIGH TECH!

*Above:* The third category of headline treatment is unifying the type and imagery into a single element, which more than doubles the impact of the elements, had they stood alone. Note that the lower corner of the "E" appears behind the glasses, an effect enhanced by having run the type in lavender.
*LA Times Magazine*; Donald Burgess, Design Director

# EASING THE IMPACT OF ROADSIDE CRASHES

*Above:* Type can be used as imagery. This effect can be done on a stat camera, on special equipment some typesetters have, with software programs on a Macintosh, and even with an ordinary photocopy machine. Use gimmicks like this with discretion and only when the effect is directly related to the point being made.
*Mechanical Engineering*; R. Scheblein, Art Director

# THE ELEPHANT MAN
*(Not to mention the Circus Maker, the Vexillologist, the Windsor-Watcher, and the Party Man)*
*By* SUZANNE WILSON

*Above:* The asymmetrically-set headline is complemented nicely by the little leafy thing, which is run in red—and there is no other reason than that it is nice. The subhead is centered in contrasting italic type.
*New England Monthly*; H. Teensma, Design Director

# SIBLING RIVALRIES

*Above:* Another example of type as imagery: The type treatment reflects the meaning of the words. The headline is easier to read in the original, which is printed in deep blue up front and aqua on the drop shadow.
*Southern Magazine*; Jeff Stanton, Art Director

# SANTA FE ENCHANTMENT
Magical scenery, architecture, art and cuisine conspire to cast spells on vacationers who seek "someplace different."
By Rochelle Reed

*Right:* Overlapping (surprinting) type over an image is standard performance, but it takes a deft touch to make it work. The danger is that the type won't be readable and that the image won't be recognizable. This beautiful example carefully positions the photo and uses muted shades of brown and blue to separate the type from the image.
*TravelLife*; Rouse Lyday, Art Director

imagery. But whatever the treatment, the best headlines are provocatively written and have a point to make. Remember that a good headline must be more than just attractive—it must say something.

## Automated Type Composition

Mergenthaler's Linotype has served the printing industry well for about 100 years, but it is losing ground to modern computer technology. *Phototypesetting,* known as *cold type* because no hot metal is involved in the process, offers greater speed and efficiency. For example, a machine that has been equipped for semiautomatic operation from perforated tape will set 18,000 to 20,000 characters an hour. The average phototypesetter today does about 1,500 characters a minute, or 90,000 characters an hour, without sacrificing quality.

Phototypesetting is a sophisticated, complex process. The earliest units were extensions of mechanical typesetters, substituting a matrix containing a negative of the characters. The type was photographed instead of being cast in metal. Computer typesetting is much cheaper than Linotype, since the operator need only be semiskilled and has few decisions to make in justifying or line spacing. (Justification refers to the fitting of a line of type exactly into a desired length.) The entire process is much faster, since no tedious molding or composition phase is involved.

## Paper

Obviously, paper is an essential factor in magazine production. The cost of paper for the average hundred-page publication using lightweight, coated paper (that containing a smooth, glossy finish) is about 30 cents a copy, or approximately 50 percent of the total production cost.

Body weights of magazine paper range from 32-pound basis to 50-pound basis. (The phrase "32-pound basis" refers to a standard; that is, a ream [500 sheets] of 25-by-38-inch paper weighs 32 pounds.) For high-run magazines, 50,000 copies and up, which print on web-fed presses, rolls of paper are used instead of sheets. This paper generally costs about two cents a pound less than sheets. For four-color printing on high-speed web presses, a waste factor of from 15 to 18 percent is built into the total cost of the paper stock. Cover weights for magazines are usually 70- and 80-pound basis in order to stand up to extra handling, especially in the binding phase.

Large-circulation weeklies, concerned with high postage costs, use paper of 32- to 36-pound basis for their body printing. Newsprint, the cheapest grade of paper, is often interspersed with coated paper. The cost of newsprint, which is mainly groundwood pulp with some chemical pulp, is substantially less than that of coated paper.

Many factors are significant in paper selection. The publisher must be concerned with the gloss, opacity, brightness, bulk, and press runability. Examine a number of your favorite magazines—you'll soon become aware of the degree of difference in the paper.

## Color

Focus your attention on a full-color ad in a magazine. You will see dozens of color variations and tones, yet in most cases the ad was reproduced in what we call *four-color process.* To understand this system let us first go back to the early history of black-and-white reproduction.

Until the middle of the nineteenth century, photography was not used in the production of line etchings (those with no continuous tones). Engraved blocks or plates, necessary for letterpress printing, were produced manually. Photographs have many tones, or gradations, which are actually tiny dots, as we can see when examining photos through a magnifying glass. An Englishman, William Talbot, in 1852 produced the first halftone photoengraving by laying a screen of fine gauze between the coated metal and negative of the original picture. Through this development printers realized the importance of breaking up the continuous tones of photographs or drawings, reproducing in effect the quarter, half, and three-quarter tones of the subject.

The early attempts to produce pictures in color consisted of painting in by hand different tints on black-and-white prints. Today we are able to reproduce faithfully all the colors in a phototransparency or piece of artwork by using only four basic colors (the four-color process): yellow, magenta, cyan, and black. Here's the way it's done.

Cameras with filters and screens screen out each of the four colors in succession. When the image passes through the screen, the negative is divided into a great number of small dots. The color of each filter is complementary to the color to be separated—that is, blue violet for yellow, green for magenta, orange red for cyan, and light yellow for black. Photographic prints are made from the four-color negatives. If the printing is to be done in letterpress, copper plates are etched from these prints; if offset, the lithographic plates are made from either negative or positive film.

To prove the results of this photomechanical process, the engraver will print test sheets in the rotation of yellow, magenta, cyan, and black. We call this stage "pulling progressive proofs." If the art director or designer requests corrections on these proofs, or "progressives," the engraver will "dot-etch" or alter the dot pattern to conform faithfully to the photo or art subject. This work is costly, but the use of sophisticated laser scanners sharply reduces the margin for error. The printer will use these progressive proofs as a guide to the proper color values. Often, the printer can attain the required result by reducing or increasing the

inking. The screens in a photo or piece of artwork are varied according to the paper stock to be used. A coarse screen, 60- to 85-line (referring to the number of cross-lines per inch), is used for newsprint and other cheap grades of paper. For coated paper a finer screen is called for: 133- to 150-line.

In figure 6–1 you see on the left a black-and-white photograph in a 65-line screen; on the right, the same photo in 133-line. Note the difference in the dot pattern.

Most magazine color presses have the capability of printing color on only sixteen out of each thirty-two-page form. Careful planning and positioning of color are therefore necessary for economy. Color gives the maximum impact and appeal to a magazine. Using it, however, entails not only the printer's added charge for color printing but also the cost of color photography or art, as well as the cost of color separations, still expensive despite modern developments in this process.

## Binding and Mailing

*Binding* refers to the finishing process after a magazine is printed. In the case of small-circulation magazines and journals with relatively few total pages, the printed paper is delivered flat and unfolded on sheet-fed presses. The sheets must then be folded into eight- or sixteen-page sections,

Figure 6–1

stitched, and trimmed. Where the paper is heavy, it is sometimes necessary to crease or score it before folding because of the bulkiness of the stock.

Web- or roll-fed presses speed up this procedure by slitting the sheets and then folding them into eight-, sixteen-, or thirty-two-page signatures at the delivery end of the press. These are then moved to a bindery line, which, in an assembly-line process, collates (gathers) the signatures, including the cover, the body, and any insert cards; stitches and trims them; and, finally, automatically bands and counts them into twenty-fives and fifties and even places the mailing sticker on the cover.

There are three kinds of binding styles. One kind is *saddle stitching,* which simply means the forcing of two or three staples through the backbone of the magazine. Modern equipment allows for saddle stitching on magazines of up to 300 pages.

An older form of binding is *side stitching,* sometimes called side wire. The folded and collated sections are first stitched together; then the cover is glued on. The backbone, often a quarter-inch or more thick, is square.

Some magazines are bound by the *perfect binding* process. It resembles side stitching but does not have stitches. The sections are held together by a flexible adhesive. The cover is glued on to the body, and the backbone is square, giving a neat, attractive appearance to the magazine.

When magazines are prepared for subscription mailing, the fulfillment house (the vendor that maintains the mailing lists) supplies the printer with the rolls or strips of names, which are broken down into an alphabetical and zip-coded arrangement. The printer then applies the tape, ties a group of magazines into bundles, and totes them off to the post office for delivery across the country.

Magazines to be sold on newsstands are tied in bundles of fifty and seventy-five copies, depending on weight, and are then labeled and shipped by rail, plane, and truck to hundreds of wholesalers who ultimately distribute them to dealers. But more about wholesalers in chapter 9.

The entire printing, binding, and mailing for a magazine with a circulation of 500,000 requires only seven or eight days. Consider, however, the logistics in producing the 17,000,000 copies of *TV Guide,* a weekly. A number of regional printers throughout the country produce this magazine, an operation based on perfect planning and timing.

## Target Marketing through Ink-jet Imaging and Selective Binding

By now we have all received those direct-mail pieces (such as the ones used by Publishers Clearing House), which personalize the mailer's message directly to us, printing our name in as many as a dozen places. As we saw in chapter 5, today's magazine publishers have jumped on the technology bandwagon and are applying data-based strategies to make their advertising and editorial efforts more effective by being better targeted.

The production terminology for these developments is *ink-jet imaging* and *selective binding.* The large magazine printer R. R. Donnelley and Sons and about nine other publication printers have pioneered these production innovations.

The key to the successful implementation of these techniques is the magazine's data base of its readers. The more a magazine knows about a subscriber, the easier it is to personalize its advertiser's sales story.

Farm Journal publishes *Beef Today, Dairy Today, Hogs Today, Top Producers,* and its largest trade magazine, *Farm Journal.* For at least ten years, with the help of its printer, R. R. Donnelley, this publisher has been personalizing its editorial content to the specific interests and focus of its readers—and in the process producing hundreds of different editions.

*American Baby* has used the technology since 1986, sending different editions to prenatal and postnatal parent subscribers. All the magazine needs to know is the subscriber's due date.

Time Inc. Magazines, our largest consumer magazine publisher, is experimenting with new versions of its magazines that would carry additional pages of editorial coverage targeted to specific readers who would pay extra for the special editions.

Buick personalized its advertising for its Roadmaster in a half-dozen major magazines by placing the ads in copies of the magazine that reach zip codes that were demographically most likely to contain people interested in large station wagons.

The end uses of this technology are infinite. It gives new meaning to the terms *niche* and *target marketing*. Of course, it requires printers willing to invest in the technology and advertisers putting it to innovative uses.

## What Will You Make in Production?

*Folio:* conducted a survey in 1992 of salaries for the two key production department functions. As with editorial and circulation jobs, production jobs pay less than advertising sales jobs do. Job security, however, tends to be more stable in production than in other areas of magazine publishing.

Here are some of the conclusions of the survey:

### Average Salaries for:

#### Production Director

| | Average | Business | Consumer |
|---|---|---|---|
| All respondents | $48,816 | | |
| Business magazines | 46,597 | | |
| Consumer magazines | 51,274 | | |
| **by Region** | | | |
| Northeast | $53,713 | $50,818 | $57,655 |
| South | 46,362 | 38,694 | 55,324 |
| North Central | 46,411 | 45,619 | 47,817 |
| West | 44,718 | 44,958 | 44,586 |
| **by Sex** | | | |
| Male | $57,106 | $53,378 | $60,176 |
| Female | 43,676 | 43,206 | 43,708 |

### Average Salaries for:

#### Production Manager

| | Average | Business | Consumer |
|---|---|---|---|
| All respondents | $31,328 | | |
| Business magazines | 30,708 | | |
| Consumer magazines | 32,329 | | |
| **by Sex** | | | |
| Male | $34,698 | $35,471 | $33,619 |
| Female | 29,964 | 28,992 | 31,714 |

Note: In certain cases the discrepancy in pay scale may reflect the production manager's supervision of a number of magazines for one company or the increased frequency of these publications.

# PRODUCTION JOB DESCRIPTIONS

**Production Director.** The director (who may be called vice-president of production) negotiates printing, typesetting, and engraving contracts and establishes production schedules. He or she oversees individual production managers, advises on technical matters, and is directly responsible for quality control.

**Production Manager.** The manager is directly responsible for daily production operations, including publication pasteup, quality control, and maintenance of production schedules. This person is the liaison with the printing plant. He or she may traffic advertising and editorial materials.

Following are random comments from production respondents in recent *Folio:* surveys:

"Achieving the successful marriage of technology and the creative process is always a challenge." (Production director in the Northeast with fifteen years' experience, earning a salary and bonus of almost $60,000.)

"Finding ways and means to improve profit by reducing manufacturing and distribution expenses is my biggest challenge." (Production director in the Midwest, earning a salary and bonus in the low sixties.)

"It's a never-ending struggle to keep manufacturing costs down while still maintaining the integrity of the product. Also, since production is not a profit-generating department, it is difficult to get approval for adequate staffing." (Production director working on a magazine with a circulation of 200,000, earning a salary and bonus in the high fifties.)

"Balancing cost, service, and quality on each job. Trying to get all three at once, that is what I am after." (Production director in the South with fifteen years' experience, earning a salary and bonus of about $70,000.)

## Interview

Irving Herschbein, vice president of manufacturing and distribution at Condé Nast Publications, brings to his position an extensive background in virtually every aspect of magazine publishing. His primary responsibility is the manufacture and distribution of all Condé Nast–owned magazine publications—*Vogue*, *HG*, *Glamour*, *Bride's*, *Mademoiselle*, *Allure*, *Self*, *Gentlemen's Quarterly*, *Vanity Fair*, *Gourmet*, *Condé Nast Traveler*, the *New Yorker*, and the Street and Smith Sport Group. He also oversees contract negotiations; the purchase of paper, printing, composition, and engravings; and the management of related manufacturing and distribution services.

A native of New York City, Herschbein attended Brooklyn College and New York University and began his career in the graphic arts at Cuneo Eastern Press.

Actively involved in a number of publishing and printing industry organizations, Herschbein is a past chairman of the Magazine Publishers of America's Production Committee. Additionally, he has held memberships on every major committee of the Association of Publication Production Managers, where he served two terms as secretary and is a past president.

*Do magazine production jobs pay the same salaries as other jobs on the business side of magazines?*

I would say that production/manufacturing jobs on magazines pay less than other positions on the business or administrative side because people in production, in the past, have had less education than people in other departments. Today, however, we are looking for a minimum of two years in a community college graphic arts course or, even better, a graduate of Rochester Institute of Technology or Carnegie-Mellon.

*To what extent do your own magazines use computer typesetting?*

All of our magazines use computer typesetting. We operate an in-house typesetting department, working three shifts a day, and, if necessary, we do work on weekends using an Atex 8000 system. Some time ago we began a three-year program of installing in all editorial departments PCs that will interface with the Atex system. We are getting into page makeup both in the editorial and art depart-

ments as well as in the typesetting department.

Our in-house system is connected to outside typesetters who currently do page makeup and generate final film. We recently pioneered the use of satellite transmission in monthly magazines. *Vanity Fair* now has the ability to produce one thirty-two-page form exactly as the news weeklies do.

*Briefly sketch a typical day in the life of a magazine production chief.*

The problem seems to be that there really is not a typical day; instead, we seem to go from one crazy thing to another.

I get in at 7:30 A.M., either at the office or at a business breakfast. The breakfast gives me an opportunity to talk to suppliers when we are fresh and alert.

The hour and a half that I'm able to get in before the phones ring and staff comes on board gives me a chance to review what happened the day before. On Mondays we have staff meetings with the director of manufacturing and distribution and the four directors who head operation, ad production, paper purchasing, and distribution. Tuesdays I meet with my boss to review manufacturing/distribution operations. Other department heads may join us, or certain key people may be brought into the meeting. One or two mornings each week are devoted to print-order meetings. These include senior management and the editor and publisher of the magazine. The editor gives a preview of the upcoming issue, and we are able to set print orders.

Once each week I meet with the personnel director to discuss problems and review salary increases or staffing changes.

Business lunches are usually with out-of-town suppliers, and, while such lunches give us an opportunity to have a quiet conversation, they also add to the growing paunch.

Afternoons are generally devoted to short meetings with editors, art directors, publishers, or ad directors to answer their questions or solve internal problems. We also see some people who would like to be added to our vendors' list. The balance of the afternoon is usually devoted to reading interoffice and regular mail and planning the next day's activities.

*Is there any specific training you would recommend for a magazine production career?*

I would suggest a degree from the Rochester Institute of Technology, Carnegie-Mellon, or Cal Poly at San Luis Obispo as a starting point. Any of these schools would give you the basics on the graphic-arts industry and enable you to move quickly. The ideal person for a top job is one who has completed undergraduate work at any of these schools and has gone on for an MBA. The two disciplines are a perfect match for what is required in production.

I met one person who did what I described above. I might add that he was the object of a bidding war by a number of major publishers, including me, because his talents were unique. I know he is going to move very quickly and very high in the industry.

*How did you progress to your present job?*

My progress was quite different. I started with a printer, having taken some courses while still in high school and having worked after hours for a weekly newspaper. The printer did magazines, and I was able to go to work as an assistant in the production department of a small magazine. In the meantime I was going to college at night with the idea of becoming the greatest writer since Shakespeare!

I quickly realized that writing was not one of my talents, but production was. I then shifted to a program that gave me at least some of the technical knowledge I needed, and, as time went on, I was able to progress to better jobs in production and in bigger publishing companies. But I continued the educational programs in parallel with my work.

I would guess that a good amount of luck, plus a fairly good education and an ability to perform in the production area, led me to my present job.

# The Desktop Revolution

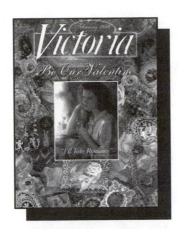

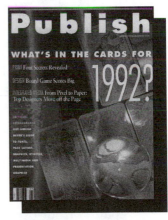

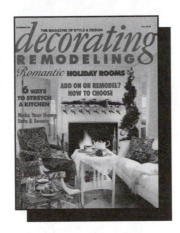

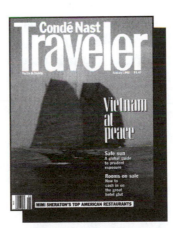

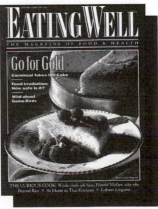

The phrase "desktop publishing" (DTP) was coined by Paul Brainerd, the president of Aldus Corporation, in 1984. A year later desktop publishing software was introduced, nearly 600 years after the invention of the printing press.

By definition desktop publishing is a publishing process that combines microcomputers and laser printers with page-layout software. It replaces the traditional methods of typesetting, pasteup, and sometimes even printing. Its benefits are increased productivity and efficiency, economies of time and money, and quality.

# THE DESKTOP PUBLISHING SYSTEM

The tools of DTP are people, a computer, and software. DTP can be as limited as computerized typesetting of text using a word processor, the text then being proofread and sent to an optical character recognition (OCR) scanning service for high-speed, high-resolution reproduction in the form of quality proofs or film. DTP can also involve sophisticated equipment for in-house typesetting, page makeup, color separating, and prepress work: in short, delivery to a printer in a form ready for the press.

Desktop publishing as we use it here refers generically to a whole range of personal computer products that automate typesetting and layout using a computer and various desktop publishing programs.

Our description of the DTP process breaks it out into three stages: input, production, and output. For our explanation of these phases, we are indebted to the people at Apple Computer for use of the material in their excellent book *The Apple Guide to Publishing, Presentations and Interactive Media*. While we make references to Macintosh computers in this discussion, there are obviously other systems available. We are further indebted to the Aldus Corporation for valuable information on its PageMaker and FreeHand software, as well as on the whole field of desktop publishing.

## Input

**Writing and Editing.** The word processor has replaced the typewriter as a tool for the writer and editor. Basically, it stores text electronically and displays it on a monitor. No paper is required until the document is complete and ready to print. Using Macintosh word processing, once text is set it may readily combine "cut and paste" segments of text, numbers, and graphics within a file.

The writer or editor also has the flexibility of using a range of typefaces, styles, sizes, and colors to punctuate the important parts of his or her work, including the body text and the headlines as well.

Some publishers claim that they have reduced their costs by as much as two-thirds since going to a desktop typesetting system.

**Text Scanning.** The process of entering text into a computer involves using a scanner and special OCR or page-recognition software. This information is "read" into a computer by use of a high-resolution scanning device and OCR software. Once the page has been scanned, the software converts the on-screen characters into text files. OCR scanning of text is a major factor in the evolution of DTP.

**Image Scanning.** A magazine page requires other elements besides text and headlines. Graphics, illustrations, and photography in black and white and color create the distinctive images that set one magazine apart from another. It is at this point that an art director takes center stage.

Scanning, such as that provided by Macintosh, enables the art director to capture the images of a line drawing or photograph and place it into the file. Where this work was traditionally done by costly, time-consuming outside services, with a scanner it can now be incorporated into a page layout in minutes.

Scanners are available to convert art, photos, and color transparencies to a computerized format in black and white, up to 256 shades of gray, or color. The Apple One Scanner handles black and white and gray, while others process colors.

**Combining Text and Graphics.** Text and graphics are brought together in desktop publishing software like Aldus PageMaker. At this point the art, editorial, and production staffs can write headlines and photo captions, draw lines and shapes, add shading, and perform any other design, layout, or formatting task to achieve the desired look. With WYSIWYG (What You See Is What You Get) capabilities, the magazine staff can see on the screen exactly how each page will look when it's printed.

Changes can be made at any time: to edit text, to change type styles, to experiment freely with placement of text and graphics, and to check the work by printing draft copies on a desktop printer.

Once this document or page is done, it can be printed to a laser printer and then photocopied or used as camera-ready art for the commercial printer.

**Clip Art.** This is an art director's essential resource. Typically, he or she will subscribe to various services that provide stock line art and photos that are used in page layouts. These are now available on disk. Using standard Macintosh "copy" and "paste" functions, they may be put into a document or imported by way of the special commands of Aldus PageMaker or another program.

## Production

**Painting and Drawing.** Capturing the input factors of text, illustrations, and photography is the starting point in the DTP process. Now we deal with the elements of production.

With technology like Macintosh's we are able to create, edit, or revise images electronically. In a paint program the mouse activates a "brush" that moves across the screen, spreading dots or screen pits in its path. Some paint programs offer the ability to create and modify images in black and white; others offer color capabilities.

You can now draw detailed, precision drawings on a Macintosh. You can even specify colors that are easily outputted on a color printer.

**Image Processing.** Retouching has always been an expensive process, used to obtain different values on a photo or piece of artwork—such as improving flesh tones or omitting a background.

Today the entire process can be done electronically.

The photos below show how, using sophisticated image processing software (such as Letraset ImageStudio or Digital Darkroom, by Silicon Beach), you can manipulate an image to attain a

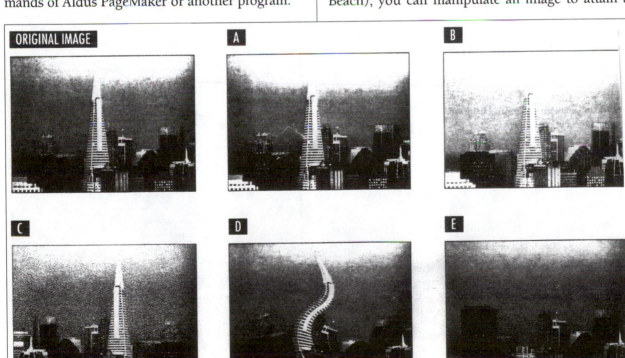

Designer of "Art of Communications" seal: Jack Herr of Clement Mok designs
Photographer of Transamerica building photo: John Ragle
Photographic manipulation by Mark Crumpacker of Clement Mok designs
Reprinted by permission of Apple Computer, Inc., © 1991.

desired effect. Contrast (A) or brightness (B) can be adjusted; dithering can be applied (C); and images can be distorted (D) or modified and retouched (E). With this equipment the art director can even airbrush on-screen flaws in a photograph.

**Typography.** Long before Mergenthaler's invention of the Linotype, designers crafted typefaces to punctuate an image or style. Many that were created 200 years ago are still with us, albeit in advanced forms. Art directors still use Bodoni, Century, Goudy, Caslon, and Garamond. We call these "faces," "typefaces," or "fonts." When the Linotype operator wanted to set 8-point Garamond Light, he took the magazine (a case, not a publication) that housed the matrices of this font and inserted it into the Linotype. As the operator punched the keys, a line of type would be cast set in 8-point Garamond Light.

Tedious, isn't it? Today the art director, using Macintosh and a LaserWriter, can experiment on his or her desktop with dozens of typefaces in a variety of sizes. Type can be bent, expanded, toned, even placed on curves. Since type libraries from the old-time type founders are being adapted to an electronic form, some of the old favorites, such as Bodoni, Caledonia, Century, and Baskerville are still available.

**Page Layout.** At *Entertainment Weekly* they call it "Jamming with Mac," says design director Michael Grossman. "Two designers work on different approaches to the same layout, or, if one comes to a creative standstill, we bounce the page back and forth between designers, who play off each other's ideas." Grossman further states, "We put out about seventy pages a week. We wouldn't be able to produce a magazine that looks like this if we were doing conventional design."

Various programs enable the art director, often working in conjunction with the editor, to shuffle type size, move copy, alter color qualities, and crop art—all at the touch of a button.

For a publication with many editorial pages and elaborate layouts, page-layout software systems are a bonanza. Such a system is particularly effective in the design of a new magazine or the redesign of an older one.

## Output

In desktop publishing it is still necesssary to see a proof. This is where laser printers and imagesetters come into play. They simply provide proof of our work.

**Printing Output and Color Prepress.** If we are preparing material for a magazine that will be printed in the offset process, we need high-resolution copy. This is accomplished by using imagesetting equipment for the final output. These machines are expensive, not always owned by a magazine publisher. Rather, this work is done by outside service bureaus. These people also do color prepress work.

This page from *Entertainment Weekly* is indicative of the kind of work Michael Grossman is able to turn out with his DTP system. It has it all, including four four-color images, two of which are positioned at an angle, requiring type kerning.

This process also involves the "separation" of a color photo or illustration into four-color film negatives. These are the four basic colors used in printing: cyan (blue), magenta, yellow, and black. With a computer like a Macintosh, a color scanner, and software, this work may be done in-house or farmed out to service bureaus. Color correcting is also done electronically before the pages go to press.

## How TV Guide Saves Millions with DTP

An article by Liz Horton in *Folio:* tells how *TV Guide,* with its circulation of more than 15 million, saved millions of dollars and cut its production time using DTP.

*TV Guide* produces more than 20,000 pages a week for its 113 regional editions, each of which has its own listings section. In 1991 the magazine purchased Optronics's PostScript laser imagesetter. With it they eliminated their previous system of typeset repro galleys that had been pasted up into mechanicals and then shot to film and stripped into printing plate–ready flats.

Today all of *TV Guide's* listing information is logged into a data base that extracts the information for the individual edition. A data base containing the magazine's advertising is fed into the system in its proper position. The imagesetter merges advertising and editorial into thirty-two-page flats for each edition; these are then sent as plate-ready film to *TV Guide's* printing locations.

The new system has reduced *TV Guide's* seven to ten days of prepress time to three to four days and will save millions of dollars.

## Who's Using DTP?

Most publishers today are using some elements of DTP. Many have converted to a total program. A number of new magazines have gone this route right from the launch. Here is a partial list of magazines that have taken the plunge:

| | |
|---|---|
| *Allure* | *Time* |
| *Esquire* | *Martha Stewart Living* |
| *Entertainment Weekly* | *Vanity Fair* |

| | |
|---|---|
| *TV Guide* | *The New Yorker* |
| *Sports Illustrated* | *MacWEEK* |
| | *PC Magazine* |

Plus eight computer and technology magazines published by Ziff-Davis.

## Recent Developments in DTP

*Adobe Illustrator* - A new version of Adobe Systems, Adobe Illustrator reached the market in late 1990. Its users are able to enter text directly and manipulate it, instead of working through dialogue boxes. Different typefaces or styles coexist within a single text block. Users are also able to adjust spacing between lines and to curve type around an initial cap (kerning). With this system graphs can be created, manipulated, and customized.

## Desktop Publishing Training

Many publishers have been making big-dollar investments in DTP technology but have fallen short in the area of training personnel. Off-site training has improved. *Entertainment Weekly* sends new designers to two different two-day training sessions, one for QuarkXpress and the other for Adobe Illustrator.

On-site training may be more expensive: $400 a day and up. What seems to work best for a large operation is a personal trainer/consultant in-house for six months or even a year.

Most design schools are emphasizing DTP training. Their graduates have a head start in entering the field, needing only on-the-job training on job-specific functions.

## Final Thoughts on DTP

There have been major changes in recent years from the traditional typesetting and printing processes into the world of desktop publishing and computer-aided art direction and design. These developments have resulted in saved time, reduced costs, and broadened creativity. As with any revolutionary change, however, the technology is not without problems.

A recent *Folio:* survey asked magazine publishing professionals for both their best and their worst thoughts on switching to desktop publishing.

Cited as the "best" is the opportunity DTP provides to implement cost-effective mini-redesigns, create ads in-house, reduce prepress costs, realize labor savings, and increase flexibility.

Named as the "worst" were technical frustrations—such as printer problems, font and software conflicts, network problems, inadequate memory, blown boards, dead monitors, and power-surge losses—as well as people problems.

How can publishers maximize the best and minimize the worst? *Folio:* advises building into DTP planning enough (a) money, (b) time, and (c) people resources to cope with whatever is going to go wrong that can go wrong.

DTP is a fast-developing technology. New hardware and software packages reach the market weekly. Clearly, costly mistakes can be made. For magazine publishers we recommend the "Tech Trends" section of *Folio:* magazine. It is crammed with important information and articles by its own staff and leading consultants. One of my favorites is Alex Brown's piece, "Desktop Publishing: Changing the Way You Work," in the May 1989 issue.

Many courses on DTP are offered by college extension divisions. We recommend the Stanford Communications Workshops, consisting of comprehensive programs in Desktop Publishing/MAC, Desktop Publishing/IBM PC, and Advanced MAC. Their address: Stanford Communications Workshops, Stanford Alumni Association, Bowman Alumni House, Stanford, CA 94305.

## Two Important Publications for the DTP Industry

*Publish!* The rapid growth of technology in electronic publishing and the increasing number of users created a significant need for a publication to service this audience. *Publish!* is the leading monthly magazine for professionals who use computer technology for publishing, presentations, and integrated media applications.

Each month *Publish!* provides in-depth coverage on how to select appropriate technologies, which products to buy, and how to use them most effectively. The magazine reports on a broad range of products and topics dedicated to communicating information through the use of computer technology.

These are publications of a division of IDG that publishes thirteen computer magazines. IMI also produces *SunWorld* magazine. *Publish!* has a paid circulation of almost 100,000.

One recent issue contained such provocative articles as "Type Troubleshooting on the Mac" and "How to Cure Font Phobia"; "Designer in Motion" described how a noted designer adapted to the new technology; and "Software Directory" presented a buyer's guide of 2,000 software products from 1,000 vendors.

The editorial mix in this issue contained ten departments, including a nuts-and-bolts piece on *Games* magazine and how it turned out an elaborate color spread for $388 using electronic color separation—which would have cost $2,780 using traditional separation techniques.

Right up front in the contents page was a column called "Toolbox." Here *Publish!* told its readers the extensive software and hardware computer publishing tools it used to produce that particular issue.

The test of a fine magazine, particularly in the business field, is that the advertising be as interesting as the editorial content. This is clearly the case with *Publish!* It is also beautifully designed and reproduced. Knowing less than a novice in this field, I found the magazine to be a liberal education in this rapidly emerging technology.

A one-year subscription to twelve issues of *Publish!* is $29.95. Write to: Publish!, Subscription Department, P.O. Box 51967, Boulder, CO 80321–1967.

*Technology Solutions* is a periodic supplement to *Publish*. A recent issue contained seventy case studies from computer technology users in banks, ad agencies, insurance companies, government agencies, and publishing companies. One study, for example, detailed the experience of the Western Sales Division of the Coca-Cola Company—a group faced with the Augean task of producing on its computers thirty to fifty publications and documents a week, ranging from fifty to a hundred pages each, plus an occasional 35 mm. slide presentation. A one-year subscription to *Technology Solutions* is supplied to subscribers of *Publish!*

**NeXTWORLD.** NeXT is the newest venture of former Apple whiz Steve Jobs. Its technology is supposed to be so advanced that it delivers today what Apple and IBM are projecting to deliver three to five years hence. *NeXTWORLD* is the quarterly publication for users of this computer technology. The basic subscription price buys four quarterly issues and eight monthly newsletters.

The address for *NeXTWORLD* is Subscription Department, P.O. Box 51967, Boulder, CO 80321–1967.

# 8

# Establishing a Subscription Base

Magazine circulation has two components: subscriptions and single-copy sales (newsstand sales). In this chapter we will explore the subscription phase; chapter 9 looks at single-copy sales.

At least once a year, almost every household in America has its mailbox stuffed with a fat envelope boldly proclaiming its hope-filled message— "CONGRATULATIONS! . . . Your recent entry put you in the only group from which our next millionaire will come. YOU CAN WIN TEN MILLION DOLLARS January 31!"

For those unfortunates who don't win the big one, there are insignificant prizes down to $10,000. These fantastic prizes are part of the subscription mailings conducted by Publishers Clearing House (PCH), the nation's largest direct-mail subscription agency. What is also amazing and true is that it's not even necessary to subscribe to any of the 132 magazines PCH offers in order to win.

Further examination of the envelope's contents reveals twelve pieces in addition to the stamp sheets and a reply envelope showing the offers of the individual magazines. On two of these inserts I saw my name, Leonard Mogel, imprinted no less than a dozen times. Clearly, this is ego appeal. One feels obligated to subscribe to a magazine simply because the company has gone to such expense.

Only three of the inserts get to the real point of the mailing—the unbeatable magazine offers whereby you can "save up to $2.00, $3.00, $4.00, and even more!" These bargains are detailed on a sheet of stamps listing the magazines participating in this program, magazines that can be subscribed to through Publishers Clearing House merely by tearing out the stamp and pasting it on an entry-order card. You will, at your option, either receive one bill for the cost of the subscription or pay one-third per month for three months—and don't forget, you're still eligible to win whether you buy a subscription or not.

Dismiss any skeptical thoughts about the practices of PCH. Its operations are totally ethical and to the consumer's and magazine publisher's advantage. PCH and a few smaller companies generate about 30 percent of all magazine subscriptions. PCH's annual sales exceed $100 million; many publishers are dependent on the organization for a substantial segment of their circulation.

The economics of this fascinating subscription business bear further study. PCH sends about twenty-five mailings a year and spends as much as 50 cents per piece for its larger mailings. Each January it mails to 75 percent of the ninety million U.S. households.

On subscribing to PCH's program, a publisher agrees to offer a magazine at its lowest rate. Why, for instance, would a publisher offer a publication at a lower rate through Publishers Clearing House than that offered in the magazine itself? The publisher receives only between 10 and 25 percent of the fee collected by PCH, yet the vagaries of publishing life make such efforts a necessity. For the whole story we must first return to the ideas discussed in the chapter on advertising sales.

Advertising salespeople need numbers. In normal circumstances the larger the circulation, the higher the rates a magazine can charge its advertisers. Since most magazines do not lend themselves to newsstand sales, it thus becomes the function of the circulation director to generate the subscriptions that will increase the circulation to the level required by the ad salespeople and keep it there. No matter that the low percentage yield received from PCH does not even pay for the postage on the subscriptions. Without those subscriptions the magazine might be forced to lower its ad rates—a thought that is anathema to any red-blooded publisher.

Consider too that business (trade) magazines (which are not sold through PCH) have no newsstand sales potential and that subscription efforts are therefore mandatory, unless the magazine chooses the free (controlled) circulation route. This decision is a difficult one for the business publication. In some professions or industries, it makes more sense to reach everyone by offering free circulation and thus affording advertisers blanket coverage than it does to reach the portion of that audience who are willing to pay the subscription price. Many business magazines, however, opt for paid circulation, on the theory that they need the additional revenue and that their advertisers will place a higher value on reaching readers who really want the magazine enough to pay for it.

Before we delve into today's arcane world of magazine subscriptions, let's review a bit of the history of circulation from *Folio:*'s wonderful March 1991 issue, 250 Years of Magazine Publishing."

### 1780s
Mathew Carey's upscale *American Museum* boasts a circulation list with prominent names, but he complains that they are deadbeats, and he is in fear of bankruptcy.

### 1799
*Port Folio,* the first national magazine, appears. Payup is abysmal. Publishers resort to desperate means to collect. Some print the names of debtors in their pages. The publisher of *Worcester Magazine* takes payment in wood, cheese, pork, and even butter.

### 1865
Premiums to subscribers are introduced. Items offered include books, tools, clothes—even pianos and church bells.

### 1865–85
Postwar industrialization increases the number of periodicals from 700 to 3,300.

### 1883
The *Ladies' Home Journal* uses reader clubs to climb to 40,000 in its first year.

### 1889
Ad rates are linked with circulation figures.

### 1920s
Professional sales agents sell subscriptions door to door, and circulation again takes a leap forward.

### 1962
*Reader's Digest* experiments with sweepstakes to attract subscribers. The strategy is tremendously successful, and others follow suit.

## Subscriptions versus Single-Copy Sales

The following chart indicates the circulation breakdown of some of our leading consumer magazines:

In the period of the ABC audit, number one hundred on the subscription list was *Hot Rod* magazine, with 655,574 subscriptions. Number one hundred on the combined list was *Food and Wine,* with a total circulation of 809,826. Number one in subscriptions was *Modern Maturity* with 22,450,003 circulation.

Generally speaking, single-copy sales are more profitable than subscriptions, yet many magazines do not have the single-copy (newsstand) potential. A magazine like *National Geographic* derives almost its total circulation from subscriptions. *Family Circle* is one of the few large-circulation magazines with an even blend of subscriptions and single-copy sales. *Time* and *Sports Illustrated* are weeklies with a predominant tilt toward subscriptions. Yet their sister publication *People Weekly* has almost a fifty-fifty split between the two sources of circulation. *Cosmopolitan* has always enjoyed a large newsstand circulation. It therefore chooses to maintain its subscriptions, a less profitable source, at only 600,000. *Vanity Fair* is chic and expensive. Most of its circulation comes from subs.

| Publication | Subscriptions | Single-Copy Sales | Total Paid Circulation |
|---|---|---|---|
| *National Geographic* | 9,679,566 | 83,840 | 9,763,406 |
| *Family Circle* | 2,256,418 | 2,808,713 | 5,065,131 |
| *Time* | 3,869,834 | 203,696 | 4,073,530 |
| *People Weekly* | 1,613,528 | 1,767,304 | 3,380,832 |
| *Sports Illustrated* | 3,175,568 | 121,925 | 3,297,493 |
| *Cosmopolitan* | 637,932 | 2,103,870 | 2,741,802 |
| *Vanity Fair* | 622,180 | 368,998 | 991,178 |

Source: Audit Bureau of Circulations, second six months 1991.

## How Publishers Achieve Subscriptions

There are more than a dozen different approaches to achieving subscription levels. Each has its limitations. Here is a brief description of some of these sources:

**Cash Field.** A cash-field agency uses high-pressure techniques, such as house-to-house calls and telemarketing, to sell subscriptions. The yield to the publisher (the amount left after the agency takes its commission) is small, from 5 to 15 percent. The renewability factor (referring to subscribers who renew their subscriptions after the term is up) is generally low because of the negative reaction to the high-pressure sales techniques.

**Catalog Sales.** Two or three catalog sales companies handle subscription sales to the 30,000 libraries of schools, government agencies, and large corporations. These libraries find it more convenient to order through the catalog sales companies than directly from the publisher. Renewals are usually made from the catalog too. The remit to the publisher is 10 to 15 percent, but the quality of these subs is high, on account of the large pass-along factor.

**Cooperative Mailings.** These generally take the form of piggyback mailings to general audiences. That is, a number of products and services combine their offers in one mailing envelope, with each paying a proportionate share of the printing, mailing, and handling costs. The packager, the company that makes all the arrangements, usually receives 15 percent of the total cost for its services. This system can be an effective source of subscriptions.

**Direct-Mail Agencies.** An example of this type of organization is Publishers Clearing House. These agencies and the publisher's own direct-mail efforts are the most important sources of magazine subscriptions. PCH mails many million pieces a year. Its main thrust in the sale of subscriptions is the sweepstakes-and-stamp approach. Here are the advantages and disadvantages of this source:

Advantages:
1. Publishers receive their net money for the entire subscription in advance.
2. There is no collection cost to the publishers.
3. Agencies' sophisticated computer operations allow publishers to control the number of mail-order subs sold. Publishers can also pinpoint the exact time they wish to receive these subs.
4. This source is beneficial to publishers whose own mail-prospecting costs (achieving subs) are high.
5. Since the basic sub offer is generally for one year, the cancellation factor is small as compared with that of the cash-field agencies, which usually sell three- to five-year subs and have a high cancellation rate after the first year.

Disadvantages:
1. The publisher often has difficulty renewing subs derived from this source, since the customer wants another chance at a sweepstakes prize and therefore will renew the sub through the agency because its prices are lower than the publishers.
2. The magazine doing business with one or two of these agencies may depend too greatly on this low-yield source.
3. The agencies offer a low remittance rate to the publisher (usually 10 percent of the yearly subscription fee), and, to make matters worse, publishers are required to charge a lower subscription rate in the agency mailing than they do in their own mailing.
4. The demographics of readers gained through these efforts are customarily lower than those of readers gained through the magazine's own direct-mail efforts.

**Paid-during-Service Subscriptions.** In this source high-pressure field agencies sell subs to customers who pay for the service monthly. The commission is high (about 85 percent), and cancellations after a few months are common. The publisher gets the money beginning with the third month of service of the sub and monthly after that. The renewability element is limited on account of subscribers' reactions to high-pressure tactics.

**School Plan.** This relates to subs sold by school-children for the benefit of the school or student groups. The operation is run by two or three organizations that remit to the publisher about 10 percent of each subscription sold by the student.

**Specialty Sources.** These are ordinarily subs sold by field agents who concentrate on doctors' offices, military posts, and so on. The publication is paid up-front for the life of the subscription. The magazine realizes only about 5 percent after the field agents take their cut but is often willing to so for the source's pass-along value. The subs are frequently sold for two or more years.

**Ads in One's Own Magazine.** This is the most favorable source of all. A magazine with a heavy newsstand sale can pull thousands of subscriptions a month from a page and inserts in its own publication. The quality of these subs is exceptional, since the purchase indicates appreciation of the magazine's editorial concept by a newsstand buyer.

A major development in the technique of promoting subscriptions is "blow-in cards"—those pesky things one finds in all magazines these days, the ones that fall on the floor as soon as you open the magazine. Well, it may be their nuisance value or some deeper psychological reason, but they do outpull by about three to one the conventional bind-in card that is stitched into magazines. Blow-in cards are particularly effective for new magazines.

## Publishers' Direct Mail

We now come to what is for most magazines the primary source of subscriptions—direct mail. Producing an effective percentage on these mailings is both an art and a science. The basic process entails the mailing of subscription offers to various lists of prospects.

The cost of these mailings is substantial. It has been estimated that the cost of acquiring a new subscription runs from $10 to $20. Careful testing procedures must be adopted in terms of copy approach, price, and the choice of mailing lists used. These lists are rented from list brokers but may also come from a magazine's own previous subscribers or as a renewal effort to the magazine's present subscribers.

We will discuss direct mail in some detail. Before we go into the nuts-and-bolts of this source, however, let's focus on some of the outstanding work done in this field in terms of creativity, technical execution, and strategy.

Here are the winners of *Folio:*'s Ninth Annual Circulation Direct Marketing Awards competition. By examining this work we will gain an understanding of the whole area of subscription direct mail. The critique shown is from a board of five prominent judges selected by *Folio:*

Reproduced with permission from *Money*, 1991

## GOLD AWARD
Renewals for magazines whose circulations exceed 250,000

*Money* "Christmas Donor Series"
Creative Team:  David L. Hecht, copywriter
                John Plunkett, art director

Suppliers:      Westvaco Envelopes
                E. L. BAS Form & Systems
                Time Customer Service
                International Paper

**Brilliantly executed. Wonderful change of copy from effort to effort. Some of the best copy lines I've seen in a long time ("May all your money worries end by November 8" and "What's really hot in August besides your free gift"). Very intriguing. Great little icons on the various order forms—Christmas trees, stripes, a beach chair. There's a sense of fun in all this. It has every whistle and bell you'd want without going overboard. The copy is wonderfully executed. It speaks to the issues, to savings. Wonderfully creative and involving.**

## GOLD AWARD

New subscription promotion, four-color or special components, 100,000 to 999,000 subscribers

Reproduced with permission from *Sports Illustrated for Kids*, 1991

*Sports Illustrated for Kids* "It's Gnarly"

Creative Team:
Kate Salovaara Brower, circulation director
Mary O'Keeffe, copywriter
Steve Hadowsky, art director

Supplier:    Metromail

The color is wonderful. The design is for children but very attractive to the parental eye also. While the package will obviously be read by the parents, parts of it appeal to both. They brought everything into play—cute little kids, clever words like "gnarly," "be a rad mom and dad," "totally tubular," "do-dos and do-dits." Really good copy in the letter, leading off with "We don't always understand our kids." It also supports the editorial inside. The package conveys fun and energy.

## GOLD AWARD

Renewal series for paid-circulation magazine

Reproduced with permission from *MacWorld*, 1991

*MacWorld* "Warranty Conversion Series"

Creative Team:
Lindsay Davidson, director of circulation
Susanna Camp, subscription promotion
                    coordinator
Elizabeth Jensen, subscription analyst
Stuart Jordan, Jordan-Savage Direct

Suppliers:    Phlum Graphics, Inc.
                    Carlson Letter Shop Services

It's colorful. Every effort in the series is different, both in type of package, color, and approach. It's urgent. It would definitely stand out in your mailbox. It's a large package renewal, which is seldom done, but it works. It's lively.

## GOLD AWARD

New subscription promotion, four-color or special components package

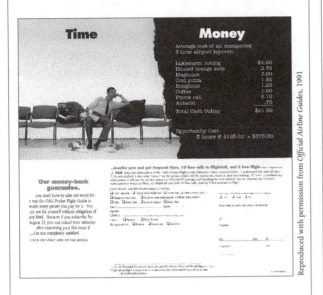

*Official Airline Guides* "Save Time and Money"

Creative Team:
Janet Libert, market sales manager

Suppliers:  Kukla Press
Executive Mailers
Database Marketing Corporation
Warren Paper

This is a self-mailer. Generally speaking they don't work too well, but this one is wonderful. It has a picture of a man on one side waiting at an airport with brilliant copy on the right, "Average cost of an unexpected three-hour layover: lukewarm hotdog $3.50, diluted orange soda $2.70"— and so on. It all adds up. Then they have a lost opportunities cost of $125 an hour. Everyone who's ever traveled on business identifies with this. It opens up and gives reasons why travelers subscribe to the OAG pocket flight guide. You want to know the most efficient connections. It works. You don't have to oversell this.

Note the credits next to each piece on these pages. These people are generally free-lancers hired by the magazine on an assignment basis. The creative team writes and designs the mailing piece, the printer prints it, and the lettershop handles the actual mailing. The list broker works with the magazine's circulation people in finding and procuring the best lists for the mailing. In the case of the renewal pieces, the magazine's in-house staff coordinates the mailing from its own list.

## Subscription Solicitation for a New Magazine

The direct-mail piece for a new magazine is vital to its success. For a magazine like *Victoria*, it had to convey the beauty and charm that are the essence of this publication. The mailing piece is particularly important before the launch because it has the advantage of the curiosity factor. At this stage potential subscribers are sold with the sizzle, since they have not yet seen the steak.

Everything about this mailing is beautiful, right from the outer envelope printed on soft, tan stock with a lone rose as a spot of color. The large, full-color folder shown in figure 8–1 does the heavy selling. In it more than a dozen full-color photos depict *Victoria*'s editorial concept, "Wondrous things to see, do, enjoy." There are six separate pieces in this mailing, including the outer

Figure 8–1

Figure 8–2

The specialists who conceived, wrote, and designed this mailing are highly paid, not usually staffers of a magazine. Although not a large field, direct-mail marketing does offer opportunities for those possessing this creative bent.

envelope. Each performs its function brilliantly.

Figure 8–2 shows the front page of the invitation letter. In it the magazine discusses its editorial features. Finally, it makes a special introductory offer—"only $5.99 for six dazzling issues."

# IMPORTANCE OF DIRECT MAIL

Direct mail is an excellent means of testing a concept for a new magazine. If we do not achieve a satisfactory response after mailing 50,000 or 100,000 pieces to fifteen or twenty different prospect lists, we had better jettison the idea and start something else. As we have seen, most subscription sources are costly and ineffectual, and so publishers must of necessity rely primarily on securing subscriptions from their own magazines and from direct mail. Some established facts on making the best use of direct mail follow:

1. The most effective time to use direct mail is in the prepublication period, when the curiosity factor is at its peak. The pull at this time may double the response generated by mail after the launching of the magazine.

2. Test mailings of less than 50,000 to fewer than ten lists are not an accurate barometer of the potential audience for a new publication. Newsletters, we are told by the *Newsletter on Newsletters,* may be tested with much smaller numbers.

3. Creative list brokers can prepare or obtain lists of every possible category or qualification. These lists generally rent for $60 to $75 per thousand names.

4. The mailing piece should be of at least the same quality as the magazine itself. It may even include sample articles, graphics—anything that will entice the prospect on legitimate grounds.

5. Be certain each list has a projectability factor of at least four or five times. It makes no sense to pull as well as 6 percent from a list of 5,000 if the expanding universe of that list is only 7,000.

6. Use specialists. Writing and designing effective direct-mail pieces is a sharply honed skill. There is no place for amateurs in this high-risk game. Dozens of fine consultants and specialists in the direct-mail field are available.

7. Test various copy and price approaches to determine the maximum response. Six issues for $10 may be more efficient than twelve issues for $15, even though the latter is more economical.

8. Experiment with innovations such as ink-jet imaging to produce letters—the kind that say, "Mr. Jones, we know that Mr. Smith on your street, Willow Road, in your hometown of Plainsville is already a subscriber to _____ magazine, and we thought you too . . .." Such letters are expensive but often bring commensurately higher results.

9. When a direct-mail test is successful, it's time for the rollout—that is, a much larger mailing to extensions of lists that worked well. For example, if a 5,000 test mailing for *Victoria* to *Cosmopolitan* subscribers pulled a 4 percent response, *Victoria* may decide to use 100,000 new *Cosmopolitan* names in the rollout. One caveat: Never change the copy or layout of a successful test mailing in the rollout. Doing so could have a negative effect.

## Copywriting for Direct Mail

We are barraged with direct mail. Each day brings a half-dozen or more pieces scrambling for seconds of our attention. The direct-mail team preparing a magazine's subscription campaign knows that to avoid the wastebasket, it must reach the prospect with provocative copy right at the outset, on the outer envelope.

In an article in *Folio:,* direct-response consultant Elaine Tyson stresses the "benefits" aspect of a mailing. How will the prospect benefit from subscribing to this magazine? On the outer envelope of the magazine *Today's Cook,* the upper-left corner states, "Free Recipe Inside," over a color photo of a basket of luscious-looking shrimp. Above the mailing window of the envelope, the attention-grabbing line in bold, black type is "UN-

WRAP LONGEVITY." Then at the bottom is a smaller line stating, "Introducing a Healthier Cuisine for 1989."

At this point there is no mention of a magazine, but the recipient's subliminal thought processes may be progressing to the possibility of eating golden shrimp and living longer. Why not open the envelope to find out about more delicious foods that will prolong life? Once inside, in a glorious color display of foods, the magazine offers its "benefits" package. Through the use of premiums and solid copy, it has a good shot at making you a believing subscriber.

Examine the next magazine direct-mail pieces you receive. The winning pieces will be those describing benefits on the outer envelope and following through on the inside. We begin to see the importance of copy in direct mail.

## The Arithmetic of Direct Mail

Today's elaborate magazine direct-mail piece may cost from $400 to $500 per thousand, or more than 40 cents each. Successful mailings for existing magazines seldom pull more than a 2 percent response.

Let's say that a magazine mails 10,000 pieces for a $14.95 trial subscription offer. At 2 percent it pulls 200 orders, for a total of $2,990. Its costs for the mailing, not including the creative costs, is $4,500. So far, not including the cost of servicing the 200 subscriptions, the magazine is in the hole $1,510. This deficit must be made up on renewals of these new subs. But remember, it often takes five or six costly renewal mailings to retain a subscriber.

This example provides only a glimpse of the many problems facing magazine direct-mail specialists. This inexact science takes careful testing, planning, and creativity. It is often daunting.

## Choosing a Winning List

The choice of lists is the essence of a magazine direct-mail campaign. A prizewinning mailing piece is only as good as the strategy used to select its lists. Choosing among lists is a challenging task.

Most magazines rent their lists of active sub-scribers to other magazines. At $75 to $90 per thousand names, such rental is a viable revenue source for the renter. When a magazine undertakes a direct-mail campaign, its in-house specialist or outside direct-mail agency will assemble a list of possible mailing lists.

Lists are always tested, since there may be a sharp variance in response rate. In addition to using related magazines in these tests, magazines will use other sources. For example, *Family Circle* uses lists of women's clothing catalogs; *Consumer Reports* uses lists of recent Black & Decker product buyers. Dr. Norman Vincent Peale's *Guideposts* magazine has successfully used a list of subscribers to *Lottery Buster,* a monthly newsletter offering tips on winning state lotteries. The key principles in list rentals are creativity in selection and careful testing.

## What Magazines Do to Increase Their Circulation Profitability

Having 400,000 subscribers, *Byte* reckons that it will be unprofitable to increase this phase of its circulation. Consequently, by mid-1991 *Byte* had begun looking to newsstands as a source of circulation.

*Architectural Record* sends out nine renewal notices to errant subscribers. It asks for the full rate in the first three or four renewal notices and then drops the price in subsequent notices. The method works for this magazine.

Since subscription revenues are generally less than newsstand income sources, many publishers reduce their cost in servicing subscription copies by printing these on lighter-weight paper. With escalating postal rates, paper weight becomes a significant factor.

*Newsweek* lowered its introductory subscription price and discontinued the use of costly premiums. Today the magazine uses only editorial premiums.

A circulation report in the May 1991 issue of *Folio:* discusses various means publishers take to increase circulation profits. Here are a few examples, along with the percentage of circulators using these strategies:

Selling active lists to direct mailers 81.7%

Streamlining through improved technology 76.8%

Reducing/eliminating unprofitable circulation sources 76.8%

Increasing subscription price 74.4%

Exchanging lists with competitors 50.0%

Reducing/eliminating gracing (servicing expired subs for two or three issues) and complimentary or promotional copies 41.5%

Reducing/eliminating subscriber discounts 28.0%

Cutting staff 24.4%

Three-quarters of publishers reported using new technology to trim fat from their departments.

## Important Facts about ABC

ABC, as mentioned in an earlier chapter, stands for the Audit Bureau of Circulations, an organization that audits the paid circulation of magazines. The results are available to advertising agencies and advertisers as an inviolable guide to a publication's numbers. The results are also available to magazines that subscribe to ABC's audit reports. In other words, nothing is secret about the numbers; any magazine can refer to them for competitive purposes. The audits are conducted annually. In the reports are noted various factors such as whether stimulants were used to sell subscriptions, the number of subs sold at lower-than-basic prices, the channels of subs sold, and the total newsstand and subscription figures by geographic regions.

## Job Opportunities in the Subscription Field

Circulation generally and subscriptions specifically offer a vast outlet for talented young people. Many MBAs entering the magazine business choose circulation as a route to the top. Although a number of undergraduate and graduate courses are offered in this specialty, courses in writing, statistics, and design are helpful.

A wide variety of jobs exist in subscription promotion—copywriting, layout, list compilation, research, statistical analysis, and fulfillment, to name just a few. Both consumer and trade maga-

---

### First Steps for the New Publisher

1. Do not go it alone. Seek the services of a skilled subscription professional. The Direct Marketing Association (DMA) can be helpful in locating these consultants.
2. Contact a representative of Publishers Clearing House or of another direct-mail agency for complete particulars on how its program works. The agency will sometimes offer increased remittance percentages to new publishers.
3. Emphasize subscription solicitation in your own magazine, especially if you sell primarily on newsstands. It is unquestionably the best source for developing your subscription base.
4. Explore every subscription medium listed in this chapter.

---

zines are deeply involved in the subscription arena, constantly providing new job opportunities in this field.

## The Direct Marketing Educational Foundation

The Direct Marketing Educational Foundation (DMEF) is an arm of the important industry organization known as the Direct Marketing Association. One of DMEF's primary activities is establishing and implementing direct marketing programs at colleges and universities. In this effort DMEF is supported by direct marketing clubs in various cities.

For information about the diverse functions of DMEF, write to the foundation at 6 East Forty-third Street, New York, NY 10017–4646; (212) 689–4977.

## Finding Circulation Recruits

In an article in *Folio:,* Michael Garry discusses the need for talented people in circulation and the path companies take to find their future stars.

Many publishers recruit at colleges; others advertise in the classified sections of newspapers like the *New York Times.* Time Inc. Magazines gets thousands of unsolicited résumés, yet the company continues to recruit on the campuses of MBA schools. Once hired, recruits may be moved to advertising and production at this multi-magazine company.

Meredith, another large publisher, seeks out MBAs and trains them in editorial, advertising, and production as well as circulation. *Business Week,* on the other hand, hires beginning marketing people who have got their start at consumer products companies like Procter & Gamble and wish to move into publishing.

Although a college degree is a must for circulation recruits, no particular discipline is favored by magazine recruiters. Good writing ability and computer literacy, however, are clearly plus factors.

## Circulation Internship and Summer Programs

The Magazine Publishers of America (MPA) places twenty to thirty college students in member firms each summer and presents a series of lectures at its headquarters. Write to the Director of Education, Magazine Publishers of America, 575 Lexington Avenue, New York, NY 10022, or call (212) 752–0055.

The Direct Marketing Educational Foundation (DMEF) runs a summer internship program. Students work for eight to ten weeks with nine companies in the New York metropolitan area. They also attend a series of lectures on direct marketing. Contact the foundation at 6 East Forty-third Street, New York, NY 10017–4646; (212) 689–4977.

New York University's Center for Direct Marketing runs a diploma program with sixteen credits of course work. The diploma is considered a postbaccalaureate credential. Write to New York University, Career Planning & Placement, 719 Broadway, New York, NY 10003, or call (212) 998–1212.

The only university offering both undergraduate and graduate degrees in direct marketing is the University of Missouri at Kansas City. Write to Career Planning and Placement, 4825 Troost, University of Missouri, Kansas City. MO 64110, or call (816) 276–1000.

The Medill School of Journalism has a master's program in direct marketing. Write to the Medill School of Journalism, Northwestern University, Kresge Hall, Room 326, Evanston, IL 60201, or call (312) 491–5091.

The National Organization for Women (NOW) runs a seventeen-week program to train entry-level people for jobs in direct marketing. Write to the Director, Direct Marketing Program, National Organization for Women, 15 West 18th Street, New York, NY 10011, or call (212) 989–7230.

Fulfillment Management Association, the organization of circulation professionals, accepts in its monthly meeting notice free ads for those seeking jobs. Call Wendy Frank (at Hearst) at (212) 649–4457.

## What Will You Make in Circulation?

*Folio:* conducted a survey of 1991 compensation for two top circulation jobs. Here are some of the conclusions of the survey:

| Average Salaries for: | | |
|---|---|---|
| **Circulation Director** | | |
| All respondents | $46,463 | |
| Business magazines | 40,707 | |
| Consumer magazines | 52,240 | |
| **by Region** | | |
| | Average | Business | Consumer |
| Northeast | $53,906 | $45,128 | $60,733 |
| South | 40,981 | 42,643 | 39,319 |
| North Central | 38,463 | 37,616 | 40,460 |
| West | 46,708 | 32,604 | 54,300 |
| **by Sex** | | |
| Male | $53,151 | $48,179 | $57,377 |
| Female | 42,535 | 36,858 | 48,758 |
| Average bonus | $6,650 | |

| Average Salaries for: | | | |
|---|---|---|---|
| **Circulation Manager** | | | |
| All respondents | $30,465 | | |
| Business magazines | 27,915 | | |
| Consumer magazines | 33,470 | | |
| **by Sex** | | | |
| | Average | Business | Consumer |
| Male | $37,832 | $34,750 | $40,143 |
| Female | 28,067 | 26,206 | 30,584 |
| Average bonus | $3,996 | | |

These salaries may not seem munificent; however, at the largest one-third of companies the average salary for a circulation director is $92,993 and for a circulation manager is $60,583. Moreover, when these managers supervise staffs of five or more people, their salaries are 20 to 30 percent higher than the average.

# SUBSCRIPTION JOB DESCRIPTIONS

**Circulation Director.** The director (or top circulation executive) plans, directs, and coordinates circulation marketing efforts. He or she is directly responsible for budgeting and analyses of single-copy and all subscription programs, list rentals, and data-base planning and maintenance. This individual is the department head in both single-magazine and multititle companies.

**Circulation Manager.** The manager is generally the second level of management in the circulation department. He or she administers circulation programs for subscriptions and single-copy sales. This individual handles all facets of circulation for one or more titles. A title is an industry term used to designate a magazine. The position is usually found in multititle companies.

Following are random comments from circulation respondents in the *Folio:* survey:

"I like what I'm doing. In the past three years we changed parts of our circulation from paid to controlled. This has added interest to the job. I am just getting a PC now and look forward to using it to produce direct-mail materials. My company will probably change fulfillment bureaus again, and I will be very involved in specifications and conversion requirements." (Circulation director in the Northeast, earning a salary in the low forties.)

"With all the doom and gloom in the trades these days, younger people don't see any future in business publishing. Keeping good people is hard." (Circulation director in the Northeast, earning more than $100,000 in salary and bonuses.)

## Interview

John Klingel is a circulation and publishing consultant who has worked with more than 200 magazines. Many circulation professionals credit him with being a major contributor to their careers. He writes often for *Folio:,* and much of that magazine's self-education material for circulation people has been written by him. Klingel is also a frequent speaker at *Folio:* seminars. He is vice-president of marketing at Time Publishing Ventures.

*What is the structure of a circulation department at a midsize consumer magazine?*

The circulation director functions as head of the department. The promotion manager is usually in charge of planning and coordinating direct-mail campaigns, insert cards, space trades, gift promotions, and other promotions. In most cases the circulation director directs most of the planning and overall strategy. The promotion manager obtains bids and selects vendors, orders lists, works with creative sources, checks mechanicals, prepares mailing instructions, and performs the many other tasks involved in coordinating promotion.

The fulfillment manager, sometimes called operations manager, is responsible for the business management of the department. This includes fulfillment, preparation of reports, and print-order management. Fulfillment is a general term for everything that happens to subscriptions after an order is received. This includes opening the mail, entering orders, sending labels to the printers, sending out bills and renewals, and generating management reports. This activity is usually performed by a service organization, with the fulfillment manager overseeing the activities of the fulfillment company.

*Briefly sketch a typical day in the life of a circulation director.*

In one word—hectic. Being a circulation director means never having a clean desk, never getting caught up. It means working on twenty or thirty projects simultaneously. Projects will include marketing, analyses of past results, meeting with creative people, fulfillment coordination, rate-base planning, and personnel management. A circulation director is in charge of a profit center that includes what is often the highest expense of any department in a magazine operation.

A circulation director has heavy financial and profit responsibilities, including both marketing and management. In addition, circulation directors are often involved in advertising planning, research, and overall magazine profit planning and strategy. There are many projects and a lot of variety; it's seldom boring.

*Direct mail is often the largest source of subscriptions for a magazine. Are the creative and planning aspects of direct mail more often done in-house or by outside specialists?*

Marketing is one of the major areas of responsibility for a circulation director. Consequently, a circulation director should be capable of planning and coordinating a direct-mail campaign. Circulation directors are not expected to be copywriters or designers, but they are expected to be able to hire creative people and to supervise the creative process.

Very few magazines use direct-response agencies. In fact, a good circulation director probably knows a lot more about direct-response marketing than the people who work at direct-response agencies.

*Is there any particular training you would recommend to someone thinking of entering the circulation field?*

There is no particular training required or available for someone who wants to enter circulation. I have an accounting and economics background, but many of my associates in circulation were history or liberal arts majors in college. It is important to be able to work with numbers and understand financial concepts.

Circulation marketing and management are heavily numbers-oriented—mostly addition, subtraction, multiplication, and division. So if you hate numbers, stay away from circulation.

*Which area of magazine circulation offers the greatest opportunities to new people?*

Most circulation people start at the bottom and work their way up. The usual entry-level job is circulation assistant, fulfillment manager, or circulation manager on a small magazine. Starting in newsstand sales is often a dead end, but a number of circulation people have started that way.

It is almost impossible to self-train in circulation. Instead, look for a magazine that has a fairly sophisticated circulation operation with people who are willing to teach. Often outside consultants serve as the principal teachers and trainers of circulation people.

*Have women achieved parity in salary and promotion in the circulation field?*

There is very little bias against women in publishing, and circulation represents a great opportunity for women. Of the more than 200 publications I've worked with, more than 50 percent employed women as circulation directors.

# ABC's of Single-Copy Distribution

The newsstand at New York's Pan Am building carries about 2,000 magazines. Most newsstands display only a fraction of this number. Given that more than 4,000 different magazines are distributed in the United States today, how do these publications find display space? Most do not.

The problem may be duplication of subject matter. According to recent reports, there are 150 crossword magazines; 220 sports magazines; 140 on home, garden, and building; more than 100 on crafts, games, hobbies, and models; more than 100 on fishing and hunting; about 80 on cars and vans; and about 50 on music.

Here are the top ten magazines sold on newsstands (in this chapter we use *single copy* and *newsstand* interchangeably) and the average number of copies they sold per issue for the second six months of 1991:

| | | |
|---|---|---|
| 1. | *TV Guide* | 6,458,237 |
| 2. | *National Enquirer* | 3,390,837 |
| 3. | *Woman's Day* | 3,375,125 |
| 4. | *Family Circle* | 2,808,713 |
| 5. | *Star* | 2,792,823 |
| 6. | *Cosmopolitan* | 2,103,870 |
| 7. | *People Weekly* | 1,767,304 |
| 8. | *First for Women* | 1,764,430 |
| 9. | *Good Housekeeping* | 1,401,546 |
| 10. | *Woman's World* | 1,279,280 |

(Source: Audit Bureau of Circulations, second six months, 1991)

It is interesting to note that some of the largest magazines in terms of total circulation have small newsstand sales. *Reader's Digest* sold only 1,019,500 copies on the newsstands out of its total circulation of 16,269,637; *Better Homes and Gardens,* only 526,333 out of its total circulation of 8,002,794.

Newsstand sales have not grown in recent years. They hit their peak in 1980 with an average monthly sale for 369 Audit Bureau of Circulations (ABC) magazines of 93,936,618. That figure had not grown significantly from 1950, when the average sale for 250 ABC magazines was 61,998,611. By 1990 the figure for more than 500 ABC magazines was down from its 1980 high to 79,000,000 copies monthly.

Newsstand sales for ABC members were off 21.1 percent in 1990 from sales in 1982. This represents a decline of 15.8 million in average sales per issue. Excluding the top-twenty magazine sellers, the balance of the industry had an average 44 percent sale (the top twenty were at 65.8 percent).

This percentage sale was off almost 14 percent since 1982. Only sixteen titles exceeded a 60 percent sale of all copies they distributed, and only three titles sold above 70 percent.

In 1991, the fiftieth-ranking magazine in terms of subscriptions was *The Workbasket* with 1,046,030. In single-copy sales, number fifty was Street & Smith's *Pro Baseball*, with only 261,942.

When I wrote the second editon of this book in 1987, the combined single-copy circulation of the top ten on the list was 35,731,904. For the second six months of 1991, that figure had plummeted to 27,142,165, a drop of 24 percent. The leader, *TV Guide,* went from 8,136,590 to 6,458,237; *Women's Day,* from 5,922,993 to 3,375,125, a drop of 43 percent.

Why the drop in newsstand sales? One answer certainly has to be fewer outlets; another, too many magazines for the amount of display space and too many on the same subject. A major reason may be the average price of a newsstand magazine, now almost double the average price of $1.21 in 1978. Even allowing for inflation, that's a huge increase. As a teenager I sold *Liberty* magazine for 5 cents a copy.

## Why Publishers Go the Newsstand Route

As we have seen in chapter 8, the average cost of acquiring a new subscriber runs about $15.00. To renew that subscription once the subscriber's in the fold costs about $2.50. Moreover, publishers reach a saturation level in their subscription efforts and need to use newsstands as an alternative.

The circulation policy of *Byte* magazine is becoming typical. In the words of Glyn Standen, its director of circulation, "When you have 400,000 subscribers, it becomes more difficult and expensive to get new ones. You find you have to do more direct mail for less return. So we have begun to switch over to the newsstand. It is definitely a cheaper way of getting circulation."

Increasing newsstand sales is done "over the long term," Standen says. "You don't have the kind of control over the numbers that direct mail offers. Locating the right chains to place magazines in, getting authorizations, and setting up discounts and promotions mean it can take a year before a significant amount of added sales registers."

# HOW THE SINGLE-COPY DISTRIBUTION SYSTEM WORKS

To comprehend the problems of this form of distribution, let us discuss the chain of events for a monthly magazine that's distributed nationally. We'll deal here with a cover date of May. The on-sale date typically is the Tuesday or Thursday closest to the fifteenth of the month preceding. Using this date will keep the magazine from becoming prematurely dated.

Why a Tuesday or Thursday? In this tradition-bound business some practices go back sixty years, a time when many wholesalers made their magazine deliveries by horse-and-wagon on Tuesday and Thursday. The procedure continues to this day, although titles (the industry's name for magazines) are delivered to newsstands daily.

The printer of the magazine, under instructions from the publisher and supplied with labels and shipping manifests furnished by the publisher's national distributor, will ship the copies all over the United States and Canada to approximately 400 wholesalers. This transportation usually takes a week to ten days. It then takes the wholesaler a week to route and bill the copies to its retail accounts. There are about 150,000 retail dealers in the United States and Canada.

The retailer, or dealer, may be a supermarket, a convenience store, a drugstore, a bookshop, a college bookstore, a smoke shop, an airline terminal, or a corner newsstand on Times Square in New York City. The dealer customarily keeps the

monthly magazine on sale for thirty days and then returns the unsold copies to the wholesaler for credit. An important note: Virtually all newsstand magazines are sold on consignment, giving the dealer the right to return all the copies received if they do not sell.

When the copies come back from the dealer, the wholesaler counts them and records the number of returns, usually by computer. The old practice was to send strips off the cover to the publisher's national distributor for credit, but that practice became unwieldy and has been replaced by a system whereby the wholesaler does not physically return the covers that have been stripped off but instead sends the distributor an affidavit attesting to the total number of returns for each magazine on an issue-by-issue basis.

The national distributor enters these data into a computer and then notifies the publisher of the total weekly returns. Ultimately, a printout is submitted that records the publication's sale for each wholesaler dealt with.

The distribution network as described here is bizarre. At times it seems to the publisher that all forces—national distributor, wholesaler, and dealer—are doing their best to see that sales are not made, but, of course, it is in everyone's interest to make sales. The function of the network will become evident to the reader as we explain the activities of each participant in the network.

### The Publisher

The publisher produces the magazine. There are about 1,000 publishers who pursue this quest for single-copy sales. The publisher traditionally deals only with the national distributor and relies on the distributor for sales and payment.

### The National Distributor

There are about 10 national distributors who service the 1,000 publishers and the 2,000 magazines that are distributed on newsstands. Some distributors operate large organizations, having many hundreds of employees; others are divisions of major publishing companies; and still others are owned by conglomerates. Warner Publisher Services, for example, is a subsidiary of Time Warner, which is involved in book and magazine publishing, records, movies, and cable TV.

The largest distributors are Curtis, Warner, Hearst, and the New York Times–owned TDS.

Some of the smaller distributors handle barely a dozen magazines, while others distribute fifty or more titles. There are also national wholesalers that distribute to a limited number of local wholesalers or retail outlets.

In a typical situation the publisher's single-copy sales manager and the national distributor's account executive meet at least once a month to decide on the number of copies to be distributed for the upcoming issue of the magazine. This "draw" (total distribution) is predicated on the distributor's record, often computerized, of previous issue sales. The publisher has a strong voice in this decision but is frequently hampered by having to base the decision on sales of an issue for a date six months prior to that of the one being planned.

For a better understanding of the distribution process, let us take a $2.00 monthly magazine that distributes 500,000 copies a month. The net to the publisher will be approximately $1.00 on all sold copies. If the publisher is on a 25 percent advance contract, he or she will receive $1.00 times 125,000 copies (25 percent), or a total of $125,000 at the time of shipping the magazines. The distributor will also advance the shipping cost of the magazines from the printer to the wholesalers, about 3 cents per copy. The distributor's share of the $1.00 remaining, after the publisher, wholesaler, and retailer get their share, is about 12 to 16 cents per copy sold.

The "sold" factor, sometimes called "sell-through," for a group of magazines in 1990 was about 60 percent—down from about 65 percent in 1980. When we delete the best-selling twenty magazines, the sell-through in 1990 was only about 45 percent.

Years ago the national distributors functioned as bankers, a practice that has been largely discontinued. When a promising new publisher approached a distributor, the publisher asked for, and often gained, a large percentage of the financing for the entire publication. At the very least the publisher would be guaranteed the paper and printing costs. This money was often assigned to the printer, who was paid directly by the distributor. These days, however, with paper and printing so highly priced, guarantees are not offered. In fact, with new publications that have no track record and are operated by inexperienced publishers, there may be no advance and certainly no financing.

The publisher who receives the 25 percent advance for his or her 500,000-copy draw will generally not derive any additional monies until ninety days after off-sale, when a settlement statement is prepared by the national distributor. If, for example, the final sale is 50 percent, the settlement for this publisher is $125,000, since the publisher has already received an advance of 25 percent on shipping. The shipping charges and any special allowances are also deducted from the settlement. If the publisher in this example has a large overhead and high editorial costs and printing charges, the final settlement may not cover the deficit. Of course, advertising sales and subscription income are additional revenue sources to single-copy sales.

The national distributor also maintains a field force that works at gaining authorizations and opening new outlets for publishers and that, in general, develops marketing programs to help publishers sell their magazines. The field people have a direct business relationship with the 400 wholesalers and in this respect are responsible for billing and collection of their publishers' sales. It is not incumbent on a publisher to have a national distributor, however, and some magazines do bypass this step in the channel of distribution.

## The Wholesalers

The wholesalers are the approximately 400 organizations whose function it is to sell magazines and paperback books within a specified locality or region. The wholesaler may receive as many as 2,000 magazines a month in addition to hundreds of new paperbacks. It is often difficult to offer publishers the individual service they require; hence many large publishers and national distributors have their own field staffs who visit dealers and wholesalers.

On a day-to-day basis wholesalers receive magazines from printers from all across the country. They allocate the quantity to be distributed to each of their dealers and then proceed to deliver and bill these dealers for their copies. When the wholesaler's truck drivers and route people visit a dealer with new copies of magazines, they also pick up the unsold copies of the previous issue. The essence of the problem with this system is that too often no attempt is made to actually sell these dealers on behalf of individual magazines. There are too many publications and books to be delivered and not enough time.

Frequently the dealer being serviced is a small-business person with little capital and a poor credit rating. Thus, the dealer is sold on a COD basis. The dealer may reject a new magazine for which he or she has no sales experience. The publisher of that new magazine doesn't have even a fighting chance to sell the product. Often a dealer who is short of cash will "premature" a magazine—that is, return it for credit before its full sales period (monthly, weekly) is up.

The wholesaler, although computerized in its operation, may not be geared to handling sellouts (all copies sold). Thus, five copies of a new magazine may be delivered by a wholesaler to a dealer and be sold out in five days. The wholesaler, however, may not be equipped to deliver additional copies to the dealer for the remainder of the monthly sales period. Compounding this problem, the wholesaler's computer may be programmed so that a sellout must occur for two or three successive months before additional copies are sent to the dealer.

The wholesaler sends an affidavit to the national distributor attesting to the number of copies sold.

(Some years ago figures developed by the Magazine Publishers of America ascertained that the paper waste for these unsold magazines shredded by wholesalers across the country had a market value well in excess of $200 million annually. And what about all those trees and spotted owls!)

The wholesaler is billed for copies sold by the national distributor at a discount of from 36 to 40 percent of the magazine's cover price. This discount is then split with the wholesaler's dealers, or in some cases a flat 20 percent discount is offered.

## The Dealer

There are an estimated 250,000 magazine dealers of all kinds in the United States and Canada. As mentioned earlier, the list includes about fifteen different categories of retailers. While some are so small they may only sell an average of two or three copies of a given magazine, others in the same city have the potential of selling one hundred copies. Rarely do publishers have contact with small dealers, confining their missionary work instead to large chains of stores or key locations. The national distributor may engage in some marketing activity directly at the dealer level, but the publisher seldom has this opportunity.

As you can now see, the distribution of single copies of magazines is fraught with problems. Some of the system's shortcomings are summarized below:

1. Because of delays in reporting sales, publishers are late to know whether a new cover approach or editing revision has borne fruit.

2. Publishers do not heed their wholesalers and will often send them more copies than they can possibly distribute in the desperate hope that they'll sell. The result? Premature returns.

3. National distributors are burdened with high overhead and a lack of influence or control over the activities of wholesalers. Often the largest accounts and those who complain most vehemently are the ones who get the best service.

4. Dealers come in all shapes and sizes. If the dealer is a supermarket, magazines represent only a tiny portion of the store's sales volume. Since space is limited on smaller newsstands, only those publications with an established track record or those whose publishers pay extra fees are given favorable display positions. This situation also leads to apathy in exploring the potential of new magazines.

5. Progressive publishers, such as those of *Fam-*

ily Circle, Woman's Day, TV Guide, and People Weekly, employ large field staffs to ensure their magazines' proper display and to open new sales outlets. Unfortunately, this arrangement entails an expense that many publishers cannot absorb.

## Where Magazine Single Copies Are Sold

According to a recent report by the Curtis Circulation Company, these are the locations where single copies of magazines are sold:

| | |
|---|---|
| Supermarket/grocery stores | 53.9% |
| Convenience stores | 10.3 |
| Pharmacies | 8.8 |
| Bookstores | 7.4 |
| Others | 19.6 |

(includes transportation outlets, newsstands, and so on)

The growth of the "Other" category is a welcome trend. On the downside, sales in convenience stores have shown a continued decline, much of it attributed to bankruptcies caused by competition from gas station stores and supermarkets.

There are thousands of newsstand magazines and only a limited amount of display space for their sale. Examine the clutter at the general rack of your favorite supermarket. At most, 200 publications are racked, usually in a disorganized display with barely an eighth of the cover showing. How can the reader get a good look at those fifteen cover lines that the editor and art director labored so long to create?

## Checkout Racks

Every publisher wants to be at the checkout rack, for it is here that the impulse buy is made. It is estimated that a magazine at the checkout counter will sell four or five times as many copies as one in a general rack. The "big four" in checkout magazines are Family Circle, Woman's Day, TV Guide, and People Weekly, after the supermarket tabloids like National Enquirer and Globe. Displaying these magazines in racks is a safe decision for the super-

market manager, since experience has proved them to be profit centers.

Some magazines have been known to offer supermarket managers a fixed amount of guaranteed income per rack. This approach may be risky business for the magazine without proven appeal.

## Display Allowances

An arrangement has been developed between publishers and dealers that calls for a dealer's display allowance for those magazines displayed in special positions or "full-face" (with the full cover showing). Magazines subscribing to this program agree to offer all participating dealers an RDA (Retail Display Allowance), usually 10 percent of the cover price, for displaying magazines in this manner. Once a magazine institutes this policy, it cannot be selective but must give every dealer the option to participate.

The program is ordinarily administered by a publisher's national distributor, who sends out the RDA contracts to dealers. But signing the contracts in no way guarantees that a magazine will actually be displayed full-face—some dealers simply won't bother to live up to the bargain. And how can any one magazine police such a vast network? Further, the distributor pays all dealers' RDA claims without supporting documentation and then deducts these charges from the publisher's settlement statements.

A long-overdue attempt at solving the problem has recently come along in the form of specialist companies whose sole purpose is to monitor these abuses. They receive a guaranteed annual fee from publishers, plus additional monies based on the amounts they recover from erroneous claims. It is still too soon to evaluate the effectiveness of these programs, but they do show promise.

## The Power of the Cover

You can sell a magazine by its cover. As we have seen in special situations, such as Sports Illustrated's annual swimsuit issue (now twenty-five years old), the difference between one cover sub-

## First Steps for the New Publisher in Developing Newsstand Sales

1. Pay a visit to your local magazine wholesaler. Let him or her explain firsthand the problems of distribution.
2. See one of the six or seven major national distributors. Ask questions about percentages of advances, promotional efforts, size of field staff, and so on. If impressed by one particular national distributor, call on a number of its major magazine accounts for their opinions.
3. Visit the regional office of a major supermarket chain. Ask about the company's attitudes on magazine sales in general, and find out how it promotes new titles and what its display policy is.
4. Study the placement of magazines and the display formats for as many retail outlets as possible. This examination of racks can also aid in evaluating which cover techniques are most effective.

ject and another can mean a difference of hundreds of thousands of copies. But cover selection is an inexact science. One certainly can't say that all celebrities are the same in their cover appeal.

Certain subjects—among them sex, making money, and losing weight—attract newsstand buyers, but constant repetition cancels their effectiveness. Surefire losers seem to be political themes and foreign politics. In one year *Business Week*'s best cover was "The Best B-Schools"; its worst, "Coup at Alcoa." *Money* paid off with "Where to Invest in the Coming Year" and missed badly with "15 Ways to Cut your Taxes."

Meanwhile, circulation directors and editors will continue to guess what cover will pull best.

## Summing Up

Single-copy sales of magazines are big business, with an annual dollar value well in excess of $2 billion. Yet the system of distribution and sales is indeed anachronistic. What other industry destroys half the product it produces?

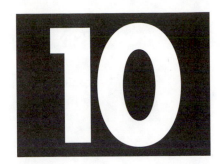

**10**

# Promotion and Public Relations

**M**agazines engage in three basic types of promotion:

- *Advertising sales promotion* to increase the sale of advertising
- *Circulation promotion* to boost newsstand sales and generate subscriptions
- *Public relations promotion* to heighten self-image.

For a clearer understanding of these functions, let us illustrate their actual use.

## Magazine Advertising Sales Promotion

In an era of highly competitive space selling, it is incumbent on a magazine's sales staff and its advertising sales promotion department to seek creative methods to market an advertiser's products. The thrust of these ongoing campaigns is directed at both the advertisers and their agencies and gives the magazine an opportunity to set itself apart from its competitors in the eyes of advertisers.

Here are some other activities performed by advertising sales promotion people on consumer and business magazines:

- Alerting advertisers to particular special issues of the magazine by use of printed material
- Arranging retail-store promotions tying in advertisers, stores, and the magazine
- Attending key industry conventions; arranging hospitality suites
- Preparing special mailings to agencies and advertisers regarding research
- Developing the media kit used by salespeople as "leave-behinds" on their sales calls
- Going on key sales calls with salespeople
- Coordinating the magazine's public relations activity as it relates to advertising

## Merchandising and Added-Value Promotions

Thirty or forty years ago, magazine advertising sales promotion was primitive compared with its sophistication today. In many cases sales promotion consisted of mounting a few thousand ad reprints, with a line at the bottom stating, "As advertised in _____ magazine." These were offered free to advertisers for use at conventions or for distribution to dealers and retailers. Or an advertiser might run a contest for its sales staff, "asking" the magazine to supply prizes, vacation trips, and the like for the contest.

Today added-value, as it is now commonly known, is a fact of advertising sales life. As William P. Hogue, a well-known magazine promotion director, points out in an article in *Folio:*, "All publishers, large and small, are now in two businesses: the publishing business and the added-value business." It's everybody—from a Goliath like *Time* to a David like *Wine Country International Magazine.*

Hogue, commenting on a 1989 *Folio:* survey, writes that "publishers' attitudes to requests for added-value falls into two camps: Enthusiasts and Resigned-to-its. However, regardless of the magazine's attitude, if the advertiser wants added-value, it gets it."

To better understand added-value promotions, consider these examples:

1. *Ad reprints.* For a publisher these are inexpensive and straightforward. Advertisers use them for many promotional purposes.
2. *Use of subscriber lists for consumer mailings.* Such use may be very practical for an advertiser and, if successful, can cement the advertiser to the magazine.
3. *Premiums to the advertiser's sales force.* Publishers may be skeptical of the benefits of this promotion, yet they are forced to go along with it.
4. *Writing/design assistance on "advertorial" projects.* An advertorial is an ad that reads like an editorial. A few years ago *Reader's Digest* did an advertorial booklet for Eastman Kodak on our national parks. A sound idea—when you visit the parks, you take pictures. And since *Reader's Digest* knows its readers better than Kodak or its agency does, why not have the publication write the booklet? For the magazine this kind of promotion offers a direct

payoff—the advertiser is buying an expensive insert in the magazine.

5. *Retail/mall events that a magazine creates and funds.* Women's and fashion magazines have been running these events for years. They're expensive in terms of time, yet they seem to be effective.

6. *High creativity in advertising sales promotion.* The Magazine Publishers of America (MPA) has been running a campaign in publishing trade magazines called "Marketing Success Stories." The thrust, of course, is that "magazines make things happen." One such ad in *Money* magazine spotlighted the success of the Dreyfus Worldwide Dollar Money Market Fund. Instead of a traditional ad insertion with a response coupon, the people at Dreyfus, their agency, and *Money's* ad sales and promotion staff came up with the gutsy and expensive idea of taking a twelve-page ad and running the entire prospectus verbatim, along with an application form. The insertion was so successful that Dreyfus did it twice.

7. Life *and McDonald's.* In the spring of 1990, *Life* ran a special issue called "The World of Children." Since McDonald's has such broad appeal within *Life's* important customer base—the American family—*Life* was able to enlist McDonald's as the sole advertising sponsor of the issue. In addition to its advertising participation, McDonald's distributed complimentary copies to its employees across the country. Here again is an example of a sound promotion that benefits the advertiser as well as the magazine.

8. Fortune *and Cleveland.* Many of our major cities have image problems. Cleveland is no exception, although in recent years it has made important economic strides. The problem: how to attract corporations to locate there. The aggressive ad and promotion people at *Fortune* convinced the Cleveland city authorities that by running an ad spectacular in their magazine, they would target a maximum specialized audience of industry movers and shakers.

A single ad or a double-page spread would not set Cleveland apart from other advertisers. Instead, Cleveland opted for an eight-page cover gatefold (the first in *Fortune's* history) and a six-page ad on the inside of the magazine. The multiple-page ad trumpeted Cleveland's message that it was indeed a terrific place to locate a business and a great place for employees to work and live.

Although no direct-response measurement is possible from such an insertion, a survey showed that 78 percent of *Fortune's* subscribers were favorably impressed. It clearly seemed to be ad money well spent.

9. Country Home *and Lexington Furniture.* Lexington Furniture Industries was launching a new collection of fine country furniture called "The World of Bob Timberlake." The target? The cosmopolitan San Francisco market. The publication Lexington Furniture chose for this particular promotion was *Country Home.*

*Country Home's* promotion staff worked with Lexington Furniture and Macy's to stage a program of events that would showcase the new collection in high-style country room settings for the California market. Timberlake, the designer of the line, along with *Country Home's* editor in chief, served as hosts and seminar presenters at four Bay Area Macy's locations.

Hundreds of *Country Home* readers came to the events, and in the best proof of an effective promotion, Macy's sold more than $1 million worth of the Timberlake line. The next stop for this advertiser and manufacturer team? Bloomingdale's in 1992.

## Low-Budget Sales Promotion

A sales promotion we did at the *National Lampoon* offers an example of a low-budget campaign. A set of very attractive bar glasses was specially designed, each glass carrying a simple line drawing depicting a form of laughter and labeled appropriately—"Laugh," "Titter," "Guffaw," and so on. The last glass in the set of eight was titled simply, "Lampoon."

The glasses were sent or hand-delivered to

about 800 advertisers and prospects, one glass per week. No sales message accompanied the gift, although recipients were aware from the package that it came from the *National Lampoon*. A brief note was stuffed into the eighth glass ("Lampoon") stating, "*National Lampoon*—there's nothing funny about the way it sells."

As an image builder, the program was a distinct success. Many requests came from advertising agencies for additional sets. We didn't deign to think that every time an advertiser downed a scotch-and-soda, thoughts would be of us. No. What we *did* think was that the set of glasses would help us convey the image of a sophisticated, adult humor magazine.

## How Business Magazines Use Advertising Sales Promotion

It is essential for the business (or trade) magazine to become an integral part of the industry or profession it serves. For example, each year in May the book publishing industry has its American Booksellers Association (ABA) convention. Here more than 700 book publishers display the books on their fall list (August through January) to an audience of about 20,000 booksellers from across the United States and Canada and from abroad. Highly visible during the ABA are the book publishing trade magazines, *Publishers Weekly* and *American Bookseller.*

These publications are basically interested in selling advertising to book publishers, as well as covering the editorial aspects of the ABA. They realize, however, that the primary purpose of the ABA for book publishers is to influence booksellers on their lines. The staffs of these business magazines therefore adopt a low-key approach, serving as message centers, giving out shopping bags, and issuing special convention programs. One is aware of their presence, but few overt advertising sales pitches to book publishers are made.

Advertising promotion people on business magazines are constantly attending technical conferences, seminars, meetings, and conventions. Often the publication itself will have a booth at an industry convention. It is the job of the promo-

tion/marketing manager to plan and manage these costly exhibits. Such events may involve the use of printed material, motion displays, or industrial films.

At an important trade event, such as the annual Consumer Electronics Show, both business and consumer magazines in the electronics field attend. For the business magazines the role is twofold. Editorially, they will report on new products and trends. Their advertising and promotion staff, however, is constantly making the rounds of manufacturers' booths to give out goodwill and arrange breakfast, lunch, and dinner dates with key personnel.

One year at a Consumer Electronics Show held in Las Vegas, *Scientific American* hired a white Rolls-Royce to chauffeur convention people to their hotels from the airport, thereby conveying a posh image for a quality magazine.

## The "Comp" Letter

Another promotion used successfuly by both business and consumer magazines is the "comp" letter. "Comp" refers to the complimentary subscriptions sent to present and prospective advertisers, opinion makers, government figures, and so on. Each complimentary mailing includes a letter that not only serves as a source of goodwill for the magazine but, more important, can be used as a vehicle for generating new advertising.

Often the comp letter is bound into a magazine between the front cover and page one. This prominent position almost always guarantees readership. The letter is sometimes printed on white paper and set in typewriter-style type to create a personal touch.

Many comp letters merely boast of a magazine's laurels—high circulation, record-breaking advertising revenues, and the like. This approach tends to become boring and does not invite readership by its busy recipients.

Figure 10–1 shows a comp letter that does invite readership: The *Reader's Digest* ad sales director asks advertising and agency people to read the piece on first aid in that isssue and to write for a free copy of the *Handbook of First Aid.* The comp

*John J. Donoghue*

You're nowhere near a doctor or a hospital. Suddenly someone you're with gets hurt. Or becomes ill.

You need to know what to do. But where do you turn for the answers? A very good place is page 144 of the March Reader's Digest. That's where we begin our fully-updated "Handbook of First Aid."

We've run it twice before. Our readers have let us know how much they value it, both with their comments, and their huge response.

They bought 11.8 million reprints of the first two first aid books.

That's the unique responsiveness and involvement you'll find among the readers of this magazine. Think a moment. Where

**Figure 10–1. Front page of a comp letter bound into the *Reader's Digest***

letter also lists that issue's prestigious advertisers and their page numbers. The theory behind this listing is that advertisers not in *Reader's Digest* will begin to wonder why their competitors advertise and they do not.

The comp list, which may include as many as 10,000 names for some large consumer magazines, is broken down into advertiser classifications so that a message from, say, the men's apparel advertising manager reaches only those manufacturers and key retailers on the men's apparel list.

The messages are customarily concise and attempt to convey to a busy recipient a simple statement from the magazine's publisher, ad director, or space salespeople.

## Walter Joyce on Merchandising

Walter Joyce made magazine promotion an art form. His long and brilliant career included top

jobs with *Playboy, The Saturday Evening Post, Psychology Today,* and *Fortune.* Joyce died in February 1991. Here are the highlights from his article in the September 1990 issue of *Folio:*

Publishers should not shy away from merchandising and added-value programs. If handled properly, they add muscle to a magazine's franchise. In fact, they may even be operated as a profit center.

*Yankee* magazine is a small but potent New England regional magazine. It competes for food advertising dollars with many larger publications. Yet its regionality is treated as a positive factor and has enabled the magazine to form alliances with major retail chains.

The magazine runs an annual *Yankee* Great New England Food Festival that draws thousands to historic Faneuil Hall in Boston. There, crowds sample the wares and hear the pitches of the twenty or so category-exclusive advertiser participants. The promotion extends to point-of-purchase through a food chain promotion with the support of newspaper advertising and a free (donated) car giveaway.

There is a payoff, of course. *Yankee* carries a special Food Festival section where a multipage commitment is required of participating advertisers.

In another brilliant *Yankee* promotion, they have signed up hundreds of inns in *Yankee's* Breakfast on *Yankee* program, through which national food advertisers have their products sampled throughout New England. It's good for the inns—free goods and a gimmick for guests. It's also good for the advertisers, but it's best for *Yankee*, which gets its name publicized and, of course, ad pages from the food advertisers.

Joyce's article goes on to discuss *GQ (Gentlemen's Quarterly)* promotion. *GQ* is a very successful magazine that has a circulation exceeding 600,000 and, with its very high pass-along of 8.69 readers per copy (according to MRI's spring 1992 estimate), has a total audience of 5.4 million readers. *GQ* has a package of in-store programs tailored to advertiser objectives. It conducts a big-time touring show that attracts thousands of consumers who pay $20 to $35 a seat. Clothes are the feature of the show, but also liquor is sampled, electronic wizardry displayed, and travel promoted. *GQ* gets the big payoff in terms of ad pages.

### Circulation Promotion

Let's look first at newsstand promotion. There aren't too many innovative schemes to improve newsstand sales. We have all seen some of the basic methods that have been in use for forty or fifty years—approaches like placing stickers on the stands themselves and displaying posters on delivery trucks. Though these strategies perhaps have a positive effect on sales, what use is made of modern promotional efforts?

TV, an immensely powerful medium, can be highly effective in increasing newsstand sales. *TV Guide* has used the medium for promotion for more than twenty years. More recently we have seen the aggressive campaigns of *People Weekly, Sports Illustrated,* and *Time.* TV commercials are often believed to have a subliminal effect. A viewer may seem oblivious to the drone of commercials, yet some subtle impression remains.

Circulation promotion takes many forms. *Time* employs effective circulation promotions at educational conventions in conjunction with its Time Education Program. The magazine takes booths at the conventions of such organizations as NACS (National Association of College Stores), NCTE (National Council of Teachers of English), and NCSST (National Council of Social Science Teachers). The premise is to encourage the use of *Time* in high school and college classrooms.

In addition, *Time* does teacher mailings and runs ads in educational journals. It also provides video programs, filmstrips, and audio cassettes.

How did *Time*'s parent company, Time Inc. Magazines, promote the launch in 1990 of its new magazine *Entertainment Weekly?* It turned to its own magazines: *Time, People, Sports Illustrated, Money,* and *Fortune.*

Bound into these magazines was a unique, twelve-page editorial insert that gave the millions of readers of these magazines a first hand look at the editorial content of *Entertainment Weekly.* A specially keyed subscription order card was bound into the issues of the magazines that carried the

inserts. More than 60,000 orders for *Entertainment Weekly,* at the full basic rate of $51.48, were received, making the insert one of the magazine's largest single sources of new subscriptions during the first quarter of 1990. *Entertainment Weekly* followed up on this profitable insertion with an eight-page ad in these magazines in February 1991.

We must also realize that the success of this promotion is measured not only in the number of direct subscriptions it pulled but also in the large audience of prospects it reached who were impelled to buy *Entertainment Weekly* on the newsstand.

### The Magazine as Advertiser

Rare indeed is the distinctive advertising campaign by a magazine for itself. The reasons are puzzling. For one, most magazine publishers—whose very existence depends on advertising sales—really don't believe in the power of advertising. Further, when it comes to advertising their own product, publishers develop a bad case of hubris. Too often they will not entrust a mere advertising agency to create an ad promoting their product. After all, many publishers reason, we are in a creative business ourselves. Yet magazines need good ads to attract readers as well as advertisers. Why not employ an agency instead of doing the ads in-house? Good, professional advertising can sell magazines as well as it sells soap and cars. What is important is for the magazine to advertise with reasonable continuity rather than on a hit-or-miss basis. And it is just as important to hire talented ad makers and pay them what they're worth as it is to advertise at all. For revealing examples of the mediocrity of much advertising by publishers, note carefully the next time you see an ad for a magazine.

## PUBLIC RELATIONS

Public relations is an oft-maligned pursuit. Most laypeople associate it with hucksterism, hype, and worse. Perhaps some of this negativism is justified, yet public relations is vital for magazines as well as for other products and services. Many aspects of PR are used by magazines; here we'll examine a few of them.

## Promoting the Lead Story or Issue Theme

The all-time champion in promoting an issue theme is *Sports Illustrated.* More than twenty-five years ago some astute *Sports Illustrated* staffer got the brilliant idea of declaring an issue in February its "swimsuit issue."

Editorially, the issue would feature scantily clad models posing on the world's greatest beaches. Of course, it is all *pour le sport.*

*Sports Illustrated* heralds the swimsuit issue with a big bash for its advertisers and agency people, all of whom get a large poster of the cover girl, the usual food and drinks, and, capping the evening, a short film featuring the models during the shooting in Bora Bora or on the Costa Brava.

The media have adopted this momentous annual event. One year New York newspapers, radio, and TV gave *Sports Illustrated*'s swimsuit issue nearly the same coverage they gave the controversial election in the Philippines and the ousting of Haiti's "Baby Doc" Duvalier.

Consider first this annual issue's financial benefits to Time's *Sports Illustrated.* In an average week it sells 100,000 to 150,000 copies on the newsstands. For the swimsuit issue it now sells ten to fifteen times that number, reaping additional revenues of more than $2 million. The issue also produces a huge increase in advertising revenues, while also providing great image building and goodwill with readers and advertisers.

*Sports Illustrated*'s swimsuit promotion is a textbook example of superb sales promotion and public relations technique.

Many mass-circulation magazines, such as *Glamour* and *American Health,* have proved to be important news sources. Their longtime outside public relations counselor, Howard Greene of Greene Inc., concentrates his agency's efforts on generating national print and broadcast publicity based on articles in each issue. Greene elaborates:

When publicizing an issue of a magazine, we first look to develop news and/or news feature stories that we feel will be appropriate for the Associated Press (AP) and the United Press International (UPI) wire services. Next we look for network television and radio opportunities. And finally for material for syndicates.

During 1991, every issue of *Glamour* and *American Health* developed several national print and/or broadcast stories. During the year AP and UPI moved 49 national stories based on editorial content; there were 69 national television segments and 134 network radio segments. Publicity on several of the issues reached a print and broadcast audience of more than 60 million.

## How to Handle Public Press Releases

An AP or UPI pickup of a story can often mean nationwide or overseas coverage. I remember being in Paris some years ago and reading in the *International Herald Tribune* a UPI story informing me that one of my magazines was being sued. Bad news travels fast, far, and wide.

Now let's look at the path of a press release first as it was sent to the media and then how it appeared in two different publications. Figure 10–2 shows a press release for *Garden Design,* an upscale garden quarterly that increased its frequency to bimonthly publication in March 1991. The release was sent to various trade publications by the magazine's PR firm, Greene Inc.

Note that while the primary subject of the release is the change in *Garden Design*'s frequency, it also covers format changes, the demography of its audience, and the background of its principals.

In figure 10–3 we see coverage of this story in *Inside Media,* an important media publication owned by Cowles Media, which also owns *Folio:. Inside Media,* on receiving the press release, decided to interview one of *Garden Design*'s principals, Arthur H. Loomis.

## GARDENDESIGN

CONTACT: Howard Greene • Greene Inc. • 219 East 31st Street • New York, NY 10016 • (212) 725-2660

FOR IMMEDIATE RELEASE (2/5/91)

"GARDEN DESIGN" TO CHANGE FORMAT, DOUBLE CIRCULATION

Frequency Increased To Bi-Monthly;
March/April Issue Sets Ad Page Record

WESTPORT, CT -- Garden Design -- the nine-year-old quarterly magazine recently purchased by Evergreen Publishing from the American Society of Landscape Architects -- has just increased its frequency to bi-monthly and will undergo a complete format change and will more than double its paid circulation effective with the March/April issue, announced Arthur H. Loomis, publisher.

"Garden Design is being positioned as an Architectural Digest for the exterior of the home," Loomis said. "It has the same production values, the same demographics and an excellent editorial environment. The magazine is not a gardening publication. It is, first and foremost, about design -- the design of gardens and landscapes, and the garden's influence on objects and material used in the daily lives of an upscale audience."

Evergreen Publishing is a recently founded company consisting of private investors with backgrounds in major publishing companies including Time Warner, Knapp Communications, Times Mirror, and Newsweek.

Format changes starting with the March/April issue include a new logo, larger trim size, and redesigned internal layout. The editorial content for the issue will feature Angela Lansbury's California gardens, the Allerton Gardens of Kauai, Hawaii, Audrey Hepburn's PBS special "Gardens of the World" and never-published autochromes of Monet and his gardens in Giverny.

The March/April issue will contain a record 54 pages of advertising, 19 pages more than any previous issue. Among the advertisers appearing for the first time in Garden Design are Absolut, Cowtan & Tout, Cunard Lines, Godiva, Grand Marnier, Jaguar, Mercedes Benz, Minolta, Monet, Orient Express, Remy Martin, Spode, and Smallbone.

more . . .

---

GARDEN DESIGN

The paid circulation for the March/April issue will exceed 70,000 (up from 30,000) and the new rate base is 65,000.

A black-and-white page costs $2,200 and four-color, $3,000. Closing date for the May/June issue is March 15.

### Demographics

According to a recent reader study, Garden Design readers:

* Have a median household income of over $60,000, with 25% more than $100,000.
* 62% are between the ages of 25 and 49.
* 55% are female, 45% male; 72% are married.
* 81% hold baccalaureate or more advanced degrees.
* 85% own homes and 24% own second homes.
* 82% own homes valued more than $76,000; 40% own homes worth more than $250,000.

### Evergreen Publishing

Two of the principals of Evergreen Publishing are Arthur H. Loomis and Rosalie E. Bruno. Loomis has been marketing director of circulation for Time Inc., executive vice president of Times Mirror Magazines and senior vice president of Lorimar Telepictures Corporation, where he helped establish a children's magazine publishing division (now Welsh Publishing). Bruno also worked at Time Inc., was senior vice president/circulation of Architectural Digest and Bon Appetit at Knapp Communications, held the same position at Newsweek and is the founder of Circulation Specialists Inc.

The editorial director of Garden Design is James G. Trulove. He was the founder of Museum Washington (now Museum & Arts) and publisher and editor-in-chief of Landscape Architecture.

# # #

**Figure 10–2**

---

# Inside Media

## Yard work

**Garden Design revamped for broader audience**

*By Maureen Goldstein*

Is the grass greener on the other side?

Arthur H. Loomis will find out when he re-launches Garden Design—the "Architectural Digest for the exterior of the home," in his words.

Loomis and a group of investors have formed Evergreen Publishing, based in Westport, Conn., which purchased the magazine from the American Society of Landscape Architects with the intention of transforming it from a guide for people with green thumbs into a magazine with broad consumer appeal.

Evergreen Publishing purchased the under-promoted and under-capitalized title last summer for an undisclosed sum.

Starting with the March/April issue, the magazine will feature a spruced-up design. Its frequency will be stepped up from quarterly to bimonthly, and the circulation will be doubled to 70,000. Garden Design is also slated to get a larger trim size, a new logo and newly designed layouts.

Agencies and advertisers will get their first glimpse of the re-styled March/April issue this month at the New York Flower Show, which is being sponsored by the New York Horticultural Society at Pier 92 March 8 through 17. Copies of the magazine will be bound into the event's program guide. The guide is being produced by Evergreen Publishing.

Under the direction of the ASLA, Garden Design had more of a vertical trade image and was primarily distributed by garden-supply manufacturers to clients.

Under Loomis's tutelage, the magazine will be transformed into a "Lifestyles of the Rich and Famous" targeted at the gardening set. It will feature articles on garden design interspersed with features on celebrity gardens and various sylvan settings from around the world. For example, the first issue will feature a visit to Angela Lansbury's California home for a view of her garden and will highlight Audrey Hepburn's PBS special "Gardens of the World" and the Allerton Gardens of Kauai, Hawaii.

"It's not a magazine that tells people how to make compost or plant a tomato," he says. "We want our readers to come away with a greater appreciation of the garden and the exterior of their homes."

Who are these readers? Loomis describes them as aging baby boomers interested in settling down. Readership data indicates that 55 percent are female; 72 percent are married and have median household incomes that exceed $60,000; 85 percent own homes and 24 percent own second homes. Loomis plans to conduct another readership study in May following the debut of the magazine's redesign.

In addition to overcoming the green thumb image the magazine had under its former owners, Loomis also hopes to change the image with advertisers. Loomis expects to augment the magazine's foundation of fence and garden supply advertisers with ads for autos, liquor, home furnishings, travel and luxury goods.

Loomis also plans to introduce a department, "A Room with a View," to showcase home furnishings. In an effort to appeal to a broader readership, he's expanded the definition of "garden" to include any item found in the home with a botanical motif, such as china.

Despite the bad economic climate that surrounds the re-launch of Garden Design, other publishing executives who have worked with Loomis say that he has several things going for him: a solid background in magazine circulation and ad sales upon which to build a magazine with an existing advertiser and reader base. "The magazines today that will be successful have a base of advertising away from an industry. Loomis already has that base and can expand on it with a base of luxury goods advertisers that are found in titles such as Arch Digest," says Don Welsh, president of Welsh Publishing. Welsh and Loomis met when the two established a children's magazine publishing division at Lorimar Telepictures.

Loomis says the first issue will feature 54 pages of advertising, including business from Cunard Lines, Smallbones kitchens, Mercedes-Benz and Absolut vodka.

But how successful Garden Design will be at cultivating long-term commitments from advertisers remains to be seen. Right now, many advertisers don't have the dollars to gamble on new ventures.

And the magazine, in straddling the horticulture and shelter categories, is competing for ad dollars against a formidable group of established and widely circulated magazines that includes Architectural Digest, Metropolitan Home, HG and Better Homes & Gardens.

"We don't have a shortage of ways to reach these people, and it's a harder group to reach than most because they spend less time with the media," says Mike White, executive vice president, media director, DDB Needham, Chicago.

Loomis is banking on the magazine's ability to provide advertisers with a new means of reaching affluent readers. "We don't pretend to offer anything unique in terms of audience, but we do offer a unique way to reach those people," explains Loomis. "We provide an alternative that's different from an HG or an Arch Digest," he says.

And he can do it cheaper—a black and white page costs $2,200, and a four-color page is a mere $3,000.

Although price did tempt Mercedes-Benz to test-drive the magazine, Tom Wilson, executive vice president and director of media services at McCaffrey and McCall, says other factors came into play.

"They have hit upon a niche that has not been cluttered like the epicurean category. The magazine is different from the horticultural magazines that are about digging in the dirt and planting seeds," he says. "Garden Design shows that gardens are an extension of a person's home." ■

Garden Design: Digging up new readers

**Figure 10–3**

## Radio and TV

Talk-show hosts always need material and will sometimes book a magazine's editor if the subject is provocative. These bookings are easier to schedule for local than for national shows. Even so, TV and radio commentators will often reflect on a newsworthy item relating to magazines.

## Dos and Don'ts of a PR Program

1. Magazines should have a consistent PR program, with an annual budget and one individual in charge. A good magazine PR person should have some college writing training and, later, magazine experience. The job requires creativity, diplomacy, aggressiveness, and the ability to write concisely and well.

2. Releases should not editorialize or state an opinion. They should be prepared as news stories and rely on the pickup to provide greater detail.

3. Releases should never be lengthy. The busy editors who read them receive hundreds of releases every day and have little time to pore over multipage tomes passing as news releases. An effective PR release should tell the whole story concisely. It should answer the questions, Who? What? Why? When? and Where? in as few words as possible.

## How Can a New Magazine Promote Itself?

The new magazine strives for identity. An early choice should be the spokesperson who can be called on for interviews, tours, and the like. Usually the editor or publisher receives this designation. It is obviously necessary for this person to be capable of effectively articulating the magazine's concept and viewpoint. One fact stands out: Publicity can far outweigh the value of advertising—and it's free.

The editor's or publisher's tour of the country is of prime significance for the new magazine. Such tours can be accomplished at relatively low cost. If the magazine is to be sold on newsstands, visits to major cities should be planned; many of the arrangements can be made from the magazine's home office. TV talk shows offer the widest exposure. Radio works well too, as do newspaper interviews.

Cities like New York, Chicago, and Los Angeles require two days for full coverage; others can be handled in a single day. For maximum effect a local PR specialist can be employed. This person will, of course, know the right interviewers and have the contacts to implement the short visit. And, of course, a number of larger PR firms will, at a fixed cost per interview, schedule the whole tour for the editor or publisher.

Timing of the tour is important. It should not be made too far in advance of the publication date of the new magazine. If a PR tour is undertaken and the magazine is to be sold on newsstands, wholesalers in the city visited should be alerted. They can achieve optimum marketing impact and dealer acceptance if they know in advance about the interviews.

As the first publisher of *Weight Watchers Magazine*, I undertook a tour of six cities. My objective was to spread the weight-control message, to emphasize obesity statistics, and to promote both the Weight Watchers classes and *Weight Watchers Magazine*. In Chicago I had two TV, three radio, and three newspaper interviews, all in one day. It was difficult enough to maintain my equilibrium, let alone to be charming and articulate, but the mission was accomplished.

What is of prime importance is that the spokesperson for a magazine be thoroughly knowledgeable about the publication's concept. Try not to let the interviewer veer off in directions other than your subject matter. If possible, don't say the same thing to two interviewers—you may be reaching the same audience, who will become easily bored with stereotyped conversation. Make notes of what you want to talk about, but never read from them.

The beginner in magazine publishing should certainly investigate the opportunities in public relations. Some key resources follow:

1. The primary national association of PR people is the Public Relations Society of America (PRSA), 33 Irving Place, New York, NY 10016.

2. A PR firm specializing in magazines is Greene Inc., 71 Park Avenue, New York, NY 10016.
3. For a list of PR firms specializing in author-editor tours contact PRSA.
4. A fine publication in the public relations field is the *Public Relations Journal,* 33 Irving Place, New York, NY 10016. This monthly deals with political, socioeconomic, and business affairs. The subscription rate is $45 a year.

The conclusion we should draw from this chapter is that promotion and public relations are a vital fact of a magazine's life. These elements should be dynamic, exciting, and designed to achieve specific results, such as increased newsstand sales or an ever-increasing flow of subscriptions. They should also serve to enhance the image of the magazine.

## Interview

Howard Greene is president of Greene Inc., a twenty-six-year-old public relations firm that specializes in national magazine accounts. Among the firm's current accounts are *American Health, American Heritage, Glamour,* and Times Mirror Magazines. During his career Greene has either worked for or represented about sixty national magazines.

*In what way does an outside PR counsel function more effectively than an in-house staff?*

The effectiveness of a public relations program is determined not by whether it is run by on-staff or outside counsel but by the skills of the personnel running the program. I know many outstanding practitioners on both sides of the aisle. All things being equal, however, outside counsel does have several advantages. Here are some major ones: Outside counsel generally brings more objectivity to the project. The agency should bring a range of experience within a subject area because it regularly deals with several clients within that general area. It should be able to recognize viable PR opportunities more easily than a practitioner with a narrower company viewpoint. It is also easier to spot opportunities from the outside without the constraints of familiarity. Outside counsel also has

a wider range of personnel and talents to draw from in servicing an account. In-house departments generally have to use full-time personnel, while an agency can assign several people with a broad base of talents to work on an account utilizing a portion of their time. Another benefit of outside counsel is a much wider range of contacts and day-to-day working relationships with these contacts, because they regularly deal with them for a range of clients. A final benefit of outside counsel is that it is generally more cost-effective for a given level of expertise. This is a function of the part-time availability of more experienced personnel.

*How do you go about providing national coverage for a magazine "event" based on an editorial story?*

The answer to this question is a definite "It depends." During the course of a year, we deal with several magazine events, some of which lend themselves to on-site coverage, and some which do not. The first step is to determine which is which. Does the event have sufficient press interest to warrant major media committing personnel to cover it? If the answer is no, treat it as just another newsworthy story (if it is indeed newsworthy) within the issue. You don't need an event to generate coverage. If the answer is yes, do whatever you can—within budget constraints (time and money)—to ensure maximum coverage. Here is a brief overview of how Greene Inc. publicized two such events that, ironically, took place within one week in November: *Glamour*'s Women of the Year Awards and *Popular Science*'s Best of What's New exhibition.

For *Glamour*'s Women of the Year Awards, held in the Rainbow Room, we decided to provide the press with two opportunities for coverage of the ten winners (including Anita Hill): a press conference one hour before the ceremony and the ceremony itself.

The first step was to put together two lists—one for press invitees to cover the event and another for media that would receive press material whether or not they attended the press conference. Next, a comprehensive press kit was developed including news stories and photographs. We then wrote a press advisory providing details of the event but withholding the names of the winners. This was serviced about two weeks before the event, followed by follow-up phone calls in which we confidentially gave the names of the more famous winners. Two days before the event, we serviced a second advisory, with the names of the ten winners (embargoed for the night of the event). Scores of follow-up calls were again made the day of the (evening) event. In all, seventy-seven print, television, and radio reporters covered the press conference and/or the ceremony. Highlights of the national press coverage included AP, UPI, and Reuters text and photo stories; news segments on "Good Morning America," "CBS This Morning," "Entertainment Tonight," and "CBS Morning News"; ten network radio segments; and photo stories in *Newsweek*, *New York* magazine, and *Interview*. Locally in New York, all four dailies covered the event, as well as most local TV and radio.

Six days after the *Glamour* event, we handled *Popular Science*'s Best of What's New exhibition of 1991's best products and technology. The basic difference between the two events was that *Glamour*'s was personality- and hard-news-based, while *Popular Science*'s was product- and news-feature-based. The steps were basically the same: press advisory, press kit, and lots of follow-up. In this case, however, the client was much more interested in product demonstrations on television. About one month prior to the event, we arranged a "Today" show segment with the editor of *Popular Science*, Fred Abatemarco, demonstrating a number of the winning products. We also started contacting a number of national television shows early to have them shoot demonstrations at the exhibition. This resulted in segments on "This Morning's Business," FNN/CNBC; "Science and Technology News," CNN; and "Steals and Deals," FNN/CNBC. In addition, six New York television stations telecast news segments. National print coverage included AP, UPI, and Reuters.

A press event, however, is not the critical ingredient for major, national press coverage of a magazine article. You'll probably remember reading, hearing, and/or watching a story based on this lead:

> NEW YORK, September 23—Bundling up helps you avoid catching a cold . . . drinking milk is good for an ulcer . . . and treat a snakebite by cutting it and sucking out the venom . . . are among some cherished medical myths debunked in the current (October) issue of American Health.

*Magazine public relations is a small field. Is it growing?*

Though I have no objective measure, it seems that many more magazines today retain outside counsel or have an internal PR department than they did five years ago.

*Is magazine PR centered in New York City?*

Yes, primarily because most national magazines are headquartered here, and New York is the major press center.

*Your organization specializes in magazine PR. What expertise is required for this field?*

At the top of the list is general intelligence (hardly specific to magazine PR, but essential). You must feel comfortable dealing with the wide range of subject matter covered by a single issue of a national magazine.

Then, in no particular order: An understanding of the needs of various media and the ability to adapt client material to these needs. An ability to recognize a viable news or news-feature story. Pragmatic creativity. An ease with written and spoken English (not so widespread as it may seem) so that you are equally comfortable pitching story ideas on the phone or by letter. An ability to prioritize and adhere to deadlines.

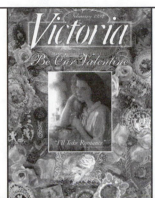

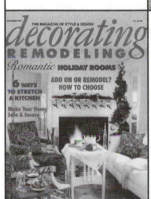

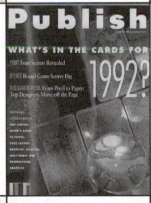

In chapter 1 we discussed the high mortality rate of new magazines. Yet each year we see two or three make it—some even make it big. Is such success attributable to talented management, strong financing, good timing, or all of these plus good luck? The one factor that is always present in a new magazine success story is a unique concept. Without it, none of the other assets can sustain the new venture.

We will examine in this chapter a number of magazines that have made it. From analyzing these publications we can gain an insight into what essential elements brought about their success.

## Sports Illustrated for Kids

Who but the gutsy people at Time Inc. Magazines would have the muscle and the moxie to launch a sports magazine for kids? All the odds are against its success. No such publication ever made it. Kids don't or won't read. Advertisers can reach this audience through TV. Yet in 1989 *Sports Illustrated for Kids* was launched, and by 1992 it already had a circulation guarantee of 750,000.

The magazine calls its prime audience "eight- to fourteen-year-old tweens," with a male-female readership ratio of 67 percent boys and 33 percent girls. If *Sports Illustrated for Kids* is to make it for the long haul, and my guess is that it will, it will do so because its editorial package is brilliantly conceived.

One recent issue had this mix:

- Nine colorful sports cards of superathletes were included to cut out and save.
- A feature called "Quick Kicks" with news of sports heroes had a frank discussion of Magic Johnson and his AIDS condition. Particularly moving were the comments of kids talking about AIDS. One eleven-year-old's message: "I wish they would find a cure so he would feel better and wouldn't die."
- The 1991 Good Sports Awards honored five sports leaders who care about kids and work hard to help them.
- Karate Kids showed kids mastering this martial art.

An admirable program conducted by the magazine is its *Sports Illustrated for Kids* Reading Team. Thirty corporate sponsors, including Pepsi, McDonald's, Hershey's, and GapKids, provide the cost of distributing 250,000 copies of *Sports Illustrated for Kids* monthly in 10,000 classrooms in poverty districts across the United States. A free monthly teacher's guide is sent to teachers in this program.

*Sports Illustrated for Kids'* circulation revenues are derived primarily from subscriptions, which, as we know, are not as profitable as newsstand circulation. Profits must therefore come from advertising revenues. A list of the magazine's 1991–1992 advertisers is impressive. Such companies as Coca-Cola, Foot Locker, Gatorade, Nike, Reebok, and Toys "R" Us have committed to the magazine, realizing what a valuable audience this is.

As a peripheral profit center for *Sports Illustrated for Kids,* the magazine has published fifty books dealing with sports subjects. One such title is *The Official Kids' Guide to the Summer Olympics.*

With its total audience of more than eight

million readers, *Sports Illustrated for Kids* is well on its way to success. If it makes it, the primary reasons will be its concept, its editorial execution, and its responsive audience.

## IB Independent Business

Few new magazines reach profitability in their first year, even if they are started by publishing giants like Time Inc. Magazines. In fact, as we have already noted, of the 500-odd new magazines launched each year, only 10 percent will make it into the second year, and, of these survivors, many will take more than four years to reach a break-even point.

Two twenty-five-year publishing veterans, Tom Sargent and Mike Carpenter, defied the odds by launching *IB* magazine in January 1990 and making a profit with their November issue the same year. How they did it is a case history in astute magazine management.

The National Federation of Independent Businesses (NFIB) is an organization of 560,000 small-business owners founded in 1943. Its typical member is a small-business person who has been in business an average of twenty years, employs nineteen people, and has average annual sales of $1.5 million.

Sargent and Carpenter were able to convince the NFIB that a quality magazine attuned to the interests and problems of its members would enhance the value of the organization. A contract was drawn whereby the magazine would be sent to NFIB members free. The parent organization would then pay the publishers a portion of members' dues for the subscription to the magazine. This, of course, both solved the problem of achieving a large circulation base and provided some of the financing for production and overhead.

The two entrepreneurs then raised $1.5 million in capital from a limited partnership and were on their way to publishing success. Their first bimonthly issue, in January 1990, had twenty-four pages of advertising. Today they carry such major advertisers as AT&T, Toyota, IBM, Avis, and the U.S. Postal Service.

*IB*'s editorial content is totally service-oriented. One recent cover story was titled "Home Office Heaven," a how-to for people who run their businesses from home. Also in this issue was an article titled "Avoiding Health Plan Ripoffs"; another wrote about taking your business on the road.

Regular editorial departments in *IB* include profiles of small-business owners with unusual occupations, how-tos on money management, and a feature on getting the most from advertising dollars.

*IB* is a money-maker because it has guaranteed circulation revenue. At the same time, it keeps its overhead down by hiring advertising sales reps instead of maintaining a costly in-house staff, employing free-lance art and makeup people, and using desktop publishing procedures to their greatest advantage.

Clearly, *IB* has competition. To an extent it competes for ad dollars with *Success, Entrepreneur,* and *Your Company*. Yet it also has advantages in terms of a strong concept, a built-in audience of 560,000 NFIB members, and the experience of its founders.

Reproduced with permission from *IB Independent Business*

### decorating REMODELING

In the Home Service and Home category of the current Standard Rate and Data Consumer Magazine listings, there are thirty-two magazines, including the formidable *Architectural Digest, House Beautiful, Better Homes and Gardens, House and Garden,* and *Metropolitan Home.* Why, then, did the astute publishers at the New York Times Company Women's Magazine group decide to launch yet another shelter magazine? The answer is that this publishing group saw a niche in the market and was willing to commit its resources to have it succeed.

Today *decorating REMODELING* is an unqualified success. In 1991 the magazine *ADWEEK* named it one of the "Ten Hottest Magazines in America" for its performance and growth in advertising sales and circulation. For 1992 *decorating REMODELING* had an advertiser rate base of 650,000.

Although the other shelter magazines cover the subject of remodeling, *decorating REMODELING* seems to approach it with an appealing, low-key flair.

The cover subjects for the issue shown on this page are indicative of *decorating REMODELING*'s winning editorial formula. The piece on "6 Ways to Stretch a Kitchen" illustrates how architectural tricks can expand a small kitchen. "Add on or Remodel?" addresses a problem faced by many people with growing families. "To Each His Own" shows how good planning can give privacy to two young boys in a small space.

In fifty years of American shelter magazine publishing, virtually every subject has been covered. I can remember editorial sessions for a decorating magazine I published more than twenty years ago. Each time an idea was proposed, it was shot down with the response, "Oh, that's been done to death." And to a great extent it's true. Nevertheless, *decorating REMODELING* is doing good, targeted, specialized publishing that works. Simply stated, in a time of financial crunch remodeling is a hot magazine concept.

*decorating REMODELING* at this writing is published only eight times a year. Its publishers

Reproduced with permission from New York Times Magazine Group

seem to be taking a conservative approach, an attitude of "Let's do what we're doing, and then we'll see what happens." My guess is that the magazine will make it.

### Entertainment Weekly

It's hard to believe that Time Inc. Magazines was willing to gamble up to $150 million in 1990 to launch yet another entertainment magazine. Movie and music industry revenues were on a downslide and the TV networks in a period of transition that promised dramatic changes in the 1990s. Moreover, in terms of coverage the world of entertainment is not shortchanged. We are barraged with news, reviews, and just plain gossip in our newspapers, on TV and radio, and in a dozen other magazines. But Time saw an opportunity and went for it.

In 1984 two Time Inc. Magazine staffers were simultaneously preparing proposals for an entertainment weekly. Jeff Jarvis was then a TV critic at *People,* and Michael Klingensmith was the general manager of *Time* Worldwide. By 1987 the two were put together to come up with an editorial prospectus/business plan, and, after management approved the plan, a "go" date of February 16, 1990, was agreed on.

Editorially, *Entertainment Weekly's* first year was an entertaining mixed bag, with the primary problem of distinguishing itself from its sister publication, *People*. This distinction was partially accomplished by focusing on entertainment, not personalities, although there was a crossover. In *Entertainment Weekly's* reviews the magazine had to make a transition from an esoteric approach to a more broad-based one. Then there was the challenging task of turning out fifty to sixty pages a week.

Klingensmith, *Entertainment Weekly's* founding publisher, had a circulation background: *Time* Worldwide, *Fortune,* and *Money*. He realized that the critical mass for a major new magazine was a circulation guarantee of at least 500,000. This was achieved through an expensive TV and direct-mail effort beginning in December 1989. A later TV-spot and direct-mail campaign in winter 1990–91, using a CD as a premium, pulled 200,000 new subscribers. These are impressive figures when one considers that a campaign does less well after a magazine has already been in circulation.

Of interest are the demographics from *Entertainment Weekly's* 1989 *Direct Mail Respondent Survey* and how these differed from the fall 1991 MRI study. Initially, *Entertainment Weekly's* stats were female, 52 percent; male, 48 percent; and a median age of 36.8 years. The 1991 MRI figures show *Entertainment Weekly's* audience as female, 45 percent; male, 55 percent; and a median age of 31.2 years. An audience more closely attuned to entertainment would tend to be younger but not necessarily more male-oriented.

*Entertainment Weekly* benefited in its sale of advertising from the median age level of its readers. Klingensmith comments, "Fortunately for us, the purchasers of advertising look a lot like the purchasers of our magazine."

The magazine carried 152 pages of advertising in its first seven issues and 1,000 pages in its first year, an impressive result.

*Entertainment Weekly's* "Special Year End Double Issue, Best of 1991" is a fat package on the personalities who made the year famous, as well as the best and worst in movies, TV, books, music, and video. Jodie Foster made it as number one Entertainer of the Year with the top movie selection, *The Silence of the Lambs,* and her directing stint on *Little Man Tate*. One must also applaud *Entertainment Weekly's* flashy and vivid graphics in this issue.

*Entertainment Weekly* was fourth on *ADWEEK's* ten-hottest-magazines list for 1991; its editor, James Seymore, was named editor of the year. In a further accolade, *Ad Age* named *Entertainment Weekly* the magazine of the year for 1991. Although at this writing *Entertainment Weekly's* success is inconclusive, the magazine has a good chance for profitability before the five years originally estimated. If it does succeed, its success will result from its sound editorial concept, its physical execution, and the investment its parent company is prepared to make to see it win. As the most expensive launch in Time Inc. Magazine's history, its career path will be carefully studied by media watchers.

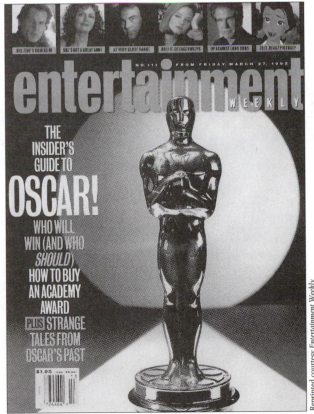

Reprinted courtesy *Entertainment Weekly*

## Midwest Living

Regional life-style magazines abound. At the top level are *Sunset, Southern Living,* and *Yankee* and below these some lesser lights, such as *Florida Home and Garden, Phoenix Home & Garden, Colorado Homes & Lifestyles,* and even *Cape Cod Home & Garden.*

The people at the Meredith Corporation, the premier magazine publisher in the Midwest, speculated that there was no one magazine dealing with the values and life-styles of America's heartland. After all, they reckoned, the roots of the Midwest run as deep as the Pony Express, the assembly line, professional baseball, and the hot dog (and I always thought it came from Coney Island by way of Frankfurt, Germany).

Meredith was the right company for the launch of *Midwest Living,* since it understood the market so well and also had recently originated publication of the successful *Country Home* and *WOOD* magazines.

Before the go-ahead for the launch was given, an extensive two-year, $500,000 research process was undertaken to determine whether the proposed audience really wanted such a magazine. Once this test proved positive, circulation marketing tests were conducted to determine readers' interest in the project and their willingness to buy. Again the news was good.

While this activity was going on, the editorial staff was engaged in its own probing, trying to find out what people wanted to see in a Midwest magazine. This search took *Midwest Living*'s editors and writers into the field in search of stories. The premier issue (April 1987) had twenty-five feature stories on such diverse subjects as a trip down the Mississippi River and jazz in Kansas City, together with a Chicago chef's piece on Midwest foods.

*Midwest Living*'s ad staff had an initial circulation guarantee of 400,000 to offer advertisers, a relatively high figure for a regional magazine. A strong PR effort didn't hurt either; the magazine was able to sell forty-five pages for the premier issue. Within a few years *Midwest Living,* published bimonthly, was selling more than 400 ad pages a year. By the March/April 1992 issue, the magazine had a circulation guarantee of 700,000 and a four-color page rate of $25,300.

To add to the magazine's laurels, for 1990 and 1991 it was cited by *ADWEEK* as one of the top-ten smaller (a circulation of less than a million) magazines.

A look at *Midwest Living*'s February 1992 issue confirms its success. Editorially, the magazine features sharp graphics and reproduction, as well as a lively writing style. Its advertisers include many who appear in our most important national magazines, among them Chevrolet, Dole, Whirlpool, Campbell's, Ford, and Toyota.

The ingredients for *Midwest Living*'s success are many. Clearly, careful research before the launch played a significant role, as did the experience and know-how of its parent, the Meredith Corporation. This is a case history of a good concept well executed. Even in a doubtful economic climate, a project like this one should succeed.

**•KEEPSAKE 5TH ANNIVERSARY ISSUE•**

# MidwestLiving

APRIL 1992 • $2.95

*Spring Magic!*

- Best Biking Trails
- Travels on Amish Byways

**Celebrity Favorites**
All-Star Recipes From Hometown Restaurants

**Home & Garden**
- Order Our New Mini Rose!
- A Country Dream House

50 TOP MIDWEST RESORTS

Vacation Guide

## Condé Nast Traveler

Although travel has grown exponentially in the past forty years, travel magazines have never been a growth category. Let's consider the field today. Here are the six leading magazines and their circulation as of December 31, 1991:

| | |
|---|---|
| *Travel & Leisure* .......................... | 1,150,000 |
| *Endless Vacation* ............................ | 811,000 |
| *National Geographic Traveler* ........ | 724,000 |
| *Condé Nast Traveler* ..................... | 716,000 |
| Reader's Digest's *Travel Holiday* .... | 568,000 |
| *European Travel & Life* ................. | 374,000 |

*Travel & Leisure*, owned by American Express, has been around for a long time and is closely involved with that company's credit-card business. Reader's Digest's *Travel Holiday* evolved through a merger of two fifty-year-old magazines, *Travel* and *Holiday*. Why, then, did Condé Nast buck an already crowded market when it decided to launch *Condé Nast Traveler* in such choppy seas in 1987?

In fairness, *Condé Nast Traveler* was not a totally new magazine. It evolved from the purchase of *Signature* (I was its first publisher in 1951) in 1986. Then, in characteristic Condé Nast fashion, the magazine underwent a complete editorial and physical overhaul—slicker paper, splashy graphics, and, most significantly, a "Truth in Travel" editorial policy. As one commentator put it, "This iconoclastic troublemaker of travel magazines has its writers travel incognito [to report on] bad airline food, questionable hygiene standards on cruise ships, and the safety of airlines."

Lest we think *Condé Nast Traveler* is the "60 Minutes" of travel, although in a sense it is that, it is also beautiful, with high editorial standards matching those in any category. One recent issue had this provocative menu:

- A charming piece on Dublin, "a city impregnated with her history." The article hailed the wonders of the Abbey Theatre, Irish Mist soufflé, and the city's smiling, freckle-faced, red-haired Irish residents.
- A main feature on Vietnam, treated with refreshing candor, including references to "the land laid waste by Agent Orange."

*Reproduced with permission from Condé Nast Traveler*

- A tip on how to cash in on the great global hotel glut by bargaining for a hotel room in Maui.
- Noted food authority Mimi Sheraton's Top American Restaurants.

The payoff for this issue was a blockbuster, sixteen-page ad spectacular for Mercedes Benz, with a cost to the advertiser of about $500,000.

*Condé Nast Traveler*'s success has been dramatic. In 1988 and 1989 it won the National Magazine Award and received three nominations in 1990. In 1989 it was also named *Advertising Age*'s Magazine of the Year. In 1991 the magazine also sold about 1,100 pages of advertising, for a total of $30 million.

Of course, with the magazine's expensive roster of writers—including James Buckley, Jr., William Styron, Joe McGinniss, David Mamet, and Arthur Schlesinger, Jr.—it still has a long road to travel to Profitland. Yet judging from its performance in its first three years, *Condé Nast Traveler* must be deemed a success story by any standards. Clearly, serving the $328-billion-a-year travel industry, the magazine is a hot ticket.

## Victoria

In 1990 *ADWEEK* named *Victoria* the "Hottest Magazine of 1989," and in 1991 the magazine ranked third in *ADWEEK*'s top ten. Here are some capsule comments on the rankings:

Media directors say: "Unique editorial. . . ." "I have no idea why it works, but it does." In categorizing *Victoria*, *ADWEEK*'s Michael Winkleman calls the magazine "a love poem to romance, to commitment, to tradition, to frills and chills and lace."

*Victoria*'s rapid rise to stardom is a tribute to both the Hearst organization and the thrust of its unique editorial concept—"women who appreciate a softer, romantic approach to living." Here's how this success story came about:

It was decided at Hearst to distribute the first issue of *Victoria* in March 1987 with its *Good Housekeeping* name on it. Newsstands were the chosen route. The company distributed 400,000 copies, of which it sold 320,000, an astounding figure for any new magazine. To add to Hearst's euphoria, 50,000 of these first-issue, single-copy buyers became subscribers.

The second issue of *Victoria* (Fall/Winter 1987) sold more than 400,000 copies on the newsstand, and direct-mail campaigns (see chapter 8) delivered 200,000 more subscribers for this issue. By July 1988 *Victoria* increased its frequency to bimonthly publication, and by the September 1989 issue it was a monthly with a circulation of 750,000. By February 1991 the magazine's circulation guarantee was an imposing 800,000, and its ABC circulation for the six months ending December 31, 1991, was 822,000, of which well over 200,000 came from single-copy sources.

Demographically, the *Victoria* audience profile shows 2.2 million women, with a median age of 40.2 years and a household income of $47,355, according to MRI's spring 1992 survey.

What is the editorial potion that has intoxicated the 2.7 million readers of *Victoria*? Perhaps the answer is that the magazine provides an antidote to the frantic pace of women's lives today. In *Victoria*, say its publishers, readers are transcended into a softer world of "beauty, tradition and femininity."

The physical look of *Victoria* is lush, full of soft-toned photographs of warm interiors and frilly fashions. One recent article was titled "A Fine Romance," after a 1930s song made famous by Fred Astaire, and featured a like-named Minneapolis gift shop that sells ribbons, tassels, tapestried pillows, and imported French photo albums. Another piece in the same issue, "A Day of Wine and Roses," told of a group of Californians who tramp the byways of their state in search of antique roses.

*Victoria* works for readers and advertisers because, in the words of agency media director Scott Morehead, "[it] doesn't analyze, preach, improve, trim or create femininity, it simply exudes the best aspects for all to enjoy." The major advertising agency Saatchi & Saatchi's senior vice-president, Irwin Srob, likens *Victoria* to a trip: "It takes women on an inexpensive vacation to a place where they can relax and be receptive to new ideas."

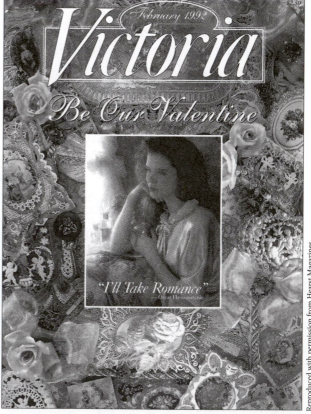

## Inside Media

*Inside Media* was launched in 1989 by Cowles Business Media, the organization that brings us *Folio:* (see chapter 17) and *Folio:'s Publishing News.* *Inside Media* is a biweekly targeted to media people at ad agencies and their clients. In a crowded field that includes *Advertising Age, ADWEEK,* and *MEDIAWEEK, Inside Media* has more than held its own in both ad dollars and reader interest.

*Inside Media* has been rewarded for its editorial excellence by being the three-time recipient of the coveted Jesse H. Neal Award, given by the American Business Press. That's pretty heady stuff for any new publication.

In 1991, a very poor year for ad-trade magazines, the sales of *Inside Media* were down only about 7 percent, while its competitors were off as much as 55 percent. How, one may ask, did *Inside Media* establish itself so quickly in this very sophisticated market? The answer seems to lie in the quality and depth of its editorial content.

The media buyer at an advertising agency who receives *Inside Media* also gets dozens of other magazines clamoring for his or her attention. Why read this one? A look at a recent issue may provide the answer.

In a piece called "Si Speaks," the magazine interviewed S. I. Newhouse, Jr., the chairman of Condé Nast, one of our largest magazine publishers. Newhouse, one of the wealthiest men in America, is rarely interviewed, but in this article he opened the doors to his cloistered kingdom without making excuses for his failures or boasting of his successes. This is the kind of in-depth article readers have come to expect from *Inside Media.*

*Inside Media* has chosen a large, tabloid-size, format for its presentation, and it works. It allows for large photos, graphics, and charts and, of course, enables the magazine to carry big splashy ads from the media companies that advertise in it. In the same issue that carried the Newhouse story were ads from *Rolling Stone,* Hachette Magazines, *ym* magazine, *Parade, Newsweek, Ladies' Home Journal, Modern Maturity,* McGraw-Hill, *Parents, Time,* and about twenty other media companies—many of these ads being two-page spreads in color.

Will the media buyer buy advertising in the *New Yorker* because he or she saw a full-color spread for the magazine in *Inside Media* that showed a baseball player making a powerful swing for the fences? Maybe not, but the ad is making an impact. It is saying that the *New Yorker* cannot be stodgy and intellectual if it runs such provocative articles as those of Roger Angell on baseball. *Inside Media* offers advertisers a large-page showcase for this kind of advertising, and that's one of the reasons it has succeeded.

From a profit standpoint, *Inside Media* must make it on advertising, since its circulation is 20,000 "qualified nonpaid," which simply means that the magazine is sent free to a selected list of media and agency people. Going the paid route might be risky. The publication would then be unable to say that it reaches all the "decision-makers in the media," a situation that might reduce its influence.

Our guess is that *Inside Media* is here for the long haul, and the reason is quality. It is proof again, along with the other success stories in this chapter, that editorial content is the single most important factor in a new magazine's reaching for the gold.

### Electronic Business Asia

In the chapter on business magazines (chapter 12), we discuss Cahners Magazine Company, a division of the giant media company Reed International. Cahners publishes such outstanding business publications as *Restaurants & Institutions, Publishers Weekly, Emergency Medicine,* and *Interior Design*. Add to this auspicious list the magazine *Electronic Business Asia*.

*Electronic Business Asia* was launched as a controlled-circulation monthly in May 1990. Its readership comprises the 41,000 corporate, engineering, purchasing, operating, and marketing managers in Asian electronics, computers, and systems companies. It is published in four separate language editions: Chinese, Korean, Japanese, and English.

Each edition contains a twelve-to-sixteen-page section in the language of that edition. Advertisers are able to buy ads on a regional (or country) basis, thus eliminating the waste factor.

Editorially, *Electronic Business Asia* focuses on in-depth reportage and analysis of its industry. The thrust of one recent cover story, "ASIA turns on to R&D," was that since Asian electronics companies have traditionally looked to the West and Japan for their technology, they now face the pressure of developing their own R&D capabilities. Two other articles in the same issue were corporate profiles of two Asian-owned electronics companies.

A full-time staff of six, headquartered in Hong Kong, is responsible for the editorial content of the magazine. In addition, free-lance correspondents in Asia and the West are employed. In my opinion one of the primary reasons for *Electronic Business Asia's* success is its no-nonsense, no-puff editorial approach. Clearly, no attempt is made to cosset its advertisers or the electronics industry. Its editorial tone matches that of our major business magazines.

All of this has made *Electronic Business Asia* a major business magazine success. In 1991 the magazine carried 740 pages of advertising, a substantial figure for a new magazine. On the strength of its success with this magazine, Cahners launched a new publication in May 1992, *EDN Asia* (*Electronic Design News*).

*Electronic Business Asia* succeeded because it represents a sound editorial concept, is regionally adapted, and is published by a skilled magazine company.

China telecoms: Round two PAGE 67    Wyse set on a turnaround PAGE 37

A Cahners Publication                    DECEMBER 1991

ELECTRONIC BUSINESS ASIA

FOR MANAGERS IN ELECTRONICS, COMPUTERS & SYSTEMS COMPANIES

**Asia's R&D race:
Survival of
the fastest**
PAGE 42
India's top
electronic makers
PAGE 37

Australia $56   Hong Kong HK$35   Indonesia 4,500 rupiahs   Japan ¥1,000   Korea 3,500 won   Malaysia M$8.50   Philippines 70 pesos   Singapore $5#   Taiwan NT$130   Thailand 90 baht

**12**

# The Fascinating Business of Business Magazines

What do *Emergency Medicine, The Logger and Lumberman, Interior Design,* and *Variety* have in common? You can guess the answer from the title of this chapter. These four—and about 3,700 others—are business publications, formerly known as trade magazines but now given a more sedate title. This major group of magazines is dedicated to the fundamental principle of bringing news, opinion, and information about an industry or specialized field to the people in that field and to those on its periphery who are concerned with its activities.

When a movie producer reads *Variety,* he or she is reading it for a number of reasons—to know the box-office grosses and what new productions have gone into principal photography, to read the latest movie reviews, and to find out who was fired at Universal Pictures.

On the other hand, the candy manufacturer who supplies movie theaters, the stock analyst who monitors the entertainment sector, and the interior designer who specializes in theaters also read *Variety,* even though they are not directly in the movie business.

Just as it does in the consumer magazine area, Standard Rate and Data Service (SRDS) publishes a business magazine directory, *Business Publication Rates and Data.* In this listing *Variety* is in a rather small classification: Motion, Talk, Sound, Commercial Pictures, and so on, with only 22 publications. But another classification of business magazines, Medical and Surgical, lists almost 500 publications. The range of business magazines, as we will see in the subsequent listings, is indeed broad.

## A Short History of Business Magazines

From *Folio:*'s "250 Years of Magazine Publishing" issue, I learned about some of our earliest business magazines. The first business "periodical" was published in 1774. It was a single sheet called *South Carolina Price-Current.* In it one could find out the price of barley, wheat, beeswax, and other staples of the day. Similar price sheets were published until the War of 1812.

As the nation's business grew, so did the flow of business magazines. By the end of the Civil War, there were about 125 publications. Some business magazines from that period still exist. *Scientific American* got its start in 1845. *American Banker* was founded as *Thompson's Bank Note Reporter* in 1836. *Hardware Age* and *Iron Age* were launched in 1855 and *Drug Topics* in 1857.

Yes, there were a McGraw and a Hill. They were competitors in the late nineteenth century until they joined forces in 1917. By 1919 there were already 1,100 business magazines, and by 1948 ad revenues were up to $255 million.

In 1984 Rupert Murdoch bought twelve Ziff-Davis trade magazines for $350 million. But in 1988 he sold a group of magazines to Reed International for $825 million. Business magazines have come a long way from the single-sheet *South Carolina Price-Current.*

## The Scope of Business Magazines Today

According to the Veronis, Suhler & Associates October 1991 *Communications Industry Report,* in 1990 the revenues of publicly reporting business and professional publishers exceeded $3 billion. The three largest publishers in the subsegment, Capital Cities/ABC, McGraw-Hill, and Reed International, accounted for 69 percent of those revenues. These three companies publish forty or more business magazines each.

Some business magazines sell thousands of advertising pages a year. For example, *PC Week,* an automatic data systems publication owned by the Ziff-Davis Company, sells more than 5,000 pages, for a total dollar figure exceeding $100 million. The *New England Journal of Medicine* sells about 5,000 pages a year, as does *Restaurants & Institutions.* A magazine as specialized as *Interior Design* sells about 3,000 pages annually. McGraw-Hill's *Engineering News-Record* sells about 3,000 pages; its *Aviation Week & Space Technology,* 1,800 pages. Business magazines as a group derive 80 to 90 percent of their total revenues from advertising.

## The Life Cycle of Business Magazines

The noted print media consultant James B. Kobak, in an article in the January 1992 issue of *Folio:*, compares two decades of business magazine data. Some important conclusions:

- Computer magazines staged the largest growth in the number of titles published since 1972. There are 181 listed in SRDS today, whereas there were only 20 in 1972. But of that original 20, only 1 is left today. From 1984 through July 1991, 244 computer magazines began publication—only 100 are still with us.
- The overall growth of all business magazines in this twenty-year period is substantial: 2,255 in 1972, 3,007 in 1984, and about 3,700 in 1991.
- The fastest-growing business magazine field in the past twenty years is health care, with a 93.3 percent growth from 1972 to 1991.
- Slow- or negative-growth fields in this period are food, energy, and government.

## Circulation and the Business Magazine

Business magazines are generally not sold on newsstands, although there are exceptions, such as the entertainment trades *Variety* and *Hollywood Reporter.* Business magazine publishers must make an important decision: Do they choose controlled—free—circulation (see chapter 8 on subscriptions), or do they go the paid route? It is a difficult decision. If a magazine's publisher opts for controlled circulation, the magazine will reach everyone in the industry but, of course, generate no revenues from this source. If the publisher chooses paid circulation, the magazine reaches only that portion of its audience that is willing to pay the subscription price.

Seventy-five to 80 percent of business magazines are distributed on a controlled basis. These publications are able to say to their advertisers that they reach every qualified individual in this industry or profession. In the medical and surgical field, for example, Standard Rate and Data Service lists about 117 that are on a paid basis and about 360 that are on a controlled basis.

Examine the following pages from SRDS showing various classifications of business magazines. One gets a sense of the diversification of these publications and, for the reader of this book, possible leads for employment. The full list is available in SRDS's *Business Publication Rates and Data,* which lists addresses and key personnel. It may be available in major journalism school libraries or from a friend who works in an advertising agency.

The degree of specialization in SRDS's list is enormous. In electronic engineering, for example, there are one hundred publications listed; in the insurance field, fifty-eight. There are twenty-seven in interior design, twenty-seven in music and music trades, and sixty-five in nursing and health. No field seems to be missing; there are even five publications dealing with the intimate-apparel industry.

The advertisers (or their advertising agencies) who buy advertising in business magazines must be able to verify the circulation of those publications; otherwise they are not spending that advertising money efficiently. For this purpose, the Business Publications Audit of Circulation (BPA) has been established.

BPA's main purpose is to audit the circulation of member publications once a year. It verifies all-paid, all-controlled, or any combination of paid and controlled circulation. Also significant about a BPA audit are the data it provides on verification of magazine staff members' names, a breakout of their occupations, and the geographic location of audited recipients. Audited circulation statements give advertisers assurance that the publications deliver their desired target audience.

# Classification Groupings

**EDITOR'S NOTE: The asterisk (*) denotes a duplicate listing.**

## 1. ADVERTISING & MARKETING
(See also: Journalism & Publishing; Sales Management.)

### AUDITED
Advertising Age
Adweek
Adweek's Marketing Computers
Agri Marketing
American Demographics
Art & Design News
Art Direction
BRAD*
Broadcasting
Business & Incentives
Business Marketing
Canadian Advertising Rates and Data*
Catalog Age
Direct
Direct Marketing
DM News
Editor & Publisher
Food & Beverage Marketing
Graphic Design: USA
How
Inbound/Outbound
Incentive
Inside Media
Licensing Book, The
Licensing International
Marketing Week
Medical Advertising News
Medical Marketing & Media
O'Dwyer's PR Services Report
Pharmaceutical Executive*
P-O-P Times
Potentials in Marketing
Print
Public Relations Journal
Sales & Marketing Management
Signs Of The Times
Standard Rate & Data Service Business Publication Rates and Data
Standard Rate & Data Service Community Publication Rates and Data
Standard Rate & Data Service Consumer Magazine and Agri-Media Rates and Data
Standard Rate & Data Service Newspaper Rates and Data
Standard Rate & Data Service Spot Radio Rates and Data
Standard Rate & Data Service Spot Television Rates and Data
Target Marketing
Telemarketing*

### NON-AUDITED
Aberdeen's Construction Marketing Today
Adcrafter
Advertising/Communications Times
Advertising Options Plus
Airbrush Action
B/PAA Communicator
Broadcasting & Cable Market Place
Catholic Journalist
Catholic Press Directory
Chicago Advertising & Media
Client Magazine
Co-op Source Directory
Communication Arts
Communication World
Confetti
Counselor, The
Creative
Daily Program Buyer
Direct Marketing Market Place, The
Editor & Publisher International Year Book, The
Editor & Publisher Market Guide, The
Exhibit Marketing Magazine
Finding
Format
Fund Raising Management
IEG Directory of Sponsorship Marketing
Inside Impact
International Archive
Journal of Advertising Research
Journal of Marketing
Journal of Marketing Research
Marketing Insights
Marketing News
Marketing Research: A Magazine of Management and Applications
Media Market Guide
MediaScope 1992 Chicago Market & Media Planner
MediaScope 1992 Florida Market & Media Planner
MediaScope 1992 Mid-Atlantic Market & Media Planner
MediaScope 1992 Southern California Market & Media Planner
MediaScope 1992: Texas Market & Media Planner
Mediaweek
MPM—Mexican Advertising Agencies Directory*
MPM-Mexican Audiovisual Media Rates & Data*
MPM-Mexican Print Media Rates & Data*
Pharmaceutical Marketers Directory
POPAI News
Product Management Today
Promo

Public Relations Journal Register Issue
Quirk's Marketing Research Review
Recruitment Solution, The
Sales and Marketing Strategies & News
Sign Business
SignCraft
Specialty Advertising Business
Sports Advantage
SRDS Media and Market Planner: Financial Markets
SRDS Media and Market Planner: Food & Food Service Industries
SRDS Media and Market Planner: Manufacturing & Processing Industries
SRDS Media and Market Planner: Technology Markets
SRDS Media and Market Planner: Travel & Tourism Industries
SRDS: Bullet
Standard Directory of Advertisers
Standard Directory of Advertising Agencies
Standard Rate & Data Service Card Deck Rates and Data
Standard Rate & Data Service Circulation 92
Standard Rate & Data Service Direct Mail List Rates and Data
Standard Rate & Data Service Hispanic Media and Markets
Standard Rate & Data Service Print Media Production Data
Standard Rate & Data Service P M P D Bulletin
Standard Rate & Data Service Special Issues
Standard Rate & Data Service Spot Radio Small Markets Edition
Step-by-Step Graphics
Television & Cable Factbook

## 2. AIR CONDITIONING, HEATING, PLUMBING, REFRIGERATION, SHEET METAL & VENTILATING
(See also: Roofing.)

### AUDITED
Air Conditioning, Heating & Refrigeration News
ASHRAE Journal
Contracting Business
Contractor Magazine
Distributor
Engineered Systems
Fuel Oil News
Fueloil & Oil Heat Magazine
Heating-Plumbing-Air Conditioning
Heating/Piping/Air Conditioning
HVAC Product News
MPC
Plumbing & Mechanical
Plumbing Engineer
Plumbing Heating Piping
Reeves Journal, Plumbing-Heating-Cooling Refrigeration
Refrigeration Service & Contracting
Service Reporter
SNIPS Magazine
Supply House Times
Wholesaler, The

### NON-AUDITED
Alabama Contractor
ASA Convention Daily
ASA Membership Directory
ASA News
Distributor Daily ARW
Distributor Daily NHAW
District Heating & Cooling
Florida Contractor
HPAC Techlit Selector
HVAC/R Directory, The News
Indiana Contractor
Indoor Comfort News
MCAA Convention Reporter
Mechanical Buyer & Specifier HVAC/Refrigeration Edition
Mechanical Buyer & Specifier Plumbing, Piping & Heating Edition
Mechanical Contractor Literature Showcase
Pennsylvania Contractor
Plumbing Business

Smacna Convention Daily
Southern Plumbing Heating Cooling
Western HVACR News
Wholesaler/ARW Convention Daily, The
Wholesaler/NHAW Convention Daily, The
Wisconsin P-H-C Contractor
Yankee Oilman

## 3. AMUSEMENTS & GAMING MANAGEMENT
(See also: Motion, Talk, Sound, Commercial Pictures, Etc..)

### AUDITED
Amusement Business

### NON-AUDITED
Amusement Industry Buyers Guide
Back Stage
Casino Gaming International
Directory of North American Fairs Festivals and Expositions
Facility Manager
Fair Times
Funparks Directory
Public Gaming International
Theatre Crafts
Theatre Journal
Tourist Attractions and Parks

## 3A. APPLIANCES
(See also: Electrical; Gas; Home Furnishings; Metal,Metalworking & Machinery; Radio, TV & Video.)

### AUDITED
Appliance
Appliance Manufacturer

### NON-AUDITED
Appliance Service News
Retail Observer

## 4. ARCHITECTURE
(See also: Building.)

### AUDITED
Architectural Record
Architecture
Building Design & Construction
Construction Specifier, The*
Metal Architecture
Progressive Architecture

### NON-AUDITED
Architecture Minnesota
Construction News Publishing Network Convention News
Design Cost & Data
Design Solutions
Fabrics & Architecture
Florida Architect
Florida Landscape Architecture
Inland Architect
Landscape Architect and Specifier News, The
Landscape Architecture
Landscape Design
Sweet's Catalog File
Sweet's Catalog Files
Technology & Conservation of Art, Architecture & Antiquities
Texas Architect
TheWoodBook
Wisconsin Architect

## 5. ARTS

### AUDITED
Art Material Trade News

### NON-AUDITED
Crafts Report, The

## 6. AUTOMOTIVE, AUTOMOBILES, TIRES, BATTERIES, ACCESSORIES, SERVICE STATIONS, GARAGES
(See also: Motor Trucks, & Accessories; Public Transportation & Mass Transit.)

### AUDITED
Aftermarket Business
American Clean Car
Auto Age
Auto Age Supplier Source & Directory
Auto Laundry News
Auto Merchandising News
Automotive Body Repair News
Automotive Engineering
Automotive Executive
Automotive Fleet

Automotive Industries
Automotive Marketing
Automotive News
Automotive Rebuilder
BodyShop Business
Brake & Front End
Business Driver
Counterman
ESD Technology
Exhaust News
Fleet Financials
Import Automotive Parts & Accessories
Import Service
Importcar & Truck
Jobber Retailer
Jobber Topics
Modern Tire Dealer
Motor
Motor Age
Motor Service
Preview
Professional Carwashing & Detailing
Service Station Management
Specialty & Custom Dealer
Specialty Automotive
Tire Business
Tire Review
Transmission Digest
Undercar Digest
Ward's Auto World

### NON-AUDITED
Aftermarket Business APAA Show Daily
Aftermarket Business SEMA/AI Show Daily
American Carwash Review
American Towman
Auto Rental News
Auto Trim & Restyling News
AutoGlass
AutoInc.
Automotive Cooling Journal
Automotive Executive Today
Automotive Marketing Who's Who APAA Show Directory
Automotive Recycling
Battery Man, The
Body Engineering
Convenient Automotive Services Retailer
Eastern Aftermarket Journal
Limousine & Chauffeur
Locator
Midwest Automotive & Autobody News
Motor Age Big "I" Who's Who
Nafa's Fleet Executive
National Guide to Vehicle Leasing Suppliers & Services
Northwest Motor
NTDRA Dealer News
Pacific Automotive News
PBE Spectrum
Performance Racing Industry
Professional Tool & Equipment News
Restyling & Accessories Marketing
SAE Update
SLIG Buyers' Guide
Supercharger
Used Car Dealer
Used Car Merchandising
Van & Truck Digest
Vehicle Leasing Today
Ward's Automotive Yearbook

## 7. AVIATION & AEROSPACE

### AUDITED
A/C Flyer
Aerospace & Defense Science
Aerospace America
Aerospace Engineering
Aerospace Products
Air Force Magazine
Air Transport World
Aircraft Technician
Airline Business*
Airline Executive International
Airport Services
AOPA Pilot*
Aviation Equipment Maintenance
Aviation International News
Aviation Week & Space Technology
Avionics
Business & Commercial Aviation
Commuter Air International
Commuter World
Controller, The
Defence Helicopter
FBO
Flight International*
Flying*
GPS World
Helicopter World
NASA Tech Briefs*
Professional Pilot
Rotor & Wing International
Space
Space News
Trade-A-Plane

### NON-AUDITED
A B D
Air Market News
Airport Journal
Aviation Ground Equipment Market
Aviators Hot Line
Conservation Aeronautics
Flight Training
1992 Helicopter Annual, The
Rotor Magazine
Vertiflite
Wings of Gold
World Aviation Directory & Buyer's Guide

## 9. BAKING
(See also: Confectionery; Food Processing & Distribution.)

### AUDITED
Bakery Production and Marketing
Baking & Snack
Baking Buyer

Milling & Baking News
Modern Baking

**NON-AUDITED**
Bakery Production and Marketing RBA
  Spotlight and Show Guide
Bakery Production and Marketing Red Book
Baking/Snack Directory & Buyer's Guide
Reference Source

**10. BANKING**
(See also: Financial.)

**AUDITED**
ABA Banking Journal
American Banker
Bank Management
Bank Marketing
Bank Marketing Magazine
Bank News
Bank Systems & Technology
Bank Technology News
Bankers Monthly
Banking Software Review
Bottomline
Credit Card Management
Credit Union Magazine
Financial Managers Statement
Mortgage Banking
National Mortgage News
Northwestern Financial Review
Savings Institutions
United States Banker

**NON-AUDITED**
Alabama Financial Directory
American Bank Directory
American Banker-Bond Buyer Newsletter
American Financial Directory
American Savings Directory
Arizona Bank Directory
Arkansas Bank Directory
Arkansas Banker
Bank Management Retail Delivery Systems
  On Site
Bankers Digest
Bankers Magazine, The
Banking Week
California Financial Directory
Credit Union Director
Credit Union Executive
Credit Union Magazine Convention Daily
Credit Union Management
Credit Union News
Credit Union Technology
Credit Union Times
Federal Credit Union, The
Florida Banking
Florida Financial Directory
Florida Mortgage Broker, The
Georgia Bank Directory
Golden States Financial Directory
Hoosier Banker
Illinois Banker
Illinois Banknews
Illinois Financial Directory
Independent Banker
Indiana Financial Directory
Journal of Retail Banking
Kentucky Bank Directory
Kentucky Financial Directory
Louisiana Bank Directory
Maryland Bank Directory
Massachusetts Financial Directory
Michigan Financial Directory
Minnesota Bank Directory
Mississippi Bank Directory
Mississippi Banker
Montana Financial Directory
New England Financial Directory
New Jersey Bank Directory
North Dakota Bank Directory
Ohio Bank Directory
Ohio Banker
Oklahoma Bank Directory
Oklahoma Banker
Oregon Financial Directory
Polk's Financial Institutions Buyers Guide
  and Services Directory
Real Estate Finance Today
Secondary Marketing Executive
Servicing Management
South Carolina Bank Directory
South Dakota Bank Directory
Southern Bankers Directory
SRDS Media and Market Planner: Financial
  Markets*
Tarheel Banker
Tennessee Bank Directory
Tennessee Banker
Texas Banking
Texas Financial Directory
Thomson Bank Directory
Utah Financial Directory
Virginia Bank Directory
West Virginia Bank Directory
Western Bank Directory

**12. BEAUTY & HAIRDRESSING**

**AUDITED**
American Salon
Modern Salon
Skin Inc.

**NON-AUDITED**
BBSI Convention Preview
Green Book
Guide, The
Nailpro
Nails

**14. BOATING**

**AUDITED**
Boat & Motor Dealer
Boat & Motor Dealer's Market Manual
Boating Industry
Boating Industry Marine Buyers' Guide

## Classification Groupings continued

Marine Business Journal
Soundings Trade Only

**NON-AUDITED**
Boat & Motor Dealer's Show Shopper
Marina/Dock Age
Marine Store Merchandising
Marine Textiles
Professional BoatBuilder Magazine
Sailing Scene
Sea's Industry West

**15. BOOKS & BOOK TRADE**

**AUDITED**
Magazine & Bookseller
Publishers Weekly

**NON-AUDITED**
American Bookseller
Bookstore Journal
Choice
Christian Retailing
Small Press

**15A. BOTTLING**
(See also: Food - Processing & Distribution.)

**AUDITED**
Beverage Industry
Beverage Industry Annual Manual
Beverage World
Beverage World Periscope
Beverage World 1992/93 Databank

**NON-AUDITED**
Bottled Water Reporter
Mid-Continent Bottler
National Beverage Marketing Directory

**16. BREWING, DISTILLING &
BEVERAGES**
(See also: Food - Processing & Dis-
tribution.)

**AUDITED**
Bartender Magazine
Beer Wholesaler
Beverage Network, The
Cheers
Jobson Beverage Group, The
Modern Brewery Age
Modern Brewery Age
New Jersey Beverage Journal
Top Shelf Barkeeping At Its Best

**NON-AUDITED**
Arizona Beverage Analyst
Atlantic Control States Beverage Journal
Beverage Bulletin
Beverage Dynamics
Beverage Journal of Spirits, Wine & Beer
  Marketing, The
Beverage Journal, The
Beverage Media
BIN Beverage Industry News
BIN Merchandiser
California Beverage Publications
Colorado Beverage Analyst
Connecticut Beverage Journal
Desktop Products Guide
Florida Food & Beverage News
Hawaii Beverage Guide
Illinois Beverage Journal
Indiana Beverage Journal
Jobson's Liquor Handbook
Jobson's Wine & Spirits Industry Marketing
Jobson's Wine Marketing Handbook
Kansas Beverage News
Kentucky Beverage Journal
Liquor Reporter, The
Maine-New Hampshire-Vermont Beverage
  Journal
Maryland-Washington Beverage Journal
Massachusetts Beverage Journal
MBAA Technical Quarterly
Michigan Beverage News
Montana Beverage News
Nebraska Beverage Analyst
Nevada Beverage Analyst
New Mexico Beverage Analyst
Observer
Ohio Beverage Journal
Ohio Tavern News
Oklahoma Beverage News
On Premise
Patterson's California Beverage Journal
Proof
Rhode Island Beverage Journal
Southern Beverage Journal
SRDS Media and Market Planner: Food &
  Food Service Industries*
Stateways
Texas Beverage News
Vineyard & Winery Management
Wines & Vines
Wines & Vines Annual Directory
Wisconsin Beverage Journal

**17. BRICK, TILE, BUILDING MATERIALS**
(See also: Ceramics; Engineering &
Construction; Stone Products, etc..)

**NON-AUDITED**
Tile and Decorative Surfaces
Tile World

**18. BRUSHES, BROOMS & MOPS**

**NON-AUDITED**
Brushware

**19. BUILDING**
(See also: Architecture; Brick, Tile,
Building Materials; Building
Management & Real Estate; En-
gineering & Construction; Logging &
Forest Products Manufacturing Market;
Roofing.)

**AUDITED**
Automated Builder
Builder
Commercial Renovation
Custom Builder
Fine Homebuilding*
Kitchen & Bath Business
Kitchen & Bath Design News
Lumber Co-Operator, The
Manufactured Home Merchandiser
Metal Construction News
MH/RV Builders News
Professional Builder & Remodeler
Qualified Remodeler
Remodeling
Rural Builder
Shelter
Sun/Coast Architect/Builder

**NON-AUDITED**
APL, Inc. Home Builder Network
Automated Builder Annual Buyers' Guide
Build/California
Build/Florida
Builder Profile
Builder/Dealer
Building Industry
Building Products
California Builder
Carpenter, The
Construction Dimensions
Construction Times
Contractors Hot Line
Custom Home
Door & Window Business
Fenestration
Florida Builder
Florida Constructor
Florida Homebuilder
Good Cents
Hot Line Construction Equipment Monthly
  Update
Interior Construction
Journal of Light Construction, The
Kitchen & Bath Design Guide
Kitchen & Bath Source Book
Kitchen & Bath Specialist
Masonry
Nation's Building News
Properties Magazine
Remodeling News
Southeast HomeBuilder & Remodeler
Sweet's Catalog File
Traditional Building
Units
Walls & Ceilings
World Fence News

**19A. BUILDING MANAGEMENT & REAL
ESTATE**

**AUDITED**
Building Operating Management
Buildings
California Real Estate
Energy User News*
Midwest Real Estate News
National Real Estate Investor
National Real Estate Investor Directory
N. Y. Habitat
Real Estate Forum
Real Estate Today
Realtor News
Southeast Real Estate News

**NON-AUDITED**
Aud Arena Stadium
Banker & Tradesman
Better Buildings
Black's Guide
BOMA International Buyers Guide
BOMA International Who's Who in the
  Office Building Industry Directory
Building Renovation and Retrofit Catalog
Business Properties
Charleston Real Estate Report
Charlotte Real Estate Report, The
Columbia Real Estate Report, The
Commercial Profile
Commercial Property News
Commercial Record, The
Common Ground
Corporate Real Estate Executive
Corridor Real Estate Journal, The
Dealmakers, The
Development Magazine
Developments
Direct Source
Empire State Realtor
First Tuesday
Fleet's Guide
Florida Realtor
Greater Los Angeles Office Market Journal
I-85 Business Belt Report, The
Inland Empire Real Estate Annual
Journal of Property Management
Kalis' Shopping Center Leasing Directory
Managers Report
Metro Chicago Office Guide, The
Metro Chicago Real Estate
Metropolitan Washington Tenant's Guide to
  Business Properties
NACORE Directory of Membership: 1992
National Relocation and Real Estate
  Magazine
National Roster of Realtors
New England Real Estate Journal
New England Real Estate News
New York Real Estate Journal

Northeast Real Estate News
Office & Industrial Guide to Broward &
  Palm Beach Counties
Office & Industrial Guide to Miami
Office Guide to Florida
Office Guide to Orlando
Office Guide to Tampa Bay
Omaha Metropolitan Office & Shopping
  Center Leasing Guide
Orange County Real Estate Annual
Perspective
Portland Metropolitan Office Guide
Property Management Monthly
Property Management News
Real Estate Business
Real Estate Finance
Real Estate Finance Journal
Real Estate News
Real Estate Newsletter, The
Real Estate Northwest
Real Estate Review
Real Estate Sourcebook, The
Real Estate Week
Real Estate Weekly
Real Estate West
Realty
Realty & Building
San Diego County Office and Business
  Parks Guide
Skylines
Southwest Real Estate News
Square Footage
Sun Belt Buildings Journal
Texas Realtor
Tri-State Real Estate Journal
Urban Land Magazine
Welcome! Nacore Annual Symposium and
  Exposition Program
Yale Robbins Office Buildings

**19B. BUILDING PRODUCTS RETAILING**

**AUDITED**
Building Material Retailer
Building Supply Home Centers
Home Improvement Center
National Home Center News

**NON-AUDITED**
Building Products Digest
Merchant Magazine, The
Northwestern Lumbermens Dealer
  Reference Manual
ProSales

**20. BUSINESS**
(See also: Business - Metro, State &
Regional; Office Methods & Manage-
ment; Professional Association
Management; Selling & Salesmanship.)

**AUDITED**
Accounting Today
Area Development
Barron's-National Business and Financial
  Weekly
Business Facilities
Business Tokyo
Business Week
Canners Magazine Network
CFO
Chief Executive
Chronicle of Philanthropy, The
CIO
CPA Journal, The
D & B Reports
Economist, The North America Edition
Entrepreneur*
Expansion Management
Export Today
Financial World*
Financier
Forbes*
Fortune*
Harvard Business Review*
HealthWeek*
Home Office Computing*
Inc.*
Independent Business
Industry Week
Investor's Business Daily
Journal of Accountancy
Journal of Commerce and Commercial, The
Kiwanis Magazine*
Leaders Magazine
Management Accounting*
Minority Business Entrepreneur
Nation's Business*
New Accountant
New York Times, The
NonProfit Times, The
P & D Magazine*
Penton Executive Network
Plants Sites & Parks
Price Club Journal
Professional Managerial Network, The
Scientific American*
Site Selection/Industrial Development
Small Business Reports
Triangle Business
U.S. News & World Report*
Wall Street Journal, The*
Washington Technology
Women In Business
World Monitor*

**NON-AUDITED**
American Food and Ag Exporter
Area Development Industrial Development
  Directory of Canada
Arizona Business & Development
ASBA Today
Asset, The
Association Source
Business Review, The
Chamber Executive
Chilton's All Business Network
Computers in Accounting
Corporate Location Bluebook
Directors & Boards

Dollars & Sense
Economic World
Economic World Directory of Japanese
    Companies in the U.S.A.
Entrepreneurial Woman*
EuroAccess
Exporters' Encyclopaedia
Florida CPA Today
Franchising World
Gaming & Wagering Business Magazine
In Business
Industrial Management
Internal Auditor
Journal of Business Strategy
Journal of Policy Analysis and Management
Journal of Taxation, The
Make Money*
Manage Magazine
Management Review
Mergers & Acquisitions
Mobility
National Business Woman
National Public Accountant
Overseas Business
Pennsylvania CPA Journal
PM Network
Practical Accountant, The
Professional Communicator, The
Project Management Journal
Quality Observer, The
Rinksider, The
Sport Construction Buyer's Guide
Sport Media Buyer's Guide
Sportbil
Standard & Poor's Register
Taxation for Accountants
Taxation for Lawyers
Tomorrow's Business Leader
Twin Plant News
Up-To-Date Price Magazine
Upside Magazine
Washington Accountant, The

## 20A. BUSINESS - METRO, STATE & REGIONAL
    (See also: Business; Office Methods &
    Management; Professional Association
    Management; Selling & Salesmanship.)

### AUDITED
Adweek/East
Adweek/Midwest
Adweek/New England
Adweek/Southeast
Adweek/Southwest
Adweek/West
Allegheny Business News
Arizona Business Gazette
Atlanta Business Chronicle
Austin Business Journal
Baltimore Business Journal
Baton Rouge Business Report
Boston Business Journal
Business Atlanta
Business First
Business First
Business First of Buffalo
Business Journal of New Jersey Magazine
Business Journal Serving Charlotte and the
    Metropolitan Area, The
Business Journal Serving Greater
    Milwaukee, The
Business Journal Serving Greater Portland,
    The
Business Journal Serving Greater
    Sacramento, The
Business Journal serving Phoenix & the
    Valley of the Sun, The
Business Journal Serving San Jose and the
    Silicon Valley
Business North Carolina
Business Press, The
Business Record
California Business
Capital District Business Review
Central Penn Business Journal
Cincinnati Business Courier
Colorado Business Magazine
Corporate Cleveland
Corporate Detroit Magazine
Corporate Report Minnesota
Corporate Report Wisconsin
Crain's Chicago Business
Crain's Cleveland Business
Crain's Detroit Business
Crain's New York Business
Dallas Business Journal
Denver Business Journal, The
Diablo Business
Enterprise, The
Executive Business Magazine
Executive Report
Florida Business/Southwest
Florida Trend
Focus—Philadelphia's Business
    Newsmagazine
Georgia Trend
Grand Rapids Business Journal
Greater Cincinnati Business Record, The
Hawaii Business
Hawaii Investor
Houston Business Journal
Indiana Business Magazine
Indianapolis Business Journal
Ingram's, For Successful Kansas Citians
Jacksonville Business Journal
Kansas City Business Journal
Long Island Business News
Los Angeles Business Journal, The
Maddux Report
Memphis Business Journal
Miami Today
Minneapolis/St. Paul CityBusiness
Nashville Business and Lifestyles
Nashville Business Journal
New England Business
New Mexico Business Journal
New Miami
New Orleans CityBusiness
Northeastern Wisconsin Business Review
Oklahoma Journal Record

Oregon Business Magazine
Orlando Business Journal
Pacific Business News
Pennsylvania Business and Technology
Philadelphia Business Journal
Pittsburgh Business Times
Providence Business News
Puget Sound Business Journal
Regardie's, The Business of Washington
Review Newspapers
San Antonio Business Journal
San Diego Business Journal
San Diego Daily Transcript
San Francisco Business Times
South Florida Business Journal
St. Louis Business Journal
Tampa Bay Business Journal
Virginia Business
Warfield's
Washington Business Journal
Western Business
Wichita Business Journal

### NON-AUDITED
Alaska Business Monthly
Arkansas Business
Business Alabama Monthly
Business for Central New Jersey
Business in Broward
Business Journal of Central New York, The
Business Leader
Business Magazines
Business New Hampshire Magazine
Caribbean Business
Carolina Business
Cleveland Enterprise
Coast Business
College Boulevard News
Colorado Springs Business Journal
Connecticut Business Times
Daily Journal of Commerce
Daily Record
Denver Business
Detroiter, The
Evansville Business Journal
Excel
Fairfield County Business Journal
Florida Independent Accountant, The
Fresno Business & Industry News
Harford Business Ledger
In Technology
Inland Empire Business Journal
Inside the Black Hills
Journal of Business
Kansas Business News
Las Vegas Business Press
Long Beach Business Journal
Long Island
Metro Jackson Business News
Mississippi Business Journal
Nevada Business Journal
New Jersey Business
North Force
Northeast Pennsylvania Business Journal
Oakland Business Monthly
Orange County Business Journal
Orange County Metropolitan
Outlook
Property Guide, The
Rochester Business Journal
Rochester Business Magazine
Santa Rosa Business Journal
Savannah Business Journal
Small Business News—Cleveland
Small Business News-Akron
SRDS Media and Market Planner:
    Manufacturing & Processing Industries*
St. Louis Countian, The
St. Louis Daily Record
State Journal, The
Successful Business
Tarrant Business
Toledo Business Journal
Valley Business Magazine
Vermont Business
Washington CEO
Westchester County Business Journal
Western New York Magazine

## 21A. CAMPGROUNDS, RECREATIONAL
### NON-AUDITED
Woodall's Campground Management

## 21B. CAMPS
### NON-AUDITED
Camp Directors' Purchasing Guide
Camping Magazine

## 25. CEMETERY & MONUMENTS
### AUDITED
American Cemetery
Southern Cemetery

### NON-AUDITED
Catholic Cemetery
Cemetery Management
Cremationist of North America
MB News
Stone in America

## 26. CERAMICS
    (See also: Brick, Tile, Building Materi-
    als; China & Dinnerware; Glass.)

### AUDITED
American Ceramic Society Bulletin
Ceramic Industry

### NON-AUDITED
Ceramic Scope
Ceramic Source '92

## 27. CHAIN STORES
### AUDITED
Chain Store Age Executive
Retail Info Systems News

### NON-AUDITED
Retail Info Systems News Directory

## 28. CHEMICAL & CHEMICAL PROCESS INDUSTRIES
### AUDITED
Canadian Process Equipment & Control
    News
CEC
Chemical & Engineering News
Chemical Business
Chemical Engineering
Chemical Engineering Buyers' Guide
Chemical Engineering Progress
Chemical Equipment
Chemical Marketing Reporter
Chemical Processing
Chemical Week
CPI Purchasing
European Chemical News*
Happi
Hydrocarbon Processing*
Industrial Process Products & Technology
Powder and Bulk Engineering
Powder/Bulk Solids
Processing
Soap/Cosmetics/Chemical Specialties
Spray Technology & Marketing

### NON-AUDITED
Chemcyclopedia
Chemical Equipment Literature Review
Chemical Packaging Review
Chemical Times & Trends
Chemical Week Buyers' Guide
Chemist, The
Chemtech
Color Research and Application
CPI Purchasing Chemicals Yellow Pages
CPI Purchasing's 1992 Equipment Buyers
    Guide
CryoGas International
Gulf Coast PetroProcess Directory
INFORM (International News on Fats, Oils
    and Related Materials)
International Fiber Journal
Journal of the Electrochemical Society
McCutcheon's Emulsifiers and Detergents
OPD Chemical Buyers Directory
Perfumer and Flavorist
Powder/Bulk Solids' Guide & Directory
RadTech Report, The

### 28A. CHINA & DINNERWARE
    (See also: Ceramics; Giftware,
    Antiques, Art Goods, Decorative
    Accessories, Greeting Cards, Etc.;
    Glass; Home Furnishings.)

### AUDITED
China Glass & Tableware

### NON-AUDITED
China Glass & Tableware Red Book
    Directory Issue

### 31. CLOTHING & FURNISHING GOODS (MEN'S)
    (See also: Department & Specialty
    Stores.)

### AUDITED
Daily News Record

### NON-AUDITED
Made To Measure
MR
Needle's Eye

### 32. CLOTHING & FURNISHING GOODS (WOMEN'S)
    (See also: Corporate Network Buying
    Opportunities; Department & Specialty
    Stores; Fashion Accessories; Textiles
    & Knit Goods.)

### AUDITED
Accessories
Apparel Industry Magazine
Apparel News South
Bobbin Magazine
California Apparel News
Chicago Apparel News
Dallas Apparel News
Fashion Market Directory
New York Apparel News
Women's Wear Daily

### NON-AUDITED
Agent, The
Bridal Apparel News
Garment Manufacturer's Index
Outerwear

### 32B. COIN-OPERATED & VENDING MACHINES
### AUDITED
American Automatic Merchandiser
Vending Times

### NON-AUDITED
Sunbelt Vending & OCS

### 32C. COMPUTERS
### AUDITED
Advanced Imaging
AI Expert
Aldus Magazine
ASIC Technology & News
Automatic I.D. News
Automatic I.D. News Reference Guide &
    Directory
Byte
C Users Journal, The
Cadalyst

Cadence
Canadian Computer Reseller
Canadian Datasystems
CIO*
Communications of the ACM
Communications Week
CompuServe Magazine
Computer
Computer-Aided Engineering
Computer Buyer's Guide and Handbook*
Computer Dealer News
Computer Digest
Computer Graphics World
Computer Language
Computer Pictures
Computer Reseller News
Computer Shopper
Computer Technology Review
Computerland Magazine
Computers in Physics
Computerworld
Computing Canada
Data Based Advisor
Data Communications
Database Programming & Design
Datacenter Manager
Datamation
DBMS
Dec Professional
Design Management
DesignNET
Digital News
Digital Review
Dowline
Dr. Dobb's Journal Of Software Tools
Enterprise Systems Journal
Federal Computer Week*
Government Computer News
Home Office Computing
HP Professional
ID Systems
IEEE Network
IEEE Software
Info Canada
InformationWEEK
Infoworld
Inside DPMA
LAN Magazine
LAN Computing
LAN Technology
LAN Times
Lotus
MacUser
MacWeek
Macworld
Microtimes
Midrange Systems
Modern Office Technology*
MSM
Network Computing
Network World
Networking Management
News 3x/400
Office Systems '92*
Office Technology Management
Office, The*
PC Computing*
PC Magazine
PC Magazine (UK Edition)*
PC Publishing and Presentations
PC Sources
PC Week
PC World
Personal Publishing
Portable Office
Processor, The
Publish
Reseller Management
Service News
SI Business
Software Magazine
SunExpert Magazine
SunWorld
Systems & Network Integration
Systems Integration
Systems 3X/400
Technical Support
UNIX Review
Unix Today!
Unix World
Varbusiness
WordPerfect Magazine

### NON-AUDITED
ABUI Network News
Access to Wang
AFSM International
AI Magazine
APL News
Better Channel, A
Bulletin, The
CA-Insight
Case Trends
CASEnews
CD-ROM Professional
Chemputer Buyers' Guide
Circuit Cellar Ink
Color Publishing
COMDEX Preview & COMDEX Show Daily
Communication & Computer News
Computer Buying World
Computer Counsel
Computer Currents
Computer Graphics World Buyer's Guide
Computer Graphics World 1991 NCGA
    Show Dailies
Computer Graphics World 1992 ACM
    SIGGRAPH Show Dailies
Computer Hot Line
Computer Security Products Report
ComputerCraft
Computers in Libraries
Computertalk Directory of Medical
    Computer Systems
370/390 Data Base Management
Data Interchange
Data Sources
Database
Database Searcher
Datamation PC Products

Desktop Communications
Desktop Publisher
DG Review
Direct Access
Document Image Automation
EDI Business Partner Directory
EDI World
Electronic Library, The
Engineering with Computers
Expert Systems
Focus
G.I.S. World
Geo Info Systems
HP Chronicle
ICP Software Directory & Information
   Service
IEEE Computer Graphics and Applications
IEEE Design & Test of Computers
IEEE Expert
IEEE Micro
Inform
Information Executive
Information Today
Information World Review
Interact
Journal of Object-Oriented Programming
Journal of Systems Management
Journal of the American Society for
   Information Science
Library Software Review
M&T Network
Macguide Report
Machine Vision & Application
MAPICS The Magazine
Mathematical Intelligencer, The
Memory Card Systems & Designs
Microsoft Systems Journal
Midrange Computing
NCR Monthly
Neural Networks
NewMedia
Object Magazine
Online
Online Review
OR/MS Today
Oracle News
Pixel
Programmer's Journal
Puget Sound Computer User
Risc World
Smalltalk Report, The
Software Maintenance News
SRDS Media and Market Planner:
   Technology Markets*
St. Louis Computing
Sun Observer, The
Supercomputing Review
Symantec
TC Interface
UniForum Monthly
UniReview
Unisphere
Unisys Open Systems News
UNISYS World
VarIndustryProducts
VAX Professional
Wang in the News
Windows Magazine
Windows/DOS Developer's Journal
WordPerfect for Windows Magazine
Workstation
Workstation News
X Journal, The
Ziff-Davis Magazine Networks, The

### 33. CONFECTIONERY
**(See also: Baking; Food - Processing & Distribution.)**

AUDITED
Candy Industry
Candy Marketer
Candy Wholesaler
Confectioner
Manufacturing Confectioner

NON-AUDITED
Candy Buyers' Directory
Candy World, Illustrated
CW Daily News

**Instrumentation/Control Headquarters**

The 63-year old leader in providing technical information to over 88,000 audited engineers responsible for industrial and process control, instrumentation and data systems.

The industry's *only* product tabloid reaching over 117,000 buyers and specifiers — with audited buying responsibility. The most efficient medium for quantity and quality sales leads.

### 34. CONTROL & INSTRUMENTATION SYSTEMS
**(See also: Fluid Power Systems.)**

AUDITED
Control
Control Engineering
Controls & Systems
I&CS

IAN
Intech
Measurements & Control/Measurement &
   Control News
Mechanical Engineering*
NASA Tech Briefs*
Sensors

NON-AUDITED
Control Engineering Hardware & Software
   Guide for Industrial Control
IEEE Control Systems Magazine
ISA Directory of Instrumentation
Motion
Motion Control
Weighing & Measurement

### 34B. COSMETICS
AUDITED
Cosmetics & Toiletries
Drug & Cosmetic Industry

NON-AUDITED
Beauty Fashion
Cosmetic World
Journal of the Society of Cosmetic
   Chemists
Nailpro*

### 34C. DAIRY PRODUCTS (MILK, ICE CREAM, MILK PRODUCTS)
**(See also: Baking; Food - Processing & Distribution; Produce (Fruits & Vegetables).)**

AUDITED
Dairy Field
Dairy Foods

NON-AUDITED
Cheese Market News
Cheese Reporter, The
Dairy Foods Market Directory
Journal of Food Protection
National Dipper, The
Southeast Dairy Outlook

### 35A. DEPARTMENT & SPECIALTY STORES
**(See also: Corporate Network Buying Opportunities; Fashion Accessories; Infants, Children's & Teen Age Goods; Linens & Domestics; Textiles & Knit Goods.)**

AUDITED
Apparel Merchandising
College Store Executive
Daily News Record*
Hosiery and Underwear
Plus Sizes
Sportswear International
Stores

NON-AUDITED
College Store Journal, The
Retail Ink

### 35B. DISCOUNT MARKETING
AUDITED
Discount Merchandiser
Discount Store News
Mass Market Retailers

### 35C. DISPLAY
**(See also: Advertising & Marketing.)**

NON-AUDITED
Exhibit Builder
TradeShow & Exhibit Manager

### 35D. DRAPERIES & CURTAINS
AUDITED
Draperies & Window Coverings
Window Fashions Magazine

### 38. EDUCATIONAL
**(See also: Campgrounds, Recreational; Educational, Adult Training, Motivation & Development; Home Economics; School Administration.)**

AUDITED
Arts and Activities
Chronicle of Higher Education, The
Creative Classroom
Curriculum Product News
Education Week
Instructor*
Learning92
Library Journal
NEA Today
School Arts Magazine
School Library Journal
School Shop/Tech Directions
Teaching K-8
Technology & Learning*
Today's Catholic Teacher
Wilson Library Bulletin

NON-AUDITED
Academe
American Annals of the Deaf
American Biology Teacher
American Educator
American Journal Of Physics
American Libraries
American Mathematical Monthly, The
American Sociological Review
Arithmetic Teacher
Art Education
Arts in Psychotherapy, The
Athletic Training
AV Guide Newsletter
Booklist

Brown's Directories of Instructional
   Programs
Bulletin of the Medical Library Association
Business Education Forum
Career Development Quarterly
CASE Membership Directory
Catholic Library World
Chance
Change
Childhood Education
College & Research Libraries
College & Research Libraries News
College Composition and Communication
College English
College Mathematics Journal
Connection
Contemporary Psychology
Counseling and Values
Counselor Education & Supervision
Counselor, The
CTA Action
Currents
Curriculum Review
Day Care and Early Education
DECA Dimensions
Directory of Libraries and Media Centers
   Including Finding a Buyer's Guide
Directory of the Medical Library Association
Educational Leadership
Educational Record
Educational Researcher
Elementary School Guidance & Counseling
Emergency Librarian
English Journal
Exceptional Children
Exceptional Parent*
Faxon Librarians' Guide to Serials
Guidepost
Health Education
Higher Education Product Companion, The
Horn Book Guide, The
Horn Book Magazine, The
Independent School
Information Technology and Libraries
Intervention in School and Clinic
JOPERD Journal of Physical Education,
   Recreation and Dance, The
Journal for Research in Mathematics
   Education
Journal for Specialists in Group Work, The
Journal of Academic Librarianship, The
Journal of Addictions and Offender
   Counseling
Journal of American History, The
Journal of College Science Teaching
Journal of College Student Development
Journal of Counseling and Development
Journal of Education for Business
Journal of Employment Counseling
Journal of Humanistic Education &
   Development, The
Journal of Learning Disabilities
Journal of Multicultural Counseling &
   Development
Journal of Reading
Journal of the American Statistical
   Association
Journal of Youth Services in Libraries
Language Arts
Library Acquisitions: Practice & Theory
Library Administration & Management
Library Resources & Technical Services
Lingua Franca
Mathematics and Computer Education
Mathematics Teacher, The
Measurement & Evaluation in Counseling
   and Development
Media & Methods
MLA News
Museum News
New York Teacher, The
NHSA Journal
Notices of the American Mathematical
   Society
NSTA Reports
Official Museum Directory, The
Phi Delta Kappan
Physical Education Digest
Physics Teacher, The
Principal*
Public Libraries
Quantum
Reading Teacher, The
Reading Today
Rehabilitation Counseling Bulletin
Rocks & Minerals
RQ
Scholastic Pre-K Today
School Counselor, The
School Library Media Quarterly
Science Activities
Science and Children
Science Scope
Science Teacher, The
Social Education
Special Libraries
SpeciaList
Teacher Magazine
Teaching Exceptional Children
Technology Teacher, The
TIES Magazine
Vocational Education Journal
Volta Review, The
Women's Studies International Forum
Words on Tape

### 38A. EDUCATIONAL, ADULT TRAINING, MOTIVATION & DEVELOPMENT
**(See also: Educational.)**

AUDITED
CBT Directions
Training
Training & Development

NON-AUDITED
Adult Learning
Data Training
Technical & Skills Training
Training Expo-Lit

### 39. ELECTRICAL
**(See also: Appliances; Automotive, Automobiles, Tires, Batteries, Accessories, Service Stations, Garages; Electronic Engineering; Home Furnishings; Telecommunications Technology.)**

AUDITED
CEE News
EC&M
Electric Light & Power
Electrical Apparatus
Electrical Contractor
Electrical Distributor, The
Electrical Manufacturing Magazine
Electrical Wholesaling
Electrical World
ElectroMechanical Bench Reference
Public Power
Public Utilities Fortnightly
Rural Electrification
Transmission & Distribution
Utility & Telephone Fleets
Utility Fleet Management

NON-AUDITED
CEE News Fast Response Pac*
CEE News 1990 Buyers' Guide
EC&M Actionpack Postcards*
EC&M 1991 Electrical Products Yearbook
   Issue
EDI—Electrical Design and Installation
Electric Perspectives
Electrical Contractor's Electri-Card*
IAEI News
IEEE Electrical Insulation Magazine
New England Buyer's Guide
Northwest Electric Utility Directory
Northwest Public Power Bulletin
T&D 1993 Specifiers and Buyers Guide
TVPPA News
Utility Construction & Maintenance

### 40. ELECTRONIC ENGINEERING
**(See also: Appliances; Electrical; Radio, TV & Video.)**

AUDITED
Assembly*
Canadian Electronics
Circuits Assembly
Compliance Engineering
Computer Design
Connection Technology
Defense Electronics
Design News*
ECN, Electronic Component News
EDN
EE Product News
EEM/Electronic Engineers Master
Electronic Business
Electronic Buyers' News
Electronic Design
Electronic Engineering Times
Electronic News
Electronic Packaging and Production
Electronic Products
Electronic Products and Technology
Electronics
Electronics Purchasing
Embedded Systems Programming
EMC Technology
Evaluation Engineering-EE
Hybrid Circuit Technology
Journal of Electronic Defense
Laser Focus World
Laser Focus World Buyers Guide
Lasers & Optronics
Lasers & Optronics Buying Guide
Microcontamination
Microelectronics Manufacturing Technology
Microwave Journal
Microwave Product Digest
Microwaves & RF
Microwaves & RF Product Extra
Military & Aerospace Electronics
NASA Tech Briefs*
PCIM (Power Conversion & Intelligent
   Motion)
Photonics Spectra
Powertechnics
Printed Circuit Design
Printed Circuit Fabrication
R. F. Design
Semiconductor International
Semiconductor International Telephone/
   FAX & Source Guide
Signal
Solid State Technology
Spectrum Magazine, IEEE*
Surface Mount Technology
Test & Measurement World

NON-AUDITED
Applied Optics
Audio Amateur
Cahners European High-Tech Network
CircuiTree Magazine
D.A.T.A. Digest
db-The Sound Engineering Magazine
ECN Literature News
EDN Info Cards*
EE Product News Direct Response Cards*
Electronic Design Direct Action Cards*
Electronic Distribution Show Daily
Electronic Distribution Show Directory
Electronic Industry Telephone Directory
Electronics Management Postcard Deck*
Electronics Source Book, The
Elektor Electronics USA
EMC Test & Design
Engineering Contacts
EOS/ESD Technology

EP&P ISHM Show Daily
EP&P NEMDE Show Daily
EP&P NEPCON East Show Daily
EP&P NEPCON West Show Daily
EP&P Surface Mount International Show
  Daily
EPRI—Electronic Product Review
Glass Audio
Hybrid Circuit Technology Supplier Source
  Book
IC Master
IEEE Circuits and Devices
IEEE Computer Applications in Power
IEEE Grid, The
IEEE Signal Processing Magazine
Information Display
Item-Interference Technology Engineers
  Master
Journal of Materials Research
Journal of the IES
Logistics Spectrum
Mectronic Buyers Directory
MRS Bulletin
OE Reports
Optical Engineering
Optics & Photonics News
Personal Engineering & Instrumentation
  News
Printed Circuit Network
Soletter
Solid State Technology Buying Guide
Speaker Builder
Spectrum, IEEE Direct Request Postcards*
SRDS Media and Market Planner:
  Technology Markets*
Tech Minnesota
Update
VMEbus Systems
Who's Who In Electronics Sources

## 40A. EMPLOYMENT OPPORTUNITIES & RECRUITMENT

### AUDITED

Careers and the College Grad
Careers and the Engineer
Careers and the MBA
CPC Annual
Engineering Horizons
Graduating Engineer
IEEE Potentials
Minority Engineer
Minority MBA
US Black Engineer
Woman Engineer

### NON-AUDITED

Affirmative Action Register
Bent Of Tau Beta Pi, The
Black Careers
Black Employment & Education Magazine
Career Woman
Careers & the Disabled
Computerworld Campus Edition
Equal Opportunity
Experienced Professional
Field Guide to Computer Careers
High Technology Careers
Hispanic Engineer
Hispanic Times Magazine
Insurance & Financial Services Careers
Job Ready
Journal of Career Planning & Employment
MS/PHD
NSBE Magazine
P-D News, The
PBL Business Leader
Placement Manuals

## 40B. ENERGY APPLICATION & MANAGEMENT
(See also: Air Conditioning, Heating, Plumbing, Refrigeration, Sheet Metal & Ventilating; Metal,Metalworking & Machinery; Plant Maintenance, Repair & Operations; Power & Power Plants.)

### AUDITED

Energy User News

### NON-AUDITED

Alternative Energy Retailer
Cogeneration
Energy Focus
Independent Energy
Solar Today
World Cogeneration
World Energy Engineering Congress
  Product Showcase Magazine

## 41. ENGINEERING & CONSTRUCTION
(See also: Building; Government (Local, State & Federal) and Public Works; Power & Power Plants; Railroad; Stone Products, etc.; Water Supply & Sewage Disposal.)

### AUDITED

Aberdeen's Concrete Construction
Aberdeen's Magazine of Masonry
  Construction
Asphalt Contractor, The
Associated Construction Publications
California Builder & Engineer
Canadian Heavy Equipment Guide
Civil Engineering
Concrete International
Concrete Products
Construction
Construction Bulletin
Construction Digest
Construction Equipment
Construction Equipment Distribution
Construction News
Construction Specifier, The
Constructioneer
Constructor

Consulting/Specifying Engineer
Dixie Contractor
Engineering Digest
Engineering Dimensions
Engineering Times
ENR
Equipment Today
Equipment World
Excavating Contractor
Geotechnical Fabrics Report
Heavy Construction News
Highway & Heavy Construction
Land & Water
Louisiana Contractor
Machinery Trader
Michigan Contractor and Builder
Michigan Roads and Construction
Midwest Contractor
My Little Salesman Heavy Equipment
  Catalog
New England Construction
Outlook
Pacific Builder & Engineer
Pipeline & Utilities Construction
Rocky Mountain Construction
Texas Contractor
Western Builder

### NON-AUDITED

Aberdeen's Concrete Repair Digest
Aberdeen's Concrete SourceBook, World of
  Concrete '92 Edition
Aberdeen's Concrete Trader
Aberdeen's Pavement Maintenance
Aberdeen's Pavement Maintenance Trader
ACSM Bulletin
AGC Directory, The
American Consulting Engineer
ASEE Prism
Blue Book of Building & Construction, The
Builder & Contractor
Builder/Architect
Cartography and Geographic Information
  Systems
CFMA Building Profits
Civil Engineering News
Civil Engineering Product Postcard Service*
Concrete Masonry News
ConnStruction
Construction Bargaineer, The
Construction Equipment Guide
Construction News West
Construction Products Review
Consulting-Specifying Engineer: Specifier's
  Guide
Cost Engineering
Daily Construction Service San Francisco
  Edition
Daily Journal, The
Daily Pacific Builder
Demolition Age
Dodge Construction News
Dodge Construction News Green Sheet
Elevator World
ENR Construction Products Postcard
  Information Service*
Florida Engineering Society Journal
Foundation Contractor
Gateway Engineer
Intermountain Contractor
Lift Equipment
Midwest Engineer
Military Engineer, The
Modern Steel Construction
National Utility Contractor, The
Ohio Engineer
P.O.B.
Parking
Parking Professional, The
Parking Technology
PCI Journal
Photogrammetric Engineering & Remote
  Sensing
Pittsburgh Engineer
Professional Surveyor
Ready Mix
Rock & Dirt
Southwest Contractor Magazine
St. Louis Construction News & Review
Subcontractor, The
Surveying and Land Information Systems
Sweet's Catalog File
Transportation Builder
Wisconsin Professional Engineer, The
Wrecking & Salvage Journal

## 44. FARM IMPLEMENTS (GENERAL)

### AUDITED

Farm & Power Equipment Dealer
Farm Equipment

### NON-AUDITED

Farm Equipment Guide
Implement & Tractor
Northwest Farm Equipment Journal

## 44B. FASHION ACCESSORIES
(See also: Clothing & Furnishing Goods (Women's); Department & Specialty Stores.)

### NON-AUDITED

Accessories Resources

## 44C. FEED, GRAIN & MILLING
(See also: Food - Processing & Distribution.)

### AUDITED

Farm Store
Feed & Grain
Feed Management
Feedstuffs
Grain Age
Grain Journal

### NON-AUDITED

Commercial Review
Feed & Grain Times Showcase

Feed Additive Compendium
Feed Industry Red Book
Feedstuffs Reference Issue
Grain & Feed Marketing
Grain Guide/North American Grain
  Yearbook
Milling Directory/Buyer's Guide
Pacific Southwest Directory

## 45. FERTILIZER & AGRICULTURAL CHEMICALS

### AUDITED

Dealer Progress
Farm Chemicals
Solutions

### NON-AUDITED

Agronomy Journal
Custom Applicator
Farm Chemicals Handbook
Farm Chemicals International

## 46. FINANCIAL
(See also: Banking; Office Methods & Management.)

### AUDITED

Barron's-National Business and Financial
  Weekly*
Business Credit
Corporate Cashflow
Corporate Finance
Corporate Risk Management
Financial Analysts Journal
Financial Executive
Financial Planning
Financial Services Week
Financial World
Futures
Global Finance
Institutional Investor
Investment Dealers' Digest
Investor's Business Daily*
Management Accounting
MoneyWorld
Pension World
Pensions & Investments
Registered Representative
Research
Stanger's Investment Advisor
Trusts and Estates
Wall Street Computer Review

### NON-AUDITED

Benefits News Analysis
Bond Buyer, The
CEA News
CFP Today
Collector
Corporate Finance Sourcebook, The
Credit
Credit World
Diplomatic World Bulletin*
Directory of Trust Institutions
Equipment Leasing Today
Equities
Estate Planning
Faulkner & Gray's Tax Publication Group
Foundation News
Global Custodian
IBIS Review
International Economy, The
Investment & Tax Shelter Blue Book
Investment Reporter, The
Investor Guide
Journal of Cash Management
Perceptions Magazine
Secured Lender, The
Securities Product News
Securities Traders' Monthly
SRDS Media and Market Planner: Financial
  Markets*
Tax Adviser, The
Technical Analysis of Stocks &
  Commodities
Traders Magazine
Wall Street Transcript, The

## 47. FIRE PROTECTION

### AUDITED

Fire Chief
Fire Engineering
Firehouse
Firefighter's News
NFPA Journal

### NON-AUDITED

American Fire Journal
California Fire Service, The
Fire Protection Contractor
Industrial Fire World
NFPA Buyers' Guide
Sprinkler Age
Sprinkler Industry Directory

## 48. FISHING, COMMERCIAL
(See also: Food - Processing & Distribution.)

### AUDITED

Alaska Fisherman's Journal
Aquaculture Magazine
National Fisherman
Pacific Fishing

### NON-AUDITED

Commercial Fisheries News
Commercial Fisherman's Guide
Fisheries Product News
Fishermen's News, The

## 48A. FITNESS PROFESSIONAL

### AUDITED

Fitness Management

### NON-AUDITED

Fitness Management Source Book
Idea Today
Tanning Trends

## 48B. FLOOR COVERINGS
(See also: Furniture & Upholstery; Home Furnishings.)

### AUDITED

Floor Covering News/U.S.A.
Floor Covering Weekly
Flooring
Hardwood Floors
Installation & Cleaning Specialist
Western Floors

### NON-AUDITED

Eastern Floors

## 49. FLORISTS & FLORICULTURE
(See also: Landscape, Garden Supplies; Parks, Public; Seed & Nursery Trade.)

### AUDITED

Florist
Flowers&
Greenhouse Grower
Greenhouse Manager
Grower Talks

### NON-AUDITED

Floral & Nursery Times
Floral Mass Marketing
Florida Foliage
Florida Nurseryman
Florists' Review
Flower News
Greenhouse Product News
Link Magazine
Michigan Florist, The
SAF Magazine
Supermarket Floral

## 50. FOOD - PROCESSING & DISTRIBUTION
(See also: Baking; Bottling; Brewing, Distilling & Beverages; Confectionery; Dairy Products (Milk, Ice Cream, Milk Products); Feed, Grain & Milling; Fishing, Commercial; Grocery; Meats & Provisions; Poultry & Poultry Products; Produce (Fruits & Vegetables); Restaurants & Food Service.)

### AUDITED

Food & Beverage Marketing*
Food Business
Food Engineering
Food In Canada
Food Processing
Food Production/Management
Food Products & Equipment
Food Technology
Frozen Food Age
Frozen Food Digest
Health Foods Business
Natural Foods Merchandiser
Prepared Foods
Seafood Business
Seafood Leader
Snack Food
Whole Foods

### NON-AUDITED

Almanac of the Canning, Freezing,
  Preserving Industries, The
Cereal Foods World
Food Engineering Master
Food Product Design
Frozen Food Executive, The
Frozen Food Report
International Food Marketing & Technology
Organic Food Business News
Quick Frozen Foods Annual Processors
  Directory and Buyer's Guide
Refrigerated & Frozen Foods
Snack World
SRDS Media and Market Planner: Food &
  Food Service Industries*
Thomas Food Industry Register
Wisconsin Grocer, The

## 52. FUNERAL DIRECTORS

### AUDITED

American Funeral Director
Southern Funeral Director

### NON-AUDITED

American Blue Book of Funeral Directors
  Director, The
Morticians of the Southwest
Texas Director, The

## 53. FUR FARMING

### NON-AUDITED

Blue Book of Fur Farming
Fur Rancher

## 54. FURNITURE & UPHOLSTERY
(See also: Floor Coverings; Home Furnishings; Interior Design / Furnishings / Space Planning.)

### AUDITED

Accessory Merchandising
Cabinet Manufacturing & Fabricating
Cabinetmaker
FDM/Furniture Design & Manufacturing
Furniture Retailer
Furniture World
Furniture/Today
Hearth and Home
Upholstery Design & Manufacturing
Wood & Wood Products
Wood & Wood Products Red Book Buyer's
  Specification Guide
Wood Digest

## NON-AUDITED
Bedroom Magazine
BedTimes
Casual Living
Custom Woodworking Business
Digest for Home Furnishers
Market Preview
Modern Woodworking
Unfinished Furniture Industry
Wood Digest Showcase

## 55. GAS
(See also: Appliances.)

### AUDITED
American Gas
Butane-Propane News
Gas Industries
LP-Gas
Pipe Line Industry*
Pipeline & Gas Journal*

### NON-AUDITED
Brown's Directory of North American and
   International Gas Companies
Sooner LPG Times
Texas LP-Gas News
Western Gas News

## 57. GIFTWARE, ANTIQUES, ART GOODS, DECORATIVE ACCESSORIES, GREETING CARDS, ETC.
(See also: China & Dinnerware; Glass; Home Furnishings; Toys, Hobbies & Novelties.)

### AUDITED
Accessory Merchandising*
Art Business News
Art Business News Buyer's Guide
Decor
Gift & Stationery Business
Gift Reporter
Gifts & Decorative Accessories
Giftware News

### NON-AUDITED
Accessories Today
Chicago Market
Columbus Market
Decor—Sources
Gifts & Decorative Accessories Buyers
   Directory
Greetings Magazine
Party & Paper Retailer
Party & Paper Retailer Source Book
Picture Framing Magazine
San Francisco Giftcenter & JewelryMart
   Buyer's Guide
Seattle Gift Center News
Souvenirs &
Souvenirs & Novelties
225 Portfolio, The
Western Show News

## 57A. GLASS
(See also: Ceramics; China & Dinnerware; Giftware, Antiques, Art Goods, Decorative Accessories, Greeting Cards, Etc..)

### AUDITED
American Glass Review
Glass Digest
Glass Industry
Glass Industry Directory Issue
Glass Magazine
U. S. Glass, Metal and Glazing

### NON-AUDITED
American Glass Review Glass Factory
   Directory Issue
Architects' Guide to Glass, Metal & Glazing
Auto & Flat Glass Journal
Glass Art
International Glass/Metal Catalog
Professional Stained Glass
Stained Glass

## 59. GOLF
(See also: Sporting Goods.)

### AUDITED
Golf Course News
Golf Industry
Golf Pro Merchandiser
Golf Product News
Golf Shop Operations
Golf World*

### NON-AUDITED
Florida Green, The
Golf Course Management
Golf Index
Golf Property
Golf Scene Magazine
PGA Magazine
Southern Golf

## 60. GOVERNMENT (LOCAL, STATE & FEDERAL) AND PUBLIC WORKS
(See also: Engineering & Construction; Water Supply & Sewage Disposal.)

### AUDITED
American City & County
Better Roads
California Journal
City & State
Civic Public Works
Congressional Quarterly Weekly Report
Contract Management
Empire State Report
Federal Computer Week
Governing
Government Computer News*
Government Executive
Government Product News
Government Technology
Nation's Cities Weekly

National Journal
North Carolina Magazine
Public Works Magazine
Public Works Manual, The
Roads & Bridges
Roll Call

### NON-AUDITED
American City & County Directory of
   Administrative Services
APWA Reporter, The
California County
Campaign Magazine
Campaigns & Elections
Cities and Villages
City & State's 1992 Resource Guide
Colorado Municipalities
Federal Managers Quarterly, The
Government Product News Literature Guide
IMSA Journal
ITE Journal
Michigan Municipal Review
Minnesota Cities
Municipal Advocate, The
Municipal Index
New Jersey Municipalities
Pennsylvania Township News
Pennsylvanian
Planning
Quality Cities
State Government News
State Legislatures
Superintendent's Profile & Pocket
   Equipment Directory
Tennessee Public Works
Texas Town & City
Virginia Review
Virginia Town & City
Western City

## 61. GROCERY
(See also: Chain Stores; Food - Processing & Distribution; Tea, Coffee, Spices.)

### AUDITED
Canadian Grocer
Convenience Store Decisions
Convenience Store News
Fancy Food
Food Distribution Magazine FDM
Food People
Gourmet News
Gourmet Retailer, The
Grocery Marketing
Non-Foods Merchandising
Private Label
Private Label Product News
Progressive Grocer
Shelby Report of the Southeast, The
Shelby Report of the Southwest, The
Supermarket Business
Supermarket News

### NON-AUDITED
American Retailer
Arizona Grocer
Beverage Aisle
California Grocer
Cleveland Food Dealer, The
Convenience Store People
DBA Deli Bake Advocate Magazine
Deli News
Florida Food Dealer
Florida Grocer
Food Broker Quarterly
Food Industry Advisor
Food Industry Skirmisher, The
Food Merchants Advocate
Food Trade News
Food World
Foodsman
Griffin Report, The
Grocers & Merchants News, The
Grocers Journal of California
Grocery Distribution
IGA Grocergram
Intermountain Retailer
International Private Label Directory
Kansas City Grocer
Kansas City Grocer Annual Food Industry
   Directory
Kansas Food News
Louisiana Grocer, The
Michigan Food News
Military Grocer
Minnesota Grocer
Modern Grocer
Modern Grocer Edicion en Espanol
Montana Food Distributor
NAWGA Review
North Carolina Association of Convenience
   Stores Annual Directory
Oklahoma Grocers Journal
Private Label International
Southern Supermarketing
Specialty Food Merchandising
SRDS Media and Market Planner: Food &
   Food Service Industries*
Texas Food Industry Association Annual
   Directory
Texas Food Merchant
Tri-State Food News
Washington Food Dealer

## 62. HARDWARE
(See also: Farm Implements (General).)

### AUDITED
Do-It-Yourself Retailing
Hardware Age

### NON-AUDITED
Doors and Hardware
Hardware Trade
Western Retailer

## 63A. HOME ECONOMICS

### NON-AUDITED
AHEA Action

Journal of Home Economics
What's New in Home Economics

## 63B. HOME FURNISHINGS
(See also: Appliances; China & Dinnerware; Electrical; Floor Coverings; Furniture & Upholstery; Giftware, Antiques, Art Goods, Decorative Accessories, Greeting Cards, Etc.; Housewares; Interior Design / Furnishings / Space Planning; Lighting & Lighting Fixtures; Radio, TV & Video.)

### AUDITED
HFD

### NON-AUDITED
Home Textiles International
HomeMarket Trends

## 64. HORSE & RIDER SUPPLIES, APPAREL & EQUIPMENT

### AUDITED
Tack 'n Togs Book
Tack 'n Togs Merchandising

### NON-AUDITED
American Farriers Journal
International Saddlery and Apparel Journal

## 66. HOTELS, MOTELS, CLUBS & RESORTS
(See also: Restaurants & Food Service.)

### AUDITED
Club Industry
Club Management
Hotel & Motel Management
Hotel & Resort Industry
Hotelier
Hotels
Lodging
Lodging Hospitality
Ski Area Management

### NON-AUDITED
Bottomline, The
California Inntouch
Club Director
Florida Hotel & Motel Journal
Hotel & Motel Management Directory of
   Hotel/Motel Management Companies
Hotel & Motel Management Show Daily
Inn Touch
Resort Development & Operation
Resorts & Parks Purchasing Guide
SRDS Media and Market Planner: Travel &
   Tourism Industries*

## 67. HOUSEWARES
(See also: Appliances; Home Furnishings.)

### AUDITED
HomeWorld Business

## 68. HUMAN RESOURCES

### AUDITED
Business & Health
Employee Benefit News
HR Magazine
Human Resource Executive
Personnel Journal

### NON-AUDITED
EMA Journal, The
HRNews
Journal of Compensation and Benefits
Managed Healthcare News*
Personnel News, The
Profiles in Human Resource: 1993
Who's Who in HR

## 69. INDUSTRIAL

### AUDITED
Adhesives Age
Adhesives Age Directory

### NON-AUDITED
Filtration News
Industrial Machine Trader
Kentucky Manufacturer, The
Lubrication Engineering
Manufacturers' Mart
Mass High Tech
P/PM Technology
Product Data Quick Metro New York
SRDS Media and Market Planner:
   Manufacturing & Processing Industries*
Surplus Record, The
Transactions of the ASME
Underground Focus

## 69A. INDUSTRIAL AUTOMATION
(See also: Control & Instrumentation Systems; Mfg. Industries, Equip., Products & Systems; Materials Handling & Distribution; Plant Maintenance, Repair & Operations; Production Engineering; Robotics.)

### AUDITED
Controls & Systems*
Industrial Computing plus Programmable
   Controls
Industrial Engineering
Managing Automation
Manufacturing Systems
Production & Inventory Management

### NON-AUDITED
APICS—The Performance Advantage
Managing Automation Literature Review
SRDS Media and Market Planner:
   Manufacturing & Processing Industries*

## 69B. INDUSTRIAL DESIGN
(See also: Product Design Engineering.)

### AUDITED
ID International Design

## 70. INDUSTRIAL DISTRIBUTION
(See also: Materials Handling & Distribution; Physical Distribution.)

### AUDITED
Industrial Distribution
Today's Distributor

### NON-AUDITED
American Fastener Journal
PT Distributor, The
Southern Industrial Supplier

## 70A. INDUSTRIAL PURCHASING

### AUDITED
Purchasing Magazine

### NON-AUDITED
Business & Industry
C.T.F.A. Buyers Guide
Chicago Purchasor, The
E.C. Industrial Report
Industrial Purchasing Agent
Kansas City Commerce
Kentuckiana Purchasor, The
Mid-America Commerce & Industry
Midwest Purchasing Management
Purchasing Management
Southern Purchaser, The
SRDS Media and Market Planner:
   Manufacturing & Processing Industries*
St. Louis Purchaser

## 70B. INDUSTRIAL PURCHASING DIRECTORIES & CATALOGS

### AUDITED
Thomas Register of American
   Manufacturers
U. S. Industrial Directory

### NON-AUDITED
Alabama Manufacturers Register
Ameritech Industrial Purchasing Guides
California Manufacturers Register
Diesel & Gas Turbine Catalog Worldwide
   Engine Power Products
Federal Buyers Guide
Florida Manufacturers Register
Georgia Manufacturers Register
Hardhat
Hawaii Buyer's Guide
Illinois Manufacturers Directory
Illinois Services Directory
Indiana Manufacturers Directory
Interstate Manufacturers & Industrial
   Classified Directory & Buyers Guide
Iowa Manufacturers Register
Kentucky Manufacturers Register
Louisiana Manufacturers Register
Mac Rae's Blue Book
Macintosh Product Registry, The
Midwest Manufacturers & Industrial
   Classified Directory & Buyers Guide
Minnesota Manufacturers Register
Missouri Manufacturers Register
Municipal Government Purchasing Directory
Ohio Manufacturers Directory
Pennsylvania Manufacturers Register
Purchasing Magazine's Metals Sourcing
   Guide*
SRDS Media and Market Planner:
   Manufacturing & Processing Industries*
State and County Government Vendors
   Registry
Sweet's Catalog File
Texas Manufacturers Register
Thomas Regional Industrial Buying Guides
West Virginia Manufacturers Register
Wisconsin Manufacturers Register

## 70C. INFANTS, CHILDREN'S & TEEN AGE GOODS
(See also: Department & Specialty Stores; Textiles & Knit Goods.)

### AUDITED
Children's Business
Earnshaw's Infants, Girls & Boyswear
   Review
Juvenile Merchandising
Kids Fashions Magazine
Small World
Young Fashions Magazine

## 72. INSURANCE

### AUDITED
American Agent & Broker
Best's Review
Best's Review
Business Insurance
Canadian Insurance
Canadian Underwriter
Contingencies
Independent Agent
Insurance Journal
Insurance Sales
Life Insurance Selling
National Underwriter
National Underwriter
Professional Agent
Risk Management
Rough Notes
Standard, The
Underwriters' Report

### NON-AUDITED
Broker World
California Broker
Calunderwriter

Claims
Employee Benefit Plan Review
Employee Benefits Network
Florida Underwriter
Focus
GAMA News Journal
Health Insurance Underwriter
Indiana Underwriter, The
Insurance & Technology
Insurance Advocate
Insurance Field
Insurance Marketplace
Insurance Product News
Insurance Record, The
Insuranceweek
International Insurance Monitor
John Liner Review, The
Journal of Risk and Insurance, The
Journal of the American Society of CLU & ChFC
Journal of Workers Compensation, The
Life Association News
Lifetimes
LIMRA's MarketFacts
Louisiana Surplus Line Reporter
Mid America Insurance
Minnesota Insurance
Ohio Underwriter, The
Professional Insurance Agents
Resource
Risk & Benefits Journal, The
Risk & Insurance
Southern Insurance
SRDS Media and Market Planner: Financial Markets*
Texas Insuror
Texas Surplus Line Reporter
Today's Insurance Woman
Underwriter Printing & Publishing Co., The

## 73. INTERIOR DESIGN / FURNISHINGS / SPACE PLANNING
(See also: Floor Coverings; Furniture & Upholstery; Home Furnishings.)

### AUDITED
Contract Design
Designer Specifier
DesignSource
Display & Design Ideas
Facilities Design & Management
Interior Design
Interior Design Buyers Guide
Interiors
Restaurant/Hotel Design International
Today's Facility Manager
VM + SD

### NON-AUDITED
A & D Business
Art Sourcebook for Interior Designers
ASID Report
Burridge Index
Contract Wallcoverings Specifier's Guide
Design Times
Designers West/Designers World
Haut Decor
IDH—The Handbook
Interior Design Market
Retail Store Image
Sweet's Catalog File

## 73B. INTERNATIONAL TRADE

### AUDITED
Florida Shipper Magazine, The
Foreign Trade
Global Trade
International Business
Shipping Digest
World Trade

### NON-AUDITED
China Business Review, The
Official Export Guide, The
Shipping Digest's Handbook for International Trade
U.S. Custom House Guide

## 73C. INTIMATE APPAREL
(See also: Clothing & Furnishing Goods (Women's); Department & Specialty Stores.)

### AUDITED
Body Fashions/Intimate Apparel

### NON-AUDITED
Body Fashions/Intimate Apparel Directory
Contours U.S.A.
Intimate Fashion News
Market Maker Body Fashions/Intimate Apparel

## 74. JEWELRY & WATCHMAKING

### AUDITED
Accent
Jewelers' Circular-Keystone
Jewelers' Circular Keystone Jewelers' Directory
Modern Jeweler
National Jeweler

### NON-AUDITED
American Jewelry Manufacturer
Fashion Accessories
Horological Times
Jewelers' Circular-Keystone September Part II
JQ Magazine
Metalsmith
Northwestern Jeweler
Watch & Clock Review

## 75. JOURNALISM & PUBLISHING
(See also: Advertising & Marketing.)

### AUDITED
Circulation Management
Columbia Journalism Review
Editor & Publisher*
Folio: The Magazine for Magazine Management
Folio's Publishing News
Magazine Design & Production
Magazine Issues
MagazineWeek
Newspapers & Technology
Presstime
Publishers' Auxiliary
Publishing & Production Executive

### NON-AUDITED
Brilliant Ideas for Publishers
CPDA News
Directory Industry Buyers Guide
Editor & Publisher International Year Book, The*
Missouri Press News
Morgan Directory Reviews
NewsInc.
PNPA Press
Quill, The
St. Louis Journalism Review, The
Technical Communication
Writer, The

## 77. LANDSCAPE, GARDEN SUPPLIES
(See also: Florists & Floriculture; Parks, Public; Seed & Nursery Trade.)

### AUDITED
Power Equipment Trade
Garden Supply Retailer
Golf & SportsTurf
Grounds Maintenance
Landscape & Irrigation
Landscape Management
Lawn and Landscape Maintenance
Outdoor Power Equipment
Park and Grounds Management
Pro
Turf
Yard and Garden

### NON-AUDITED
California Landscape Magazine
Interior Landscape Industry
Interiorscape
Landscape Contractor, The
Northern Turf Management
Nursery Retailer
Servicing Dealer, The
Southern Turf Management
Turf
Turf Central
Turf News
Turf West
Western Turf Management

## 78. LAUNDRY & DRYCLEANING

### AUDITED
American Coin-Op
American Drycleaner
American Laundry Digest
Coin Launderer & Cleaner
Laundry News

### NON-AUDITED
Drycleaners News
Journal, The
National Clothesline, The
National Coin Operators Reporter
New Era Laundry & Cleaning Lines
Textile Rental
Western Cleaner & Launderer

## 79. LEATHER, BOOTS & SHOES

### AUDITED
Footwear News
Footwear Plus

### NON-AUDITED
American Shoemaking
Journal Of The American Leather Chemists Association
Leather Manufacturer, The
Shoe Service
Show Reporter
World Leather

## 80. LEGAL

### AUDITED
ABA Journal
American Lawyer
Barrister
California Lawyer
CBA Record
Chicago Lawyer
Law Practice Management
Lawyers Alert
Legal Management
Los Angeles Lawyer
National Law Journal, The
New Jersey Law Journal
New Jersey Lawyer
New York Law Journal
San Francisco Daily Journal
Student Lawyer
Trial

### NON-AUDITED
ACCA Docket
American Lawyer Media, L.P.
Arizona Attorney
California Paralegal Magazine
Champion, The
Chicago Daily Law Bulletin
Connecticut Law Tribune, The
DCBA Brief
Docket, The
Family Advocate
Florida Bar Journal, The
Florida Bar News, The
Fulton County Daily Report
Illinois Bar Journal
Kentucky Bench & Bar
Law Office Computing
Lawyers Weekly Publications
Legal Assistant Today
Legal Times
Manhattan Lawyer
Massachusetts Lawyers Weekly
National Paralegal Reporter
National Trial Lawyer
New Jersey Trial Lawyer
Ohio Lawyer
Practical Lawyer, The
Practical Real Estate Lawyer
Probate & Property
Recorder, The
Rhode Island Lawyers Weekly
Texas Bar Journal
Texas Lawyer
Trials Digest
Virginia Lawyers Weekly
Washington Lawyer, The
Wisconsin Lawyer

## 81. LIGHTING & LIGHTING FIXTURES
(See also: Appliances; Home Furnishings.)

### AUDITED
Architectural Lighting
Home Lighting & Accessories

### NON-AUDITED
Lighting Design & Application
Lighting Dimensions

## 81A. LINENS & DOMESTICS
(See also: Department & Specialty Stores.)

### AUDITED
Home Fashions Magazine
Home Textiles Today
LDB/Interior Textiles

### NON-AUDITED
Bedroom Magazine*

## 82. LOGGING & FOREST PRODUCTS MANUFACTURING MARKET
(See also: Building; Woodworking.)

### AUDITED
Arbor Age
Forest Industries
Logger and Lumberman, The
Northern Logger and Timber Processor, The
Panel World
Southern Loggin' Times
Timber Harvesting
Timber Processing
Tree Care Industry

### NON-AUDITED
Alabama Forests
American Christmas Tree Journal, The
Crossties
Directory of the Forest Products Industry
Forest Farmer
Forest Products Journal
Forests & People
Journal of Forestry
Loggers World
National Hardwood Magazine
Pacific Forests
Pallet Digest
Pallet Enterprise
Softwood Forest Products Buyer, The
Southern Lumberman
Timber Equipment Trader
Timber/West
Tree Farmer, The
Virginia Forests
Western Mills Today

## 83. LUGGAGE & LEATHER GOODS

### AUDITED
Travelware

### NON-AUDITED
Showcase
Travelware Resources
Travelware Suppliers

## 83A. MAINTENANCE

### AUDITED
Cleaning Management
Installation & Cleaning Specialist*
Maintenance Executive
Maintenance Sales News
Maintenance Supplies
Maintenance Technology*
Pest Control
Pest Control Technology
Sanitary Maintenance
Services

### NON-AUDITED
American School & Hospital Maintenance
Cleanfax Magazine
Environmental Management
Executive Housekeeping Today
Maintenance & Modernization Supervisor
Pest Management
Professional Cleaning Journal
Sanitary Show Daily

## 83B. MFG./INDUSTRIES, EQUIP., PRODUCTS & SYSTEMS
(See also: Plant Maintenance, Repair & Operations.)

### AUDITED
Cleanrooms
Industrial Equipment News
Industrial Product Bulletin
New Equipment Digest
New Equipment News
Plant, Canada's Industrial Newspaper*

### NON-AUDITED
American Industry
Compoundings
Industrial Literature Review
Industrial Product Bulletin Catalog Review
Job Shop Technology
Lit for Industry
Michigan Industry
Ned's Literature Digest
New Equipment Reporter
SRDS Media and Market Planner: Manufacturing & Processing Industries*

## 84. MARITIME, MARINE, SHIPBUILDING, REPAIR & OPERATING

### AUDITED
Marine Log
Maritime Reporter and Engineering News
Pacific Maritime Magazine, The
Waterways Journal
WorkBoat

### NON-AUDITED
Inland River Guide
Inland River Record
International Dredging Review
Marine Equipment Catalog
Marine Technology
MRAA Newsletter
Seaway Review
World Dredging, Mining & Construction

## 85. MATERIALS

### AUDITED
Advanced Composites
Advanced Materials & Processes

### NON-AUDITED
Journal of Materials Engineering
Journal of Materials Shaping Technology
SRDS Media and Market Planner: Manufacturing & Processing Industries*

## 85A. MATERIALS HANDLING & DISTRIBUTION
(See also: Industrial Distribution; Motor Trucks, & Accessories; Moving & Storage; Physical Distribution; Transportation, Traffic, Shipping & Shipping Room Supplies.)

### AUDITED
Material Handling Engineering
Material Handling Product News
Modern Materials Handling

### NON-AUDITED
Material Handling Wholesaler
Network
SRDS Media and Market Planner: Manufacturing & Processing Industries*

## 86. MEATS & PROVISIONS
(See also: Food - Processing & Distribution.)

### AUDITED
Meat & Poultry
Meat Processing
National Provisioner, The

### NON-AUDITED
Meat Business Magazine

## 88. METAL,METALWORKING & MACHINERY
(See also: Appliances; Energy Application & Management; Fluid Power Systems; Product Design Engineering.)

### AUDITED
Advanced Materials & Processes*
American Machinist
American Metal Market
Assembly
Canadian Machinery & Metalworking
Cutting Tool Engineering
Fabricator, The
Fastener Technology International
Finishers' Management
Foundry Management & Technology
Heat Treating
Industrial Heating
Iron & Steelmaker
Iron Age
Light Metal Age
Manufacturing Engineering
Metal Center News
Metal Center News' Metal Distribution
Metal Finishing
Metal Finishing Guidebook Directory
Metalworking Digest
Metlfax Magazine
Modern Applications News
Modern Casting
Modern Machine Shop
Modern Metals
Production
Products Finishing
Recycling Today
Scrap Processing and Recycling
33 Metal Producing
Tooling & Production

## NON-AUDITED
ASM News
Automatic Machining
Casting Source Directory
Die Casting Engineer
Die Casting Industry Buyers Guide
Die Casting Management
Diemaking, Stamping & EDMing
Directory Iron and Steel Plants
Ductile Iron News
Forging
Gear Technology
Industrial Laser Review
Industrial Market Place
International Journal of Powder Metallurgy
Iron and Steel Engineer
JOM
Metal Forming
Metal Statistics
Metalworking Digest Literature Review
Modern Machine Shop Guidebook To CNC
   Technology & Manufacturing Software
Nonferrous Edition of 33 Metal Producing
Ornamental and Miscellaneous Metal
   Fabricator
Plating & Surface Finishing
Powder Coating
Products Finishing Directory
Purchasing Magazine's Metals Sourcing
   Guide
Quality in Manufacturing
Sources
Springs
SRDS Media and Market Planner:
   Manufacturing & Processing Industries*
Stamping Quarterly
Tool & Die (TAD) Magazine
TPQ, The Tube & Pipe Quarterly

## 90. MILITARY & NAVAL (ACTIVE & INACTIVE SERVICE)

### AUDITED
Air Force Magazine*
Armed Forces Journal International
Army
Army Times Military Group
Defense News
Exchange & Commissary News
Military Market
National Defense
Sea Power

### NON-AUDITED
Almanac of Seapower, The
Amphibious Warfare Review
Army Aviation
Defense Housing
Hook, The
Interservice
Marine Corps Gazette
Military Club & Hospitality
Military Clubs & Recreation
Military Retailing Brand Name Directory
Military Retailing Directories
National Guard
Naval Engineers Journal
Officer, The
Shipmate
U. S. Naval Institute Proceedings

## 93. MINING (COAL, METAL & NON-METALLIC)
(See also: Stone Products, etc..)

### AUDITED
Coal
Coal Voice
Engineering & Mining Journal*
Mining Engineering

### NON-AUDITED
American Mining Congress Journal
California Mining Journal
Coal Journal, The
Coal People
Mine & Quarry Trader
Mines Magazine, The
Mining Record
Mining World News
Pay Dirt
Skillings' Mining Review
Western Mining Directory

## 95. MOTION, TALK, SOUND, COMMERCIAL PICTURES, ETC.

### AUDITED
AV Video
Boxoffice
Daily Variety
Hollywood Reporter, The
Location Update
Post
Variety

### NON-AUDITED
American Cinematographer
American Cinemeditor
Back Stage/SHOOT
Chicago Film & Video News
Cinematographers Product Designers,
   Costume Designers & Film Editors
Detroit Film & Video News
Faces International
Film Composers Guide
Film Directors: A Complete Guide
Film Journal, The
Film Producers, Studios, Agents & Casting
   Directors Guide
Film Writers Guide
In Motion
Location Production Guide
Locations
Markee
Official Southwest Talent Directory, The
Producer's Master-Guide, The
Reel Southeast
Screen

Special Effects & Stunts Guide
Television Directors Guide
Television Writers Guide

## 96. MOTOR TRUCKS, & ACCESSORIES
(See also: Automotive, Automobiles, Tires, Batteries, Accessories, Service Stations, Garages; Public Transportation & Mass Transit; Transportation, Traffic, Shipping & Shipping Room Supplies.)

### AUDITED
Commercial Carrier Journal
Diesel Equipment Superintendent
Fleet Equipment
Fleet Owner
Go West Magazine
Heavy Duty Trucking
Independent Trucker
Land Line
Modern Bulk Transporter
Motor Truck
My Little Salesman Truck Catalog
Over the Road
Overdrive
Owner Operator
P & D Magazine
Pro Trucker
Refrigerated Transporter
Road King
Southern Motor Cargo
Successful Dealer
Today's Trucking
Trailer/Body Builders
Transport Topics
Truck Paper, The
Truck Parts & Service
Truck Sales & Leasing
Trucker's News
Trucks Magazine

### NON-AUDITED
Allied Truck Publications
Caltrux
Downtime
Fastline Publications, Inc.
Florida Truck News
Hildy's Ford Blue Book
Illinois Truck News
Lifting & Transportation International
Mid-America Transporter
Milk and Liquid Food Transporter
Movin' Out
Nebraska Trucker
Ohio Government Directory
Private Carrier, The
Rand McNally Motor Carriers' Road Atlas
SCTA Hi Lights
Silver Book Chevrolet Dealer Guide For
   Special Bodies & Equipment
Tow Times
Transport Fleet News
Truck & Commerce
Truck News/Truck West
Truck Trader
TRUCKcat
Truckers/USA
Vehicle, The
Vocational Equipment Directory for GMC
   Truck Dealers

## 97. MOTORCYCLE & BICYCLE

### AUDITED
American Bicyclist
Bicycle Dealer Showcase
Dealernews
Motorcycle Industry Magazine
Motorcycle Product News
Motorcycle Product News Trade Directory

### NON-AUDITED
Bicycle Business Journal, The
Dealernews Buyers Guide

## 97A. MOVING & STORAGE

### NON-AUDITED
American Mover
Mini-Storage Messenger
Self Storage Journal

## 99. MUSIC & MUSIC TRADES

### AUDITED
Billboard
Music Trades Magazine
Music, Inc.
Musical Merchandise Review

### NON-AUDITED
Academy of Country Music Awards
   Program
American Music Teacher, The
American Organist, The
1992 Billboard's Country Music Sourcebook
1993 Billboard's International Buyer's Guide
1993 Billboard's International Recording
   Equipment & Studio Directory
Campus Activities Programming
Cavalcade of Acts and Attractions
Clavier
Diapason, The
DJ Times
Instrumentalist, The
International Musician
Music & Sound Retailer
Music Educators Journal
Pastoral Music
Piano Quarterly, The
Pollstar Magazine
Purchaser's Guide to the Music Industries
Southwestern Musician Combined with the
   Texas Music Educator
Symphony Magazine
1992 Tape/Disc Directory
1993 Billboard's International Talent &
   Touring Directory

## 100. NEWSLETTERS

### NON-AUDITED
Academic Physician
C + + Report, The
Freelance Writer's Report
Hair International News
Linked Ring Letter, The
Maturity Market Perspectives
Mid-Atlantic Archivist
Mini' App'les
NCOA News
Nordic Network
Priority Parenting
R.S. Wavelength
Radio Business Report
Recreation Advisor, The
Social Science Division Bulletin
Teaching Elementary Physical Education
Women With Wheels

## 101A. NUCLEAR SCIENCE & ENGINEERING

### NON-AUDITED
Journal of Nuclear Materials Management

## 102B. OCEAN SCIENCE & ENGINEERING

### AUDITED
Sea Technology

### NON-AUDITED
Sea Technology Buyers Guide/Directory

## 103. OFFICE EQUIPMENT & STATIONERY

### AUDITED
Business Machine Dealer
Geyer's Office Dealer
Office Dealer '92
Office Products Dealer
Office World News

### NON-AUDITED
Educational Dealer
Geyer's Who Makes It Special Issue
Marking Industry
Mid America Banner
NOMDA Spokesman
NOPA Membership Directory & Buyers'
   Guide
NOPA Official Convention Guide
Office Market Update
Western World

## 103A. OFFICE METHODS & MANAGEMENT
(See also: Business - Metro, State & Regional; Printing & Printing Processes; Reproduction - Inplant & Commercial.)

### AUDITED
Modern Office Technology
Office Systems '92
Office, The

### NON-AUDITED
Facilities Planning News
Forms and Label Purchasing
Journal of Court Reporting
mast Magazine
Secretary, The

## 104. OILS (VEGETABLE)

### NON-AUDITED
Soya Bluebook

## 107. PACKAGING (MFRS.) PAPERBOARD, WOOD BOXES & BARRELS

### AUDITED
Boxboard Containers
Converting Magazine
Package Printing and Converting
Paper, Film and Foil Converter
Paperboard Packaging

### NON-AUDITED
Board Converting News
International Paper Board Industry
Official Container Directory

## 107A. PACKAGING (USERS)

### AUDITED
Canadian Packaging
Food & Drug Packaging
Good Packaging Magazine
Packaging
Packaging Digest

### NON-AUDITED
1992 Blue Book: The Buyer's Guide for
   Pharmaceutical Packagers
Journal of Packaging Technology
Packaging Digest Machinery/Materials
   Guide

## 108. PAINT & WALLCOVERINGS, PAINTING & DECORATING

### AUDITED
American Paint & Coatings Journal
American Paint & Coatings Journal
   Convention Daily
American Painting Contractor
Decorating Retailer
Industrial Finishing
Journal of Coatings Technology
Modern Paint & Coatings
Paint & Coatings Industry
Painting & Wallcovering Contractor
Wall Paper, The
Wallcoverings, Windows & Interior Fashion

## NON-AUDITED
Decorating Retailer's Directory of the
   Wallcoverings Industry
Federation Year Book
Paint Red Book

## 109. PAPER

### AUDITED
American Papermaker
NPTA Management News
Paper Age
Paper Industry
PIMA Magazine
Pulp & Paper
Pulp & Paper Buyers Guide
Pulp & Paper Journal
Tappi Journal

### NON-AUDITED
American Paper Convention Daily
Fibre Market News
Lockwood-Post's Directory of the Pulp,
   Paper and Allied Trades
Mill Trade Journal's Recycling Markets
Paper Age Convention Daily
Paper Sales Convention News-NPTA
Paper Sales Convention News-API
Paper Stock Report, The
PIMA Catalog
PIMA Conference Daily
PIMA Membership Directory
Sources of Supply/Buyers Guide
TAPPI Journal Directory Issue
Walden's ABC Guide and Paper Production
   Yearbook
Walden's Paper Catalog

## 110. PARKS, PUBLIC
(See also: Landscape, Garden Supplies.)

### AUDITED
Parks & Recreation
Recreation Resources

## 111. PETROLEUM & OIL

### AUDITED
Energy Network, The
Hydrocarbon Processing
Journal of Petroleum Technology
JPT/SPE PetroMedia
National Petroleum News
Ocean Industry
Offshore Incorporating The Oilman
Oil & Gas Journal
Oil and Gas Investor
Oil, Gas & Petrochem Equipment
Petroleum Engineer International
Petroleum Management
Petroleum Marketer
Petroleum/C-Store Products
Pipe Line Industry
Pipeline & Gas Journal
Pipeline Digest
World Oil

### NON-AUDITED
AAPG Bulletin
AAPG Explorer
American Oil & Gas Reporter, The
Composite Catalog
Drilling Contractor
Fuel Reformulation
Geobyte
Geophysical Directory, The
Geophysics
Geophysics: The Leading Edge of
   Exploration
Gulf Coast Oil Directory
Gulf Coast Oil World
Houston Oil Directory
Independent Gasoline Marketing
International Petroleum Encyclopedia
International Pipe Line & Offshore
   Contractors Association Membership
   Directory
International Tradequip
Journal of Petroleum Marketing, The
Journal of Petroleum Technology Annual
   Review and Membership Directory
Michigan's Oil & Gas News
Midcontinent Oil World
Modern TruckStop News
NLGI Spokesman
Northeast Oil World
O & A Marketing News
Offshore Services & Equipment Directory
Oil Daily, The
Oil Marketer, The
Oil World Network
Pacific Coast Oil Directory
Pacific Oil World
Pacific/Mountain Oil Directory
Petroleum Independent
Petroleum Marketing Management
Southwest Oil World
SPE Drilling Engineering
SPE Formation Evaluation
SPE Production Engineering
SPE Reservoir Engineering
Tipro Reporter, The
Today's Refinery
Truckstop World
Well Servicing
Western Oil World

## 112. PETS

### AUDITED
Pet Age
Pet Business
Pet Dealer, The
Pet Product News
Pets/Supplies/Marketing

### NON-AUDITED
Groom & Board

Petfood Industry

## 113. PHOTOGRAPHIC

### AUDITED
Industrial Photography
Minilab Developments
Photo Business
Photo District News
Photo Electronic Imaging
Photo Lab Management
Photo Marketing
Photographic Processing
Photographic Trade News PTN
Professional Photographer
Rangefinder, The
Studio Photography

### NON-AUDITED
News Photographer
Photo/Design
Photopro
PTN/Photokina News
PTN/PMA Convention Daily
PTN/PP of a Convention Daily
Who's Who in Professional Photography

---

## Industrial Maintenance and Plant Operation

Serving the Plant Engineering, Maintenance and Operations Market for 50 years.

---

## 113B. PLANT MAINTENANCE, REPAIR & OPERATIONS
(See also: Energy Application & Management; Fluid Power Systems; Mfg./Industries, Equip., Products & Systems; Power Transmission Components & Systems.)

### AUDITED
AIPE Facilities
Engineer's Digest
Health Facilities Management
Industrial Maintenance and Plant Operation
Machinery & Equipment MRO
Maintenance Technology
Materials Performance
New Equipment Digest*
PEM Plant Engineering & Maintenance
Plant Engineering
Plant Services
Plant, Canada's Industrial Newspaper

### NON-AUDITED
SRDS Media and Market Planner: Manufacturing & Processing Industries*

## 114. PLASTICS & COMPOSITION PRODUCTS

### AUDITED
Aerospace Composites & Materials
Modern Plastics
Modern Plastics Encyclopedia
Plastic Trends
Plastics Compounding
Plastics Engineering
Plastics Machinery & Equipment
Plastics News
Plastics Technology
Plastics Technology Manufacturing Handbook and Buyers' Guide
Plastics World
SAMPE Journal

### NON-AUDITED
IAPD Magazine, The
Journal of Cellular Plastics
Plastics Compounding Redbook
Plastics Distributor and Fabricator Magazine, The
Plastics World 1992 Plastics Yellow Pages
PM/USA The Green Sheet
SRDS Media and Market Planner: Manufacturing & Processing Industries*

## 115A. POLICE, LAW ENFORCEMENT & PENOLOGY
(See also: Security.)

### AUDITED
Law and Order
Law Enforcement Technology
Police
Police Chief, The

### NON-AUDITED
Corrections Today
Law Enforcement Action Deck*
Law Enforcement Product News
Police And Security News
Sheriff

## 115B. POLLUTION CONTROL (AIR & WATER)
(See also: Energy Application & Management; Waste Management; Water Supply & Sewage Disposal.)

### AUDITED
Canadian Environmental Protection
Econ: The Environmental Magazine for Real Property Hazards
Environment Today
Environmental Protection
Environmental Waste Management
Hazardous Materials Control
HazMat World
Pollution Engineering

Pollution Equipment News
Pollution Equipment News Buyer's Guide

### NON-AUDITED
Air Pollution Control
American Environmental Laboratory
Archives of Environmental Contamination and Toxicology
Biocycle
Environment
Environmental Buyers' Guide
Environmental Careers
Environmental Lab
Environmental Management
Environmental Science & Technology
Journal of Environmental Health
Journal of the Air & Waste Management Association
Microbial Ecology
Resource Recycling
SRDS Media and Market Planner: Manufacturing & Processing Industries*
Waste Tech News

## 116. POULTRY & POULTRY PRODUCTS
(See also: Food - Processing & Distribution.)

### AUDITED
Broiler Industry
Egg Industry
Meat & Poultry*
Poultry Digest
Poultry Processing
Poultry Times, The
Turkey World

### NON-AUDITED
International Poultry Exhibition Guide
Poultry and Egg Marketing
Watt Poultry Yearbook: USA Edition, The
Who's Who in the Egg and Poultry Industries

## 117. POWER & POWER PLANTS
(See also: Engineering & Construction.)

### AUDITED
Diesel & Gas Turbine Worldwide
Electric Light & Power*
Gas Turbine World
Nuclear News
Nuclear Plant Journal
Power
Power Engineering
Turbo Machinery International

### NON-AUDITED
Electric Power International
Radioactivity & Radiochemistry

## 118. PRINTING & PRINTING PROCESSES
(See also: Office Methods & Management; Reproduction - Inplant & Commercial.)

### AUDITED
American Printer
Copy Magazine
Flexo
FormsMfg.
Graphic Arts Monthly
Graphic Arts Monthly Printing Industry Sourcebook 1991
Graphic Arts Product News
High Volume Printing
In-Plant Printer & Electronic Publisher
In-Plant Reproductions
Instant and Small Commercial Printer
Plan and Print
Pre-
Print-Equip News
Printing Impressions
Printing Journal
Quick Printing
Screen Printing Magazine
Southern Graphics
SPN
TypeWorld

### NON-AUDITED
American Ink Maker
Business Forms, Labels & Systems
Craftsmen Review, The
Dealer Communicator
FORM
Forms & Direct Mail Manufacturer's Marketplace
Graphic Arts Blue Book
Lewiscards*
New England Printer & Publisher
Post Gutenberg
Prepress Bulletin, The
Print & Graphics
Print Buyers Review
Printers Hot Line
Printing Impressions First of the Month News
Printing News East
Printing News Midwest
Standard Rate & Data Service Print Media Production Data*
Standard Rate & Data Service P M P D Bulletin*
Trade Show Times
Trade West
Typographer, The

## 119. PRODUCE (FRUITS & VEGETABLES)
(See also: Dairy Products (Milk, Ice Cream, Milk Products); Food - Processing & Distribution; Poultry & Poultry Products.)

### AUDITED
Packer, The
Produce News, The

### NON-AUDITED
Export Buyer's Guide

Fresh Trends Magazine
Produce Availability and Merchandising Guide
Produce Business
Produce Merchandising
Produce Packaging Digest 1991

## 120. PRODUCT DESIGN ENGINEERING
(See also: Fluid Power Systems; Industrial Design; Metal,Metalworking & Machinery; Power Transmission Components & Systems.)

### AUDITED
Agricultural Engineering
Appliance*
Appliance Manufacturer*
Design Engineering
Design News
Designfax
Diesel Progress
Hydraulics & Pneumatics
Machine Design
Materials Engineering
Materials Selector, The
Mechanical Engineering
NASA Tech Briefs
OEM Off-Highway
Plastics Design Forum
Power Transmission Design
Product Design & Development
Sound and Vibration

### NON-AUDITED
ASME News
Casting Design & Application
Design News Information Card Packs*
Fluid Power Handbook & Directory
Innovation

## 120B. PROFESSIONAL ASSOCIATION MANAGEMENT
(See also: Business; Business - Metro, State & Regional.)

### AUDITED
Association Management

### NON-AUDITED
Association Trends
Executive Update
Forum
U.S. Association Executive
Who's Who in Association Management

## 121. PUBLIC TRANSPORTATION & MASS TRANSIT
(See also: Automotive, Automobiles, Tires, Batteries, Accessories, Service Stations, Garages; Motor Trucks, & Accessories.)

### AUDITED
Mass Transit
Metro Magazine

### NON-AUDITED
Bus Operator
Bus Ride
Bus Tours Magazine
National Bus Trader
National School Bus Report
Passenger Transport
School Transportation News

## 121A. QUALITY ASSURANCE

### AUDITED
Quality
Quality Progress

### NON-AUDITED
PIQuality

## 122. RADIO, TV & VIDEO
(See also: Appliances; Electrical; Electronic Engineering; Home Furnishings.)

### AUDITED
AudioVideo International
AV Video*
AVC/Presentation Development&Delivery
Broadcast Engineering
Broadcast Engineering's Equipment Reference Manual
Broadcasting*
Cable World
CableVision
CED
Communications Technology
Dealerscope Merchandising
Electronic Media
Installation News
Millimeter
Mix
Multichannel News
Presentation Products Magazine
Private Cable Magazine
Pro Sound News
R E P
Rental Dealer News
Sound & Communications
Sound & Video Contractor, S&VC
Studio Sound & Broadcast Engineering
Television Broadcast
TV Technology
Twice
Via Satellite
Video Business
Video Digest
Video Insider
Video Software
Video Store
Video Systems
Video Times
Videography

### NON-AUDITED
Buying Group News
Cable & Station Coverage Atlas

CableFAX
CES Daily News
CES Trade News Daily
College Broadcaster
Current
Electronic Servicing and Technology
Emmy
In Motion*
International Cable
InView
LPTV Report, The
Mobile Electronics Specialist
Narda News
NATPE Programmer's Guide
Official Video Directory & Buyer's Guide
Photofact Annual Index
Producers Quarterly
Professional Electronics
Professional Electronics Yearbook
Pulse of Radio, The
Radio & Records
Radio Only
Radio World
Religious Broadcasting
Retailing News
RTNDA Communicator
SMPTE Journal
Sound Management
Spec-Com Journal, The
TV Executive Daily
TV Executive, The
Twice Today
Video Business Show Daily
Video Extra
Video Retailer Showcase
Video Vision

## 124. RAILROAD
(See also: Engineering & Construction; Public Transportation & Mass Transit; Transportation, Traffic, Shipping & Shipping Room Supplies.)

### AUDITED
Pocket List of Railroad Officials
Progressive Railroading
Railway Age
Railway Track & Structures

### NON-AUDITED
Track Yearbook

## 126. RELIGIOUS

### NON-AUDITED
Catechist
Church Management: The Clergy Journal
Homiletic and Pastoral Review, The
Official Catholic Directory, The
Priest, The

## 126A. RENTAL & LEASING EQUIPMENT

### AUDITED
Rental
Rental Equipment Register
Rental Management

### NON-AUDITED
Progressive Rentals
Rental Equipment Register California Rental Association Show Daily
Rental Equipment Register Show Daily
Rental Showcase

## 126B. REPRODUCTION - INPLANT & COMMERCIAL
(See also: Office Methods & Management; Printing & Printing Processes.)

### NON-AUDITED
AIIM Show Program, The
Conference Daily, The
Information Management Sourcebook
International Imaging Source Book

## 127. RESTAURANTS & FOOD SERVICE
(See also: Hotels, Motels, Clubs & Resorts; Institutions; School Administration.)

### AUDITED
Airline, Ship & Catering Onboard Services Magazine
Canadian Hotel & Restaurant
Catering Today
Chef Institutional
Food Arts
Food Industry News
Food Management
Foodservice and Hospitality
FoodService Director
Foodservice Distributor, The
Foodservice Equipment & Supplies Specialist
Foodservice Product News
Institutional Distribution
Journal of the American Dietetic Association
L'Hospitalite*
La Carta
Nation's Restaurant News
NightClub & Bar
Pizza & Pasta
Pizza Today
Restaurant Business
Restaurant Hospitality
Restaurants & Institutions
School Food Service Journal
Special Events
Sunbelt Foodservice

## continued

**NON-AUDITED**
Asia Pacific Foodservice Product News
College Union & On-Campus Hospitality
Cooking for Profit
Culinary Trends
Empire State Food Service News
Equipment Show Daily
FEDA News & Views
Florida Restaurateur, The
Food & Service
Food—Service East
Hospitality Management
Mid-Atlantic FoodService News
Midwest Foodservice News
Modern Food Service News/Restaurant
   Exchange News
Northeast Foodservice Buyer's Guide
Restaurant Digest
Restaurant News of the Rockies
Restaurant Show Daily—CRA
Restaurant Show Daily—NRA
Server Pennsylvania, The
Southeast Food Service News
Spice
SRDS Media and Market Planner: Food &
   Food Service Industries*
Tennessee Restaurateur
Wisconsin Restaurateur, The
Yankee Food Service

**128. ROBOTICS**
**(See also: Metal,Metalworking &
   Machinery; Science, Research &
   Development.)**

**NON-AUDITED**
Robotics World

**129. ROOFING**
**(See also: Air Conditioning, Heating,
   Plumbing, Refrigeration, Sheet Metal &
   Ventilating; Building.)**

**AUDITED**
Contractors Guide
Professional Roofing
R S I
Roofer Magazine

**NON-AUDITED**
Florida Forum
Handbook of Commercial Roofing Systems
NRCA Convention Program Book
NRCA Membership Directory
RSI Extra
Western Roofing/Insulation/Siding

**130. RUBBER**
**(See also: Automotive, Automobiles,
   Tires, Batteries, Accessories, Service
   Stations, Garages.)**

**AUDITED**
Elastomerics
Rubber & Plastics News
Rubber World

**NON-AUDITED**
Elastomerics Rubber Red Book
Rubber Chemistry and Technology
Rubber World Blue Book

**131. SAFETY, ACCIDENT PREVENTION**

**AUDITED**
Industrial Hygiene News
Industrial Safety & Hygiene News
Occupational Hazards
Occupational Health & Safety
Occupational Health & Safety Purchasing
   SourceBook
OHS Canada
Professional Safety

**NON-AUDITED**
Best's Safety Directory
Chemical Safety
Industrial Hygiene News Buyer's Guide
9-1-1 Magazine
Safety & Health

**131A. SALES MANAGEMENT**

**AUDITED**
Personal Selling Power

**NON-AUDITED**
Agency Sales Magazine

**132. SCHOOL ADMINISTRATION**
**(See also: Educational.)**

**AUDITED**
American School Board Journal
American School & University Magazine
Athletic Business
Athletic Management
Electronic Learning
Executive Educator, The
School Administrator, The

School And College
School Bus Fleet
School Business Affairs
T.H.E. Journal
Technology & Learning

**NON-AUDITED**
Beckley-Cardy Quarterly, The
California School Boards Journal
Child Care Information Exchange
Community, Technical, and Junior College
   Journal
Early Childhood News
Momentum
NASSP Bulletin
Principal
Swimming Technique
Thrust for Educational Leadership

**132A. SCIENCE, RESEARCH &
   DEVELOPMENT**

**AUDITED**
American Biotechnology Laboratory
American Laboratory
American Scientist
Analytical Chemistry
Journal of NIH Research
Lab Animal
Laboratory Equipment
Laboratory Product News
LC:GC
Materials Evaluation
Nature
Physics Today
Research & Development
Science
Science News*
Scientific Computing & Automation
Spectroscopy
Test Engineering & Management
Trends in Biochemical Sciences

**NON-AUDITED**
Academic Digest
ACS Laboratory Guide
American Antiquity
American Chemical Society Research
   Journals
American Industrial Hygiene Association
   Journal
American Laboratory Buyers' Guide and
   International Laboratory Buyers' Guide
American Laboratory News
Analytical Biochemistry
Applied and Environmental Microbiology
Applied Occupational and Environmental
   Hygiene
Applied Spectroscopy
ASM News
ASTM SN
Bio/Technology
Biochemistry
Bioscience
Biotech Buyers' Guide
Biotechnology Week
Cell
Chemical Reviews
Cytokine
Einstein Quarterly, The
EMSA Bulletin
EOS
FASEB Journal, The
Fundamental and Applied Toxicology
Geology
Health Physics
Infection and Immunity
Inorganic Chemistry
Intelligent Instruments & Computers
International Journal of Systematic
   Bacteriology
Journal of Agricultural & Food Chemistry
Journal of Analytical Toxicology
Journal of AOAC International
Journal of Biological Chemistry, The
Journal of Chemical Education
Journal of Chemical Information &
   Computer Sciences
Journal of Chromatographic Science
Journal of Medicinal Chemistry
Journal of Membrane Biology
Journal of Organic Chemistry
Journal of Physical Chemistry
Journal of the American Chemical Society
Journal of Vacuum Science and
   Technology
Journal of Virology
Laboratory Digest
Macromolecules
Magnetic Resonance in Medicine
Management Science
Materials Characterization
Microbiological Reviews
Microscope Book, The
Neuron
Noise Control Engineering Journal
ORSA/TIMS Bulletin
Powder Diffraction
Proceedings of the Society for Experimental
   Biology and Medicine
Review of Scientific Instruments, The
Scanning
Scientist, The
Superconductor Industry
Toxicology and Applied Pharmacology
Weatherwise

**132B. SECURITY**

**AUDITED**
Access Control
Locksmith Ledger International
Locksmith Ledger International Directory
National Locksmith, The
Security
Security Dealer
Security Distributing & Marketing
Security Management
Security Sales

**NON-AUDITED**
CCTV Applications & Technology Magazine
Controls & Security Systems Catalog
Keynotes
Security Industry Buyers Guide

**133. SEED & NURSERY TRADE**
**(See also: Florists & Floriculture;
   Landscape, Garden Supplies.)**

**AUDITED**
Seed Trade News
Seed World

**NON-AUDITED**
American Nurseryman
Nursery Business Grower
Nursery Manager
Nursery News
Ornamental Outlook
Pacific Coast Nurseryman and Garden
   Supply Dealer
Plantfinder
Seed Industry Journal
Seed Trade Buyers Guide
Southern Nursery Digest

**134. SELLING & SALESMANSHIP**
**(See also: Business - Metro, State &
   Regional.)**

**NON-AUDITED**
Money Making Opportunities
Spare Time

**135. SHOPPING CENTERS**

**AUDITED**
Monitor
Shopping Center World
Shopping Centers Today

**NON-AUDITED**
Directory of Major Malls
Shopping Center Digest
Shopping Centers Today Convention Show
   Daily

**137. SPORTING GOODS**
**(See also: Golf.)**

**AUDITED**
American Firearms Industry
American Firearms Industry S.H.O.T. Show
   Issue
Archery Business
Fishing Tackle Retailer
Fishing Tackle Trade News
Outdoor Retailer
Scholastic Coach*
Shooting Industry, The
Shooting Sports Retailer
Ski Business
Ski Tech
Skiing Trade News
Snowmobile Business
Sporting Goods Business
Sporting Goods Dealer, The
Sports Trend
SportStyle
Tennis Buyers Guide
Tennis Industry

**NON-AUDITED**
Action Sports Retailer
Army-Navy Store and Outdoor
   Merchandiser
Bowlers Journal
Bowling and Billiard Buyers Guide
Bowling Proprietor, The
Fitness Equipment Dealer
Lifestyle Apparel News
Official Sports Product Guide & Super
   Show Directory
Stringer's Assistant, The
Swim Fashion Quarterly
Team Licensing Business Magazine
Team Sports Business
Wear Magazine

**139. STONE PRODUCTS, ETC.**
**(See also: Brick, Tile, Building Materi-
   als; Engineering & Construction; Mining
   (Coal, Metal & Non-Metallic).)**

**AUDITED**
Pit & Quarry
Rock Products

**NON-AUDITED**
Dimensional Stone
Stone Review
Stone World

**140. SUGAR & SUGAR CROPS**

**AUDITED**
Sugar y Azucar

**NON-AUDITED**
Sugar y Azucar Yearbook

**140A. SWIMMING POOLS**

**AUDITED**
Aqua
Aquatics International
Pool & Spa News
Swimming Pool/Spa Age
Swimming Pool/Spa Age Product Directory

**NON-AUDITED**
Aqua Industry Guide
Pool & Spa News Source Book

**141. TEA, COFFEE, SPICES**
**(See also: Food - Processing & Dis-
   tribution; Grocery.)**

**AUDITED**
Tea and Coffee Trade Journal
World Coffee & Tea

**142. TELECOMMUNICATIONS
   TECHNOLOGY**
**(See also: Radio, TV & Video.)**

**AUDITED**
Business Communications Review
Cellular Business
Cellular Marketing
Communications
Communications News
Communications Week*
CommunicationsWeek International*
Data Communications*
Fiberoptic Product News
4th Media Journal, The
IEEE Communications Magazine
Lightwave
Mobile Product News
Mobile Radio Technology
Network World*
Outside Plant Magazine
Procomm Enterprises Magazine
RCR—Radio Communications Report
Satellite Communications
Telecommunications
Teleconnect
Telemarketing
Telephone Engineer & Management
Telephony
Telephony's Buyers Guide
Voice Processing Magazine

**NON-AUDITED**
APCO Bulletin
Audiotex Directory & Buyer's Guide
Business Radio
Fiber Optics Magazine
Fiber Optics Sourcebook, The
IEEE LTS
Infotext
OPASTCO Roundtable
Payphone Exchange/O+ Magazine
Phone+
Public Communications
Radio Resource
RCR's Cellular Handbook
Rural Telecommunications
Satellite Directory, The
SRDS Media and Market Planner:
   Technology Markets*
Telecom Gear
Telecom Trader
Teleconference Magazine
Telephone Engineer & Management
   Directory
Telephone Industry Directory & Sourcebook
TeleProfessional
Telocator

**143. TEXTILES & KNIT GOODS**

**AUDITED**
America's Textiles International
American Dyestuff Reporter
Carpet & Rug Industry
Industrial Fabric Products Review
Industrial Fabric Products Review Buyer's
   Guide
Nonwovens Industry
Press Magazine, The
Printwear Magazine
Textile Chemist and Colorist
Textile World

**NON-AUDITED**
Dalton Carpet Journal
Davison's Textile Blue Book
Davison's Textile Buyers Guide
Hosiery News
IAWCM Bulletin
Impressions
Knitovations
Knitting Times
Screenplay
Southern Textile News
Stitches Magazine
T-Shirt Retailer & Screen Printer
Textile Manufacturing

**145. TOBACCO**

**AUDITED**
Tobacco International Magazine
Tobacco Reporter
United States Distribution Journal

**NON-AUDITED**
Retail Tobacconist
Smokeshop
Tobacco World Illustrated

**147. TOYS, HOBBIES & NOVELTIES**
**(See also: Chain Stores; Giftware, An-
   tiques, Art Goods, Decorative Accessories, Greeting Cards, Etc..)**

**AUDITED**
Craftrends
Creative Products News
Playthings
Profitable Craft Merchandising
Toy & Hobby World
Toy Book, The

**NON-AUDITED**
Craft & Needlework Age
Hobby Merchandiser
Miniatures Dealer
Model Retailer
Playthings Who Makes It Special Issue
Selling Christmas Decorations
Selling Halloween
Toy & Hobby World Show Daily

## 147A. TRAILERS & ACCESSORIES

### AUDITED
RV Business
RV News
RV Trade Digest

## 148. TRANSPORTATION, TRAFFIC, SHIPPING & SHIPPING ROOM SUPPLIES
(See also: International Trade; Maritime, Marine, Shipbuilding, Repair & Operating; Materials Handling & Distribution; Motor Trucks, & Accessories; Moving & Storage; Physical Distribution; Public Transportation & Mass Transit; Railroad.)

### AUDITED
Air Cargo News
Air Cargo World
American Shipper
Container News
Distribution
Inbound Logistics
Jet Cargo News
Journal of Commerce and Commercial, The*
Pacific Shipper
Traffic Management
Traffic World
Transportation & Distribution

### NON-AUDITED
ACCA Express
Airport Press
CNS Focus
Coast Marine & Transportation Directory
Daily Shipping News
Defense Transportation Journal
Hereford's Americas
Journal of Commerce Transportation Telephone Tickler, The
Journal of Commerce, The International Edition*
OAG Air Cargo Guide
Official Directory of Industrial and Commercial Traffic Executives, The
Official Motor Carrier Directory
Official Motor Freight Guide
Official Shippers Guide, The
Port of Baltimore
Professional Broker
Purchasing Magazine's Transportation Sourcing Guide
"QC" Quick Caller Air Cargo Directories
Seaports of the Western Hemisphere
Southern Shipper
Via Port of New York-New Jersey
Weekly Commercial News
WWS/World Wide Shipping
World Wide Shipping Guide

## 149A. TRAVEL, BUSINESS CONVENTIONS & MEETINGS
(See also: Travel, Retail.)

### AUDITED
Business Travel Management
Business Travel News
Corporate & Incentive Travel
Corporate Meetings & Incentives
Corporate Travel
Incentive*
Medical Meetings
Meeting News
Meetings & Conventions
New Jersey Metro Meeting Planning Guide
Sales & Marketing Management*
Successful Meetings

### NON-AUDITED
ABC Corporate Rate Hotel Directory
ABC Preferred Rate & Availability Directory
Association Executive, The
Association Meetings
Byways
Convene
Conventionsouth
Courier
Destinations
Exhibit Review
Florida Official Meeting Planners Guide
Group Travel Leader, The
Health Care Pocket Survival Guide
Insurance Conference Planner
Mature Group Traveler
Meeting Manager, The
Meeting Planners Guidebook
Motorcoach Marketer, The
1992-1993 MPI Membership Directory
Nashville Travel Guide
Official Meeting Facilities Guide
Official Meeting Facilities Guide—Europe
Pocket Survival Guide
Professional Meeting Planners Guide
Religious Conference Manager
SRDS Media and Market Planner: Travel & Tourism Industries*
Tennessee Travel Guide
Texas Tour & Meeting Guide
Trade Show Times Chicago
Tradeshow & Exhibit Manager Directory
Tradeshow Week
Tradeshow Week Data Book
Tradeshow/Convention Guide
Travel Management Convention Daily
Western Association News

## 149B. TRAVEL, RETAIL
(See also: Travel, Business Conventions & Meetings.)

### AUDITED
ASTA Agency Management
ASU Travel Guide
Canadian Travel Press Weekly
Canadian Traveller
Discover Hawaii Sales Planner
Honeymoon Destinations

Hotel and Travel Index
JAX Fax Travel Marketing Magazine
OAG Business Travel Planner
OAG Travel Planner Hotel & Motel RedBook (European Edition)
OAG Travel Planner Hotel & Motel RedBook (Pacific Asia Edition)
Recommend Magazine
Tour & Travel News
Travel Agent Magazine
Travel Courier
Travel Trade
Travel Trade Personnel Sales Guide
Travel Weekly
Travel World News
TravelAge East
TravelAge MidAmerica
TravelAge West

### NON-AUDITED
Air Charter Guide
Airair Interline Magazine
ASTA Congress Daily
Caribbean Gold Book
Consolidated Tour Manual
Cruise and Vacation Views
Cruise Trade
Latin Travel Review
OAG Cruise & Shipline Guide-Worldwide Edition
OAG Desktop Flight Guide North American Edition
OAG Desktop Flight Guide-Worldwide Edition
Official Handbook of Travel Brochures
Official Hotel Guide
Official Railway Guide Travel Edition
Official Tour & Travel Reference Manual
Official Tour Directory
Pocket Flight Guide
Pocket Flight Guide
Pocket Flight Guide
Pocket Flight Guide
Pocket Flight Guide
Southeast Travel Professional
Specialty Travel Index
SRDS Media and Market Planner: Travel & Tourism Industries*
TIA International Travel News Directory
Tour & Travel Marketplace*
Tour Trade
Travel Counselor
Travel Digest
Travel Industry Personnel Directory
Travel New England
Travel Planning Guide
Woodside Annual Directory of Hotel Corporate Rates

## 152. VETERINARY

### AUDITED
Agri-Practice
American Journal of Veterinary Research
Compendium on Continuing Education for the Practicing Veterinarian
DVM
Equine Practice
Equine Veterinary Journal
Journal of the AVMA
Large Animal Veterinarian
Pet Veterinarian
Veterinary Economics
Veterinary Forum
Veterinary Medicine
Veterinary Product News
Veterinary Technician

### NON-AUDITED
California Veterinarian
Canine Practice
Equine Athlete, The
Feline Practice
Journal of Equine Veterinary Science
Journal of the American Animal Hospital Association
New Methods
Pulse
Seminars in Avian & Exotic Pet Medicine
Swine Practitioner
Texas Veterinary Medical Journal
Trends
Veterinary Practice STAFF
Wildlife Rehabilitation Today Magazine

## 154. WASTE MANAGEMENT
(See also: Energy Application & Management; Pollution Control (Air & Water); Water Supply & Sewage Disposal.)

### AUDITED
Environmental Waste Management*
Pollution Engineering*
Recycling Today
Waste Age
World Wastes, The Management of

### NON-AUDITED
Environmental Careers Bulletin
MSW Management
Solid Waste & Power
Waste Business West
Waste Management

## 155. WATER SUPPLY & SEWAGE DISPOSAL
(See also: Engineering & Construction; Government (Local, State & Federal and Public Works; Pollution Control (Air & Water).)

### AUDITED
Journal American Water Works Association Public Works Manual, The*
Water & Wastes Digest
Water Conditioning & Purification
Water Engineering & Management
Water Environment and Technology

Water Technology
Water Well Journal

### NON-AUDITED
Florida Specifier, The
Ground Water Age
Ground Water Monitoring Review
Irrigation Journal
Journal American Water Works Association Buyers' Guide
National Drillers Buyers Guide
Operations Forum
Research Journal of the Water Pollution Control Federation
Texas Water Utilities Journal
U.S. Water News
Ultrapure Water
Waterworld News

## 156. WELDING

### AUDITED
Welding Design & Fabrication
Welding Journal

### NON-AUDITED
1992/93 Welding & Fabricating Data Book
Welding Distributor, The

## 158. WIRE & WIRE PRODUCTS

### AUDITED
Wire Journal International
Wire Technology International

### NON-AUDITED
Wire Journal International Reference Guide
Wire Rope News & Sling Technology

## 159. WOODWORKING
(See also: Building; Logging & Forest Products Manufacturing Market.)

### NON-AUDITED
Cutting Tool Business
Millwork Manufacturing

# Healthcare Section
## (See Part II)

## H1. BIOTECHNOLOGICAL SCIENCES

### AUDITED
Biomedical Products
BioPharm
BioTechniques
Genetic Engineering News

### NON-AUDITED
AgBiotechnology News
Bio/Life Digest
Biotechnology Week*
BioWorld Magazine
Diagnostic Cytopathology
Fisheries
IEEE Engineering in Medicine and Biology Magazine
Journal of Histochemistry & Cytochemistry
Journal of Molecular Evolution
Peptide Research

## H2. DENTAL

### AUDITED
Dental Economics
Dental Products Report
Dental Teamwork
Dentistry Today
Journal of Clinical Orthodontics, The
Journal of the American Dental Association, The
RDH

### NON-AUDITED
Access
ADA News
AGD Impact
American Journal of Orthodontics and Dentofacial Orthopedics
Anesthesia Progress
ASDA Handbook
CDS Review
Compendium Of Continuing Education In Dentistry, The
Cranio: The Journal of Craniomandibular Practice
Dental Assistant, The
Dental Lab Products
Dentistry '90
Esthetic Dentistry Update
General Dentistry
Illinois Dental Journal
Journal of Dental Education
Journal of Dental Hygiene
Journal of Dental Research
Journal of Dentistry for Children
Journal of Endodontics
Journal of Esthetic Dentistry
Journal of Oral and Maxillofacial Surgery
Journal of Periodontology
Journal of Prosthetic Dentistry, The
Journal of the California Dental Association
Lab Management Today
New York Journal of Dentistry
New York State Dental Journal
Northwest Dentistry
Oral Surgery, Oral Medicine, Oral Pathology
Practical Periodontics and Aesthetic Dentistry
Proofs, The Magazine of Dental Sales
Quintessence International
Trends & Techniques

## H3. DRUGS, PHARMACEUTICS

### AUDITED
American Druggist

BioPharm*
Chain Drug Review
Drug Store News
Drug Store News for the Pharmacist
Drug Topics
Pharmaceutical Engineering
Pharmaceutical Executive
Pharmaceutical Processing
Pharmaceutical Technology
Pharmacy Times
U. S. Pharmacist

### NON-AUDITED
American Druggist Blue Book
American Journal of Hospital Pharmacy
American Pharmacy
Annals of Pharmacotherapy, The
California Journal of Hospital Pharmacy, The
California Pharmacist
Clinical Pharmacy
Computertalk for the Pharmacist
Connecticut Pharmacist
Consultant Pharmacist
Drug Information Journal
Drug Store News Annual Reference For Patient Counseling RX and OTC
Drug Topics Red Book
Hospital Pharmacist Report
Hospital Pharmacy
Journal Michigan Pharmacist
Journal of Pharmaceutical Sciences
Journal of Pharmacy Practice
NARD Journal
New York State Journal of Pharmacy, The
New York State Pharmacist/Century II
Pharmacy Counselor
Pharmacy Practice News
Pharmacy West
Southern Pharmacy Journal
State Pharmaceutical Editorial Association (Group)
Washington Pharmacist
Wholesale Drugs

## H4. HEALTHCARE

### AUDITED
Contemporary Long Term Care
Continuing Care
Employee Assistance
Health Industry Today
Home Health Care Dealer
Homecare
McKnight's Long-Term Care News
Medical Products Sales
Provider
Rehab Management

### NON-AUDITED
Addiction & Recovery
Addiction & Recovery's National Treatment Resource Issue
Adolescent Counselor
American Journal of Health Promotion
Caring
Case Manager, The
EAP Digest
Employee Services Management
Gerontologist, The
Health Industry Buyers' Guide
Healthcare Marketing Report
HMO Magazine
Home Care News
Independent Living*
Journal of Gerontology
Looking Fit
Managed Healthcare News
N.A.H.C. Report
NHHCE Show Daily
Nursing Homes and Senior Citizen Care
Nutrition & Dietary Consultant, The
Nutrition Counselor
Professional Counselor
Rehabilitation Today
TeamRehab Report
Today's Image

## H5. HOSPITAL ADMINISTRATION

### AUDITED
Computers in Healthcare
Health Progress
Health Systems Review
Healthcare Financial Management
Healthcare Forum Journal
Healthcare Informatics
HealthWeek
Hospital Purchasing News
Hospitals
Journal of Healthcare Materiel Management
Modern Healthcare
Trustee

### NON-AUDITED
Buyers Guide for the Health Care Industry
Catholic Health World
Chicago Healthcare
Extended Care Product News
Health Care Strategic Management
Healthcare Executive
Hospital Blue Book
Hospital Blue Book
Hospital News of Minnesota
Materials Management in Health Care
Medical Device Register
Medical Group Management Journal
Southern Hospitals Magazine

## H6. MEDICAL & SURGICAL

### AUDITED
Administrative Radiology
American Clinical Laboratory
American College of Physicians Observer
American Family Physician
American Journal of Ophthalmology
American Medical News
Annals of Emergency Medicine
Annals of Internal Medicine

Applied Radiology
CAP Today
Cardio
Cardiology Board Review
Cardiovascular Reviews & Reports
Clinical Cardiology
Clinical Chemistry
Clinical Chemistry News
Clinical Lab Products
Clinical Pediatrics
Consultant
Contemporary Gastroenterology
Contemporary Ob/Gyn
Contemporary Orthopaedics
Contemporary Pediatrics
Contemporary Surgery
Contemporary Urology
Cutis
Dermatology Times
Diagnostic Imaging
Diagnostic Imaging International
Dialysis & Transplantation
Diversion
DO, The
Drug Therapy
Ear, Nose and Throat Journal
Emergency
Emergency Medical Services
Emergency Medicine
Emergency Medicine News
Family Practice Recertification
Female Patient, The
Geriatric Medicine Today
Geriatrics
Hearing Instruments
Hearing Journal
Hippocrates
Hospital Formulary
Hospital Medicine
Hospital Physician
Hospital Practice
IM—Internal Medicine
Infections in Medicine
Infectious Disease News
Infectious Diseases in Children
Internal Medicine News & Cardiology News
Internal Medicine World Report
JAMA: Journal of the American Medical Association
JEMS
Journal of Critical Illness, The
Journal of Dermatologic Surgery & Oncology, The
Journal of Family Practice, The
Journal of Musculoskeletal Medicine, The
Journal of Osteopathic Medicine, The
Journal of Respiratory Diseases, The
Journal of the American Osteopathic Association, The
Laboratory Medicine
MD Magazine
Medical Aspects of Human Sexuality
Medical Device & Diagnostic Industry
Medical Economics
Medical Economics for Surgeons
Medical Electronics/Medical Electronic Products
Medical Equipment Designer
Medical Physics
Medical Product Manufacturing News
Medical Tribune
Medical World News
Medicine and Science in Sports and Exercise
MLO/Medical Laboratory Observer
Modern Medicine
Monthly Prescribing Reference
Nephrology News & Issues
New England Journal of Medicine
OBG Management
Ocular Surgery News
Oncology Times
Ophthalmology Times
Orthopaedic Review
Orthopedics
Orthopedics Today
P & T
Patient Care
Pediatric Annals
Pediatric News
Physical Therapy Forum
Physician and Sportsmedicine, The
Physician Assistant
Physician's Management
Physicians Financial News
Physicians' Travel & Meeting Guide
Podiatry Today
Postgraduate Medicine
Practical Gastroenterology
Primary Cardiology
Private Practice
Psychiatric Annals
Psychiatric Times, The
Radiology Today
Resident & Staff Physician
Surgical Rounds
Texas Medicine
U. S. Medicine
Urology
Urology Times
VA Practitioner
Varia

## NON-AUDITED

AABB News Briefs
AARC Times
ACA Journal of Chiropractic, The
Academic Medicine
Acta Cytologica
Adolescent and Pediatric Gynecology
Advance for Radiologic Science Professionals
Advance for Respiratory Care Practitioners
Aesthetic Plastic Surgery
AIDS
AJDC: American Journal of Diseases of Children
Alcoholism: Clinical and Experimental Research
Allergy Proceedings
American Chiropractor, The

### Classification H6—Continued

American Clinical Laboratory Buyers' Guide
American Heart Journal
American Journal of Asthma & Allergy for Pediatricians
American Journal of Cardiac Imaging
American Journal of Cardiology, The
American Journal of Clinical Nutrition, The
American Journal of Clinical Pathology
American Journal of Contact Dermatitis
American Journal of Cosmetic Surgery, The
American Journal of EEG Technology, The
American Journal of Emergency Medicine, The
American Journal of Gastroenterology, The
American Journal of Gynecologic Health
American Journal of Hospice and Palliative Care
American Journal of Hypertension
American Journal of Kidney Diseases
American Journal of Knee Surgery
American Journal of Medicine, The
American Journal of Obstetrics and Gynecology
American Journal of Occupational Therapy
American Journal of Otolaryngology
American Journal of Otology, The
American Journal of Pathology, The
American Journal of Pediatric Hematology/Oncology, The
American Journal of Perinatology
American Journal of Physical Medicine & Rehabilitation
American Journal of Physiology
American Journal of Psychiatry
American Journal of Public Health
American Journal of Rhinology
American Journal of Sports Medicine
American Journal of Surgery, The
American Journal of Surgical Pathology, The
American Psychologist
American Review of Respiratory Disease
American Surgeon
Anesthesia & Analgesia
Anesthesiology
Anesthesiology News
Anesthesiology Review
Angiology
Annals of Allergy
Annals of Neurology
Annals of Ophthalmology
Annals of Otology, Rhinology & Laryngology
Annals of Plastic Surgery
Annals of Surgery
Annals of Thoracic Surgery, The
Antimicrobial Agents and Chemotherapy
AOA Yearbook and Directory
APA Monitor
APMA News
Archives of Dermatology
Archives of Environmental Health
Archives of General Psychiatry
Archives of Internal Medicine
Archives of Neurology
Archives of Ophthalmology
Archives of Otolaryngology-Head & Neck Surgery
Archives of Pathology & Laboratory Medicine
Archives of Physical Medicine and Rehabilitation
Archives of Psychiatric Nursing
Archives of Surgery
Arteriosclerosis and Thrombosis
Arthritis and Rheumatism
Arthroscopy
Asha
AUA Today
Audecibel
Aviation, Space and Environmental Medicine
Biomedical Instrumentation & Technology
Biotechnic & Histochemistry
Birth
Blood
Blood Cells
Bulletin
Bulletin, The
Buyer's Guide of Cardio-Respiratory Care Equipment and Supplies, The
CA—A Cancer Journal for Clinicians
Calcified Tissue International
California Physician
Cancer
Cancer Nursing
Cancer Research
Cardiology, The Newspaper of
Careers in Respiratory Therapy
Catheterization and Cardiovascular Diagnosis
Chest
Chiropractic
Chiropractic Economics, The Digest of
Chiropractic Journal, The
Chiropractic Products
Chiropractic Sports Medicine
Chiropractic Technique
Chiropractic, Dynamic
Choices in Cardiology
Choices in Respiratory Management
Circulation
Circulation Research
CLAO Journal, The
Cleveland Clinic Journal of Medicine
Clinical Chemistry News Convention Dailies
Clinical Consultations in Obstetrics and Gynecology
Clinical EEG
Clinical Infectious Diseases
Clinical Laboratory Management Review
Clinical Laboratory Marketplace
Clinical Laboratory Science
Clinical Management
Clinical Nephrology
Clinical Nuclear Medicine

Clinical Pharmacology & Therapeutics
Clinical Psychiatry News
Clinical Research
CLR/Clinical Laboratory Reference
Computerized Medical Imaging and Graphics
Contemporary Dialysis & Nephrology
Contemporary Internal Medicine
Cortlandt Forum
Cosmetic Dermatology
Critical Care Medicine
CRNA: The Clinical Forum for Nurse Anesthetists
Current Microbiology
Current Podiatric Medicine
Current Surgery
Cytometry
Dermatology Clinical Digest Series
Desk Reference and Directory of the American Podiatric Medical Association
Diabetes
Diabetes Care
Diabetes Spectrum
Digestive Diseases and Sciences
Diseases of the Colon & Rectum
Doctor's Orders
Doctor's Shopper
Dysphagia
Ear and Hearing
Echocardiography
Endocrinologist, The
Endocrinology
Endoscopy Review
Epilepsia
Experimental Hematology
Family Medicine
Family Planning Perspectives
Family Practice News
Fertility and Sterility
Foot and Ankle
Gastroenterology
Gastroenterology & Endoscopy News
Gastrointestinal Endoscopy
General Surgery News
Glaucoma
Group Practice Journal
Group Practice Managed Healthcare News
Head & Neck
Headache
Headlines
Hearing Instruments Convention News
Hepatology
HMO Practice
Hospital & Community Psychiatry
Human Pathology
Hypertension
ICCN/Outpatient Care
Illinois Medicine
Immunology & Allergy Practice
In Vitro Cellular & Developmental Biology
Infection Control & Hospital Epidemiology
Internal Medicine Resident, The
International Journal of Dermatology
International Journal of Radiation Oncology Biology Physics
Internist, The
Investigative Ophthalmology & Visual Science
Investigative Radiology
Journal of Acquired Immune Deficiency Syndromes
Journal of Allergy and Clinical Immunology, The
Journal of Applied Physiology
Journal of Bacteriology
Journal of Bone & Joint Surgery-American Volume
Journal of Bone and Joint Surgery British Volume
Journal of Burn Care & Rehabilitation
Journal of Cardiac Surgery
Journal of Cardiopulmonary Rehabilitation
Journal of Cardiothoracic and Vascular Anesthesia
Journal of Cardiovascular Electrophysiology
Journal of Cardiovascular Management, The
Journal of Cataract and Refractive Surgery
Journal of Clinical Anesthesia
Journal of Clinical Endocrinology & Metabolism
Journal of Clinical Engineering
Journal of Clinical Gastroenterology
Journal of Clinical Immunoassay
Journal of Clinical Immunology
Journal of Clinical Investigation
Journal of Clinical Microbiology
Journal of Clinical Monitoring
Journal of Clinical Neurophysiology
Journal of Clinical Oncology
Journal of Clinical Psychiatry, The
Journal of Clinical Psychopharmacology
Journal of Clinical Ultrasound
Journal of Computer Assisted Tomography
Journal of Craniofacial Surgery, The
Journal of Critical Care
Journal of Diagnostic Medical Sonography/JDMS
Journal of Electron Microscopy Technique
Journal of Emergency Medicine, The
Journal of Foot Surgery, The
Journal of General Internal Medicine
Journal of Hand Surgery, The (American Volume)
Journal of Hand Therapy
Journal of Heart and Lung Transplantation, The
Journal of Histotechnology
Journal of Immunology, The
Journal of Infectious Diseases
Journal of Intensive Care Medicine
Journal of Interventional Cardiology
Journal of Invasive Cardiology, The
Journal of Investigative Dermatology
Journal of Laboratory and Clinical Medicine, The
Journal of Lithotripsy & Stone Disease
Journal of Magnetic Resonance Imaging

Journal of Manipulative and Physiological Therapeutics
Journal of Neuroimaging
Journal of Neurophysiology
Journal of Neuroscience, The
Journal of Neurosurgery
Journal of Nuclear Medicine
Journal of Nuclear Medicine Technology
Journal of Nutrition
Journal of Occupational Medicine
Journal of Orthopaedic and Sports Physical Therapy, The
Journal of Orthopaedic Research
Journal of Parenteral and Enteral Nutrition (JPEN)
Journal of Parenteral Science and Technology
Journal of Pediatric Gastroenterology & Nutrition
Journal of Pediatric Oncology Nursing
Journal of Pediatric Ophthalmology & Strabismus
Journal of Pediatric Orthopaedics
Journal of Pediatric Surgery
Journal of Pediatrics, The
Journal of Perinatology
Journal of Pharmacology & Experimental Therapeutics
Journal of Reconstructive Microsurgery
Journal of Renal Nutrition
Journal of Reproductive Medicine, The
Journal of the American Academy of Child and Adolescent Psychiatry
Journal of the American Academy of Dermatology
Journal of the American Academy of Physician Assistants
Journal of the American Board of Family Practice, The
Journal of the American College of Cardiology
Journal of the American Geriatrics Society
Journal of the American Medical Women's Association
Journal of the American Podiatric Medical Association
Journal of the American Society of Echocardiography
Journal of the American Society of Nephrology, The
Journal of the National Medical Association
Journal of the Student National Medical Association
Journal of Thoracic and Cardiovascular Surgery, The
Journal Of Trauma
Journal of Ultrasound in Medicine
Journal of Urology, The
Journal of Vascular and Interventional Radiology
Journal of Vascular Surgery
Journal of Voice
Kidney International
Laboratory Investigation
LACMA Physician
Lancet The
Laryngoscope
Lasers in Surgery and Medicine
Life Sciences
Lung
M.D. Computing
Magnetic Resonance Imaging
Mayo Clinic Proceedings
Medical Decision Making
Medical Device Technology
Medical Dosimetry
Medical Electronics & Equipment News
Medical Essentials Directory—Gastroenterology
Medical Grand Rounds
Medical Interface
Medical Problems of Performing Artists
Medical Sonography
Medico Interamericano
Metabolism
Micron and Microscopica Acta
Microsurgery
Military Medicine
Molecular and Cellular Biology
Mount Sinai Journal of Medicine
MR
Muscle & Nerve
Nation's Health, The
National Directory of Chiropractic, The
Neonatal Intensive Care
Neurology
Neuroscience
Neurosurgery
New Jersey Medicine
New Physician, The
New York Doctor, The
New York State Journal of Medicine
News in Physiological Sciences (NIPS)
NN&I ESRD Product & Service Directory
Nutrition
Nutrition in Clinical Practice (NCP)
Ob. Gyn. News
Ob/Gyn Resident, The
Obstetrical & Gynecological Survey
Obstetrics and Gynecology
Occupational Therapy Forum
Ohio Medicine
Oncology
Operative Techniques in Orthopaedics
Operative Techniques in Otolaryngology/Head & Neck Surgery
Ophthalmic Surgery
Ophthalmology
Orthopaedic Physical Therapy Practice
Orthopedic & Sports Medicine News
Orthopedic Resident, The
Otolaryngology—Head and Neck Surgery
Pacing and Clinical Electrophysiology
Pain Management
Pediatric Cardiology
Pediatric Emergency Care
Pediatric Infectious Disease Journal, The
Pediatric Management
Pediatric Physical Therapy
Pediatric Pulmonology
Pediatric Research

Pediatrics
Pennsylvania Medicine
Peptides
Pharmacotherapy
Physical Therapy
Physical Therapy Products
Physical Therapy Today
Physicians & Computers
Plastic & Reconstructive Surgery
Plastic Surgery News
Pneumogram
Podiatric Products
Podiatry Management
Prehospital and Disaster Medicine
Primary Care & Cancer
Progress in Cardiovascular Diseases
Progress Report
Psychiatric Hospital, The
Psychiatric News
Psychiatric Resident, The
Psychosomatics
Quality Assurance and Utilization Review
RadioGraphics
Radiologic Technology
Radiology
Radiology Management
1993 Radiology Reference Guide
Radiology Specialty Group
Refractive & Corneal Surgery
Regional Anesthesia
Relax
Rescue Magazine
Rescue—EMS Magazine
Respiratory Care
Respiratory Practitioner, The
Retina
Rocky Mountain E.M.S.
RT
Science Illustrated
Second Source Biomedical
Second Source Imaging
Seminars In Anesthesia
Seminars in Arthritis and Rheumatism
Seminars in Arthroplasty
Seminars in Colon & Rectal Surgery
Seminars in Dermatology
Seminars in Diagnostic Pathology
Seminars in Dialysis
Seminars in Hearing
Seminars in Hematology
Seminars in Interventional Radiology
Seminars in Nephrology
Seminars in Neurology
Seminars in Nuclear Medicine
Seminars in Oncology
Seminars in Ophthalmology
Seminars in Orthopaedics
Seminars in Pediatric Infectious Diseases
Seminars in Perinatology
Seminars in Radiation Oncology
Seminars in Reproductive Endocrinology
Seminars in Respiratory Infections
Seminars in Respiratory Medicine
Seminars in Roentgenology
Seminars in Spine Surgery
Seminars in Thoracic and Cariovascular Surgery
Seminars in Thrombosis and Hemostasis
Seminars in Ultrasound CT and MR
Seminars in Urology
Seminars in Vascular Surgery
Skin & Allergy News
Skull Base Surgery
Sleep
Southern Medical Journal
Spine
State Journal Group
Stroke
Surgery
Surgery, Gynecology and Obstetrics
Surgical Neurology
Surgical Products
Survey of Anesthesiology
Survey of Ophthalmology
Texas Heart Institute Journal
Thrombosis Research
Today's Chiropractic
Transfusion
Transplantation
Transplantation Proceedings
Ultrasound in Medicine & Biology
Vascular Surgery
Western Journal of Medicine
World Journal of Surgery
Wounds

**H7. NURSING & HEALTH**

AUDITED
American Journal of Nursing
Nursing92
Nursing Management
RN

NON-AUDITED
AANA Journal
AAOHN Journal
AJN Guide, The
American Journal of Infection Control
American Nurse, The
ANNA Journal
AORN Journal
California Nursing
California School Nurse
Clinical Nurse Specialist
Critical Care Nurse
Decubitus
Dermatology Nursing
Diabetes Educator, The
Florida Nursing News
Focus on Critical Care
Gastroenterology Nursing
Geriatric Nursing
Healthcare Trends & Transition
Heart and Lung: The Journal of Critical Care
Home Healthcare Nurse
Imprint
Journal of American College Health
Journal of Emergency Nursing

Journal of ET Nursing
Journal of Gerontological Nursing
Journal of Intravenous Nursing
Journal of Neuroscience Nursing
Journal of Nurse-Midwifery
Journal of Nursing Administration, The
Journal of Obstetric Gynecologic and Neonatal Nursing
Journal of Ophthalmic Nursing & Technology
Journal of Pediatric Health Care
Journal of Pediatric Nursing
Journal of Post Anesthesia Nursing
Journal of Practical Nursing, The
Journal of Psychosocial Nursing and Mental Health Services
Journal of School Health
Journal of School Nursing, The
MCN The American Journal of Maternal/Child Nursing
Medical Care Products
NASnewsletter
Neonatal Network
Nurse Anesthesia
Nurse Practitioner Forum
Nurse Practitioner, The
NurseWeek
Nursing '92 Career Directory
Nursing Economic$
Nursing Opportunities
Nursing Outlook
Nursing Research
Nursingworld Journal
Nursingworld Journal Nursing Job Guide
Oncology Nursing Forum
Orthopaedic Nursing
Ostomy/Wound Management
Pediatric Nursing
Plastic Surgical Nursing
Professional Medical Assistant, The
Rehabilitation Nursing
Seminars in Oncology Nursing
Seminars in Perioperative Nursing
Southwest Medical Opportunities
Surgical Technologist, The
Today's OR Nurse

**H8. OPTICAL & OPTOMETRIC**

AUDITED
Contact Lens Spectrum
Eyecare Business
Frames
Optometric Management
Review of Optometry
20/20

NON-AUDITED
AOA News
Argus
Journal of the American Optometric Association
OAA News
Optometric Economics
Southern Journal of Optometry
Texas Optometry
Vision Monday

(Courtesy Business Publication Rates and Data, December 1991 edition; reproduced with permission from Standard Rate and Data Service, Inc.)

## New Business Magazines

Each month *Folio:* lists the new business magazines. The list for a typical month shows how broad the base is for these magazines. *Treasury* is a quarterly publication started in October 1991 by the Economist Group, which also publishes *CFO*, a monthly for chief financial officers. *Treasury's* audience is corporate treasury officers.

*Educational IRM Quarterly* was started in late 1991 for the information resource managers of school districts. Its initial circulation is 10,000 controlled. In March 1992 American Hospital Publishing, Inc. kicked off *Material Management in Health Care*, a monthly targeted at buyers of medical equipment and supplies. Almost a hundred new business magazines are launched each year.

# PORTRAITS OF THREE BUSINESS PUBLISHING GIANTS

If you're intent on making it in magazines, and specifically in business magazines, you'd be wise to consider the giants—stable, diversified companies with a success orientation. Let's look at three of them.

## Capital Cities/ABC, Inc.

The parent company is a diversified organization that in 1990 had total revenues of $5.4 billion and after-tax profits of $477 million. It is engaged in the ownership of the ABC-TV network, TV and radio stations, newspapers, and consumer and business magazines. The business magazine group is composed of these companies:

*Agricultural Publishing Group*—nine farm publications in the Midwest

*Chilton Company*—twenty-four publications in various industrial classifications

*Communications and Commodities Group*—five publications

*Hitchcock Publishing Company*—nine industrial publications

*Fairchild Fashion and Merchandising Group*—twelve publications, including the *Daily News Record* and *Women's Wear Daily*

*Financial Services and Medical Group*—including the domestic and international editions of the influential *Institutional Investor,* as well as six medical-news publications

In addition to their magazine publishing operations, these groups are also involved in book publishing and in conducting meetings, seminars, and trade shows.

## McGraw-Hill, Inc.

McGraw-Hill is a 102-year-old, multimedia publishing and information services company. Its publishing efforts are in books, magazines, and newsletters. In 1990 the company had revenues of almost $2 billion and a net income of $172 million. The business magazine operations of McGraw-Hill are divided into five groups:

*Aviation Week Group*—*Aviation Week & Space Technology* being the lead publication, plus five others

*Computers and Communications Group*—with *BYTE* being the standout in this group, which publishes magazines as well as providing information and electronic services

*Construction Information Group*—with *Architectural Record* being the major publication in this group

*Science and Technology Group*—publishing six business magazines, including *Chemical Engineering, Modern Plastics,* and *Electrical World.*

*Professional Publishing Group*—including four business magazines, book publishing, software, and book clubs for the health-care industry

## Reed International

Reed is one of the world's leading publishing and information companies. Headquartered in London, the company operates in Australia and the

**Figure 12–1**

United States as well. It is engaged in book, newspaper, and magazine publishing and in subscription-based information publishing.

In the United States Reed's magazine publishing entity is Cahners Publishing Company, which publishes sixty-nine business magazines and newspapers and thirteen consumer special-interest magazines. Prominent in Cahner's business magazine lineup are *Interior Design, Restaurants & Institutions, Professional Builder, Publishers Weekly,* and the show business bible, *Variety.*

Cahners has been in business since 1946; in the years since then, it has been busy acquiring other magazines. In 1987 the company was acquired by Reed International. With its recent entry into consumer magazine publishing (thirteen titles), Cahners is becoming one of the largest publishing firms in the nation.

As a possible employer, Cahners would be an excellent choice. It employs 3,000-plus highly skilled professionals in the field of business journalism, producing more than eighty magazines in specialized business and consumer publishing. Cahners is located in New York, Chicago, and Newton, Massachusetts. It offers the kind of diversification not usually found in other publishing companies.

## Careers in Business Magazines

An editorial director at a large business magazine company recently discussed with me his problems in attracting bright young editorial talent. The company publishes many magazines, pays well, and provides ample opportunities for growth. Yet the notion persists that business magazines are dull places to work, places where one is buried in boredom for the rest of his or her working life. Nothing can be further from the truth.

Here are examples of the kind of investigative reporting, human-interest stories, and information-packed pieces turned out by journalists who work in the specialized business press:

- "Commercialization of Space" is a special issue of *Aviation Week and Space Technology* that explores the mind-boggling outlook for conducting manufacturing operations in outer space.
- "The Right to Die" in *Nursing Life* magazine probes the feelings of nurses and relatives of patients on this highly emotional issue.
- "The Counterfeiting of America and Elsewhere" in *Commercial Carrier Journal* is an exposé of the flood of counterfeit merchandise pouring into the United States from the Far East. Posing as New York businessmen, two *CCJ* editors traveled thousands of miles—from the back alleys of big-city Chinatowns to Hong Kong, Singapore, and Taiwan—tracking down the purveyors and financiers of counterfeit products.

The basic advantage of journalists working for specialized business magazines is the opportunity to write—an opportunity frequently denied to writers on consumer magazines, where editing is the primary activity. The journalist's goal on a business magazine is to become so knowledgeable about some field or function of business—be it computers, entertainment, or chemicals—that his or her writing is essential for the specialists in that field.

Breck Henderson was a successful engineering graduate who joined the Navy, became expert in nuclear power work, and found similar work in the civilian sector. Later, he decided to go back to school for a master of journalism degree from Louisiana State University. He was recommended for the BPEF internship with McGraw-Hill's *Aviation Week* in their Washington, DC, bureau.

He was then hired permanently by the San Francisco office and later became the military electronics editor for the magazine.

"I love this job," he said. "They call me an editor, but I'm really reporter and writer. This is the kind of job I always wanted. I get to go to a lot of interesting places and see a lot of high-tech equipment. People I went to school with were focused on newspapers for a career, but after a few years they get tired of the low wages and poor working conditions."

Wendy Bishop, a 1987 University of Missouri journalism school graduate, was the first intern from her school to be placed by the BPEF. Today she works as an associate editor for Intertec Publishing's *Lawn & Garden Marketing,* where she is involved in design, editing, and production.

"I wouldn't consider working in any other form of journalism," she said. "I'm gaining a broad knowledge of publishing and handling a lot of responsibility. I'm really exposed on all fronts, and I do it because I love business journalism."

Suzette Hill graduated in 1990 from California State University at Long Beach, where she majored in magazine journalism. While doing an internship at Bobit Publishing Company, she was offered a full-time job. A year later she became editor of *Nails Magazine,* where she now writes stories, lays out pages, deals with free-lancers, proofs copy, and does all of the other editorial functions.

"I'm definitely staying in the business press. There are a lot more job opportunities and a chance to do many more things than in the consumer magazine field," Hill comments.

## The Business Press Journalists

In 1988, with funding by the Association of Business Publishers, Dr. Kathleen Endres of the University of Akron in Ohio conducted a major study of business press journalists. Here is the conclusion of her study:

> This study indicates that the business press has much in common with journalism in general. Yet business journalists indicate that they are striving for a higher level of professionalism and respectability within the journalism community.
>
> In background, the business press reporters and editors have much in common with their brothers and sisters in other journalistic positions. The business press journalists are likely to be males in their mid-thirties with bachelor's degrees.

Women in the field appear to be facing some less than conducive conditions. They are less apt to hold higher positions on the editorial staffs and are likely to be paid substantially less than the men.

On the job, the business press field appears to be ideal for the skills generalist as opposed to the specialist. Small staffs mean that editors do many different types of jobs during the course of the day. The clear demarcation between editor and reporter has not developed in most business publications.

The business journalists have developed a sense of responsibility to their readers. Even if they work for a publication sent free of charge to qualified individuals, business journalists feel that their primary responsibility is to the reader, not the advertiser. Indeed, business journalists appear to be quite sensitive to potential problems when faced with advertiser interference and disavow such attempts. Respondents, promised anonymity, were vocal in their criticism as well as their praise for the field. In general, however, most journalists thought the business press did a good job covering their industries.

A number of journalists responding, however, said they did not think the business press was taken seriously by journalists outside the field. As one editor explained, "The trade press is generally a second-class citizen compared to the consumer press as far as public/trade/retail perceptions go." This study indicates that this perception—if it indeed exists—appears to be off the mark.

## Career Opportunities on the Business Side

Although most journalism school graduates think primarily of writing careers, the jobs on the business side—in marketing, circulation, or production—should not be overlooked. In other chapters we discuss in detail the positions and functions within these areas of publishing; still, a basic understanding of how those areas relate to business publishing is valuable.

Circulation identifies the people within an industry or profession who should receive the publication. It creatively markets the relevance of its editorial content to that target audience. Circulation people sell new and renewal subscriptions for paid publications and certify that individuals requesting nonpaid publications are qualified to receive them because of the nature of their jobs or businesses.

"As a career opportunity, it is an undiscovered gold mine," says Gloria Adams, corporate circulation director for Penton.

The marketing staff in business publications requires high-caliber people who can unite specified sellers with specialized buyers. Says Ben Miyares, executive editor of *Food & Drug Packaging,* "The business press is a unique proving ground for marketing skills; only the best marketers survive. Our customers are too intelligent, too well informed to be taken in by hokum."

Selling advertising space is an art. Salespeople have to thoroughly understand the readers and their jobs or businesses to transmit to advertisers what readers need in terms of products and services and what their buying patterns are. These salespeople rely heavily on research. Researchers also track the readership of advertising (as well as editorial material) and conduct opinion polls that tell advertisers how magazines are regarded by their readers. Research too can be a rewarding career path.

The production staff works closely with the editorial, marketing, and circulation departments and transforms its efforts into a final product. This is the team that must know the best in paper, ink, type, and printing techniques. The production group purchases the printing, paper, and distribution services in a highly competitive environment. On a continuing basis it is involved in the meticulous monitoring of suppliers and the skillful negotiation of prices.

"You're challenged by Murphy's Law at every turn," says Bill Budusky, production manager at *Industry Week.* "And believe me, there is no greater satisfaction than beating Murphy at his own game."

## Intern Program of the Business Press Educational Foundation (BPEF)

The Business Press Educational Foundation is affiliated with the American Business Press (ABP), the prestigious organization that speaks for the entire business press. In a partnership with journalism schools nationwide and specialized business publishers of ABP, BPEF places about twenty-five interns each summer. These faculty-recommended interns, representing nineteen universities, hold paid editorial positions of ten to twelve weeks' duration at twenty-one companies serving forty-six publications from Massachusetts to California.

For further information about this program, write to Phyllis Reed, Director, BPEF Student Intern Program, 675 Third Avenue, New York, NY 10017–5704.

## ABP's Employment Roundup

ABP performs a valuable service for its member publishers and for those seeking employment in the business publishing industry. Each month it furnishes its members with a listing of help-wanted and situation-wanted ads. No fees are charged for this service.

For those publishers looking for people, ABP's *Employment Roundup* shows listings by various publishing categories and invites publishers to call ABP for further information on particular listings.

For those looking for a position, ABP's *Employment Roundup* lists ads and then sends an applicant's résumé to interested publishers. For information about the monthly report, readers should call Phyllis Reed at (212) 661–6360.

## The Quality of Art Direction in Business Magazines

Business publications, along with their consumer magazine brethren, are vying for the reader's time and attention. In addition to quality writing and reportage, many business magazines employ excellent art direction and design to attract readers to their pages. They use graphics, illustrations, and photography with the highest degree of expertise.

Figure 12–2 provides an example of a business magazine whose art direction is outstanding.

Cahners's *Interior Design* carries advertising from resources in the design business that is as beautiful as its own editorial content. Here is a spread (run in color) from the issue on hotel design. Note the excellent choice of typefaces and the effective use of a photograph of a hotel lobby.

Among the many other well-designed business publications are *School Arts, Emergency Medicine, Institutions* (covering the food-service industry), *Geriatrics, Learning,* and *Professional Builder.*

## Summing Up

As we have seen in this chapter, the field of business magazines is dynamic and prosperous, offering great possibilities for talented people in both the editorial and the business phases. One favorable aspect is the locus of employment; business magazines are not nearly so Northeast-oriented as consumer magazines. Here's the breakdown on business magazines: Northeast, 40 percent; Midwest, 25 percent; other areas, 35 percent.

When applying for employment in business magazines, consider the larger companies—Cahners, McGraw-Hill, Edgell, Penton, Gralla, Lebhar-Friedman, Ziff Communications, and Cap Cities/ABC Publishing. Lists of their publications can be found in the SRDS business magazine directory. Keep in mind what we have stated elsewhere in this book: A star on one magazine in a chain will be recognized by top management and be considered for promotion on others in the company's roster.

Again, in addition to applying to personnel or human resources departments of a publishing company, proceed wherever possible through an individual editor or publisher.

The almost-4,000 business magazines in the United States employ more than 100,000 people. These magazines attract more than 70 million readers and sell almost 2 million advertising pages annually. Business magazine publishing is a rewarding field to consider for one's lifework.

**Figure 12–2**

## Interview

Today it is difficult to predict where your first job may lead you. Many journalism school graduates do not go to work in the business magazine field. More and more, however, the leading schools are encouraging their graduates to take this option.

Stacy Gordon earned her master's degree with honors from the Medill School of Journalism at Northwestern University in December 1986. Weighing a number of attractive offers, she chose to accept a job as an assistant copy editor at *Business Insurance,* a Crain Communications publication. Crain publishes *Ad Age* and about twenty other influential business magazines.

In five years at the magazine, she was promoted to copy editor, associate editor, and New York bureau chief, a managerial position where she supervises a staff of New York reporters and assists reporters nationwide. As a legal reporter, Gordon writes about judicial decisions involving insur-ance, product and environmental liability, and toxic torts. We asked Stacy Gordon about her job.

*Compare your experiences at a leading business magazine to those of friends or fellow Medill graduates who opted for the consumer magazine route, with respect to salaries and job responsibilities.*

Business journalism allows me the opportunity to become an expert in the areas I report on. I regularly read legal publications and attend legal conferences in an ongoing effort to stay on top of the field. My expertise allows me to write complex and technical legal stories that my readers can rely on when making important business decisions. There is a satisfaction in knowing how much my readers depend on my work in performing their jobs.

The salaries in business journalism are better than the salaries in the consumer press. I estimate that I earn twenty percent more than my counterparts at consumer magazines and newspapers.

And in five years I have achieved a position within the senior management of my magazine—something unheard of in the consumer press.

*We are told that one of the benefits of business magazine employment on the editorial side is the opportunity to investigate topics thoroughly and then write about them in depth. Give an example of a typical assignment. How long did it take to research and then to write about it?*

I can spend four to five days working on an important story for the magazine. Unlike my counterparts at the *Wall Street Journal* and the *New York Times,* I have the ability to *study* judicial briefs filed in a case or travel nationwide to view trial proceedings. One of my favorite assignments is to attend arguments at the U.S. Supreme Court. I also have the time to interview five to six people for a story (sometimes ten to twelve people). An average story is about 1,000 to 1,500 words, which gives me the opportunity to thoroughly explore all its aspects. I am also able to follow an important story as it develops. I have written three to four stories about the same case as it evolves.

*What are the benefits of working for a multi-magazine publishing company?*

The benefits of working for a multimagazine publishing company are twofold. First, I have access to stories written by reporters at several magazines who share their work on an intracompany computer system. Second, I have the added prestige of working for a nationally renowned publishing company. If a source does not know the name *Business Insurance,* they will know the name Crain Communications.

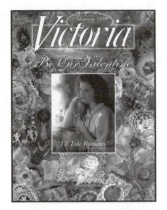

# 13

# Starting a New Magazine, Part I

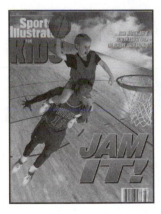

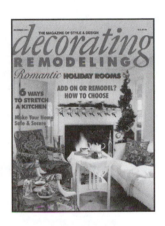

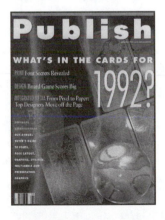

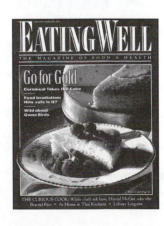

An article in *Folio:*'s July 1989 issue is titled "Launches: Learning from the Pros." The subhead reads "Nine Seasoned Publishers Reveal Their Strategies for Starting New Magazines, Sharing Their Experience and Expertise." Two of the magazines cited, *Victoria* and *Premiere*, went on to become major successes. Unfortunately, two years later four of the nine magazines discussed in the *Folio:* article had failed. One of these failures, *7 Days*, had more than adequate financing, an excellent concept, and a fine editorial product. Why, then, did it go under?

Having had controlled (free) circulation, *7 Days* was actually delivered to the homes of 75,000 Manhattanites who were hand-picked by the publishers. Unfortunately, the magazine ran into a down economic climate that curtailed the amount of advertising it received. Moreover, the publishers soon realized that to be successful with a controlled-circulation magazine, they needed a huge number of advertisers. Advertisers want numbers, and a city magazine like *7 Days*, reaching an upscale audience, could not deliver those numbers.

Have we already begun to make our point on the precariousness of starting a new magazine? Well, here's more. The "Magazine World 1991" issue of *ADWEEK* ran a page titled "In Memoriam." Under illustrations of the grim reaper and skeletons blowing trumpets, the magazine listed twenty-six magazines that bit the dust in the previous year. Many of them were published by major publishing companies. *BW's Assets* was put out by McGraw-Hill's *Business Week*; *Egg* by Forbes; *Men's Life*, by Murdoch Magazines. *Games, Manhattan, inc., Savvy Woman*, and *Taxi* were also the products of substantial organizations.

Husni's *Guide to New Consumer Magazines* lists 541 launches in 1991; 265 of them were consumer magazines. We don't have any accurate statistics, but we'll certainly speculate that 90 percent of these startups did not make it into a second year, particularly those with titles like *Bikini Style, Confetti Connections, Contemporary Doll, Hard Rock Magazine, Joe Franklin's Nostalgia*, and *Official International Wrestling Insider*. Yet there are always winners. In that same year *Eating Well, Elle*

*Decor, Entertainment Weekly, In Health*, and *Martha Stewart Living* made their successful debuts.

One of the primary reasons for the failure of new magazines is the lack of adequate financing, but we have seen situations where financially secure projects have still failed. Time Inc. Magazines invested huge sums in *TV Cable Week* and *Picture Week* without success. It poured $30 million (a large sum at the time) into *Sports Illustrated* before it went into the black. And, as we have noted, the company is prepared to lose $150 million on *Entertainment Weekly* before it moves into the profit column.

In two articles in *Folio:* in late 1991, Samar Husni, an authority on magazine statistics, points out that one of the major problems is overkill. Of ten computer magazines started up in 1985, only two were still publishing in 1991, and of ten launched in 1987, only one made it to 1991. Of eighteen sports titles originating in 1987, only five were still published in 1991, and of twenty in 1988, only four lasted into 1991.

Lest we be accused of sabotaging the interests of printers and paper mills, let us say that new magazines *can* succeed, but one must be aware of the dangers before stepping out onto the ice. We will discuss the necessary ingredients for a successful venture, but we will also point out the problems faced by new magazines.

# MAJOR PROBLEMS IN STARTING A MAGAZINE

## The Editorial Concept

"The wrong editorial concept is the main reason magazines fail," observes magazine consultant James B. Kobak. "Entrepreneurs' biggest problem is thinking they've got a great idea for a magazine the world needs. The question isn't whether the world needs it, but whether it wants it," he says.

Kobak cites the example of three houseplant magazines published in the early 1980s: *Houseplants and Porch Gardens, Plants Alive*, and *Popular Gardening Indoors*. "Each got 300,000 in circulation. None survived. There are only two things you do with plants, water them and talk to them. What else is there to say after that?"

Eric Schrier is one of the founders of *Hippocrates* (now *Health*). His magazine was purchased by Time Inc. Magazines. These days he reviews new magazine ideas for that company's Time Publishing Ventures subsidiary. In a three-month period in 1991 he saw about one hundred professionally produced new magazine ideas but acted on none.

Most consultants and executives who evaluate new magazine ideas advise the entrepreneur to submit his or her ideas to as many professionals as possible. No one steals ideas. The more guidance and opinion one gets on a magazine idea, the more time and money will be saved.

Often a magazine professional will advise the entrepreneur to consider starting the magazine idea as a newsletter. This route is much less expensive and frequently can be used to build an audience that may be converted to magazine readers.

A final note on this subject: Bear in mind that even the largest, most experienced publishers misjudge an editorial concept; then consider how much higher the odds are for the less experienced.

## Lack of Advertising Support

Consumer magazines depend on their revenue from circulation and advertising. Business magazines often choose to pursue a controlled-circulation policy, whereby all their revenues come from advertising sources. It is extremely difficult for a new magazine to achieve substantial advertising revenues.

Media departments at ad agencies are usually kind enough to listen to pitches from all new magazines, but they seldom react positively, unless a large company is behind the publication. The predominant attitude of these agencies is a conservative wait and see. Their only impetus to advertise in a promising magazine is to tie up preferred positions, such as second and back covers.

Further, new magazines seldom guarantee their circulation. Much depends on the success of direct mailings and newsstand sales, and we al-

ready know how precarious these activities are. The new publication cannot be audited by ABC until it is published for three or four issues, and then it takes a few more months for the audit to be completed. The vital consideration of pass-along readership cannot be effectively measured for at least a year. Meanwhile the pioneer advertiser is gambling on the magazine's survival.

## Reader Apathy

Readers may be attracted to a new magazine on the newsstand by the meretricious appeal of a cover. The true test, however, comes when the first-time reader buys the second issue, and then the third and fourth. Or, better yet, will the first-time reader of a new magazine fill out one of those pesky blow-in cards and subscribe to the publication for a year or two?

And among subscription buyers of a new magazine, disappointment abounds. How many charter subscribers to consumer and business magazines alike were attracted by prepublication offers but sadly disenchanted when the magazine finally arrived? When renewal time comes around, the true test of a magazine's acceptance is met.

## Lack of Viable Testing Procedures

Testing a new magazine concept is very difficult. Newsstand magazines can sometimes be pretested in a limited number of markets by distributing them in only two or three large cities. This method is expensive, since the editorial package must be tooled up with the same effort expended on a national launch. Then too, heavy promotional efforts must accompany these limited tests if a true barometer of success is sought.

Direct-mail testing is a more accurate procedure but still has its shortcomings. Because of a limited universe (expansion factor) for individual lists, an inadequate number of subscriptions may result from this source, thus requiring numerous follow-up mailings once the magazine is started. We also know that once a magazine begins regular publication, the direct-mail response declines.

## Newsstand Problems

The following scenario, enacted at least once a week on a typical newsstand, illustrates the perils of this form of distribution. For this example we will choose a tobacco and magazine stand in the lobby of a major office building. The business seems to be doing well, but the owner has not been paying his wholesaler promptly and is therefore sold to on a COD basis. Enter the wholesaler's routeman:

> Routeman: *Here's $168.62 worth of magazines, Willie.*
> Willie: *But I only have $111 in cash.*
> Routeman: *OK, which ones don't you want?*
> Willie: *Well, take back the new magazines. They won't sell anyway, and here's $30 worth of that new junk you brought me last week.*

Exit the busy routeman, while Willie goes back to enjoy his half-lighted cigar. This little story is not funny if you are the publisher of the new magazines the routeman brought the newsdealer this week and last.

## Attracting Talented Personnel

Some years ago William Blair, a veteran publisher, and Richard Ketchum, a longtime editor, joined forces to publish *Country Journal.* The merger of these two talents resulted in a solid success. Unfortunately, however, that situation is rare. Seldom is there such a fortuitous match. More often people without extensive publishing experience are determined to break the odds against making it. They seldom do.

For a new magazine to succeed, it must have not only a strong editorial concept but also talented people to execute the concept. If the entrepreneurs are not experienced in this area, they must recruit such people from other publications. This effort may require offering not only high salaries and incentive packages but also a piece of the action.

Similarly, on the business side skilled management is a must factor. The business head of the magazine is responsible for the vital areas of circulation, production, advertising sales, and even financing. Here there is no substitute for talent and experience.

Hiring recent MBA graduates and expecting them to have an immediate grasp of the complex problems of magazine publishing are unrealistic. It may be wise instead to hire a magazine consultant in order to gain an overall perspective on the numerous issues faced by the new magazine, although these services are expensive.

## Lack of a Business Plan

A real business plan, prepared by magazine specialists, is a sine qua non for the new magazine. It is essential in the search for money, as well as in the early operations of the new magazine. A typical business plan is detailed later in this chapter.

## Capitalization

When we started the *National Lampoon* in 1970, we were undercapitalized. Our newsstand sales were excellent for the first issue but went on a downward spin for the next six issues. Fortuitously, just when we were running out of money the eighth issue had good sales, and we were able to survive. Our problem was similar to those of many new magazines: We didn't raise enough money, and we were eager to get started. Remember, it is very difficult to go back to investors for additional funding. Raise enough money or don't do it at all.

# GETTING STARTED

If you are convinced by now that it is impossible to start a new magazine, stay with us. It can be accomplished. Here is a brilliant example of how one publisher got started:

Robin Wolaner, the former publisher of *Mother Jones,* was thirty-one when she got the idea for *Parenting* in 1985. With so many double-income parents, Wolaner reckoned there would be a need for an upscale magazine for upscale parents of young children. In what is an amazing publishing coincidence, she was developing the concept at the same time the mighty Time Inc. Magazine organization was developing its own upscale parents' magazine with the very same name, *Parenting*.

Rather than this female David taking on the Time Goliath, Wolaner proposed that Time fund her launch for $5 million. She would retain the majority interest and control of the publication. Time agreed to her terms, basically because she was far ahead of them in developing her version of *Parenting* and also because their own estimate for the launch was $25 to $30 million; hers was a bargain. It was the first time Time had backed a venture it did not itself conceive.

Perhaps Wolaner's weightiest sales tool in selling Time was the direct-mail test she had conducted in 1986, spending $175,000 raised from ten Silicon Valley investors (later bought out for $500,000). The test, using twenty-seven different lists, pulled a 5.7 percent response, a rate Time executives claim is one of the highest they had ever seen.

Wolaner, in keeping with Time procedures, had prepared a five-year business plan calling for the magazine to break even at the third year, with a circulation of 400,000. The first issue of *Parenting* came out in 1987, with a circulation of 200,000. In its first year the magazine had a whopping 539 pages of advertising; by August 1988 it had 350,000 in circulation; and by 1992 its circulation was 758,000, with a total audience of 5.14 million.

What can we learn from Robin Wolaner's successful venture? Clearly, an idea can be developed through direct-mail testing for under $200,000. With a successful test you can then sell the magazine idea to a large publisher, investment banker, or venture capitalist.

If you don't have this seed money, or first-stage financing, yourself, you will have to raise it from friends, relatives, and even your mother-in-law. Don't give away too large a percentage of the venture for this seed money, since you will have to relinquish a large portion when the real money is invested.

The structure of the operation is not too important at this stage, because it can always be changed. At this juncture find a lawyer who is familiar with publishing situations. Doing so might be expensive but can save a lot of grief later on. If you are going to call on banks, insurance companies, private investors, or venture capitalists, you will need a document called a *business plan*. Here is what it is all about.

## The Business Plan

The business plan is an important document that states the principles, concept, scope of market, table of organization, cash projections, and assumptions on which those projections are based. Although it may be only twenty-odd typewritten pages, it tells the sophisticated investor what the new product is all about. Unless you are highly skilled in all the phases of magazine publishing and can prepare a business plan yourself, it should be entrusted to a skilled magazine consultant. The document contains several essential elements.

**The Concept.** In a page or two concisely written, this section articulates the concept of the magazine—how it differs from others already published, what areas of interest it will cover, and the like.

**The Editorial Need.** The entreprenuer here positions the proposed magazine against its competition. He or she should avoid pie-in-the-sky statements, such as "The whole world is waiting for this magazine" or "None of the dozens of _____ publications does an adequate editorial job; they don't fill the gap that _____ magazine will." Instead, the would-be publisher should state clearly why his or her new magazine should be published.

**Editorial Content.** In this section the publisher deals with the nuts-and-bolts of the proposed editorial package. To provide an example, we will outline the contents of a hypothetical magazine called *TV Sports*.

Generally, *TV Sports* will do the following:
1. Instruct viewers in the rules of the games they are watching
2. Inform readers with carefully researched statistics on their favorite sports

3. Entertain readers with high-quality photography that figuratively transports them to the stadiums and arenas of the sports they watch on television

4. Provide in-depth interviews with sports personalities and broadcasters

Even more important in the section on editorial content is a selection of titles for actual or proposed articles to be carried in the new magazine. It indicates to the investor the specific editorial objective of the magazine. It might read like this:

*TV Sports* will cover these topics in its early issues:

• The Charm and Excitement of Wimbledon
• Inside Soccer
• Golf Tips from the Top
• How to Be an Armchair Quarterback
• Is Harness Racing Fixed?
• Are Hockey Fights Staged?
• The Professionalism of the Olympics

This section should include as many as thirty or forty editorial ideas and, if known in advance, the names of the authors who will write these articles. It impresses the investor with the degree of long-range planning that went into the preparation of the business plan and, in particular, the editorial content portion.

**Reader Potential.** This section attempts to answer for the skeptic where the readers for the proposed magazine will come from. It will answer some of these questions:

1. What is the age-group of this audience?
2. What are their demographics?
3. How many of them are there in the United States?
4. What other magazines do they read, and what is the circulation of those magazines?
5. What are the circulation objectives of the new magazine for its first three or four years?

**Advertising Potential.** If advertising is to be sold in the new magazine, the publisher must detail the primary and secondary classifications for these sales. One can then state the total amount of ad dollars spent by these groupings on magazine advertising.

Since our hypothetical magazine, *TV Sports*, appeals to the sports-minded, it would be wise to list the ten or fifteen most important sports publications and state the number of ad pages and total yearly revenue they carried in the previous year. Obviously, the would-be publisher intends to derive an ad income from budgets currently allocated to the existing sports magazines.

A listing of the primary target advertising areas is valuable for this section. For example:

• Alcoholic Beverages
• Automotive
• Home Entertainment
• Men's Apparel
• Sports Clothing
• Sports Equipment
• Sports Book Publishers

**People Involved.** Along with the financial information that follows, this portion of the business plan is the most important. The serious and sophisticated investor is concerned with who is going to run the show. Actual names of key staffers, together with details on their background, should be included. Do not overstate the case. A false credential could undermine the whole effort.

If certain individuals are currently employed by other companies, the publisher should be prepared, in confidence, to submit their résumés. Of course, this is a sensitive area.

Go down the line of key personnel. List the names of the publisher, editor in chief, art director, advertising director, circulation director, editorial advisory board members, production manager, consultants, even the lawyers and accountants. If prestigious, these last named can enhance the credibility of the entire operation. Complete this section with a table of organization. Investors will want to know each person's function and the total number of people on the magazine's staff.

## Basic Assumptions

We are dealing with the financial segment of the business plan, which starts with the basic assumptions on which the cash projections are derived. These are broken down into the following:

## Basic Assumptions

| | Test Period | Year 1 | Year 2 |
|---|---|---|---|
| A. Number of issues | | 6 | 12 |
| B. Average circulation | | 110,000 | 215,000 |
| C. Subscription price (one year only) Regular | $12.00 | $12.00 | $21.00 |
| D. Total mailings (in millions) | .140 | 4.0 | 4.0 |
| E. Average percentage of return on mailings (gross) | 4.0% | 4.5–2.8% | 2.8% |
| F. Renewal percentage Regular renewal | | 65% | 65% |
| G. Newsstand draw (in thousands) | | 50.0–75.0 | 100.0 |
| H. Newsstand percentage of sale | | 30–40% | 40% |
| I. Newsstand price/copy | | $2.00 | $2.00 |
| J. Average total pages/issue | | 100 | 116 |
| K. Average advertising pages/issue | | 20–25 | 30–35 |
| L. Advertising CPM/black-and-white page | | $22.00 | $22.00 |
| M. Cost/copy of printing and paper | | $ .52 | $ .49 |
| N. Number of full-time employees | | | |
|     Mechanical and distribution | | 1 | 1 |
|     Editorial | | 4 | 7 |
|     Advertising | | 6 | 6 |
|     Circulation | | 1 | 1 |
|     General and administrative | | 4 | 4 |

Test Period
Year 1
Year 2
Year 3
Year 4

It is my opinion that projecting a third and fourth year for a new publication is a bit of whimsy. There are far too many variables, making these figures unpredictable. Yet investors want these projections, and so they must be calculated. We outline above a sample page of assumptions for a better understanding of their meaning. This model has been adopted by my friend Jim Kobak, the dean of magazine financial consultants. We borrow it with his approval.

Now for an explanation of each item:

A. The proposed magazine will be bimonthly for the first year and monthly for the second.

B. The average circulation will be 110,000 for the first year and, for the second, 215,000—almost double.

C. Since there are subscription mailings in the test

period, we see the price of $12 for six issues, the same for Year 1, and $21 for twelve issues in Year 2.

D. There will be 140,000 pieces of subscription mail sent out during the test period, increasing to four million in Year 1 and the same for Year 2.

E. The test mailings of 140,000 will pull 4 percent (not bad) and will vary for the rollout (the large mailing of four million) from 2.8 percent on some mailings to 4.5 percent on others. In Year 2, when the better lists are used up, the average percentage will drop to 2.8.

F. Of the charter subscribers, 65 percent will renew in Years 1 and 2. This is a rather high percentage to project.

G. Recalling chapter 9 on single-copy distribution, we know that all newsstand copies are on consignment. Thus the assumptions given are for 50,000 to 75,000 copies distributed in Year 1 and for 100,000 copies in Year 2.

H. The assumptions are realistic, projecting only a 30 to 40 percent sale on newsstands for the first year and 40 percent for the second. These percentages are slightly lower than the national average for all newsstand magazines.

I. The newsstand price per copy is $2.00.

J. In Year 1 the publisher will produce an issue with 100 pages (96 body pages plus cover); in Year 2, 116 pages plus cover.

K. Here one must resist the urge to overstate the amount of advertising pages to be sold—20 to 25 per issue in Year 1 and 30 to 35 in Year 2. This estimate seems to be on the high side for a new magazine.

L. The reader should remember about CPM (cost per thousand). If the black-and-white CPM is $22 and the circulation base is 100,000, the page will cost $2,200.

M. The cost per copy for manufacturing, printing, and paper is 52 cents in Year 1 and 49 cents in Year 2. The drop in cost of 3 cents in Year 2 is attributable to the larger number of copies printed. Paper cost would probably increase 10 percent but startup time and plate cost on the presses would be amortized over a larger print run.

N. We note here that there are no full-time people on the staff during the test period and a relatively small complement in Years 1 and 2. The increase

in editorial staff is no doubt due to the increased number of pages to be produced.

Once the assumptions are made, the publisher, accountant, or consultant will draw up a statement showing the cash projections. This chart is extremely necessary for the publisher's own use, but more so for prospective investors. See the example on the opposite page.

We will now analyze this all-important statement. Bear in mind that on an existing magazine, these reports are prepared monthly, as well as budgeted for future years.

A. Since few mailings were made in the test period, we see only $3,000 in these receipts. This increases to $26,000 in the prepublication period, which is generally three months before the first issue comes out. The test period may be as long as a year before the first issue. In Years 1 and 2, there are many new subscription mailings, plus the revenue from subscription renewals. Thus the big numbers.

B. This magazine is obviously not newsstand-oriented. We therefore see only $98,000 in newsstand receipts for Year 1 and $359,000 for Year 2.

C. "Advertising (net)" means net of agency commission (15 percent).

D. Other can refer to receipts from mail-order sales, list rentals, and the like.

E. "Mechanical and distribution" refers to the cost of printing, paper, typesetting, color separations, and the charge the printer applies to the shipping and handling of newsstand copies.

F. Editorial disbursements would include the cost of outside manuscripts, photography, and illustrations, as well as the salaries of the editorial and art staff.

G. Advertising disbursements would include the salaries of the ad sales staff and the costs of advertising sales promotion.

H. This item refers to the cost of subscription mailings. Note the heavy increases in Years 1 and 2, when 4 million pieces are mailed annually.

I. Circulation fulfillment costs include the postage for the magazine's subscriptions, the maintenance of the sub list, the running off on tape of the names for the printer each issue, and the printer's

## Cash Projections (in thousands)

| Receipts | Test Period | Prepublication | Year 1 | Year 2 |
|---|---|---|---|---|
| A. Subscriptions | $ 3 | $26 | $1,459 | $2,675 |
| B. Newsstand | — | — | 98 | 359 |
| C. Advertising (net) | — | — | 144 | 880 |
| D. Other | — | — | 15 | 72 |
| Total receipts | 3 | 26 | 1,716 | 3,986 |
| **Disbursements** | | | | |
| E. Mechanical and distribution | — | $ 4 | $ 478 | $1,389 |
| F. Editorial | — | 23 | 168 | 294 |
| G. Advertising | — | 34 | 234 | 321 |
| H. Circulation promotion | $45 | 10 | 1,283 | 1,410 |
| I. Circulation fulfillment | — | — | 63 | 107 |
| J. General and administrative | 8 | 62 | 249 | 275 |
| Total disbursements | 53 | 133 | 2,475 | 3,796 |
| K. Net cash flow | ($50) | ($107) | ($ 759) | $ 190 |
| L. Cumulative cash flow | ($50) | ($157) | ($ 916) | |

High point of negative cash flow in Year 2—$1,374,000.

charge for affixing the name strips on the printed copies and then following them through to the post office.

J. "General and administrative," generally shortened to G&A, is a catchall for many expenses. They would include executive salaries, rent, utilities, supplies, payroll taxes, and a dozen other miscellaneous expenses.

K. The net cash flow, when it appears in parentheses, pertains to a negative amount. Thus in the test period the venture has a deficit of $50,000; in the prepublication period, $107,000; in Year 1, $759,000; and in Year 2, finally, a positive cash flow of $190,000.

L. This line states the *cumulative* cash flow, which is negative $50,000 in the test period, increases to negative $157,000 in the prepublication period, and climbs to negative $916,000 by the end of

Year 1. We are also told that the high point of negative cash flow is reached sometime in Year 2, with $1,374,000.

It is hoped that since Year 2 actually took in $190,000 more than it expended, in subsequent years the $1,374,000 will be reduced. But this example shows the necessity of adequate financing to sustain the venture through this rocky period on its way to safer ground. We also learn that it is hardly possible for the investor to allocate a small sum of money subject to "calls" for larger amounts, since almost $1 million is required by the end of Year 1.

The magazine consultant John Klingel makes an important point about raising capital: "If you need to raise $1 million, your projections will usually have to show a potential fifth-year profit of $1 million for the deal to be attractive to investors. Under current market conditions, a magazine earning $1 million would be worth $10 million to $15 million. You want to keep 30 percent to 40 percent of the equity and the investors are going to want a substantial return on their investment."

We have referred in this chapter to a direct-mail test for a new magazine. Robin Wolaner's test for *Parenting* enabled her to achieve Time Inc. Magazine's financing. Here are a few considerations when making such a test:

1. An accurate indication of the potential market for a new magazine is a mailing of a total of 100,000 pieces to twenty different lists—about 5,000 to each list.

2. Be certain there is a large enough, ongoing universe (expansion factor) for each list used. It makes no sense to pull a high 10 percent on a list of 5,000 when the total number of names on that list is only 10,000.

3. A "cold" test without asking for money far in advance of publication may yield inconclusive results. That is, it is the wrong approach to say to the prospect, "Don't send me any money, but when I do publish the magazine a year from now, I'll send you a bill." The prospect may forget all about the offer and need to be resold.

4. You can use a "hot" test—that is, asking for money in advance of publication—if you are absolutely certain the magazine will be out in three or four months from the time you collect the money. A longer period can bring trouble from the Better Business Bureau or your state's attorney general.

5. Timing, as we pointed out in chapter 8 on subscriptions, is very important. A good month for a test is September, with a rollout in January. In January you may be competing in the mails with white sales but not Christmas catalogs.

We have progressed now with the business plan and the direct-mail test to the stage where we are ready for the next major move—the search for money to finance the venture. First, however, I would advocate the preparation of a printed dummy. But more about that in the next chapter.

# 14

# Starting a New Magazine, Part II

When I was actively publishing magazines, at least once a month I received a phone call from a would-be publisher who eagerly tried to convince me of the attributes of his or her "great new magazine idea." Since it made good business sense to see each of these entrepreneurs, I would arrange a meeting.

Invariably, the neophyte publisher arrived armed with reams of financial data but seldom with the necessary business plan outlined in the previous chapter. I was usually presented with an amateurish pasted-up dummy of the proposed magazine. It contained an artist's rough layout of stories, articles, and advertisements clipped from other magazines. At the conclusion of the meeting, the aspiring publisher quickly informed me that this magazine idea was the most remarkable phenomenon since the discovery of Halley's comet. I was usually unimpressed.

### The Printed Dummy

If one is seeking large-scale financing for a visual product like a magazine or is attempting to sell advertising long in advance of a magazine's publication, it is essential to prepare a *printed dummy*. Doing so may be expensive and time-consuming but is unquestionably the most professional approach.

A number of techniques can be used in producing a printed dummy. In its simplest form a representation of the cover is used, with a bare indication of the inside editorial pages. Another approach is that taken by Condé Nast Publications when it started *Self* in the late 1970s. In this case the publisher used an actual cover and mock type for a number of the inside layouts. Finally, some publishers use a full-dress representation of the magazine exactly as it will ultimately be published.

Although a number of years have passed since *Self* was launched, the printed dummy Condé Nast used for the publication serves as an outstanding model of what a dummy should be. The magazine went on to achieve major success, with a circulation at this writing of more than 1.15 million and advertising revenues of about $40 million.

The company produced an outstanding printed dummy. In this case, the expensive presentation was created not for financing purposes but rather to sell advertising space.

The entire dummy promotion was a class act. Hundreds of advertisers and their agencies received the dummy in an attractive orange box, with the title, *Self,* being the only piece of copy. A simple letter of introduction from *Self*'s publisher at the time, Peter Diamandis, was inside the box. The recipients were invited to enter a contest to win a *Self* warm-up suit. Both pieces were color-coordinated in orange and black. Figure 14–1 shows the elements discussed.

Accompanying the letter and contest form was an elegant wrapper, opening to the dummy magazine itself.

The cover of the dummy for *Self,* reproduced in figure 14–3, shows a natural-looking model who conveyed the desired image of health and vivacity. The cover lines tell the newsstand browser that this magazine relates to "self-help."

The contents page for the dummy lists subjects likely to appear in the first issue (fig. 14–2). With over twenty articles and a dozen features, readers of this dummy know exactly what the magazine's editorial concept is all about. I cannot say that similar articles have not appeared in other magazines, but as a total unit, they successfully promote the new publication's image.

The ads in this dummy were representative of those the *Self* people expected to sell in their early issues. Since Condé Nast publishes many other magazines, it was no problem for them to borrow these ad plates.

It is extremely difficult to be innovative about beauty spreads. In figure 14–4 we see an effective demonstration of such a spread. The cost entailed the actual photo shootings, model fees, and color separations. Since the people at *Self* did not want to tip off too much of the editorial content, they chose to use mock type unrelated to the piece.

The dummy of *Self* was 128 pages plus cover. I found the whole presentation excellent. Founding editor Phyllis Starr Wilson and art consultant Bea Feitler created a package that was certain to impress potential advertisers. It took planning, talent, and money, but then, Condé Nast always

**This is it!**

The one and only "SELF Starter" contest. Designed by so-called experts to give you a shot at winning what you've always dreamed of owning (a smashing "SELF Starter" warm-up suit shown here in living color).

Study SELF's editorial statement on Page 1 of the magazine, scan the enclosed rate card (that's always a lot of fun) and then complete this entry blank carefully, pop it into the pre-paid, pre-addressed envelope and drop it into the mail. Anyone answering all questions correctly (we have our standards) is eligible for our drawing that will produce at least 200 winners. These lucky people will be notified on or about July 1, 1978 and be invited to a party.

Figure 14–1

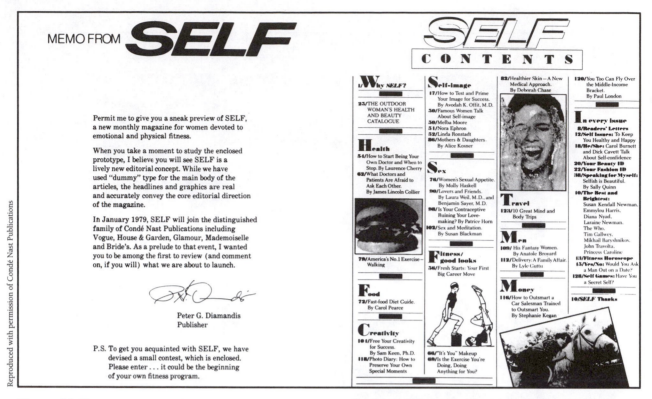

MEMO FROM **SELF**

Permit me to give you a sneak preview of SELF, a new monthly magazine for women devoted to emotional and physical fitness.

When you take a moment to study the enclosed prototype, I believe you will see SELF is a lively new editorial concept. While we have used "dummy" type for the main body of the articles, the headlines and graphics are real and accurately convey the core editorial direction of the magazine.

In January 1979, SELF will join the distinguished family of Condé Nast Publications including Vogue, House & Garden, Glamour, Mademoiselle and Bride's. As a prelude to that event, I wanted you to be among the first to review (and comment on, if you will) what we are about to launch.

Peter G. Diamandis
Publisher

P.S. To get you acquainted with SELF, we have devised a small contest, which is enclosed. Please enter . . . it could be the beginning of your own fitness program.

**SELF**
CONTENTS

Figure 14–2

Figure 14–3

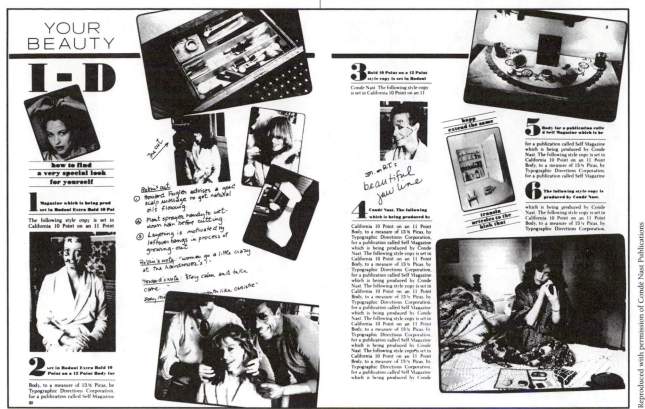

Figure 14–4

travels first-class. Although most new publishers cannot enjoy the luxury of such a presentation, with modifications this *Self* dummy can be emulated on a lesser budget.

## EATING WELL, The Magazine of Food & Health

Telemedia Communications in Charlotte, Vermont, already published the successful *Harrowsmith Country Life* magazine when it decided to launch *EATING WELL* in July 1990. Telemedia is a large Canadian media company.

Since the magazine wanted to establish an image of high graphic and editorial quality, the publisher decided to produce a full-blown preview issue a year prior to publication. The purpose was (a) to conduct in-depth market research of product appeal and market acceptance; (b) to use indirect-mail testing; and (c) to give advertisers an accurate idea of what the editorial product would contain.

Figure 14–5 shows the cover of *EATING WELL*'s preview issue. Its editorial premise is clear-cut: beautifully prepared food that is also healthy to eat. Figure 14–6 depicts the contents page, which illustrates the diversity of the magazine's editorial package. Figure 14–7 displays a letter of introduction from the magazine's publisher, clearly outlining the magazine's purpose. Figure 14–8 illustrates the magazine's well-devised use of a food piece with a travel orientation.

*EATING WELL* went on to become a success story. By its January/February 1992 issue, it had a rate base of 400,000, almost double the circulation at its launch. Surely, the decision to produce a full-blown dummy was integral to this early success.

## Essential Steps in Producing a Printed Dummy

Have definite plans for the entire editorial portion. Use four-color only if there will be four-color in the actual issue.

Figure 14–5. The cover of preview issue

Figure 14–6. The contents page of this issue

Figure 14–7. An introductory letter from the magazine's publisher

Figure 14–8. This travel piece emphasizes the mood of the magazine: eating quality food that is also healthy

**Figure 14–5**

**Figure 14–6**

**Figure 14–7**

**Figure 14–8**

Unless a skilled art director is on your team at the outset, engage the services of one at a fixed price. Request a budget from the art director for all costs—typesetting, photography, color separation, pasteup.

Shop for a competitively priced, quality printer. When you have found one, sell the printer on doing a printed dummy at cost.

Visit the production managers at large advertising agencies and ask for the use of their black-and-white and color film of ads you select for the dummy. Sometimes a printer can help in this regard.

Print the correct number of copies the first time—it's expensive to go back to press. Remember, you may be using these dummies for potential investors, advertisers, staff, and so on.

Finally, make sure the dummy is professionally executed. Do not opt for easy substitutes. Make certain the quality of the writing is indicative of what will appear in the real magazine. Go to the expense of making color separations. Do not lift them from other magazines. Stress the authenticity of the contents page. Maintain the same level of pacing you would in the actual magazine. In short, make the dummy a true representation of your first issue.

## Time and Money

Now that you have seed money, a business plan, the results of a direct-mail test, and a printed dummy, you are in business—or are you? There is still the Herculean task of raising the real money for the venture. This task can take months, and even years.

One consultant who has worked on many new magazines traced the history of a venture from concept to first issue. It took almost three years. The first year was spent developing the concept and completing the business plan; another year was consumed raising the seed money, revising the business plan, and planning the direct-mail test. After mailing 200,000 pieces with spectacular results in the first month of the third year, the entrepreneur started a round of fund-raising for major financing. This and other organi-

zational efforts took nine months and culminated in the publication of his first issue. Is it worth it? We think so. The magazine business is like few others. Unlike the manufacturer of other consumer products, the "manufacturer" of magazines puts himself or herself on the line with a new product every week or month. The sheer excitement of a magazine's creation and marketing is unmatched by any other pursuit.

## Financial Arrangements

Before calling on investors or other money sources, it is judicious to frame some idea of what the general relationship of all parties involved in the publication will be. It is much simpler to negotiate with an investor if you realize how much you are prepared to give up.

These days major investors are hard-nosed about new magazine ventures, a factor that may cost you 70 percent or more of the ownership of the publication, thereby reducing the equity interest of all the other participants proportionately. Where are the places to go for money? A list of possibilities follows.

**Venture Capital.** Certain companies are in business primarily to invest in new ventures. They invest the money of wealthy individuals, trusts, and even banks.

Venture capitalists are highly sophisticated, and although they generally see every new idea, they accept just a few each year. If they are enamored of the concept and the entrepreneurial team and decide to fund the project, they will ask for 60 to 70 percent of the venture for their investment.

**National Distributors.** In the old days when magazine launchings cost a fraction of what they do today, the place to go if you planned to publish a newsstand magazine was to a national distributor. In return for a contract, the distributor would advance enough money to pay for each issue's printing bill. This advance was usually treated as an assignment, money the printer could draw on at completion of the issue. All the publisher had to do was finance the editorial and overhead expenses of the magazine.

Those days are gone forever. Distributors may, if they love a magazine idea, offer an advance of 10 to 15 percent on shipping an issue, but this sum hardly covers the cost of printing and paper. I do know, however, of at least two major magazines that were partly funded by a distributor. Although this information is confidential, I can say that one of them was a women's magazine.

**Use a Name or Lead Investor.** Another possibility involves finding a socially or financially prominent individual who will invest in a project in its early stages and allow his or her name to be used in attracting other investors. In money circles the "sheep" principle seems to prevail, with subsequent prospects saying to themselves, "What does _____ know that I don't?"

When we started raising money for our first publishing venture, *Weight Watchers Magazine,* we were fortunate to be able to convince a leading Wall Street broker to join our group. His respected name brought at least four other investors into the project. These investors in turn were able to interest other money people. It is worthy of a strong effort, therefore, to bring a "name" into the magazine launching at the outset.

## Banks and Insurance Companies

Although most big banks and some insurance companies maintain communications loan departments, the odds are decidedly against their financing a new magazine. They are very conservative and seem to have a bias against publishing in general as being too risky.

There is, however, cash to be found. The reader is directed to Margaret E. Popper's article "How to Find the Money You Need to Grow" in the December 1991 issue of *Folio:*.

## Magazine Publishing Companies

Although magazine publishing companies are generally poor prospects for backing an outside magazine idea, there are exceptions (see chapter 13 for *Parenting*'s story). Further, most communi-

cations companies have corporate development departments whose staff may be willing to listen to new ideas.

A few years ago a student of mine at New York University spoke to me after class about an idea he had for a magazine. The young man had no magazine experience but was working in the field of paramedicine. He informed me that there was no specific publication covering this important new field and that he would like to start such a magazine but had no money.

I suggested that he take the idea to a large trade magazine publisher and be willing to accept a good job and a small percentage of the profits if the publisher accepted the new magazine proposal. My student was fortunate in being able to find a publisher for his idea. The magazine was published and, to my knowledge, is successful.

Magazine publishing companies prefer buying an established magazine rather than a new one from an entrepreneur. In this way they are dealing with proven entities.

## Suppliers

As a consultant to a new magazine a few years ago, I was able to convince a printer to invest a portion of his profit margin in the magazine. He agreed to invest up to a certain sum in the project, and for doing so he received an equity interest in the venture. The publisher made similar arrangements with other suppliers, which helped him survive his first year.

It may be difficult to convince potential suppliers of the merits of this kind of investment, but the prospect of acquiring an important new account by gambling profits can be appealing to printers, direct-mail organizations, and even consultants.

One last tip on raising money: Do not underfinance a magazine because you have difficulty attracting the required amount. Some years ago I consulted on a magazine project geared to young single people who were "living the new life-style." The concept was sound, but the magazine failed. The plan called for raising about $600,000, and the publisher could raise only $350,000, part of this in credit from a printer for a portion of his bill. I urged the neophyte publisher to wait until he had the additional funds—but to no avail. He started the magazine in a poor financial condition and never got past the first year. It was too late to go back to his original investors for more money. It is worth the additional time and effort to raise the required amount of capital at the outset. Secondary financing is a difficult procedure.

## Entrepreneurs and the Deals They Cut

An article in *Publishing News* for June 1989 lists the arrangements made by six entrepreneurs with established magazine companies:

## Legal Forms for the Venture

Now that you have the money, what are the best legal forms for the venture to take? Here are a few:

**Limited Partnership.** The entrepreneur puts up no money and becomes the general partner, receiving a fixed share of the profits. The investors put up all the money and become limited partners, their liability being limited to the amount of their investment. For tax purposes all losses go to these limited partners. Profits can be apportioned among partners in any way they agree at the start of the project.

**Subchapter S.** This form limits the venture to ten shareholders. For wealthy individuals in a high

| Title | Launch Date | Entrepreneur | Corporate Arrangement |
|---|---|---|---|
| *Practical Homeowner* | 1980 | Harry Egner | Egner formed the firm with Capital Cities/ABC and others to buy *PH* from Rodale Press in 1989 and to operate independently. |
| *Details* | 1982 | Annie Flanders | Following a series of investment bankers, Condé Nast paid $2 million in 1988 for *Details*, retaining Flanders. |
| Whittle Communications | 1986 | Chris Whittle | Time Inc. Magazines paid $185 million in 1988 for a 50 percent share, with additional payments and ownership contingent on Whittle's growth through 1993. |
| *Hippocrates* (now *Health*) | 1987 | Eric Schrier | In 1988 Time, Inc. paid $9 million for a 50 percent share. |
| *Parenting* | 1987 | Robin Wolaner | Time Inc., put $5 million into startup for a minority position and a buyout option, later picked up. |
| *Sazz* | 1988 | Mary Ann and Edgar Holley | Fairchild contributed $1.8 million and retained the right to buy 100 percent of the magazine. |

tax bracket, this type of investment is appealing, since they are able to pick up the magazine's losses on their current year's taxes in proportion to their share of stock. This plan is practical for a new magazine, which customarily loses money in its early years. When the magazine begins to show a profit, the corporate form can be changed.

**Public Financing.** Here the new publisher and a group of insiders hold 100 percent of the stock but agree to sell some percentage of their interest to the public to gain additional financing. Under the Securities and Exchange Commission Act of 1933, this financing requires a registration of the stock, which is costly. The *National Lampoon* was formed as a Subchapter S entity and a few years later went the "public" route. As previously stated, however, these offerings are difficult to put over these days.

## Some Key Points

If the material in these two chapters on starting a new magazine is put to use and you manage to get through all the necessary steps with success, it will still be only the beginning. You must now go ahead with the business of actually publishing the magazine. Here are some important points to follow:

1. Try to charge a realistic price for the magazine on the newsstand and, particularly, for subscriptions.
2. If you are going the newsstand route, get a reputable distributor.
3. When selling advertising for a new magazine, offer charter rates, but have a uniform policy for all advertisers.
4. Hire the best art director and editor you can afford. No amount of preparation and financing will make a new magazine succeed if the editorial package is not superior.
5. Make sure your promotion and PR efforts are top-flight.
6. Don't load yourself with unnecessary overhead, especially in the early stages of a venture. Fancy offices mean little to a new magazine. Don't put people on the payroll too far in advance of your publication date.

## Tips on Purchasing a Magazine Property

Even in a slumping economy, there are companies that want to buy magazines, particularly if they are successful. Acquiring an existing publication may be an easier approach than starting one. A magazine in the consumer or business sector that has a franchise position in its field (that is, controlling its classification or industry) will, however, command a high price.

Most investors searching for magazines are seeking out specialized publications, those whose audiences can be clearly identified for advertisers. Such magazines can draw premium rates. The demand for acquisitions is expected to remain strong for some time.

If a magazine you are considering is not in a franchise situation and is number one or two in its field, think about starting a new magazine aimed at the same audience rather than buying one.

If the magazine is losing money, consider a token payment and then a payout based on future profits. This formula has been used frequently in acquisitions.

When a magazine is heavy in subscriptions, realize that you will inherit these obligations and take this factor into account in your cash-flow projections. If the magazine is audited by ABC, you can obtain an accurate record of its subscription activity. An examination of the publication's own records will readily determine how many subscribers renew.

Check the source of these subscriptions—many can have a low yield to the magazine.

Retain the top management of the acquired magazine for at least three years if their performance is good.

Finally, hire the very best consultant you can afford to analyze the multitudinous factors involved in measuring a magazine's worth. One of the best we know is James Kobak. His astute "What's Your Magazine Worth" in *Folio:*'s September 1986 issue provides advanced education on the subject.

If you want to buy a major existing magazine property, we recommend the preeminent investment bankers in this field, Veronis, Suhler & Associates, 350 Park Avenue, New York, NY 10022.

In these chapters we have dealt with the complex yet fascinating subject of starting a new magazine. In the next chapter we will look at the legal questions of magazine publishing, and in the final chapters we will discuss women in magazine publishing and the future of magazines as a communications medium.

## Interview

James B. Kobak started James B. Kobak & Company in 1971. A consulting firm, the company specializes in magazine, book, and other communications companies and is active throughout the world. Mr. Kobak himself is a director of a number of companies in the field, writes articles, and speaks frequently to various groups. He conducts courses in such subjects as "Starting a New Magazine" and "Buying, Selling, and Merging Companies."

A CPA prior to starting his consulting business, he was from 1946 to 1971 the managing partner of J. K. Lasser & Company, a major international accounting firm. He was one of the founders in 1974 of James B. Kobak Business Models, a firm that markets financial models and systems to publishers throughout the world.

He sometimes invests in communications properties and is the owner of Kirkus Reviews, Inc., which reviews books prior to their publication for libraries, booksellers, film producers, and others.

*Starting any new business is extremely difficult. What factors are responsible for the reported 90 percent failure rate of new magazines?*

By far the most frequent reason for the failure of new magazines is that the subject matter is not something about which people want to read. The most important reason for a magazine's success is the field it serves. If people do not *want* a magazine about the subject, even though the publisher feels that the world *needs* such a magazine, it will fail. And if people *do* want a magazine about a subject, you can publish a pretty bad product and still be successful.

The second most frequent reason is that the editorial matter does not serve the field well. This is usually because the purpose of the magazine has not been defined. If you cannot state the purpose of a magazine in less than ten words, then you don't know what you are doing and the magazine will not have a sharp enough focus to be of interest.

You will frequently hear people say that they failed because they were inadequately financed. This is an excuse, not a reason. The truth is that either they planned very poorly and thus did not know how much financing would be needed, or they started even though they knew they didn't have enough money, which is just plain dumb. And then in some cases, the publishers are just inept and do a poor job of publishing.

While the failure rate overall is 90 percent or so, for those magazines which are carefully planned and tested the answer is just the opposite—70 percent succeed.

*You are probably asked this question every day. We'll ask it again: Is there a minimum amount of capital needed to start a new magazine?*

To answer this one I first must point out that there is no magazine business. Every magazine is in a different business, appealing to different readers and different advertisers. Consider whether there are any common characteristics between *Playboy* and *Ms.* Of course not, except that they are printed on paper.

Because of this there really is no answer to the question. The amount needed is different in each case and can range from the few who find a way for $10,000 all the way up to the many millions.

*Are there categories in publishing that are still undeveloped and open for magazine ideas?*

Of course there are—and there always will be. But I can't tell you what they are. Magazines exist because people have interests. Those interests are constantly changing; therefore, the desire for different magazines is also constantly changing. During the past ten years or so, there has been a large expansion of people's interests. This should continue for the foreseeable future. The reasons? More education, more affluence, more travel—and, more than anything else, the televison tube. Television has aroused new interests of all kinds. And the present proliferation of channels will continue this.

New magazines are started by people who have a feeling about when these interests are becoming important. The strange thing is that usually people come from different places but seem to get the feeling at about the same time. The concepts for new magazines usually spring up like tulips all at once—and I often hear within a couple of months from people in California, Georgia, and Philadelphia about the desire to start magazines for the same field.

*If readers of this book have uncovered what they think is a brilliant idea for a new magazine that does not duplicate anything now published, would you advise them to find a group of private investors for funding, or to go to a large publishing company to try to sell the idea?*

It is hard to raise capital for any new venture. But raising it for a new magazine is particularly difficult. It is a little-understood business. And if the financial people do not relate to the subject matter of the magazine, financing may be impossible.

I advise people to go in every conceivable direction in raising money. This starts with family, friends, your doctor and dentist, venture capital firms, wealthy individuals, Wall Street firms, banks (for references), lawyers, accountants, small publishers, large publishers, and anyone else who might have an interest.

*Briefly explain what a business plan is and why it is so important for new magazine development.*

A business plan is vital for any new venture. How else can you—or anyone else—know what you are going to do? The blueprint of the operation for the first five or six years, it consists of several parts:

The concept—a brief statement of what the magazine is all about

Editorial content—a brief statement of what the contents will be

Market for readers—a quantification of who the potential readers are and the ways to obtain them

Market for advertisers—who the logical advertisers are

Competition—description of the magazines with which you will compete and some vital statistics about them: amount of circulation and advertising, prices, history, and so on

People involved—brief biographies of who is on the team; include outside helpers such as consultants, lawyers, accountants, bankers, and the like

Financial projections—for the first six years, prepared on the cash basis; these may be presented in summary form but should be based on careful, detailed calculations of every item of income and expense

The plan will show the amount of financing you anticipate will be needed and also the profits you expect to earn for the period covered. Aside from being necessary for you, the plan is essential in the money-raising process. It is also helpful in luring key employees and in talking with potential suppliers.

*I have written briefly about the Time Inc. organization and its failures,* Picture Week *and* TV Cable Week. *What went wrong?*

I do not consider *Picture Week* a failure. They went through a very thorough (and possibly overly expensive) testing procedure in several cities and decided not to publish it nationwide. The failure of *TV Cable Week* is well documented in the book *The Fanciest Dive*. It is the typical large-corporation screwup. The same type of thing happens at General Motors, Xerox, and Boise Cascade. While Time has had some wonderful startup successes (*Time, Life, Fortune,* and *People*), some of its now-successful magazines were launched very poorly. *Sports Illustrated* lost money for some thirteen years; *Money,* about ten. *Discover* was never able to make money, and it was sold.

The real point is that large publishing organizations are no better at launching magazines than anyone else. All of them have had failures—consider the *Reader's Digest* and *Families,* Rodale Press and *Spring,* McCall's and *Your Place,* Triangle and *Good Food* (first-time launch).

Some two-thirds of successful magazines have been started by people who have never been in the magazine business.

# Publishing and the Law

Through my affiliation with the *National Lampoon,* I have acquired a working familiarity with publishers' legal problems. I know that sooner or later, and more often sooner, most publishers are confronted with legal problems in several areas. In this chapter we will explore some of the more common problem areas.

### Libel

The threat of a libel suit is always present for any publisher who is at all controversial. Almost any statement that could injure someone's reputation leaves the publisher potentially the defendant in a lawsuit. The observation is vague, I know, but the law is equally so. Generally, specific allegations that could cause a loss of reputation can be libelous, while commentary or factual statements of little consequence cannot. For example, calling someone a crook (when the person is not one) is almost certainly libelous; calling someone a bore is probably not. What you say and how you say it not only are a question of style and journalism but also may be a question of law. Accordingly, editorial staffs of magazines often find themselves huddled with their legal counsel over a particularly sensitive allegation.

Nor is insurance likely to be much help in this area. While libel insurance *is* available (although if you are particularly controversial, you may not be able to obtain it), it is expensive and may carry a very high deductible—perhaps more than $100,000. And it probably won't cover the generally heavy legal expenses of defending a lawsuit.

A magazine's publishing schedule does not always leave time to check with counsel; moreover, it's not always the obviously risky statements that come back to haunt the publisher. To avoid endless legal hassles and the substantial risk of a large judgment, a certain amount of preventive medicine and common sense should be exercised. Any statement, whether true or untrue, that could be damaging to someone's reputation should be backed by evidence that it *is* true before being printed. As Harold Hayes, former editor of *Esquire,* has observed, "You must have evidence to justify your interpretation. A magazine should be able to document sufficiently whatever interpretation it is going to make. . . . If it goes beyond what the evidence suggests, it would be my responsibility to restrict the degree of the author's comment."

To a large extent good journalism is also a good legal defense—if it does not prevent a lawsuit, it can often prevent losing a lawsuit. Of course, any true statement is absolutely protected by the courts, but it is often difficult to prove truth in court. The law provides, however, substantial protection to publishers who print allegations about public officials or important or well-known people (called "public figures" by the courts). Publishers of such statements are required to prove not the truth of the statement but that they reasonably believe it, or at least did not entertain serious doubts about its truth. A few examples might illustrate this point.

Ralph Ginsburg, in a publication entitled *Fact Magazine,* printed a "Goldwater" issue on the eve of the 1964 presidential election. It revolved around the theme that Barry Goldwater was mentally unstable and that a majority of American psychiatrists believed him to be psychologically unfit to be president. Goldwater lost the election but won the lawsuit (the jury awarded him damages totaling $75,000). The "poll" turned out to be a mailing of a simplistic questionnaire that went largely unanswered or, if returned, was unsigned. It was condemned by psychiatric groups as being completely invalid *prior* to the publication of the "results" of the poll. Goldwater, being beyond a doubt a public figure, had to prove not only that the statements made about him were untrue and therefore libelous (the latter was not very difficult—the law in New York and most other states holds that any false accusation that someone is mentally ill is libelous) but that Ginsburg *knew* they were untrue. The evidence showed that Ginsburg worked on the poll without any expert help, knew that many of the responses were unreliable because they were completely untraceable, was aware that the poll had been dismissed as scientifically worthless, and published many of the "responses" only after they were heavily edited and embellished but nevertheless printed the "results" without qualification.

Similarly, University of Georgia football coach (and public figure) Wally Butts brought and won a libel suit against the *Saturday Evening Post* for printing an article accusing him of fixing a football game by giving the rival coach a detailed description of Georgia's play, calls, and strategy. The article was based solely on the statement of a single person—someone known to be on probation in connection with bad-check charges—who claimed to have "accidentally" overheard a telephone conversation between the two coaches. The *Post* printed the story without checking with football experts or making any other attempt to confirm the story. It appeared, as the U.S. Supreme Court found, that the *Post* was searching for a "controversial" image and had allowed itself to get sloppy in apparent hunger for a quick scoop.

On the same day that the *Post* lost its case, the Associated Press won a reversal of a libel judgment awarded to General James Walker, a right-wing extremist figure of the 1960s (and a public figure). The AP sent out a story to the effect that Walker had led a group of anti-integration demonstrators against U.S. marshals at the University of Mississippi. Walker claimed that actually he had tried to calm the crowd. The issue was not who was right but whether the AP could rely on its reporter on the scene—the Court said it could, since AP had no reason to doubt his story and, being a news service, operated a very tight schedule when reporting hot news.

The press scored a clear victory when the U.S. Supreme Court in 1988 unanimously struck down a lower court's $200,000 award to televangelist Jerry Falwell in his case against Larry Flynt's *Hustler*. Falwell initially sued for libel and emotional distress after the magazine ran a cartoon parody depicting him in drunken incest. The libel claim was thrown out when the jury found that no one would believe the parody, but Falwell won an appeal on the charge that the satire was "intentional infliction of emotional distress." The Supreme Court's overruling was based heavily on *The New York Times* v. *Sullivan*, which states that a publication can be found guilty only if it contains a false statement of fact made with actual malice.

The Falwell parody, the Court said, was an "opinion" and therefore could not contain a "false statement" or "false idea." The *Hustler* decision, protecting even "outrageous" speech, "absolutely blows out of the water any idea that the Rehnquist court would dismantle the *Sullivan* principle," claims media attorney Jason Meyer. He further speculates that this may put to rest the idea that opinions containing malice can be applied to public-figure cases. Media attorney Slade Metcalf cautioned that, even though he believes the Court will not refuse to hear cases attempting to change the breadth or basis of the *Sullivan* rule, publishers must be as careful as ever when covering individuals not in the public eye.

While there is no formula that can tell you when to cross-check before rushing into print, caution may be the better part of valor, especially if your publishing schedule gives you the chance to make sure, or to be as sure as you can, that you can back up your story.

Although no checklist can cover every situation, the following guidelines may be of use to the publisher before printing a story or allegation:

1. Is the statement libelous in character? As I have said, there is no clear-cut guide here, but in most cases common sense, and perhaps a call to your lawyer, should provide an answer.

2. Is the statement made about an identifiable person? Simply "changing the names to protect the innocent" may not always be enough if other facts make it clear who is being referred to.

3. Is the person about whom the statement is made a public official or public figure? If the person is not well known or clearly involved in a news event that makes him or her newsworthy, you may be held to a stricter standard than you would be if the story concerned a public figure. There is a lot of case law, not always consistent, about who is or is not a public figure. For example, a relatively well-known socialite involved in a particularly nasty divorce action sued when certain details (which she claimed to be false) of the proceedings were reported in a national newsmagazine. The court held that the divorce proceeding was an essentially private affair,

that she was not so well known as to make details of her marital strife a matter of public interest, and that accordingly she was not a public figure. On the other hand, Johnny Carson *was* held to be a public figure with regard to a story about *his* marital difficulties. It is obviously worth a call to your lawyer for an opinion when in doubt, because the answer may well determine what kind of risk you are prepared to take with a statement you cannot absolutely prove.

4. Is the author or source reliable? Generally, under the law you are stuck with your employees' mistakes, but at least you can send them out to check again. In the case of submission, you are not always able to check the reliability of every statement made. Courts do understand this and to some extent allow the publisher to rely on the author's accuracy, but it is not safe to treat every word as golden. When possible, check with the author on statements you think are sensitive. You can place quite a bit of reliance on an author with whom you have dealt before and found reliable, or who has a good reputation. Be *very* wary, however, of unsolicited submissions—someone else's grudge piece may become your lawsuit. A written guarantee (discussed later in this chapter) is also advisable when dealing with authors not on the payroll.

One final point: Most statutes of limitation for libel actions (and normally for invasion of privacy as well—see the next section) are relatively short—one or two years. If you are not sued for a year or two after the offending issue hits the newsstands, you are probably home free, even if you still sell an occasional copy to readers who request back issues. But remember, if you reprint an article—in an anthology or in a new issue of the magazine, for example—you run the risk of giving a potential plaintiff a second chance to sue you.

## Invasion of Privacy

The right of privacy, with its lawsuits brought by those who claim that this right has been violated,

seems to be expanding. This right has been defined as the right to be left alone, and while publishers can hardly turn out a magazine by leaving people alone, it is becoming increasingly important to know just how far you can go.

It may be useful to divide lawsuits under the right of privacy into two broad categories: commercial appropriation and public disclosure of private facts.

**Commercial Appropriation.** It is the law in some states that you have to get someone's permission before you can print his or her name or picture in a magazine that is sold to the public. The exception to this rule—and it's a huge exception—is that you can publish a name or picture in connection with a newsworthy event, and the term *newsworthy* has been given a very broad meaning. As a rule, celebrities are fair game for true reports about their comings and goings even if the "news" is really little more than gossip. The fact that your magazine can sell more issues if someone's name or picture appears in it is not necessarily damning so long as there is some reasonable connection with a story that is arguable "news," even if it is of the entertainment variety. Robert Goulet, for example, lost a case against *Confidential,* which printed a "lurid" story about his private life. Some publishers have gone a little too far, though. Carroll O'Connor (Archie Bunker) sued a magazine that featured prominently on its cover an "interview" with O'Connor that never took place.

Using someone's name or picture in an advertisement without his or her permission can be an invitation to a lawsuit—but using that person's name or picture in connection with an advertisement for your magazine is probably permissible, if that person "appeared" in one of your editions. Joe Namath brought and lost a suit against *Sports Illustrated* when it ran a subscription advertisement showing a picture of him taken from an earlier edition. If the original story was newsworthy, advertising the content of the magazine is permissible as long as there is no attempt to imply that the celebrity endorses the magazine.

The publisher should not be lulled into thinking that *every* use of a famous person's name or likeness is going to be protected under the "newsworthy" exception. Remember, celebrities are now selling the use of their names and faces for astronomical sums. A famous person's name can be a very valuable piece of property, and courts have recently begun to agree with celebrities that this property cannot be used without payment. Cary Grant sued *Esquire* for using his face on another model's body in an article on men's fashion. The court held that while Cary Grant was certainly famous, and men's fashions certainly "news," there was no real newsworthy connection between the person and the "event," and that in effect *Esquire* was using Grant as a fashion model without paying him.

Speaking of models, some states (New York in particular) require a written release before a model's picture can be used to illustrate a magazine. Even where not required, a written release is a good idea and is normally customary where the model is paid for posing. Not every picture requires a release, however, even where the picture is not of a celebrity. *New York* magazine ran a photograph on its cover of a man in a green "Irish" outfit at the Saint Patrick's Day parade, using it to illustrate an inside story on the Irish in New York. The court held that it was not an invasion of privacy, since the photo was taken at a public event and was used to illustrate, and had a valid connection to, an article of "newsworthy" significance.

**Public Exposure of Private Facts.** Even a true statement about someone can, when published in a magazine distributed to the public, be the basis of a lawsuit in some states. Courts have recognized that at least some right to stay out of the public eye is accorded to the private citizen, especially where facts of a potentially embarrassing nature are revealed. While it is fairly safe to publish the details of a *celebrity's* sex life (leaving the question of libel aside), it may be asking for trouble to do the same for your next-door neighbor. Normally, most stories interesting enough for your readers will concern people who either are well known or are caught up in events that make at least a limited inquiry into their life "newsworthy." It will not hurt, however, to disguise the identity

of "unimportant" people where the story does not require their real names. In California a court held that the *Reader's Digest* should have considered not using a criminal's real name in reporting a crime that had been committed more than ten years before and was used only to add color to an article on truck hijacking in general. Of course, if you can get written permission to use a person's real name, then there will be no problem.

## Obscenity and Censorship

The law regarding obscenity is, to put it simply, a mess. As of now, each locality can determine, within certain limits, what is obscene, so that a magazine issue that goes unnoticed in New York may be pulled off the stands by a zealous prosecutor in Dubuque. Local standards can go only so far, however. While the U.S. Supreme Court has deliberately refused to be explicit about what is obscene, certain broad interpretations are clear: Scenes of cutting off people's heads are not considered obscene; depiction of sex is.

Unless you plan a fairly explicit sexual theme for your magazine, *successful* obscenity *prosecution is unlikely.* But there is always the chance that your magazine may be subject to a degree of harassment by overzealous local officials.

## Copyright Law

Copyright law determines who owns the right to publish an author's, photographer's, or illustrator's work. The magazine publisher should quickly establish what rights are being bought from the contributor. As a general rule, the publisher owns the copyright to work created by salaried employees, but even here it is not a bad idea (and relatively easy to implement if you are just starting) to obtain a written agreement from editorial employees that they understand they have no copyright on any work they do for the magazine.

What is generally at stake here is the right to use of the work after it has been published in the magazine. Normally, the nonemployee contributor of a piece to the magazine retains the copyright and can proceed to resell it to whomever he or she

## AUTHOR'S/ARTIST'S RELEASE

The undersigned hereby grants to _____ one-time magazine publication rights in the article/art work tentatively entitled _____. The undersigned acknowledges receipt of full payment for such rights. The undersigned warrants originality, authorship, and ownership of the aforesaid article/art work, that it has not been heretofore published, and that its publication will not infringe upon any copy-right, proprietary, or other right.

The undersigned further grants to _____ the exclusive right to negotiate and to sell reuse of the above titled article/art work for one-time use in foreign publications including, but not limited to, those with which _____ may have a regular working relationship. It is understood that the undersigned will be entitled to 50% of the gross amount paid to, and actually received by, _____ for such foreign reuse. _____ agrees to pay all transaction costs (including, but not limited to, cable fees, reproduction of negatives and film, shipping, insurance where appropriate, telephone calls, etc.) involved in negotiating such reuse.

This purchase also gives _____ the right to select and republish your material as part of any of _____ anthological collections. For this reuse you will receive your pro-rata share of 5% of the gross sales of such special edition which is reserved for distribution among all contributors. Such payments will be made in two parts: the first, at the time of off-sale of such publication and the second at approximately 90 to 120 days off-sale. The first payment to be publisher's estimate of anticipated sale. It is further understood that if the above titled article/art work is the acknowledged collaborative product of more than one author and/or artist, then the author/artist's share described above shall be distributed among such authors and/or artists on a pro rata basis.

SIGNED: _____  DATE: _____

ADDRESS: _____
             (Street)              (City)        (State)      (Zip)

PHONE: Home    (        )          Business    (        )
              area code                        area code

SOCIAL SECURITY or ID No.: _____

pleases. At the very least you should secure, in writing, rights to magazine publication in North America. If you expect to anthologize articles or illustrations appearing in your magazine, you should secure those rights at the time of submission as well. It is also a good idea to include in the same agreement a warranty on the part of the author that the work is original with him or her (that is, that it doesn't violate someone else's copyright) and that it does not violate other rights (such as the right of privacy). If possible, couple this warranty with an indemnification clause— while few contributors can as a practical matter be expected to defray the costs of a lawsuit, the prospect of being held accountable for a judgment or legal fees may discourage obvious plagiarism or libel. Remember that the contributor is still free to publish his or her work in book form, movie form, or any other form unless you contract otherwise. Of course, the more rights you contract for (including assignment of the whole copyright), the more, presumably, you will have to pay, and better-known contributors may be planning anthologies of their own.

The previous page shows a sample form used by a national magazine to secure one-time rights from authors and artists.

To obtain complete protection of your own magazine from copiers, it is highly advisable that you have each issue registered with the Copyright Office promptly on publication. This is done by filling out the appropriate form and submitting two copies of the magazine to the Copyright Office. In addition, you should place a notice of copyright in a prominent location in the magazine (generally the table of contents page). The notice should include the copyright symbol (©) or the word *copyright*, together with the year of publication and the name of the copyright owner.

# 16

## Foreign Licensing and Publishing

In this chapter we will examine the business of American publishers and their investment in launching magazines abroad. We will also discuss the sale of American magazines in overseas markets, as well as the sale of subsidiary rights to foreign publishers.

## Serial Rights

Very often a book publisher will sell serial rights of a portion of a book to a magazine publisher. The book publisher regards magazine exposure as a valuable promotional adjunct in the sale of a book. We have seen a spate of articles derived from books written by key members of a presidential cabinet or executive team. The "inside" nature of these pieces makes them attractive to magazines. Serial-rights sales in six figures are commonplace in this era of stratospheric book projects where author advances sometimes reach $1 million.

A "first" serial right refers to an excerpt, article, or story published in a magazine *before* the book is published. The magazine will customarily pay a higher price for this right than it will for a "second" serial right, an excerpt published in a magazine *after* a book is published. The book's author will share with the publisher a percentage of the revenue from these serial rights. Book publishers maintain extensive subsidiary-rights departments to sell their works to magazines, book clubs, television, and filmmakers.

Magazines sometimes publish anthologies of the "best" of their works. These are usually in book form and contain collections of an annual or biennial nature. Some magazine editors buy outside articles on an all-rights, "buyout" basis, whereby the author receives one fee only, regardless of the further use of his or her work.

Book publishers will occasionally anthologize magazine articles from a number of publications into a book. Since these are "second" serial rights, the fees paid are minimal. Some magazines split these fees with the article's author; others retain this revenue, especially if the pieces are written in-house.

An example of a first serial right would be the publication of a magazine article by a former White House official before it appeared in book form. First serial rights like this are expensive. The publisher of a smaller magazine can, however, secure excellent material at low cost from books about to be published.

Magazine editors should establish relationships with the subsidiary-rights people at book companies as well as with the leading authors' agents. The editor can sometimes convince the book publisher that prepublication of an article in his or her magazine will create advance interest for the book.

## Sales of U.S. Rights Abroad

It is not always possible for an American publisher to license an entire magazine abroad. An active market has been therefore established for the sale of individual articles to foreign publishers. Here, rather than a royalty percentage, a flat price is negotiated for each transaction. The American publisher will usually ship the article to the foreign publisher, who is then responsible for the translation and the editing.

The sale of U.S. rights abroad can be lucrative to the small and large magazine publisher alike. Many foreign magazine publishers have offices in this country. Others employ scouts in the United States to seek out provocative pieces they can use in their own publications. There are also agencies that represent U.S. magazines all over the world in the sale of their material to foreign publishers. These agencies generally split the revenues received with their American clients.

## Foreign Invasion

The Paris-based Hachette Group is a giant magazine publisher in its own country, with additional interests in TV, radio, and books. In April 1988 Hachette made its bid to become the number one magazine publisher in the world by purchasing the New York–based Diamandis Communications for $712 million. This acquisition added to Hachette's base such publications as *Woman's Day, Car and Driver, American Photographer, Road &*

*Track, Audio, Stereo Review, Popular Photography, Flying and Boating, Cycle,* and even some crossword and astrology magazines.

From Diamandis's standpoint, this was a gigantic coup. He had bought all these magazines from CBS only six months earlier and reaped a $303 million profit on the transaction.

Hachette joined with the Australian-born Rupert Murdoch to introduce to American audiences the French publications *Premiere* and *Elle*. Later *Premiere* was spun off to Murdoch and *Elle* to Hachette.

In 1986 Hachette bought controlling interest in Curtis Circulation, one of the largest U.S. distributors of newsstand magazines. In Europe Hachette not only is a newsstand distributor but operates a chain of about 1,500 retail stores.

A week before announcing the Diamandis acquisition, Hachette plunked down $450 million to buy the American book publisher Grolier, publisher of the *Encyclopedia Americana*.

By the late 1980s Rupert Murdoch's News Corporation Ltd. had become a major player in the magazine business, but financial pressures forced Murdoch in June 1991 to sell a block of magazines, including *European Travel & Life, New Woman, New York, Premiere,* and *Seventeen* to K-III Holdings for $650 million.

The British multimedia company Reed International has made a major foray into the American consumer and business magazine market. Its Cahners division (see chapter 12) is one of our largest business magazine publishers.

## American Publishing Investment Abroad

American magazine publishers have been publishing foreign editions for some time. The *Reader's Digest* has forty-one international editions in seventeen languages, with a circulation of thirty million and more than one hundred million readers throughout 163 countries. The Great Britain edition was established in 1938, the Brazil edition in 1942, the French edition in 1947, the Hong Kong edition in 1965, and the Arabic edition in 1978.

Some of these *Reader's Digest* international editions—United Kingdom, Latin America, and Asia/Pacific—have circulations in excess of one million.

These international editions offer excellent opportunities for U.S. advertisers who want to reach foreign audiences and for foreign advertisers who want to reach prospects in their own countries.

*Time* has an ambitious international publishing program, producing fourteen separate editions in Europe, Africa, and the Middle East; eight in Latin America; and twelve in Asia and the South Pacific.

*Family Circle,* one of the two major supermarket magazines in the United States (the other is *Woman's Day*), initiated a Japanese edition in 1978, a time when there were more than 4,000 supermarkets in Japan. The magazine also has an Australian edition.

In the women's magazine category, *Vogue* is represented in Australia, Britain, France, and Italy and is exploring publication in Japan. *House and Garden* publishes in Britain and France; *Cosmopolitan* has twenty-three international editions in eleven languages and is sold in eighty-three countries. Interestingly, the British *Cosmopolitan* carries only 10 percent of the editorial content of the American edition, yet the Greek version carries 90 percent.

*Playboy* has been very active on the foreign-edition front, with licensed editions in Germany, France, Italy, Brazil, Mexico, the Netherlands, Hungary, Czechoslovakia, and Japan. *Playboy's* foreign editions do not contain the identical editorial content of their American counterpart. Censorship and local customs play an important role in what appears in the magazine—even in the famous centerfold.

In late 1986 McGraw-Hill published in China *International Business and Management*, a compendium of articles from *Business Week* translated into Chinese. This move furthers China's attempt to tap America's know-how, particularly in the area of economic expansion. *Business Week* has recently begun publishing editions in Eastern Europe and the emerging federations of the former Soviet Union.

Lee Hall, one of the foremost authorities on international book and magazine licensing, writes in an article in *Folio:* of the difficulty in making publishing deals with the Japanese. Hall claims that his first such deal was signed only after twenty-one trips to Tokyo.

But when Japanese publishers finally do consummate an arrangement, they really mean business. In 1990 the publisher Kadokawa Showten licensed the American magazine *Premiere,* choosing to treat it as virtually a Japanese translation of the English-language title. Within three weeks of the first issue's publication, 150,000 copies had been sold on the newsstands.

*Scientific American,* which has been continuously published since 1845, has been aggressive on the foreign-licensing front. The signing of a Polish edition in 1991 brought the magazine's total to eleven foreign-language editions. In April 1990, with the support of the magazine's German owners, *Scientific American* launched *Scientific European.* At this writing its circulation is up to 360,000.

Lest these successes seem to make foreign licensing a breeze, consultant Lee Hall points out that launching a foreign edition is actually harder than launching the original U.S. edition. The odds against success, he maintains, are 200 to 1. Yet for matters of prestige and profit, magazine publishers actively seek out these arrangements, particularly in the newly fertile fields of Eastern Europe.

It is important to understand that foreign editions of American magazines are published under various types of arrangements. In most cases the edition is licensed by a publishing company in a particular country. There is customarily a minimum dollar guarantee against a percentage of the circulation and/or advertising revenue. Some editions, however, such as those of *Time, Newsweek,* and *Reader's Digest,* are wholly owned by the American publisher.

## How American Magazines Are Sold Abroad

In the feature-film business, a successful movie can count on 30 to 50 percent of its sales coming from foreign sources. Although the magazine business has not developed its distribution to this point, it nevertheless actively promotes worldwide

sales. How is this accomplished by American publications?

There are distributors and wholesalers in each country who specialize in these sales. For a larger-than-usual discount (usually 60 percent), a publisher can sometimes sell its magazine to the foreign distributors on a firm (guaranteed-sale) basis. That is not the usual practice, however; consignment sales are the most prevalent.

A more effective procedure than marketing individually is to deal with one international distributor, who functions very much like a distributor in the United States. These international distributors have offices and representatives in most parts of the world. Copies of magazines are shipped to their warehouses and forwarded to the foreign wholesalers. The fee for this service is approximately 8 percent on all sold copies.

An active market exists for American magazines among U.S. service people stationed abroad. These sales are coordinated by two quasi-military organizations, Stars and Stripes Europe and Stars and Stripes Pacific. The two groups manage the post exchanges at military installations, where magazine sales are an integral part of total sales.

An international convention of distributors, called Distripress, is held annually, in a different country every year. Here publishers with major foreign distribution are afforded the opportunity of meeting their global wholesalers to discuss problems and future prospects. I have attended a number of these conventions and found them most productive.

Serial sales, foreign licensing, and acquisitions are a fascinating avenue in the magazine publishing world. The degree of activity increases dramatically each year. An understanding of the nuances is vital to every magazine practitioner.

**17**

# Trends and Countertrends Today

James Kobak made an informal study of the consumer magazine industry in the twenty-five years from 1963 to 1988. His significant conclusions appeared in an article in *Folio:*'s March 1990 issue. Here are some highlights:

During that period the industry

- put out three times as many titles as there were in 1963;
- had about twice the circulation—540 million versus 270 million; and
- increased to 125 the number of magazine copies that went through each door.

There has been good growth in these twenty-five years in the number of larger-circulation magazines, as follows:

| Circulation | Number of Magazines | |
| --- | --- | --- |
| | 1963 | 1988 |
| Up to 100,000 | 215 | 661 |
| 100,000–499,999 | 142 | 414 |
| 500,000-1,000,000 | 38 | 100 |
| Over 1,000,000 | 50 | 100 |

## Changing Fields

**Senior Citizens.** In 1963 there were no magazines for seniors. In 1988 there were seventeen, with a total circulation of more than 38 million. The two titles published by the American Association of Retired Persons have circulations exceeding 15 million each.

**Computers.** In 1988 some forty-two computer magazines had a total circulation of 4.5 million. Many have come and gone in recent years. Of the forty-two in 1988, forty made their debut that year. By the end of 1991, there were seventy-seven computer magazines. They sold an average of 1,300 ad pages per year.

**City or Metropolitan.** *New York* magazine started in 1968, and a few other of these publications existed before that year. In 1988 Standard Rate and Data (SRDS) listed 129 magazines in this category.

**Home Service** (sometimes known as shelter). There were nine home service titles in 1963, compared with eighty-three in 1988. Some important introductions in this period: *Southern Living, Architectural Digest,* and *Metropolitan Home.*

**Epicurean.** In 1963 the field belonged to *Gourmet.* By 1988 *Bon Appétit, Food & Wine, Weight Watchers,* and eleven others entered the competition.

**Sports.** In this fast-growing field, there were thirty-four titles, with a total circulation of 2 million, in 1963; by 1988 there were 100 titles, with a total circulation of 24 million.

**Fitness and Health.** Nine titles existed in 1963, with only 600,000 in total circulation. By 1988 there were twenty-six magazines, with a total circulation of 20 million. Some important new ones: *Prevention, Health,* and *American Health.*

**Business.** Seventeen magazines in 1963, with a total circulation of 1.8 million grew to thirty-three titles in 1988, with a total circulation of 8.2 million. *Inc., Venture, Black Enterprise,* and *Entrepreneur* are relative newcomers.

**Women's.** There were only seventeen women's magazines in 1963 compared with fifty-seven by 1988. Many have come and gone with fashion's tide in this twenty-five-year period. Promising newcomers: *Essence, New Woman, Mirabella, Lear's,* and *Self.*

It's not all a growth pattern, however. Five fields have suffered a decline in number of titles between 1963 and 1988—men, youth, and children; romance and fan; religious; and civic and fraternal. Alas, *Argosy* is no more—but, fortunately, *Boy's Life* is still with us.

## Teens and Their Magazines

By 1991 the U.S. teen market numbered twenty-seven million. In the previous seventeen years, there had been no growth in the size of this audience, although demographers predict increases in that age group between 1992 and 2005.

In terms of spending, in 1990 teens spent about $79 billion, of which $29 billion was discretionary. How does this spending relate to teen-oriented magazines? Magazines dealing with this vast audience, such as *Seventeen, Teen, Sassy,* and *ym (young modern)*, suffered in 1990 and 1991 from reduced spending by teen-product advertisers. These magazines should clearly benefit from the increased size of the teen market, as should such magazines as *Rolling Stone* and *Spin,* which have large numbers of teenage readers.

## Hard Times

What do magazine publishers do when things get tough, as they did in 1990 and 1991? To survive one of the worst advertising droughts in recent memory, publishers coped by using various measures:

- Many publishers opted for "trimsizing," which means cutting the physical trim size of a magazine, thereby saving paper costs.
- In the months of September and October 1991 alone, 1,200 magazine jobs were eliminated. Time, Inc., Magazines laid off 105 editorial and 500 business employees at six magazines.
- *Business Week* closed three news bureaus and put a hold on any new launches.
- Magazines changed their traditional 60 percent ads/40 percent editorial ratios by cutting back on editorial content.
- *Money* even resorted to selling General Mills copies of the magazines to be distributed with packages of their Total cereal.

Meanwhile other publishers still pursued the risks of starting new magazines, among them *Allure, Martha Stewart Living,* and *Eating Well.*

## Magazines for the Older Set

The top two magazines of the top ten in circulation are, according to the January–June 1991 ABC report, *Modern Maturity,* with a circulation of 22,450,000, and *NRTA/AARP Bulletin,* with a circulation of 22,174,021. Both of these magazines are published by the American Association of Retired Persons (AARP). No competitor comes even close to these two leaders in the retiree market.

*Reader's Digest* puts out *New Choices for the*

*Best Years* to reach the active age-group of persons fifty-five to sixty-five years old. The magazine's circulation is about 600,000.

All three of these magazines are gearing up for the baby boomers, who will begin hitting the age-fifty mark by 1996.

## Comparing the Newsweeklies

*Time, Newsweek,* and *U.S. News & World Report* compete vigorously for advertisers and subscribers. In circulation *Time* is ahead, with 4,287,000 to *Newsweek*'s 3,295,000 and *U.S. News*'s 2,347,000. The total adult audience for the three is 58 million. All have large editorial staffs—*Time* about 390, *Newsweek* 300, and *U.S. News* 220—who turn out about fifty pages a week. *Time* and *Newsweek* each have ten domestic bureaus; *U.S. News* has five.

When it comes to advertising revenues, *Time* led its two competitors in 1991 with $327 million, followed by *Newsweek*'s $229 million and *U.S. News*'s 173 million. In terms of operating profits, *Time*'s is about $88 million, *Newsweek*'s $29 million, and *U.S. News*'s about $18 million.

## Special Sections and Advertorials

Special issues, special sections, and advertorials are produced for additional ad revenue. Their format is as varied as the imagination of the ad directors and promotion people that conceive them. Here are some examples.

The *Reader's Digest* has done more special sections than anyone else—almost 1,000 since the whopping thirty-six-page "Buyers Digest" it ran for Ford in the May 1959 issue. One of the nine special sections it ran in 1991, called "Full Life Program," was geared to seniors. These special sections can even be international in scope. One twenty-four-page section called "What's Behind the Name?" tells the stories of famous-brand products and has appeared in twenty-three countries.

*New Yorker* purists were shocked when a few years ago publisher Steven Florio began running special sections on travel and other subjects. I doubt that the magazine lost any subscribers as a result of this "crass commercialism."

Other magazines active on the special section and special issue front are *Life, Business Week, Fortune,* and *Road & Track.*

Although the American Society of Magazine Editors takes exception to these "advertorials," or special sections, saying they look too much like the magazine's editorial pages, as long as they're profitable, publishers will continue running them.

## K-III Magazines: A New Publishing Giant

The parent company of K-III is a partnership headed by Henry Kravis, the company who owns R. J. Reynolds and General Foods. In June 1991 K-III became a major magazine player by virtue of its $650 million acquisition from Murdoch Magazines of eight magazines—*New York, Soap Opera Digest, Soap Opera Weekly, Seventeen, European Travel & Life, New Woman, Automobile,* and *Premiere.*

Although ad revenues and profit margins were way down in 1991, K-III is actively pursuing acquisitions. With the lower price tags on magazines, the company may soon become a major presence in the magazine business.

## The New World of Corporate Magazines

The newest phenomenon in publishing is corporate magazines that accept advertising. For example, in early 1992 IBM launched two publications, *Profit* and *Beyond Computing.* Both accept advertising from outsiders and will have a controlled circulation of 200,000 each. *Profit* deals with small businesses; *Beyond Computing,* with large and midsize IBM clients.

Benetton, the trendy Italian-based clothing manufactuerer and retailer, began distributing *Colors* magazine in summer 1992. Distribution is through the company's 6,300 retail outlets in eighty-five countries. So far Benetton is not accepting outside advertising for *Colors.*

Pillsbury's *Fast and Healthy* is a new bimonthly with a goal of targeting health-conscious consumers. It will be sold at newsstands and by subscription and has a guaranteed circulation of 100,000. Pillsbury is treating the venture as a profit center and is uncertain whether it will advertise its own products: a pretty cool attitude.

## Rodale's New Life-Style Magazine

Rodale is a low-profile publisher known for its roster of health, fitness, and gardening magazines. Its big ones are *Prevention* and *Organic Gardening,* with a combined circulation of over 4 million. In early 1988 Rodale purchased *Backpacker, Adventure Travel,* and *Ski X-C* from Diamandis Communications. Rodale had previously bought the *Runner* from CBS in 1987 and merged it with its own *Runner's World* with great success.

In the mid-1980s Rodale attempted to capitalize on the health and fitness boom with a newsletter, *Men's Health,* geared to men with a median age of thirty-nine (why not forty?) Defying the odds against the success of men's magazines evidenced by the demise of Rupert Murdoch's *Men's Life,* Forbes's *Egg,* and Business Week's *Assets*—Rodale slowly groomed *Men's Health* as a full-scale magazine.

As the first service magazine for men, *Men's Health* contains an editorial mix of health tips, sex information, success-oriented pieces, and fun. The formula seems to be working. By early 1992 *Men's Health* had a circulation of 500,000 and was publishing on a bimonthly basis.

## The Ten Hottest Magazines of 1991

Each year *ADWEEK* selects the ten hottest magazines. For 1991 they gave the listing a subhead, "Hot Books for Cold Times," in recognition of the sour state of the magazine business in this period. These ten, however, buck the trend.

1. *Parenting*
2. *Parade*
3. *Automobile*
4. *Entertainment Weekly*
5. *Outside*
6. *U.S. News & World Report*
7. *Child*
8. *Scientific American*
9. *The Economist*
10. *Penthouse*

*Parenting* made the list for the second year in a row, reaching 750,000 in circulation. In advertising it was up 12.6 percent over the previous year.

*Parade* is a Sunday newspaper supplement owned by the Newhouse family of companies. It is seventh among the top magazines in terms of gross revenues.

*Automobile* is owned by K-III, a fast-moving newcomer in the magazine sweepstakes. Its circulation is about 480,000.

*Entertainment Weekly* is one of our recent success stories. At this writing its circulation is up to 800,000, and it is selling over 1,000 ad pages a year.

*Outside* competes favorably with the other outdoor life-style publications. Its circulation is 325,000.

*U.S. News & World Report* gained 0.6 percent in advertising pages in 1991. Its two competitors, *Time* and *Newsweek*, were both down.

*Child* is an upscale magazine owned by The New York Times Magazine Group.

*Scientific American* has been a hardy perennial for more than 100 years. Today its circulation is about 500,000, and it continues to be the classiest science magazine.

*The Economist* is another of the "think" books in the business field. Its circulation price is $110 a year.

*Penthouse* has 1,230,000 circulation to its rival *Playboy's* 3,500,000. *Penthouse* sells more ad pages, but *Playboy* has higher ad revenues.

## Ad Age's *Best Magazines of 1991*

Not to be outdone by its competitor, *ADWEEK, Ad Age* selected its Magazine of the Year for 1991 and five runners-up. As we noted in chapter 11, *Entertainment Weekly* was *Ad Age's* top selection. Next best were *Outside, Country America, Parenting, U.S. News & World Report,* and *Cooking Light.*

It is significant that three of these titles, *Entertainment Weekly, Parenting,* and *Cooking Light* are publications of Time Inc. Magazines. All six magazines on the *Ad Age* list achieved success in a dismal economic climate.

## When the Going Gets Rough

The year 1991 will go down in infamy in magazine advertising history. Reduced advertising spending affected every category of magazines. Here is an indication of the extent of these losses, which, of course, reduced magazine profits enormously.

1991 Paid Ad Pages

| Magazine | versus 1990 Figures |
| --- | --- |
| *Working Woman* | -20.73 % |
| *Metropolitan Home* | -21.15 |
| *European Travel & Life* | -21.66 |
| *Elle* | -22.10 |
| *American Health* | -24.86 |
| *Life* | -24.90 |
| *Esquire* | -26.41 |
| *Financial World* | -26.78 |
| *Self* | -27.34 |
| *Town & Country* | -28.36 |
| *Architectural Digest* | -31.47 |
| *Discover* | -37.11 |

Note that a number of these are upscale magazines, yet they, too, suffered. Were any magazines *unaffected* by this economic downturn? Yes, just a few. Ad revenues at *Success* magazine were up 14.47 percent; at *National Geographic,* up 2.54 percent; and at *Scientific American,* up 8.18 percent.

# IMPORTANT PUBLISHING ORGANIZATIONS

## Magazine Publishers of America

Magazine Publishers of America (MPA) has been the premier consumer magazine publishing organization since 1919. Today the MPA serves more than 200 domestic and 36 international companies publishing a total of 1,200 magazine titles. Here are some of its principal activities:

1. *Representation*—Advocates the industry's interests at all levels of government. Champions publishers' First Amendment rights.

2. *Marketing Promotion*—Seeks to increase magazines' share of advertising dollars and the amount of time people spend reading magazines.

3. *Education*—Sees to the proper preparation of people entering publishing as well as to the continuing professional development of established staffers.

4. *Research*—Measures and evaluates magazine readership and the effectiveness of magazine advertising.

5. *Information*—Serves as a primary source of information and expertise about the publishing industry for both MPA members and the public at large.

In addition to these activities, MPA cosponsors with *Folio:* several conferences/trade shows across the country. These attract thousands of magazine executives and hundreds of exhibitors each year.

The MPA and the American Society of Magazine Editors (ASME) jointly sponsor the American Magazine Conference, a three-day meeting that includes general sessions and subject-specific workshops.

To promote the excellent career opportunities available in magazine publishing, each year MPA recruits college juniors and first-year MBA students from universities throughout the country. In this summer program the selected interns work for magazine publishers and attend MPA-conducted seminars and lectures by the industry's leading publishing executives and editors.

The American Society of Magazine Editors (ASME) is affiliated with and supported by MPA and is housed at MPA's headquarters. ASME honors magazines for editorial excellence with its National Magazine Awards.

ASME also conducts an intern program for fifty or more college juniors each summer. The program involves a ten-week work experience that is preceded by a four-day orientation program. ASME interns receive a minimum of $275 per week before taxes.

Both the MPA and ASME can be reached at 575 Lexington Avenue, New York, NY 10022; (212) 752–0055.

## American Business Press

The American Business Press (ABP) is the professional association for the nation's business publications, trade journals, and technical journals. ABP has more than one hundred domestic members who publish a total of 703 magazine titles. In many respects the ABP is the business magazine counterpart of the MPA.

Here are some of ABP's activities and services:

1. Sponsors meetings, seminars, and workshops.

2. Issues major management studies on costs, compensation, and benefits.

3. Sponsors important research and information reports.

4. Promotes the use of business publication advertising.

5. Produces films and presentations on the role of business-to-business advertising in the marketing process.

6. Gives awards for editorial achievement.

7. Supports the Business Press Educational Foundation (BPEF), which encourages journalism students to enter the business magazine profession. BPEF also conducts an internship program.

Both the ABP and the BPEF can be reached at 675 Third Avenue, New York, NY 10017–5704; (212) 661–6360.

## Publications Offering Internship Information

The following publications offer internship information. They may be available at university libraries:

*Internships*
c/o Peterson's
202 Carnegie Center
P.O. Box 2123
Princeton, NJ 08543–2123
(609) 243–9111

*Internships, Volume 2*
The Career Press, Inc.
P.O. Box 34
Hawthorne, NJ 07507
(800) CAREER–1

*Journalism Career and Scholarship Guide*
Dow Jones Newspaper Fund
P.O. Box 300
Princeton, NJ 08543–0300
(609) 452–2820

*The National Directory of Internships*
National Society for Internships
  and Experiential Education
3509 Haworth Drive, Suite 207
Raleigh, NC 27609
(919) 787–3263

*Scholarships, Fellowships, and Loans*
Gale Research Inc.
835 Penobscot Building
Detroit, MI 48226–4094
(313) 961–2242

*The Student Guide to Mass Media Internships*
School of Journalism and Mass
  Communication
University of Colorado
Boulder, CO 80309
(303) 492–5007

# THE ROLE OF WOMEN

As we have seen in the salary statistics throughout this book, women are still making less than men for doing the same jobs. But this situation is changing. Each year we see women's compensation coming closer to parity with that of their male counterparts. And just as important, women are being given the opportunity to hold leadership positions.

On many consumer magazines women now hold top editorial jobs in every category. On business magazines women are closing the gap for the top editorial jobs. In some classifications, such as science and medicine, retail, and the service industries, women outnumber men. On many ad sales staffs, women hold the majority of jobs.

Here, for example, is a list of some of our largest magazines and the names of their key women editors, ad directors, and publishers as of this writing. What is of greater importance to women coming into the magazine field is that just below these leaders are dozens of female associate publishers; managing editors, and advertising sales managers poised for that rapid move to the corner office.

| Magazine | Name and Title |
| --- | --- |
| Allure | Linda Wells, editor in chief |
| American Express Publishing Group | Pamela Fiori, editorial director |
| American Health | Susan Baron, publisher |
| Architectural Digest | Paige Rense, editor in chief |
| Arts & Antiques | Allison Bliss Selover, publisher |
| Bon Appétit | Polly Perkins, publisher |
| Bride's | Barbara D. Tober, editor |
| Cosmopolitan | Helen Gurley Brown, editor |
| Discover | Nina Halsey, advertising director |
| Ebony | Linda Johnson Rice, president |
| Elle | Gail Stone, publisher |
| Esquire | Nancy Nadler LeWinter, publisher |
| Essence | Barbara Britton, national advertising director |
| Family Circle | Valerie Salembier, publisher |
| Flying | Patricia Luebke, vice-president, advertising director |
| Gourmet | Gail Zweigenthal, editor in chief |
| HG (formerly House & Garden) | Nancy Novogrod, editor in chief; Susan Rerat, advertising director |
| House Beautiful | Carole Ference, publisher |
| Ladies' Home Journal | Donna Galotti, publisher |
| McCall's | Barbara Littrell, publisher; Madelyn Alpert Roberts, advertising director |

| | |
|---|---|
| *Mademoiselle* | Julie Lewit-Nirenberg, publisher; Ruth Kauders, advertising director |
| *Metropolitan Home* | Jamella Maloof and Laura Jennings, advertising directors |
| *Money* | Betsy Martin, ad sales director |
| *National Geographic* | Joan McCraw, vice-president, advertising director |
| *New Republic* | Joan Stapleton, publisher |
| *New Woman* | Lori Zelikow Florio, publisher |
| *Penthouse* | Audrey Arnold, director of advertising |
| *People* | Ann Moore, publisher |
| *Premiere* | Susan Lyne, editor |
| *Rolling Stone* | Susan Gold, advertising director |
| *Sassy* | Linda Cohen, publisher |
| *Self* | Marianne Howatson, publisher; Victoria Lasdon, advertising director |
| *Seventeen* | Janice Grossman, publisher; Amy Churgin, advertising director |
| *Sports Illustrated for Kids* | Susan Sachs, publisher |
| *Stereo Review* | Louise Boundas, editor in chief |
| *Time* | Lisa Valk, publisher |
| *Travel Holiday* | Patricia Haegele, publisher |
| *Travel & Leisure* | Alexandra Golinkin, vice-president/publisher |
| *TV Guide* | Anthea Disney, editor in chief |
| *Vanity Fair* | Fran Orner, advertising director |
| *Victoria* | Katherine Mountain, publisher; Nancy Lindemeyer, editor |
| *Vogue* | Anne Sutherland Fuchs, publisher |

Conclusion: These women have made it. There is definitely a place for you on this star roster.

## Jobs in Ad Sales

There are two major resources for women seeking those lucrative ad sales jobs. Both combine job training with a referral service. One is in New York; the other, in Beverly Hills. Here are their addresses:

David King, Careers for Women, 80 Fifth Avenue, New York, NY 10011, (212) 807–7633; Kathy Aaronson, The Sales Athlete, 9808 Wilshire Blvd., Beverly Hills, CA 90212, (310) 275–8900.

## Folio:—The Magazine for Magazine People

*Folio:*, the most important trade publication for magazine publishers, was started by Joe Hanson in 1972. I have been a loyal reader of the publication since its inception. For me, as well as for a legion of *Folio:* subscribers, it has served as an advanced education in the magazine business.

Until 1977 *Folio:* was published on a controlled (free) circulation basis. During those first five years, it was more important for Hanson to reach all the influential business and consumer magazine publishing and editorial staffers than it was to have a paid circulation and serve only a limited number. The only revenue came from advertising sales. *Folio:* was also a bimonthly until 1977, when it became a monthly and began charging a subscription fee. As of this writing, *Folio:* has a circulation of 11,000 and a subscription rate of $68 per year.

Realizing that ad revenues from his magazine were not sufficient to support his operation, Hanson in 1975 launched the first Face to Face Publishing conference. These conferences were an instant success and soon expanded to other cities, where they attracted large numbers of professional magazine people to attend lectures and participate in discussions with industry leaders.

In 1989 *Folio:*'s conferences were merged with those of the MPA to create a powerful educational and training source for magazine professionals. Today there are *Folio:* conferences in Chicago; Los Angeles; Washington, D.C.; and New York. At the fall conference in New York, more than 180 full-

Courtesy Folio: magazine

and half-day seminars are conducted, covering seven aspects of magazine publishing: management, editorial, ad sales, marketing, production, design, and circulation. Also at this November *Folio:* show is a three-day exhibition of publishing products and services.

*Folio:* additionally publishes the annual *Folio: Source Book.* This important reference book is a comprehensive source of magazine publishing industry suppliers. It also contains special tabbed editorial sections with essential reference material for management, production, and circulation executives. One handy highlight of the *Folio: Source Book* is a complete editorial index to all articles published in *Folio:* and *Publishing News* in the previous eighteen months. Subscribers to *Folio:* receive the *Source Book* free; others can purchase it for $35.

### Folio:'s Publishing News

This sister publication to *Folio:* is a controlled-circulation newsmagazine published monthly. Its circulation is 27,000 qualified magazine publishing managers. Its tabloid format and newsmagazine ed-

itorial thrust make *Publishing News* an important adjunct to *Folio:.* Both publications have been of invaluable service in the preparation of this book.

In January 1988 the Cowles Media Company acquired the Hanson Media Group. Cowles also publishes *Direct, Catalog Age,* and *Inside Media.* The company's chairman and CEO is magazine industry veteran Hershel Sarbin.

For information about subscriptions to *Folio:* or the magazine publishing seminars, write to *Folio:*, Six River Bend Center, Box 4949, Stamford, CT 06907–0949.

### Magazine Week

*Magazine Week* is a concise, well-edited, nuts-and-bolts weekly serving the magazine industry. Competing head-on with competitors *Folio:* and *Folio's Publishing News, Magazine Week* has established itself as an important source of industry news.

*Magazine Week* features six regular columns in each issue: Magazine Marketing, Magazine Trends, Magazine Production, Circulation Management, Direct Marketing, and Magazines and the Law. In addition *Magazine Week* covers new developments in the magazine business.

A highlight of *Magazine Week* is its "Profit Profile," in which the publication determines the yearly net profit/loss and profit margin percentage for a different magazine in each issue. We found it interesting that although most magazines have profit margins in single digits, *Magazine Week's* coverage of Hachette's *Stereo Review* showed it to have a profit margin of 27.3 percent.

*Magazine Week* also conducts forums on subjects of interest to publishers. One recent topic was advertising rate negotiations, moderated by Donald L. Nicholas, editor in chief of *Magazine Week.* For information on subscriptions, write to *Magazine Week*, P.O. Box 53463, Boulder, CO 80323–3463.

### The Two Most Important Advertising/Marketing Publications

Although they are not totally dedicated to magazines, two trade publications devote considerable coverage to this medium. We highly recommend them.

*ADWEEK* is a weekly, published in six regional editions. What distinguishes *ADWEEK* is its liberal use of four-color and its breezy, hip, but editorially relevant style. *ADWEEK* publishes a variety of special reports throughout the year that are bound into the publication. In 1991 the company purchased *Marketing and Media Decisions* and renamed it *MEDIAWEEK*. This excellent publication presents news about all the media from a market perspective.

For information about a subscription to *ADWEEK*, write to *ADWEEK*, 49 East Twenty-first Street, New York, NY 10010.

*Advertising Age*, or *Ad Age*, as those in the industry refer to it, has been around for sixty years. It comes out weekly and contains news, industry analysis, and articles on the fields of marketing, advertising, sales promotion, direct mail, and magazines. A standout feature of the publication is its in-depth special reports.

*Ad Age* is also broken out into four regional editions for editorial emphasis. It leads its competitor, *ADWEEK,* in circulation (90,000) and in advertising revenues ($25 million).

For information about subscriptions write to *Ad Age*, Circulation Department, 965 Jefferson Avenue, Detroit, MI 48207–9966.

Both *ADWEEK* and *Ad Age* are available in well-equipped libraries.

## Washington Journalism Review

For provocative reportage and opinion about magazines and the media, we suggest reading the *Washington Journalism Review*. This outstanding publication presents an insider's view of the whole communications industry. It is the kind of provocative journalism that can only be written by working professionals and leading consultants in the media. For information about subscriptions, write to *Washington Journalism Review,* P.O. Box 51017, Boulder, CO 80321–1017.

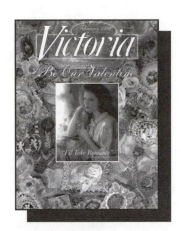

# 18

# Getting a Job and Moving Ahead

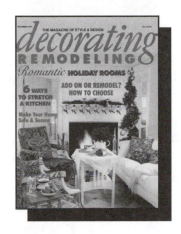

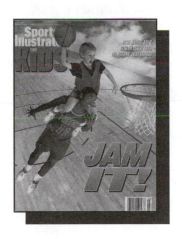

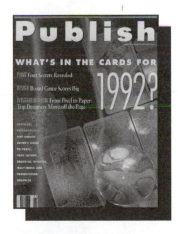

At this writing the outlook for the magazine business is dim. Many marginal magazines are folding. Even larger-size magazines are downsizing. More and more employees are being asked to increase their responsibilities.

Yet as we know, our economy moves in cycles. We have had recessions in the past and have always recovered. While we may see a momentary lull in magazine launches for a time, surely that pattern will change and again result in 300 to 400 new magazines being published each year.

This chapter is directed to three groups: (a) college students who plan to enter the magazine field on graduation; (b) those who are already working on magazines and need guidance on moving ahead; and (c) those employed in other areas who wish to make a career change into magazines.

# TWENTY-FIVE TIPS FOR OPENING DOORS

1. Read any current books you can find about the magazine business and related fields. Often such books contain good information about résumés and the hiring process.

2. Learn how to write an excellent résumé. Make sure it is career-specific and contains accurate, verifiable information. The best résumés exude a sense of energy and leadership. Be sure to include information about your degree of computer literacy. Send a short cover letter accompanying the résumé.

3. Don't try to avoid the human resources department of the publishing company you're interested in. At the same time, however, there's nothing wrong with corresponding with specific department heads or executives.

4. Exploit any personal contact, whether or not the person is at the top. A college friend or a relative who works in the media department of an ad agency may be a good source for ideas and leads about magazine sales jobs.

5. Contact your college's alumni association. There you can track people from your school who have gone to work at a magazine company that interests you.

6. Attend job fairs where magazine companies are participating. Ask specific questions about hiring procedures and company policies.

7. Seek out job opportunities at metropolitan and business magazines. They may offer the best possibilities if you choose to work outside New York and other large cities.

8. Once you have graduated from college and are working at the entry level in magazines or a related field, take one of the fine extension courses offered by many colleges, such as the School of Visual Arts and New York University in New York; the Medill School of Northwestern University in Evanston, Illinois; and UCLA in Los Angeles.

9. Contact the leading magazine publishing organizations for information about jobs, training, and internship programs. Write to Magazine Publishers of America, 575 Lexington Avenue, New York, NY 10022 or American Business Press, 675 Third Avenue, New York, NY 10017.

10. Consider taking one of the excellent comprehensive summer magazine publishing programs discussed in chapter 3. A prospective employer will certainly regard this attendance as a plus.

11. You'll probably get your first job by cold calling, letter writing, and networking. Make sure you are adept at each.

12. Focus on all the major magazine companies mentioned in this book. There is clearly an advantage to working for a big company versus a small one. The big ones have their own training programs, provide educational benefits, and offer the important opportunity to move from one magazine to another within the company.

13. A graduate degree in business is important if you wish to reach for the gold. It may, however, be a good idea to first work in publishing

for a few years and then take a leave of absence with your company's permission. Many companies encourage this practice.

14. If you want to write, your chances are better if you work for a business or trade magazine. Follow Howard Rauch's sage advice in chapter 3 of this book.

15. Beware of phony employment agents who promise jobs but really can't deliver. There are only a handful of executive recruiters who specialize in publishing and the media industry. One such company is The Howard-Sloan-Koller Group, 545 Fifth Avenue, New York, NY 10017.

16. Become familiar with the magazine publishing business by reading the best publications available. *Folio:* and *Folio:'s Publishing News* are a must. It's also a good idea to read *Advertising Age* and *ADWEEK,* both of which contain valuable information about magazine publishing as well as coverage of advertising and broadcasting. Most good libraries have these publications on file.

17. Don't lie or exaggerate on your résumé. If your prospective employer is seriously interested in you, he or she will undoubtedly check references, education, and job experience.

## On Interviews

18. Be prepared for the interview. Learn as much as you can about the parent company and the specific magazine to which you are applying for a job.

19. If you are seeking an ad sales job, you must demonstrate that you are a forceful communicator with a people-oriented personality. If the magazine is considering you for a sales job and you lack prior magazine experience, be ready to prove that you have other qualifications that will support your quest for the position.

20. In his book *Who's Hiring Who?*, Richard Lathrop refers to a number of considerations to make before "stepping up to the plate." These include appropriate clothing, good grooming, a firm handshake, pertinent humor and a readiness to smile, a genuine interest in the employer's operations and alert attention when the interviewer speaks, the display of sound ideas, and the ability to take control when employers fall down on the interviewing job.

Lathrop also advises the interviewee to send a follow-up letter thanking the interviewer for his or her time and consideration and stressing the interviewee's high interest in the job and ability to produce strong results.

21. Be prepared, even on the first interview, to speak to an individual at a much higher level than the first interviewer. At one very large publishing company, with almost 3,000 employees, the president insists on personally interviewing each sales candidate for an hour and a half, after he or she has been interviewed by four or five other people.

22. Be prepared to ask hard questions about the job and all its duties.

23. Don't be afraid to ask about perks, benefits, tuition reimbursement, and vacations.

24. When applying for a specific job, ask about the pecking order in that department.

25. Expect that the interviewer will go down the line on your résumé and ask specific questions about your education and previous jobs.

# GLOSSARY

**AA** Author's alteration, made in the copy by the author and marked on the galley proof, after a manuscript has been set in type.

**AAAA** The American Association of Advertising Agencies, the membership organization of American advertising agencies. Member agencies conform to a code of rules and procedures.

**ABC** The Audit Bureau of Circulations, the group formed by advertisers, agencies, and the media to audit the circulation statements of its media members and release this information to advertisers and advertising agencies.

**Account** The client of an advertising agency, market research firm, or media-buying service.

**Account Executive** The representative of an advertising agency who acts as a liaison between the agency and its client.

**Advertising Agency** A company set up to create and place advertising in the various media. It also serves its accounts by evaluating the results of the ads.

**Advertising Budget** The detailed breakdown of the costs involved in advertising a product, including agency expenses and time charges and costs for space in print media and for time on TV and radio.

**Advertising Director** The executive of a magazine who directs and coordinates all advertising sales.

**Advertising/Editorial Ratio** In a magazine, a ratio representing the percentage of advertising space to editorial pages.

**Advertising Linage** The number of advertising pages carried by a magazine in a given period.

**Agency Commission** The commission paid by the media to the advertising agency (usually 15 percent) for its services.

**Audience Composition** The classification of individuals or households into various demographic characteristics, such as age, education, sex, and income.

**Basic Paper Weight** The designation of the weight of paper. For example, 50-pound basis means that 500 sheets of 25-by-38 inches weighs 50 pounds.

**Benday** A method of laying a screen (dots, lines, and other textures) on artwork to show various shadings and tones.

**Bind-in Card** An insert card in a magazine that is stitched in with the printed pages and is often used to sell subscriptions. It is called a *bingo card* when it serves as a reader's request form for information on products and services advertised in the publication.

**Binding** The finishing process following printing, which involves folding, collating, stitching, gluing or stapling, and trimming the pages into a complete magazine.

**Binding Edge** The inside edge of the page of a magazine, containing the fold and sometimes the stitches.

**Black-and-White Pages** Pages that utilize no color except black.

**Bleed** The extension of illustrations, photos, or copy to the edge of a page.

**Blow-in Card** A loose insert in a magazine, used primarily to sell subscriptions. Blow-in cards are effective because of their nuisance value.

**Blueprints** The final proof pulled by a printer before a magazine goes to press. Sometimes known as *brownlines*.

**Body Typeface** The typeface, usually no larger than 14-point, in which the text of a magazine or book is set.

**Boldface** The designation for a typeface that has a heavy or dark stroke.

**Broadcast Media** The category of media that includes radio and television.

**Bulk Discounts** The discounts offered by the media to advertisers who place large orders. They are measured by the number of pages or total linage placed by one advertiser in a given magazine.

**Business Magazine** Sometimes called a *trade magazine*. This classification represents the nonconsumer publication that serves the interest of a particular industry or profession.

**Business Plan** A document prepared by the publisher of a new magazine outlining its editorial content, staff, market, and financial projections.

**Call Report** The daily or weekly reports, submitted by space salespeople on a magazine to their superiors, that convey the results of particular sales meetings.

**Center Spread** The facing pages in the exact center of a magazine. This spot is desirable for advertisers because of its high visibility.

**Charter Rate** The reduced rate given to subscribers or advertisers of a new magazine.

**Checkerboard Ad** The innovative placement of portions of an ad in a checkerboard fashion, alternating with the editorial content of the page.

**Checkout Racks** The racks placed at checkout counters of supermarkets or convenience stores. These racks are advantageous in producing impulse sales.

**Circulation** The number of copies sold by a publication through subscription and/or newsstand sales.

**Circulation Director** The individual on a magazine with the responsibility of maintaining and increasing the level of subscriptions and newsstand sales.

**Circulation Guarantee** The minimum total circulation of a magazine offered to its advertisers.

**City Magazines** Sometimes referred to as *metropolitan magazines*. They deal with the special interests of readers in a particular geographic area.

**Class Magazines** Special-interest consumer magazines that treat their subject matter in a sophisticated manner. Their circulation often reflects a high socioeconomic group.

**Closing Date** The last date on which an agency can submit advertising material for a particular issue of a publication.

**Coated Paper** Sometimes known as *slick paper*. It refers to paper that has been chemically treated in its manufacture to create a shiny effect.

**Color Proof** A full-color representation of an image before printing.

**Comp Letter** A sales letter bound into a magazine that is sent to its complimentary or free subscribers.

**Consignment** Referring to the trade practice in single-copy or newsstand distribution whereby magazines are offered to dealers with the option of returning unsold copies for full credit.

**Consumer Magazines** The class of magazines that are sold directly to consumers, as distinguished from business/trade magazines, which deal with readers' business or professional interest.

**Contract Year** The twelve-month running period of an ad that an advertiser and its agency contract for. It can be on a calendar- or fiscal-year basis or effective with the first appearance of the ad.

**Controlled Circulation** A circulation practice, usually for a business/trade magazine, whereby the publication is sent free to specific individuals who are selected because of their job titles or function.

**Convenience Stores** The category of grocery or variety store that has less square footage than a supermarket and carries fewer items. These stores generally are open seven days a week and for long hours each day. In recent years they have become valuable outlets for the sale of magazines and paperback books.

**Conversion Factor** A phrase used in subscription solicitation relating to the number of "leads" that are converted to actual subscribers.

**Copy Editing and Copyreading** The stage in a magazine's editorial preparation where the raw manuscript is carefully examined for grammar, spelling, and correct usage.

**Cover Lines** Often called *sell lines*, these are adjuncts to the photo or illustration on a cover of a magazine. They tell the reader about some of the contents in a particular issue.

**Cover Positions** The premium-priced cover space in a magazine. The second cover is the inside front; the third cover, the inside back; and the fourth cover, the outside back cover.

**CPM** Cost per thousand, a dollar figure used by agencies and advertisers to evaluate the relative cost of various media within a selected audience criterion. It is achieved by dividing the audience or circulation of a publication by its cost per page.

**Demographic Characteristics** The phrase used to categorize the various social and economic characteristics of a group of households or individuals. It refers to such statistics as sex, age, size of family, education, and economic levels of the audience of a magazine.

**Direct Mail** Advertising sent by mail to the consumer's residence, often used to generate magazine subscriptions and containing a response mechanism for ordering by return mail.

**Distributor** The term in newsstand distribution referring to the national organization that distributes magazines to the hundreds of local wholesalers.

**Dot Pattern** The coarseness or fineness of a screen in a photo or illustration. It is measured by the number of dots per given area.

**Double Spread** Two facing advertising or editorial pages.

**Dummy** The prototype of a new magazine in either artist's roughs or printed form.

**Face** The designation of type style.

**Four-Color Page** An advertising or editorial page that utilizes black and three other basic colors: magenta, yellow, and cyan.

**Four-color Process** The process of color printing using four engravings or films, each with a different color ink, to reproduce color artwork, which has been reduced to its basic colors by a filtration and separation process.

**Fractional Page Space** Advertising space measuring less than one full page, usually one column, a half-page, or two-thirds of a page.

**Free-lance Writer** The outside contributor to a magazine's editorial content.

**Frequency Discount** A rate discount allowed to an advertiser who purchases a specific amount of space within a given period of time.

**Fulfillment** The process of maintaining and running off the subscription names of a publication.

**Galley Proof** The proof of a page or quantity of type. Galley proofs are sent to a magazine's proofreading staff for checking and correction.

**Gatefold** An additional leaf, usually on a magazine's front cover, that is attached to an advertising page and folds over to partly or fully cover the page.

**General Magazine** A consumer magazine that has a broad editorial appeal and is not directed at a specific or specialized audience.

**Gravure** One of the three major printing processes. Utilizes a depressed or cell-like area to produce an impression.

**Greek Type** Type, often used in a dummy of a new magazine, that is not meant to make sense.

**Grid** The design pattern of an editorial page of a magazine.

**Halftone** The tonal variation used for the reproduction of black-and-white photographs. The original graphics are photographed through a halftone screen, which breaks down the image into a small, varied dot pattern.

**House Agency** An advertising agency that is controlled in full or owned by one advertiser.

**House Organ** The in-house publication of a business organization or union, often used to improve employee relations.

**Ink-jet Imaging** Technology used, along with selective binding, by magazine publishers to target their editorial and advertising content to readers.

**Insert** A preprinted advertisement supplied by an advertiser to a publication and bound into its pages.

**Insertion Order** The form or document sent to a publication by an advertising agency that contains information relating to an ad's placement—its size, rate, frequency, date, and any other special information.

**Kill Fee** The fee paid to a free-lance writer by a magazine when the assigned article or story is not used.

**Layout** The rough designation by an art director or designer of what will appear on a printed page.

**Letterpress** One of the three major printing processes. Uses a raised or relief plate for the printing impression.

**Libel** A term in law relating to a written defamatory statement that conveys an unjustly unfavorable impression or tends to expose another individual or group to public contempt.

**Lightface** Designation for type that has relatively light, thin lines.

**Linotype** The typesetting machine that casts characters of a given typeface into a line or slug of metal type.

**List Broker** The clearinghouse or compiler of mailing lists for a direct-mail subscription campaign.

**Logo** A single piece of type or art indicating the name of a publication or a trademark.

**Mail-Order Ads** Advertisements that solicit direct response by mail for merchandise or services.

**Make Good** Repeat of an ad in a magazine to compensate for an error in the original insertion.

**Mass Circulation** Denotes consumer magazines with large circulation and distribution.

**Masthead** The page or section in a magazine set aside to list the publication's title, personnel, and publishing policies. Often it appears alongside the table of contents.

**Mechanical** The composite of the elements of an ad or editorial page. It is sometimes called a *pasteup*.

**Media Kit** A package used by magazines in advertising sales. It contains a rate card, survey results, demographics, and often publicity about the magazine.

**MPA** The Magazine Publishers of America, the official organization of major consumer publications.

**MPX** Magazine page exposures, denoting how thoroughly a consumer reads magazines.

**MRI** Mediamark Research Inc., a major syndicated research organization that measures the size and characteristics of the audience of major magazines.

**National Advertising** The class of advertising that deals with nationally distributed advertisers, as distinguished from local or mail-order advertisers.

**Newsletter** A small publication, not usually sold on newsstands, that concerns itself with the special interests of a particular group.

**OCR** Optical character recognition, the advanced technique that uses a computer to read a page of manuscript and reproduce it on paper or film.

**Offset** One of the three major printing processes. Photographically reproduces from a flat plate.

**One Shot** A special edition of a regularly published magazine.

**Out of Register** Poor lineup (registration) of color plates in a printed reproduction; a color ad that appears blurred.

**Pass-along Readers** The secondary audience, composed of readers who did not actually purchase the publication.

**PE** Printer's error, a mistake on a galley proof that is the fault of the typesetter, not the magazine's editorial staff.

**Perfect Binding** The process of binding that uses glue rather than staples or stitching and results in a square spine. Also called *adhesive binding*.

**Photoengraving** The process by which black-and-white and color artwork is made into plates and film.

**Phototypesetting** The typesetting technique that eliminates the casting of metal.

**Pica** A printer's unit of type size, equal to 12 points.

**Point** The basic unit of typographical measurement; 72 points equal one inch.

**PR** Public relations, used on magazines for image building and the promotion of newsstand and advertising sales.

**Premature** In newsstand distribution, the early return of a magazine by a dealer before the end of the magazine's on-sale period.

**Prepress** The preparatory process, such as typesetting and camera work, done before a magazine goes to press.

**Print Order** The document sent to a printer by a magazine stating the print quantity, delivery instructions, and other pertinent information.

**Production Manager** The individual on a magazine assigned the responsibility for typesetting, printing, and binding functions.

**Progressive Proofs** A set of proofs of color film and plates, serving as a guide for a magazine's art staff and printer.

**Promotion Director** The magazine executive charged with the task of promoting its subscription, newsstand, and advertising sales efforts. Often the function of public relations is assigned to the promotion department.

**Psychographics** A measurement of a publication's audience as to attitudinal and personality criteria that affect life-style and purchasing behavior.

**Rate Card** The magazine's detailed document listing its ad rates, frequency, closing dates, and other production information.

**RDA** Retail display allowance, given to dealers who agree to display a magazine full face.

**Regional Edition** A breakout of a magazine's circulation to smaller geographic areas than its national distribution.

**Rep** An advertising sales representative of a publication who is not a full-time member of its staff.

**Repro Proof** A perfect type proof on good-quality paper, suitable for photographic reproduction.

**Research Director** The individual with the responsibility of developing information that can be used to promote circulation and advertising sales.

**Rollout** The large mailing of a direct-mail campaign, conducted after a test.

**Roman Typeface** A style of type that appears straight up and down. The ordinary type style, as distinguished from italic.

**Saddle Stitching** The binding process whereby a publication is held together by staples at the folded edge.

**Sans Serif** Letter or characters of a typeface that are devoid of the short finishing strokes of a serif face.

**Schedule** In advertising, the complete list of publications in which the advertiser schedules its advertising.

**Seed Money** Venture money for a new magazine.

**Selective Binding** A method that implements ink-jet imaging in targeting readers.

**Sell-through** The number of single copies distributed that are actually sold.

**Serif** The designation of a typeface that has short lines stemming from and at an angle to the upper and lower ends of the main strokes of a letter.

**Side Stitching** The binding process whereby a publication is held together by stitches or staples a fraction of an inch in from the folded edge.

**Signature** The name given to a printed sheet of a magazine or book after it comes off the press and has been folded into eight, sixteen, or thirty-two pages.

**Simmons** A syndicated media research organization that measures product usage, demographics, and so forth of a publication's audience. Now merged with TGI.

**Single-copy Sales** The current phrase denoting newsstand sales of magazine.

**Space** Term used to denote advertising linage.

**Specialized Magazines** The classification of publications geared to the special interests of a group of readers.

**Special Position** The result of a special request of an advertiser for an ad to appear in a specific place in a magazine. Usually involves a higher ad rate than regular space does.

**SRDS** Standard Rate and Data Service, the organization that lists and categorizes the media.

**Subscription Director** The executive of a magazine's circulation department assigned the function of generating and maintaining subscription sales.

**Tabloid** Format used primarily by newspapers and some trade publications. In magazines this is a large format; in newspapers it is smaller.

**Target Marketing** Advertising or sales promotion keyed to a specific group or regional area.

**TGI** Target Group Index, another of the major syndicated research organizations that measure the audience of national magazines. Now merged with Simmons.

**Title** Designating a given magazine, such as *Good Housekeeping* or *Life*.

**Total Audience** Combined total of a magazine's paid circulation and its pass-along readership.

**Trade Magazine** Another popular phrase for *business magazine*, used to designate nonconsumer publications that serve the interests of an industry or professional group.

**Trading Out** The practice by which one magazine exchanges space with another, with no cash involved.

**Typography** General term for the typesetting function.

**Waste Circulation** That portion of a magazine's circulation who are not prospects for a particular advertised product or service. Includes circulation in an area where an advertiser does not have distribution.

**Wholesaler** The local marketing organization that distributes newsstand magazines within a given geographic area.

# RECOMMENDED READING

Barnhart, Helene Schellenberg. *How to Write and Sell the Eight Easiest Article Types.* Cincinnati, Ohio: Writer's Digest Books, 1985.

Bruno, Michael H. *Pocket Pal.* New York: International Paper Company, 1986.

*Business Publication Rates and Data.* Standard Rate and Data Service. Published monthly.

Byron, Christopher M. *The Fanciest Dive: What Happened When the Media Empire of Time/Life Leaped without Looking into the Age of High-Tech.* New York: Plume/New American Library, 1987.

Claxton, Ronald H. *The Student Guide to Mass Media Internships.* Boulder, Colo.: University of Colorado, School of Journalism, 1983.

Click, J. W., and Russell N. Baird. *Magazine Editing and Production,* 2d ed. Dubuque, Iowa: W. C. Brown, 1979.

*Consumer Magazine Rates and Data.* Standard Rate and Data Service. Published monthly.

Cool, Lisa Collier. *How to Sell Every Magazine Article You Write.* Cincinnati, Ohio: Writer's Digest Books, 1986.

Cutlip, S. *Effective Public Relations,* 6th ed. Englewood Cliffs, N.J.: Prentice Hall. 1988.

Delton, Judy. *The Twenty-Nine Most Common Writing Mistakes and How to Avoid Them.* Cincinnati, Ohio: Writer's Digest Books, 1985.

*Direct Mail List Rates and Data.* Standard Rate and Data Service. Published semiannually.

Emerson, Connie. *The Writer's Guide to Conquering the Magazine Market.* Cincinnati, Ohio: Writer's Digest Books, 1991.

Jean M. Fredette, ed. *Handbook of Magazine Article Writing.* Cincinnati, Ohio: Writer's Digest Books, 1991.

Gordon, Josh. *Competitive Selling: A Fundamental Approach.* Stamford, Conn.: Hanson Publishing Group, 1991.

Hubbard, J. T. W. *Magazine Editing: How to Acquire the Skills You Need to Win a Job and Succeed in the Magazine Business.* Syracuse, N.Y.: Syracuse University Press, 1988.

*Internships: 16,000 On-the-Job Training Opportunities for All Types of Careers.* Cincinnati, Ohio: Writer's Digest Books. Published annually.

Jacobi, Peter. *The Magazine Article: How to Think It, Plan It, Write It.* Cincinnati, Ohio: Writer's Digest Books, 1991.

Kevles, Barbara. *Basic Magazine Writing.* Cincinnati, Ohio: Writer's Digest Books, 1986.

Koff, Richard M. *Strategic Planning for Magazine Executives,* 2d ed. Stamford, Conn: Hanson Publishing Group, 1987.

Koller, Edward. *The Hiring Challenge.* Stamford, Conn.: Hanson Publishing Group, 1991.

Lieberman, Seymour. *How and Why People Buy Magazines.* New York: Publishers Clearing House, 1977.

*Literary Market Place/Directory of American Book Publishing.* New York: R. R. Bowker. Published annually.

Love, Barbara. *Handbook of Magazine Publishing: Selected articles from "Folio:",* 3d ed. Stamford, Conn.: Hanson Publishing Group, 1991.

Mainstream Access. *The Publishing Job Finder.* Englewood Cliffs, N.J.: Prentice Hall, 1981.

Mann, Jim. *Magazine Editing: Its Art and Practice.* Stamford, Conn.: Hanson Publishing Group, 1985.

*Newsletter on Newsletters.* Rhinebeck, N.Y.: The Newsletter Clearinghouse. Published monthly.

Paine, Fred K., and Nancy E. Paine. *Magazines: A Bibliography for Their Analysis, with Annotations and Study Guide.* Metuchen, N.J.: Scarecrow Press, 1987.

Parnau, Jeffery. *The Handbook of Magazine Production.* Stamford, Conn.: Hanson Publishing Group, 1985.

Rogers, Geoffrey. *Editing for Print.* Cincinnati, Ohio: Writer's Digest Books, 1985.

Schein, Eliot DeY. *Renewals.* Stamford, Conn.: Hanson Publishing Group, 1992.

Scherman, William H. *How to Get the Right Job in Publishing.* Chicago: Contemporary Books, 1983.

Stone, Bob. *Successful Direct Marketing Methods.* Chicago: Crain Books, 1975.

Strunk, William, Jr., and E. B. White. *Elements of Style.* 3d ed. New York: Macmillan, 1979. Paperback.

Teeters, Peggy. *How to Get Started in Writing.* Cincinnati, Ohio: Writer's Digest Books, 1986.

White, Alex. *How to Spec Type.* New York: Watson-Guptill, 1987.

———. *Type in Use.* New York: Design Press, 1992.

White, Jan V. *Designing for Magazines.* New York: R. R. Bowker, 1982.

*Writer's Market.* Cincinnati, Ohio: Writer's Digest Books, 1992. Published annually.

# INDEX